THE KONSO OF
ETHIOPIA

Presented to the Prime Warden and Wardens of the Worshipful Company of Goldsmiths with the respectful compliments of the Author.

C. R. Hallpike.

Konso Landscape

THE KONSO

OF

ETHIOPIA

A Study of the
Values of a Cushitic People

BY

C. R. HALLPIKE

OXFORD
AT THE CLARENDON PRESS
1972

Oxford University Press, Ely House, London W. 1

GLASGOW NEW YORK TORONTO MELBOURNE WELLINGTON
CAPE TOWN IBADAN NAIROBI DAR ES SALAAM LUSAKA ADDIS ABABA
DELHI BOMBAY CALCUTTA MADRAS KARACHI LAHORE DACCA
KUALA LUMPUR SINGAPORE HONG KONG TOKYO

PRINTED IN GREAT BRITAIN
AT THE UNIVERSITY PRESS, OXFORD
BY VIVIAN RIDLER
PRINTER TO THE UNIVERSITY

ACKNOWLEDGEMENTS

THE fieldwork on which this book is based was made possible by a Studentship from the Worshipful Company of Goldsmiths, and I am glad to have this opportunity of thanking them for their generosity, and also my parents, who provided the necessary financial support for writing up my field-notes. The final revisions have been completed during my tenure of a Killam Fellowship at Dalhousie University. I am indebted to the members of the Norwegian Lutheran Mission in Konso, and in other stations, for their help and hospitality on many occasions, which made my stay in Konso much easier and pleasanter then it would otherwise have been. I am also obliged to Dr. Richard Pankhurst for his advice and assistance, and for making the facilities of the Institute of Ethiopian Studies available to me. That I ever went to the Konso at all is due to Mr. Wilfred Thesiger, and I am grateful to him for first drawing them to my attention. I am particularly obliged to Dr. David Elliott for analysing the various Konso generation-grading systems by computer, which has greatly added to our knowledge of their operation. Dr. Rodney Needham and Dr. James Fox, who read the typescript, made a number of valuable suggestions, and Mr. F. White, Curator of the Forestry Herbarium of Oxford University, kindly identified the plants to which I refer in this book. Finally, my thanks are due to the Konso people themselves, not only for bearing so tolerantly with my incessant questions, but also for having evolved such an interesting culture, without which the best efforts of the anthropologist would be in vain.

C. R. H.

West Lawrencetown
Nova Scotia
April 1969

CONTENTS

LIST OF PLATES

LIST OF FIGURES

LIST OF MAPS

For reasons which are explained in the text, it was necessary to use a scale based on paces for some maps; 20 paces = 54 feet.

LIST OF TABLES

ORTHOGRAPHIC NOTE

I HAVE tried to keep vernacular terms to a minimum, except where there is no suitable or concise English translation. Phonetic symbols can be irritating to the reader, and I have therefore used the conventional alphabet, only modified by a few diacritical marks, which nevertheless give a close approximation to the correct pronunciation. It is hoped to publish an account of the Konso language elsewhere.

The English phonemes

k,g	s,z
p,b	t,d

are not clearly distinguished in the Konso language, though I believe that some differentiation is made; my rendering of words with these sounds should therefore be accepted with this qualification in mind.

VOWELS

a   as in Italian
e   ε
i   as in English 'sit'
o   as in 'hot'
u   as in 'full'
ā   as in 'path'
ē   as in 'late'
ī   as in 'tight'
ō   as in 'hope'
ū   as in 'fool'

CONSONANTS

¨   glottal stop
'b implosive b
'd implosive d
'g implosive velar g
ĝ   velar fricative, voiced
ħ   velar fricative, voiceless

’j   implosive j
r   is a flapped sound between l and r
ř   rolled r
ñ   Spanish ñ
Long consonants are doubled
All other consonants as in English

RULES OF STRESS

1. Two syllables—stress on first syllable.
2. Three syllables—stress on second syllable.
3. Four syllables—stress on first and third syllables.

II. Elder

I

INTRODUCTION

I. KONSO IN RELATION TO THE REST OF ETHIOPIA

IN the far south-west of Ethiopia[1] among the barren mountain ranges of that region can be found the minute territory of the Konso.[2] A watcher in the Konso Highlands, looking north, along the floor of the Rift Valley sees spread below him the great plain of Gomīda, dominated by the Gidole mountains on the left. Beyond the plain the distant gleam of Lake Shamo will catch his eye, and, remoter still, the towering mass of the Chencha mountains, sixty miles away, will terminate his view. About thirty miles to the east are the precipitous and rain-scarred heights of the Amarro mountains, the home of the Burji people, and also used for grazing by the Guji division of the Galla. Over the Sagan River, to the south, are the lands of the Borana Galla who roam the hot low plain of Sāba, and its adjacent mountains, that runs down to Moyale and Kenya. The dark jagged outline of the Hummer range can be glimpsed forty miles to the west, across the humid depths and haze of the Woito valley, through which the Woito River runs down to Lake Stephanie, receiving the waters of the Sagan on its journey.

The vast distances which the eye can travel over mountain and lowland are in striking contrast to the narrow limits within which the Konso[3] themselves have always lived. The Konso Highlands are a narrow range, between 5,000 and 6,000 feet in altitude, running with the path of the sun, from east to west; five hours walking are

---

[1] Latitude 5°30 N., longitude 37°30 E.

[2] The name 'Konso' is almost certainly derived from 'Ḥonso' which is the name of a great wooded hill overlooking the markets of Omboko and Bakaule. This has always been one of the most important centres of trade, and explains why the name is so widely used outside the district. Strictly, it should be spelt 'Konzo', but as 'Konso' is now the accepted spelling it would be confusing to alter it.

[3] Their present population is about 55,000–60,000. The Government census, which was completed just before I left, gave the figure as 55,701 but this is almost certainly an underestimate.

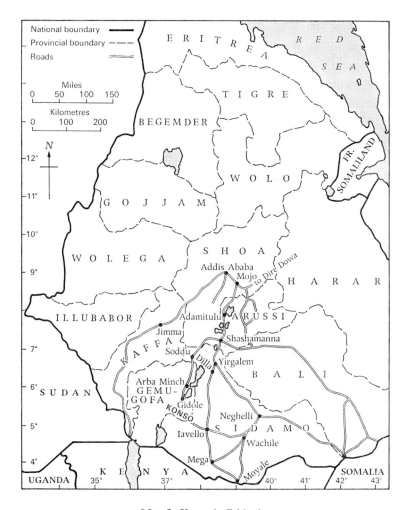

MAP I. Konso in Ethiopia

enough to pass from one end to another of the inhabited portion, and only four would cover their breadth. The Konso now extend in scattered settlements considerably beyond these limits, but this expansion, with one exception—that of Turo region, which extends for about three hours' journey to the north from the main massif— is of recent origin. From ancient times the hostile Guji and Borana prevented any casual travelling to the south and east across the Sagan River, or even north to Gidole, across the Gomīda plain, and the heat and disease of the lowlands in which these pastoral tribes graze their cattle did not attract Konso settlement. The Gauwada, another agricultural tribe to the west, on the hills overlooking the Woito valley, also prevented expansion in that direction, though south of the Gauwada there has been room for expansion towards the Woito. The Konso say that they are friends with other agricultural peoples, and enemies with cattle peoples, but this is not strictly true; they have fought many times with the Gauwada for instance.

The Konso have thus tilled their fields and evolved their remarkable culture in a high degree of isolation, through the many centuries that they have occupied their land. Trade, of course, there has always been, especially with the Borana, who brought the vital salt, unobtainable in Konso, cowrie shells, and other attractive rarities, often for ritual purposes, from the coast. Iron ore came from Gofa to the north, and there has always been a demand for Burji women as potters. But these contacts are not the only links between the Konso and their neighbours, since they are related both to the pastoral and the agricultural tribes of the area by common origins.

Konsiña[1] is an East Cushitic language, like Galliña, and the Konso believe that they were descended from the Borana in the distant past, and also from the Ala and Gauwada; they also have some close cultural and linguistic similarities to the Gidole. The relationship between the Konso and the Galla peoples is most obviously displayed in the linguistic evidence.

Using Swadesh's 200-word list, Konsiña has 46 per cent of cognates with Galliña. The language of the Gidole[2] people, on the other

[1] The suffix -iña is Amharic, and means 'language'.

[2] I am obliged to Messrs G. Linton, and R. Kaley, of the United States Peace Corps, and to Mr. D. Coolidge, for putting their linguistic data on the Gidole and neighbouring tribes at my disposal.

hand, who live only about twenty-five miles away, and whom the Konso consider their closest neighbours culturally speaking, has only 31 per cent of cognates with Konsiña, and 19 per cent with Galliña. Calculations by glottochronological techniques[1] give the time lapse since the original Konso separated from the Galla as approximately 1,800 years, but in view of the large amount of contact between different cultures in this area, this is likely to be an over-estimate.

This relationship with the Galla is not just linguistic but also cultural. Knutsson's description of the Macha Galla[2] makes it clear that the Konso are squarely in the Galla cultural complex; this is supported not only by their common possession of generation-grading systems of the *gada* type,[3] similar types of high priests, and an obsession with phallicism and peace, but by Konso tradition. But while there is a clear relationship between Konsiña and Galliña, as well as obvious cultural similarities, we should beware of thinking in terms of a basic Konso stock which split off from a proto-Galla people, wandered around in southern Ethiopia, and finally came to rest in Konso. Konso family traditions show that the present Konso population is derived from all the surrounding areas. Moreover, the Konso are markedly shorter and more negroid than the Borana. They are clearly an amalgam, both physically and culturally, in which other stocks than Galla are represented. I shall refer below to the Mādo people, who are said to be the predecessors of the Konso and are credited in particular with having dug a number of deep wells. There are a number of other aspects of Konso culture which are analogous to the digging of wells. In one region, Takadi, clay for pots is mined, rather than dug, although my own inspections of the site suggest that an 'open cast' form of digging would be equally effective. In Takadi also there are a large number of stone houses which are constructed by excavating large holes in the rock, facing the cavity with stone, and roofing the resulting house with a kind of volcanic earth. There is also a sacred stone called the Kidoma, whose origin no-one knows, which suggests that it was placed there by the same Mādo people. It is possible, therefore,

[1] See Sarah Gudschinsky's article, 'The ABC's of Lexicostatistics (Glottochronology)', in *Language in Culture and Society*, ed. Dell Hymes (1964).

[2] Knutsson, *Authority and Change* (1967).

[3] *Gada* systems are chiefly distinguished from true age-grading systems by the principle that recruitment is based not on age, but upon the position of the father in the system.

that they were of 'megalithic'[1] culture, and also small, black, and negroid.

While the Konso partake of many elements of that Cushitic culture whose peoples form the majority of the population of modern Ethiopia, their way of life appears to owe little or nothing to those outside influences which have shaped traditional Abyssinia. Judaism and Christianity, Moslem and Galla invasions, the Portugese, Italians, and other Europeans, have largely passed them by. Indeed they were independent within living memory; in 1897, during the last phase of the expansion which was to define the boundaries of modern Ethiopia, the armies of the Emperor Menelik II, armed with rifles, passed through Konso, and subdued it by their usual policy of promising that if tribute were paid no violence would be done to the people, but that any resistance would be crushed. In general the Konso accepted these terms, but at least two of the towns fought for their independence, and were only taken after bloody fighting, in which the houses were burned and many people killed. But their inclusion within the Ethiopian Empire did not produce any marked changes in their traditional way of life. In those days there was neither the wish nor the administrative machinery to Amharicize what were considered to be remote and barbarous peoples. According to Konso traditions a large number of slaves was taken, but to judge from the present slight depopulation of the towns it is likely that only a small proportion of the people was enslaved. The principal token of Amhara rule was the presence of a local governor, and the obligation to pay taxes. Colonizers from other parts of Ethiopia seem only to have arrived after the defeat of the Italians, and even today they are very few, chiefly comprising the families of policemen and government clerks.[2] Nor has the Coptic Church sought to convert the Konso, having contented itself with receiving their tithes.

The transitory and hard-pressed Italians—another potential source of social change—in fact did no more than build a few roads; they brought no school, mission, or clinic.

The Amhara governor who took over after their departure continued the traditional policy of maintaining law and order, and

[1] For a discussion of 'Megalithic Cushites', see Murdock's *Africa. Its Peoples and their Culture History*, and many references in Haberland's *Galla Süd-Äthiopiens*.

[2] Kluckhohn's statement that the Amhara have taken one-third of productive Konso land is gross exaggeration. Most Konso own their land.

collecting taxes, without interfering much with their traditional mode of life.

Again, the geographical position of Konso has meant that it has been less affected by the development of roads in Ethiopia than many other regions. This is because it lies off the main route from Addis Ababa to Kenya which runs through Iavello to the east of the lakes Margherita and Shamo: the western route, through the new provincial capital of Arba Minch, Gidole, and Konso, is very little used in comparison.[1]

2. SOCIAL CHANGE

The most recent and active outside influences have been the missionaries and the government school. The Norwegian Lutheran Mission arrived in 1954 and in the following year established a school and clinic. The school now has about 130–40 pupils, and at present teaches up to the sixth grade, but most pupils only complete the second grade. A government school was also established some time later, and now has about the same number of pupils. The mission clinic treats about 70 out-patients a day from all parts of Konso, besides its in-patients. While both school and clinic are flourishing, however, and have made considerable impact on the people, the religious efforts of the missionaries have had less success. At present (1966) the number of converts is about 400, and half of these were made in 1965 and 1966. It does not appear to be the policy of the Norwegian Lutheran Mission for its members to learn the local languages, or live among the people and understand their life. Preaching in the district is done only by locally recruited evangelizers, and the increase in the number of these in the last few years has been reflected in the number of converts. The preachers are young and poorly paid, however, and thus not well qualified to command the respect or attention of the people.

The mission is concerned to preserve good relations between its converts and the rest of the people, and explicitly tells them to respect the things which the pagans hold sacred. They are merely forbidden to attend pagan ceremonies. There is, I think, no idea among the converted Christians that the beliefs of their ancestors are wicked; the present missionary tells me that he has never heard

---

[1] Only a few years ago the road between Arba Minch and Gidole was so bad that the missionaries in Konso and Gidole were forced to come from Addis Ababa through Iavello.

from a potential convert that he wanted to become a Christian because the Konso religion was bad. One should not forget that their
new Christianity is of a very simple type, added on to, rather than
replacing, their fundamental beliefs. While there have been a few
violent incidents between converts and their pagan fellows, such
converts as there are, therefore, do not differ from their neighbours
in any contentious or revolutionary mood, but are quite well integrated with them. I hardly ever found that, as a result of mission
teaching, my sources were confused in such a way that I found it
hard to decide whether a particular practice or belief was indigenous or the result of the mission. In religious terms, then, the
Konso are almost unaffected by recent influences.

But the imposition of law and order by the Amhara and the
pacification of the region has had important effects on their society.
In the past the towns[1] were autonomous and would, if necessary,
settle their differences by battle, wrong-doers were beaten or exe-
cuted, and revenge was exacted in blood. Now Amhara courts,
which apply Ethiopian law and do not recognize local law, have
been established with the power of an armed police force to support
them. This has greatly diminished the power of the elders' councils, which used to be the only judicial bodies, and removed the
opportunity for fighting in defence of home and town; warriorhood is now more of an ideal than the necessity of life which it was
in the past. More generally, it seems that the loss of their independence has weakened their confidence in and devotion to their
own institutions, since more powerful ones are now available. The
effects of Amhara rule can be seen in the fact that the walls
surrounding the towns have in many cases been allowed to become
ruinous, and the gates which were once barred and guarded at night
are now left open and unwatched. (I was told by some people that
this was the result of a government prohibition on any maintenance
of defensive works, and by others, that as the government had
established peace, they were no longer necessary.)

Whereas, in the past, travel was severely limited by banditry,
such that in times of famine it was impossible to import grain, the
pacification of the area has allowed Konso to be linked with the

[1] I use the word 'town' in preference to the more usual 'village' since their
large and dense populations, their defensive walls, and the fact that in pre-
Amhara times they were sovereign units, distinguish them from most other African settlement patterns. In English usage one of the distinctive criteria of towns
has always been their self-governing status, as opposed to that of villages.

rest of Ethiopia by trade. While this has been greatly to the advantage of the Konso—which they freely acknowledge—it has also helped to erode traditional social ties.

They themselves said that whereas in the past people had a strong sense of corporate duty, now it was every man for himself. A good example of this was the town of Idigle where I lived for some weeks. Here many men had taken up the weaving of cotton cloth which was bought by two local traders with lorries who sold it in other parts of Ethiopia. The money the men of Idigle received from this was largely spent on drink, and the result was that their fields were neglected and full of weeds, and the town resounded with quarrelling and recrimination. They were able to buy beer[1] because of the surplus of grain, which came from Gidole. Before the Amhara, grain was often in short supply, as it was hard to go to Gidole because of the Borana and Guji in the lowlands. The beer that was made was the prerogative of the old men.

Thus the pacification of the region and the greater opportunity for trade, in cotton as well as grain, has led, in Idigle and other towns, to a decay in social order and the traditional values. Not only is there less exclusiveness among the towns, though this is still strong, and less confidence in general in their institutions, but many of the old restrictions in social intercourse have become less rigid. In the past it is said that there was more deference to the aged, and men and women mixed less freely than they do today. Cultivators used not to eat or drink with craftsmen but now they do. In general I had the feeling that while in many ways the ideas, beliefs, and institutions were still there, relatively unchanged, some of the old fire and spirit had gone out of them. But this was more evident in some towns than in others. I spent my first nine months in a town called Būso, which still retained much of its old self-reliance, where there was very little drunkenness, and the voice of the elders was heard and respected. So in spite of some corroding influences, their beliefs and institutions are still functioning in most parts of Konso with

[1] Beer (made from malted millet) seems invariably to make the Konso morose and quarrelsome, though when sober they are fairly jovial. On the rare occasions when I drank deeply, of a particularly good brew, I found that it produced in me a rather unhappy state of mind. *Tej*, the Amhara honey wine, on the contrary, always induced in me a state of almost seraphic benevolence. It may be, therefore, that there are certain alkaloids or similar substances in these two drinks that can affect the mind in diverse ways, or it is possible that the tensions generated by their urban life, which are repressed by traditional restraints when they are sober, are released under the influence of alcohol.

some vigour; I think that nothing of any importance has vanished, or is likely to do so for some time to come.

I should state here that while many Konso have emigrated to Iavello, Mega, and Marsabit in Kenya, there is no question of an emigrant labour force periodically leaving to seek work in other parts of Ethiopia, and returning when it has saved enough money. Those who have emigrated seem to be mainly craftsmen, who are traditionally more mobile than the cultivators. They are an insignificant percentage of the total population, and seem to have lost contact with those who have remained. Nor are there enough Amhara or missionaries to create a significant local market for labour.

3. THE CIRCUMSTANCES OF MY FIELDWORK

I arrived in Konso on 21 May 1965, and left on 23 January 1967; during that time I spent about sixteen and a half months in actual fieldwork. I lived for my first nine months in Būso, one of the most isolated towns, simply to sink myself in the traditional atmosphere of the people and get a good grounding in the language, in which I attained a fair competence after about four or five months. After six months of living in a deserted men's clubhouse, I was then invited by a prominent priest to come and live in his compound, which I did for three months. I then moved on to another town, Degato, where I lived for two months with another family, and made, among other things, a special study of the craftsmen, a despised group. So far I had only been living in the eastern part of Konso, called Garati, and since there are important variations in the customs and beliefs of the three regions, I moved on to Gaho in the western (Takadi) region for three months, to make a special study of the generation-grading system there, and of its differences from that of Garati. From Gaho I went back to Idigle, in Garati, to clarify some refinements of social organization and ritual, and thence removed north to Turo, the third and most inaccessible region of Konso, which differs more from the other two than they do from each other. Here again my chief interest was in their form of generation-grading system, but, as in every case, I collected as much information as possible on other aspects of their lives.

The Konso are a friendly people, quite ready to talk on general matters and answer questions, and accepted me without having any idea at first why a white man should be so eccentric as to come and live among them. Perhaps I was helped in this respect by the earlier visit of Jensen in 1935 to Būso, where he left a favourable impression. One of my first experiences of their geniality was on my fourth day in Būso. I was attending an important sacrifice when it came on to rain, and one of them volunteered to hold an umbrella over me as I wrote to keep my notebook dry. Everyone who came to speak to me catechized me about the words for parts of the body and other familiar objects which they produced, and were delighted if I gave the right answer. They were clearly pleased that a *ferenji*[1] was trying to learn their language, which is usually despised and ignored by outsiders.

But they are very resistant to questions about personal matters, such as the amount of land they hold, and I never attempted any investigation of land tenure for this reason, apart of course from establishing the general principles of their laws relating to it. Making maps or taking a census also upsets them as they have a general fear that all outside investigation of their possessions, or even the number of children they have is the prelude to more taxation, an attitude which, on their past experience of the Amhara, is very justifiable. And while these fears can be partially overcome when one has their confidence, they always maintain a fundamental reserve about their personal affairs, which it would not only be impertinent but ultimately self-defeating for the outsider to try to penetrate with his questions.

A more impenetrable barrier for the anthropologist studying the Konso is that they are, compared with many primitive peoples, relatively inarticulate, in the sense that they have remarkably few legends or stories either about the world around them or themselves, in which their hopes and attitudes are portrayed for others to see. They have no folk-heroes, and no tradition of heroic recitation; story-telling as a pastime is very little developed among them. Nor do their songs, what there are of them, convey much of interest. They have no proverbs which in other cultures provide such a wealth of insight into their beliefs. I took down many texts, when I either asked people to 'tell me a story', leaving the subject to them, or asked them to talk in their own way about topics which interested me. Out of the 91 texts I obtained in this way, only 28 were real stories, many of them very short. The most interesting of their oral possessions are their riddles, which are often extremely subtle

---

[1] The word for 'European' in Amharic.

and ingenious, showing that they have an abundance of talent for inventing legends and stories should they wish to do so.

There is no written dictionary or grammar of Konsiña, and indeed I am the first European ever to have learnt their language, though four short word-lists have been published.[1]

I was fortunate in being able to obtain a preliminary word-list from a teacher at the mission, who was a Konso by birth and upbringing, but I had to acquire most of my knowledge of the language by living with the people. I never used an interpreter at any time. While Konsiña lacks the inflections, tones, and syntactical complexity of many other languages studied by ethnographers, its very vagueness and the indifference of its speakers to things like prepositions, number, and pronouns often makes the sense very hard to understand with any exactitude. Again, the only way of grasping words which are not easily demonstrable by pointing to physical objects or miming is by comparison of the contexts in which they occur, and this can be a very long process. It is a matter of logic that unless a difficult word is used by the natives several times in informative contexts the anthropologist cannot possibly guess its meaning, and this limitation applies even to those persons who undoubtedly have a genius for absorbing unwritten foreign languages. The problem occurs more acutely when the people are talking among themselves, since often one may not know the subject of their conversation. When they are answering questions, and the investigator is setting the topic, it is much easier to guess what the unknown word or words may be, especially if the same topic is discussed on several occasions. To understand speeches on religious or other public occasions, when the words are often recondite, even to them, takes a great deal of labour, not all of it conclusive. I used a tape-recorder to collect speeches and prayers, and worked over them at great length with my friends afterwards.

Anthropologists in their writings often give the impression of having been faced, in their initial contact with the natives, with a bewildering complexity of behaviour. When I first went to Būso, however, nothing at all seemed to be going on, beside the simple and universal processes of domestic life—women grinding millet, and fetching water, animals being taken out to graze, children playing, and men sitting and spinning their cotton. The atmosphere was one of stillness and mystery, not of lively and bewildering

---

[1] See bibliography.

activity. Simply by observing their behaviour I should have learned little. I learnt most about them in fact by asking questions. One gathers a certain amount from listening to them talk, but their conversation is generally very trivial—for the anthropologist's purposes—'Did you put the cotton out to dry this morning?', 'There is a snake over at Gutchulo's house', 'Look, the *ferenji* is scratching his nose', and so on. It is only in clumsy novels that the characters tell each other what to them are well-known facts for the information of the reader, which in real life they would never bother mentioning. Questions were usually essential to stimulate conversation on those 'high matters' which like most other ordinary people everywhere they are not normally interested in discussing.

I preferred to work with a few informants whom I came to know well. In this way I could form an estimate of their biases and reliability. They also got to know me and what I was interested in, and often became quite enthusiastic in talking about the topics raised. I taught some of them to speak at dictation speed, and acquired a large number of texts. These were an invaluable complement to the material provided by questions, since they were talking in their own idiom, which gave me an insight into associations of ideas which were important to them. I paid small sums for these texts, and often distributed cigarettes, for example, in the course of a discussion to those sitting with me. The anthropologist should not flatter himself that his company is in itself sufficient recompense to the natives for the time and attention they give him. But eventually as I learnt more I found that a carefully prepared series of questions, on the more technical aspects of the institutions, was the only way of getting the information I wanted. To check against deceit or simple error I would compare what a man said on one day with what he said in a month's time, or with what someone else said. Moreover, when one is dealing with highly complex systems such as the generation-grades, one can exclude certain statements simply on the grounds that if they were true the system could not possibly work, or would not be consistent with the distribution of the actual ages of the people in the grades. I always tried to obtain at least two independent accounts of anything important, and if they agreed I found that where I could check them by observation they were nearly always true. Another useful technique was to start an argument about something and listen while they wrangled it out. Fortunately, while they tended to be deferential to me, as a white man, they were quite prepared to contradict me if they thought I was wrong about some aspect of their life or beliefs, or laugh at suggestions they thought absurd, or reprove me if I offended against their code of behaviour.

4. PREVIOUS KONSO ETHNOGRAPHERS

Konso, like the rest of Ethiopia, has attracted few professional anthropologists. The late Professor Adolf Jensen was the first to arrive, and he spent less than five weeks there in January–February 1935. The results of his researches were published in *Im Lande des Gada* (1936), and in an article 'Elementi della cultura spirituale dei Conso nell'Etiopia meridionale'[1] in 1942. After the war he returned to Konso in 1951 for two months. Apart from one short article nothing of this later research has yet been published by him or his colleagues at the Frobenius Institute. Jensen was an ethnographer of the *Kulturkreis* school, and not trained in the British tradition of the meticulous study of a single tribe, and his theoretical preoccupation with the cultural traits of Cushitic Ethiopia, and the very short time he spent in Konso perhaps explain the disappointing quality of his ethnography. Not speaking the language, he was obliged to converse in Galliña, and derived much of his information from someone who was not a Konso at all, but a Borana living in Konso.[2] In view of this it is not surprising that he ascribes many Borana traits to the Konso which they do not possess at all. We are told that the age-grading (*altersklassen*) system and its ceremonies are called 'Jila', a Borana word quite alien to the Konso, and that they have borrowed a special kind of age-grading system called '*harriyāda*' from the Borana, based on a cycle of thirteen years. In fact there is no cycle of thirteen years among the Konso and their *harriyādas* work in a totally different fashion from that which he describes; nor do the Borana have a thirteen-year cycle, so the Konso could hardly have copied it from them. If anything, they have merely borrowed the Borana word *harriyāda*, meaning 'age-mate', and this is perhaps the source of Jensen's idea that they copied the whole institution from the Borana. But shortage of time can hardly have been responsible for an error of a simpler nature, which occurs in his plan and three-dimensional drawing of the Mora Murgito (a sacred place) in Būso, where he resided for

---

[1] See bibliography.　　[2] *Im Lande des Gada*, p. 349.

some weeks, reproduced in *Im Lande des Gada*[1] and in the Italian
article. Three monoliths are shown in the plan and drawing,
orientated towards the home of the Bamalle (a great priest). Actually, in the Mora Murgito there are and always have been, only *two*
monoliths, and they are orientated in quite a different direction. They
represent past victories, and there is no possibility that there were
ever three. Among other things, the ground is very rocky here, and
the socket would still be visible if a stone had been removed. So,
in spite of his praiseworthy industry, his account of the Konso does
not contain much useful or reliable information. Nevertheless,
there are a number of excellent drawings of huts and artefacts, and
some photographs which are good, for the period.

The other anthropologist to visit the Konso was Dr. R. P. R.
Kluckhohn, who spent between two and three months there in
1960. So far, unfortunately, the only fruit of his research which
has appeared is an article, 'The Konso Economy of Southern
Ethiopia', in *Markets in Africa*, edd. Bohannan and Dalton (1962).
In the short time available he seems to have concentrated, no doubt
wisely, on the more easily observable aspects of their economy and
material culture, relying on Jensen and Murdock for assertions of
a more ambitious nature, but even at this practical level there are
some elementary errors. On p. 413, for example, he says that in the
past donkeys were used for pulling ploughs. But ploughing was
introduced relatively recently into Konso by the Amhara, and any
ethnographer should know that donkeys are never used to plough,
as they are far too light for the job. In Konso, bulls are the only
draught animals. Also on p. 413 he refers to the Konso as building
walls in which a simple mortar is used. One minute's inspection of
a Konso wall would have shown him that they are of dry-stone construction, and one minute's thought should have convinced him
that in a country where water is as scarce as in Konso they would
not be likely to waste thousands of gallons making mortar, even if
they had the materials and the knowledge to do so. To my regret,
therefore, I was not able to make much use of my predecessors'
work.

5. THE AIMS OF THIS MONOGRAPH

The object of this study is to examine how the social institutions
of the Konso and their religious rituals are given coherence by their

[1] *Im Lande des Gada*, p. 445.

values. I am aware that such emphasis upon values is a fairly radical departure from the traditional concerns of British social anthropology. The influence of Radcliffe-Brown and the organic model of society which was the core of his social theory, while a stimulus to field-studies of the interaction of social institutions, has retarded the study of values and belief systems as integral elements of society.

But the organic model is not just an analogy which can only be pushed so far; it is, I suggest, something very much worse than that—a fundamental source of illusion. In the first place, social institutions are not physical aggregations of individuals, as the organs of the body are physical aggregations of cells. Institutions are of a different logical order to people, because they are concepts. As Nadel says, 'All such names, [marriage, family, chieftainship, etc.] as we shall see, stand for normative concepts; the institution represents, for the actor, a rule or norm, and has that kind of reality, that is, the non-spatial and in a sense timeless validity of concepts.'[1] In the second place, the organic model cannot assimilate the existence of rules. The interaction of the organs of the body occurs on the level of physical cause and effect. But societies, while they are indeed systems of action, are also systems of meaning. Not only do individuals act in a manner prescribed by rules and norms, but also institutions themselves encapsulate rules and norms. In the third place, the organic model, if it does not assume some definition of 'health', must at least posit that the system as a whole has demands which must be met by the characteristics of its component parts. While this is true of physical organisms and machines, it is untrue of societies, for two reasons. The first is that, as historical examples show, it is possible for one social order to change over a period of time into another of quite a different type, and even though the process causes social unrest and confusion we would not be inclined to say that a society undergoing such a transition had ceased temporarily to be a society. Secondly, what actually constitutes social harmony, or 'health', to use the organic analogy, is not an unvarying empirical fact, but relative to each culture. Evans-Pritchard describes how violence is endemic among the Nuer, where not only members of the same village fight among themselves, but even brothers may come to blows over cattle and separate; for them this is a 'normal' state of society. But to the

[1] S. F. Nadel, *Foundations of Social Anthropology*, p. 107.

Borana, another pastoral people of East Africa, this would appear as total anarchy and social disintegration. The Borana regard even angry words as a dangerous event, and violence among them is almost unthinkable.[1] Social solidarity therefore is culturally relative, and cannot be appealed to as an 'end' to which institutions contribute.

Another assumption, closely related to the organic model, is that societies are *basically* composed of people on the ground interacting, exchanging goods, and competing for women and other desirables. From this assumption derives a model according to which there is on the one hand 'reality', consisting of people doing things to one another, to animals, and the physical world, and on the other, ideas, beliefs, cosmologies, and values which, if they do not 'reflect' the society, are at least intrinsically separable from it. But a society is composed not only of people doing things, but of people assembled into a series of groups and categories, each with its rules of recruitment and norms of behaviour. If we must depend on analogies in social anthropology, I would suggest that we use that of the 'game' rather than the 'organism'. Games, unlike organisms, are both systems of action and systems of meaning; that is, they are not just systems of interaction, but interaction taking place according to rules of which the players are aware. In a game we are aware of the necessity of studying the rules, as well as the behaviour of the players if we are to reach a full comprehension of what is going on, and, like societies, but unlike organisms, games are capable of drastic structural modification without ceasing to be playable.

The process of understanding a society, our own or an alien one, involves reducing a great complexity of data to certain basic principles which may be in some instances ethical, and in other cases relate to beliefs, or techniques of action. This is not a statement about the nature of 'science', but about the nature of human beings in society. Chaos is unliveable; communication whether in words, goods, or expectations of behaviour, demands adherence to certain rules and I would suggest that it is an essential aspect of explaining a society to set out the rules which have the widest application, and see how they are worked out in social relations.

In this study of the Konso I therefore place great emphasis upon

---

[1] For an account of Borana values, see P. Baxter's paper 'Repetition in Certain Boran Ceremonies', in *African Systems of Thought*, edd. Fortes and Dieterlen (1965).

Konso values because it seems to me that they are not only norms governing personal relations, but also partially explain the forms their institutions have taken, and in some cases the very existence of these institutions. Of course, each institution is also governed by rules of recruitment and behaviour which are peculiar to it alone, and the interaction of social groups has a logic of its own which may in some cases be largely independent of basic values. But their values are, in the first place, general to the whole range of their institutions and ritual, so that a single value may underly a wide variety of institutions, and, secondly, values must be taken as 'given', in the sense that one cannot go behind them and ask, for example, why the Konso should place such emphasis on peace, or virility. The Konso just do, and there is no more to be said. In these two respects, therefore, they are analogous to the rules of a game.

Perhaps I should emphasize that I do not regard my list of Konso values simply as the analytic concepts of an ethnographer used for heuristic purposes, but as vital, explicit elements of daily existence. I believe that if the relevant chapter on values were translated to an intelligent Konso, he would say 'Yes, you have got it right, these are the things we Konso admire'. In short, they talk about peace, and manliness, and reasoned discussion, and truth, and the admirable nature of hard work; and when they make choices and decisions, or react to some government decree, they will do so partially in terms of these values. The present characteristics of Konso institutions (like those of every other people) are the result of choices and decisions—many of them minor, but others of great importance—which must have been taken in the light of the values obtaining at the time. It is not, therefore, in the least surprising that they constantly refer to these values in explaining their institutions. Of course, I am not saying that their values have been the sole dynamic agency in their social development, and are in themselves sufficient to explain contemporary Konso society. Population density, the kinship system, residence patterns, modes of agriculture, trade, immigration, famine, and disease, are all essential aspects of their world, which they have to contend with, and which also partially explain their present society. Equally important are certain beliefs about the world; for example, that God withholds the rain from towns which quarrel too much, that it is possible to divine the future, and that one man may bless or curse another. Any theory which seeks for ultimate determinants of a single type, whether they be values, or child-rearing techniques, or ecology, is fundamentally misconceived.

This concept of society as a system of meaning as well as of action is, of course, by no means new. But the general theoretical awareness among social anthropologists of the fallacy of treating society as an organism has not been reflected in the contents of ethnographic monographs. Monica Wilson's study of the Nyakyusa, *Good Company*, is the only monograph on an African people which attempts to give a proper place to values, and thirteen years elapsed between this book and Campbell's masterly study of Greek shepherds, *Honour, Family, and Patronage*. Even in the symposium *African Worlds*,[1] while some contributors show a keen awareness of the importance of values, they do not make full use of this form of analysis in their ethnography.

As Beattie says,

> Indeed it may be said that despite the great advances in our understanding of the working of small-scale societies due to the development of functional and structural theory, this development has on the whole tended to distract attention from the equally important problem of how to understand other peoples' systems of beliefs and values. . . . There has been a tendency to regard ideas and values as 'cultural' data, and for many years 'culture' has been regarded as at best a peripheral interest of structurally oriented social anthropologists.[2]

I must defer a full description of Konso values until the reader is familiar with their mode of life and their basic institutions, but it will obviously clarify the following chapters if I summarize these values briefly here.

They believe that rainfall, the fertility of women, animals, and crops, and success in war and hunting, depend on the maintenance of social harmony and peace; and so Life in all its various manifestations, and peace are two of their most dominant values. Consistently with their high evaluation of peace, they admire sociability, co-operation, discussion, and a just subordination according to age and seniority, as sanctioned by ancestral tradition. They reject the idea of being governed by one man, and of arbitrary personal authority in general, but there are recognized outlets for individual enterprise, and they place a high value on the worth of the person, one of the worst crimes in their eyes being to put a price on someone's head, by blood money, or by selling one's children.

[1] Ed. D. Forde (1954).   [2] *Other Cultures*, pp. 63-4.

Life, as I have already said, is manifested for them in the fertility of women, animals, and crops; the *poĝalla* or priest is preeminently the bringer of Life, in his role as sacrificer. The grave is the symbol of Death, and there is a symbolic opposition between it and the priest, who ideally should kill no living thing, except when sacrificing.

One of their chief concerns is masculinity, especially as expressed in warfare, hunting, and work in the fields. The phallus is the focus of this esteem for manhood, and it appears in symbolic form throughout their culture. Women are seen as the weakeners of men, whose vitality is drained by sexual intercourse, and for this reason married men as well as bachelors often spend the night in special men's houses, to preserve their virility. Women are also regarded as socially unstable, leaving their lineages and natal towns at marriage to form unions with outsiders. A number of myths suggest that they are regarded in consequence as in some ways anti-social.

This brief summary, which does not do justice by any means to the full subtleties of the reality, must suffice for the time being, but it should provide a useful guide to the chapters which follow.

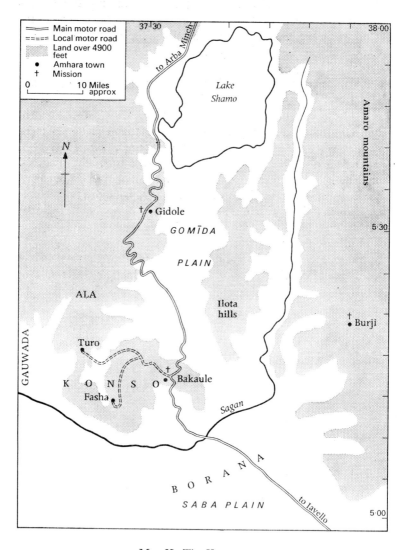

MAP II. The Konso area

II

KONSO LAND AND LIFE

THE Konso Highlands are rugged and stony, cut by deep valleys that reach far into the heart of the country. To maintain the soil of their fields on the steep slopes the hills have been contoured with terraces 4 or 5 ft. high, and double that in width, from base to summit. Perhaps nowhere else in traditional Ethiopia has the hand of man so impressed itself on the landscape as in Konso. Built of dry-stone wall, the terraces are still recognizable, even after decades of neglect, where the dryness of the soil or other factors have led to their disuse, and so the whole extent of the Konso Highlands bears witness to the almost unthinkable toil of unnumbered generations.

The Konso are a small and wiry people varying in colour from reddish-brown to almost black, but they are on the whole brown. Some have the thin lips and tallness of the Borana, while others are distinctly more negroid, and shorter, but prognathism is slight even among these. They tend to have high cheek-bones and pointed chins. Negroid characteristics are more marked among the women than the men.

Their lives are devoted to their fields and crops, and every traveller has remarked on their love of work. They recognize their own pre-eminence in this respect, and boast of their endurance and hardihood in the fields as other people do of warfare or riches. As the working parties move in line over the terraces, hoeing and weeding under the burning sun, they keep up their spirits by intermittently bursting into choruses of ferocious whoops and yells, that suggest the battle cries of a charging army, and are in strange contrast to the peaceful nature of their work.

From the overflowing abundance of stone, basalt in most cases, they derive the material not only for terraces, but also for walls to protect the fields against floodwater and cattle, and to encircle their towns. Stone is as much a part of their life as soil, and although basalt cannot be dressed they are highly skilled in using it as far as its limitations permit. Stone is used for grinding corn, in the form of columnar basalt as phallic emblems, for sharpening knives, as anvils, for throwing at enemies and birds, for building dams in streams, for housebuilding in some parts, and for defence, in the form of town walls, as well, of course, as being essential for agriculture. I am told that in the past, when iron was rarer, they also made knives from obsidian blades. Their use of stone gives a clarity and definition to their towns and homesteads which is extremely striking to the observer; it conveys a sense of harmony, order, and industry, and is in these respects a true expresssion of their values.

There are many groves of trees in Konso, and some large juniper woods, belonging to priests. This tree flourishes in most of their land, and is of great significance in ritual and housebuilding. Large quantities of wood are used for the latter, and some of the timbers are massive; juniper is only one of the trees used, and the Konso are familiar with the properties of many woods in relation to durability, strength, and other qualities. The fields are dotted with trees, especially of the *shelaĝda* variety (see the Glossary of plant names). This tree is generally specially planted, since its foliage is used for food.

While Konso soil is extremely stony it is nevertheless fertile, constantly enriched as it is with rotted animal dung and human faeces. It supports an ample crop of millet—the staple food—of which they grow at least twenty-four varieties, though not all in the same area. They also sow maize, peas, beans, marrows, and bananas, which were introduced by the Amhara. On the lower slopes cotton and coffee both grow prolifically, and are the two cash crops. On the higher ground, which has a dry montane climate, wheat and barley flourish but *ensete*[1] is hardly cultivated at all, partly due to the dryness of Konso, but also because the people prefer a crop that yields a quicker return for the labour of growing it. Three types of tuber, *pagana*, are grown everywhere; these are crushed with clubs and laid out on stones to dry in the sun, in order to remove the poison they contain, and then ground into flour, from which beer or food can be made after mixing with millet or maize. Their particular virtue is the ability to survive dry weather, and they are thus a form of insurance against a bad millet crop. The *shelaĝda* tree is grown in every homestead for its succulent green leaves, *mida*; these are plucked down with long hooks and used as a relish with the balls of cooked millet dough that are the basic form of Konso food. There are a few other plants cultivated for their food value, the yam, taro

[1] The 'false banana' of Ethiopia.

(used in flavouring beer), another sort of small potato, flax, and the sunflower, but their principal food has always been millet.

There are two crops of this, the first being sown in February and March, when the heaviest rains of the year begin to fall. These continue through April and May, and peter out in June. The second crop is not sown freshly, but derives from the secondary sprouting of the millet roots that have been harvested in July and August. The second and slighter rains begin to fall at the end of September and continue sporadically until December. This crop, which may include some freshly sown maize, is harvested in December and January.

Rain in Ethiopia does not fall steadily from leaden skies, that remain overcast for weeks at a time. Rather, it is a sudden and violent affair, the offspring of black thunder clouds that can be seen making their slow approach over the mountains, grumbling with thunder, their rain falling in dark pillars that sweep over the land with the noise of a great waterfall. Storms seldom last more than an hour or two, until the clouds pass over, and the sun reappears. But in that short time an immense volume of water has poured onto the soil, some of it to penetrate its depths and nourish the crops, or replenish the sources of the vital wells, and some of it to pour into the dry river-beds in furious red torrents that die away not long after the rain has ceased. Rain is of deep emotional and religious significance to the Konso. Seldom do they merely say 'It is raining', but usually 'God is raining'. These thundershowers are often extremely localized. When I was in Buso we often saw them pass by only two hundred yards or so away, up the Garfura valley to Takadi, but leaving us completely dry. They believe that God, Waĝa, withholds the rain from towns which are disturbed by too much internal quarrelling, and the localized nature of rainfall lends some plausibility to this most important religious belief. Hardly any of their fields has permanent water from streams, so without the rain they will die. No one who lives among them can remain unaffected by their deep and passionate preoccupation with rain.[1]

[1] In the dry belt of South-west Ethiopia of which Konso is part, annual rainfall is approximately 26 inches. Unfortunately only the figures for three months, February, March, and April 1966, are available:

III. Approaching rain

For about seven months of the year there is little rainfall, and the only drinking water for men and beasts is that which is drawn from the wells or from a few permanent streams. In a few places huge reservoirs have been constructed, to contain the rain-water for cattle in the dry months. The dams are as much as 40 ft. high, and sometimes more than 200 ft. in breadth; they must contain many hundreds of thousands of gallons when they are full. One or two towns have excavated deep tanks out of the solid rock, for the same purpose, and there are many smaller pools which have been dug and walled, and which keep their water for several weeks. Wells are of two kinds, most commonly in the form of bucket-shaped and stone-lined cavities perhaps 20 ft. deep, and 10 ft. across, with a few feet of water in the bottom. They are invariably situated beside a watercourse, and rely on tapping the subterranean water that saturates the rock, and runs down below the surface from higher ground. Even though the stream beds are quite dry, the wells will be constantly replenished by a small trickle. Sometimes the water has dried up unaccountably, and returned equally unexpectedly, and for this reason among others, wells have a mysterious quality in their eyes. Another and rarer kind, which I only found in the areas around Bakaule, was quite different, resembling the wells familiar to Europeans. These wells are narrow stone-lined holes which go down to a depth of 30 ft. or more, though they can be quite shallow, and are shaped like bottles, with narrow necks that widen considerably after descending for a few feet, being closed by a slab at the top. Water is, of course, drawn up on a rope. These wells seem always to be private property, unlike the larger types, or else are

Feb.   Total: 3·8 in. Max. 1·3 in.   8 days of rain 2 thunderstorms
Mar.   Total: 6·2 in.   1·3 in. 12 days of rain 6 thunderstorms
Apr.   Total: 10·0 in.   1·55 in. 15 days of rain 5 thunderstorms
(This rainfall was exceptionally heavy, however.)

These are the only rainfall measurements made in Konso. The mission, where they were taken, is one of the dryer parts. In the higher regions especially, rainfall is heavier. Average maximum daily temperatures taken during these three months at the mission were as follows: February, 87·5 °F.; March, 83·0 °F.; April, 79·0 °F. When I was in Gaho on the plateau my records of the average maximum daily temperature for two months, September and October 1966, were: September, 76·6 °F.; October, 74·5 °F. The lowest maximum daily temperature I recorded was 64·0 °F. and the highest 83·0 °F. At night during these cool months the temperature can fall to 58·0 °F. or perhaps lower. We can say that temperatures range from below 60·0 °F. at night in the higher regions, during the cooler months, to over 90·0 °F. in the lower hotter regions at the hottest time of the year.

shared between a few families. It is said that the deepest ones were
dug by the Mādo people, the ancient predecessors of the Konso.
There are no deep wells of the Borana type in Konso, however.
Often, because towns are situated on high ground and stream beds
lie in the surrounding valleys, the wells are at a considerable
distance from the towns. Those at Degato, for example, are half
an hour's walk in each direction, and at Būso they are about 200 ft.
below the town.

The Elbola stream below Būso, which runs all the year round, is
used for irrigating a few fields. Elaborate stone leats or *kaba* allow
the water to pass through series of walled gardens, which grow
prolific crops of taro, banana, pawpaw, and potatoes, as well as
maize and millet. But such amenities are very rare, and this type of
permanent irrigation is quite untypical.

In their fields, however, they must still take pains to see that the
rain-water is properly distributed, and the run-off from paths is
carefully channelled, through leats, onto the land. Even in the night,
if there is a thunderstorm, the men turn out in the dark, and run
naked through the pouring rain to their fields, to see that the water
is flowing well over the soil and not running to waste. When these
fields are near a river-bed such work can be dangerous. I well
remember going down with them through a thunderstorm to the
Elbola, and listening as the boom of the approaching flood water
grew nearer out of the darkness. These great walls of water often
sweep men away and dash them in pieces on the boulders.

There are cattle in plenty, as well as sheep and goats, but they
have none of the mystique with which pastoral tribes like the
Borana or Nuer endow cattle. While they figure prominently in
ritual and a brave man is called '*horma*', a bull, their principal function in daily life is to provide manure, and meat, the greatest delicacy for the Konso. There is no idea of improving the breed, and
no castration.[1] The sparsity and dryness of grazing land means that
their yield of milk is very small, and what is left for their owners to
drink is given to the children or made into butter. For this reason it
is never sold in the markets and forms a very inconspicuous item
of food. Milk in the markets is bought from Guji women. Most commonly it is made into butter, another luxury, that keeps well and
commands a high price. Livestock cannot be allowed into the fields,
where they would eat the crops, and knock down the terrace walls,

---

[1] They are aware, however, of the physiological function of the testicles.

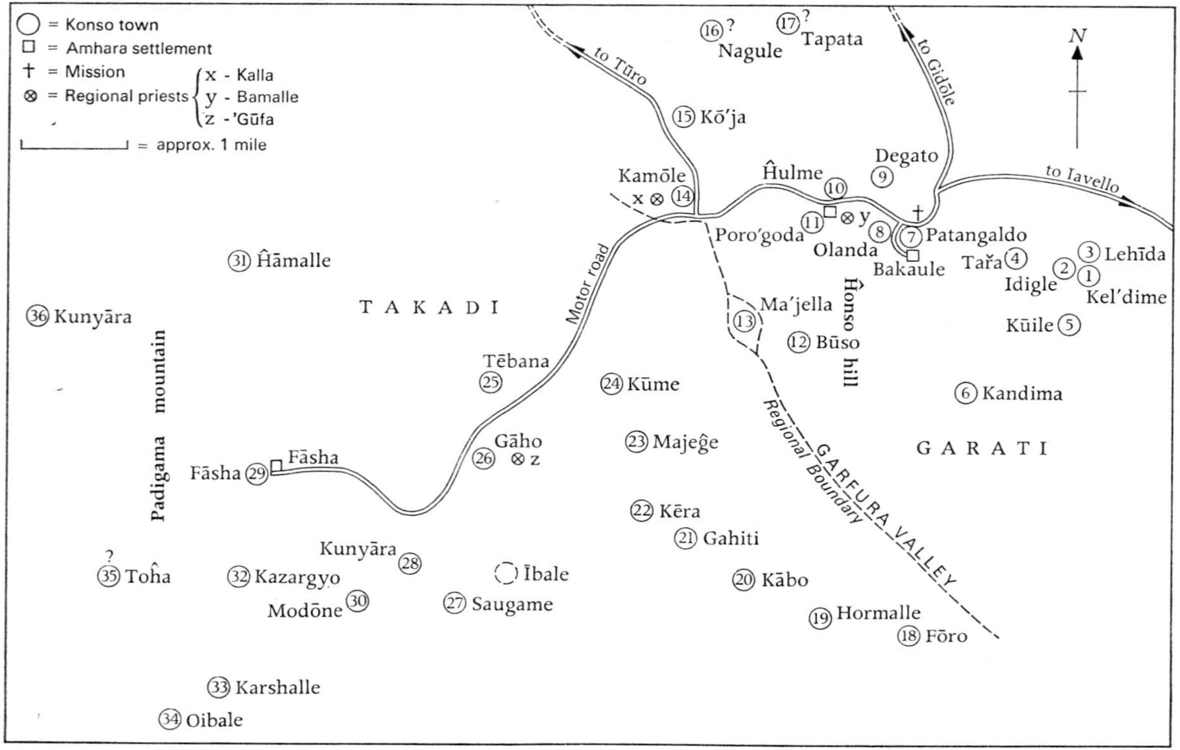

MAP III. Konso towns

Legend:

○ = Konso town
□ = Amhara settlement
+ = Mission
⊗ = Regional priests

x - Kalla
y - Bamalle
z - 'Gūfa

⎿_____⏌ = approx. 1 mile

to Javello

③ Lehīda
① Kel'dime
② Idigle
④ Tařa Tařa
⑤ Kūile

GARATI

⑥ Kandima

to Gidōle

+ Patangaldo
⑦ Bakaule
⑨ Deĝato
⑧ Olanda
⑩ y

Ĥonso hill

⑪ Poro'goda
Ĥulme
Ĝ Ma'jella ⑫ Būso
Tapata
⑰? Nagule
⑯?

GARFURA VALLEY

Regional Boundary

⑮ Kō'ja
⑬

to Tūro
Kamōle
x ⊗ ⑭

Motor road

⑳ Kābo
⑲ Hormalle
⑱ Fōro

㉑ Gahiti
㉒ Kēra
㉓ Majeĝe
㉔ Kūme

TAKADI

Tēbana
㉕

Gāho
㉖ ⊗ z

○ Ibale
㉗ Saugame

㉛ Ĥamalle

Kunyāra
㉘

㉚ Modōne
㉜ Kazargyo

㉝ Karshalle

Fāsha
□ Fāsha ㉙

Padigama mountain

㉟ Toha
?

㉞ Oibale

㊱ Kunyāra

N

and for much of the time are kept penned and hand fed in the stalls inside their owners' homesteads, where their manure can be easily collected, and are only taken out under careful supervision along special walled routes to the grazing land. They are enthusiastic bee-keepers, putting their cylindrical hives up in the branches of large trees, and protecting them with little thatched roofs. (Such hives can be seen in the tree in Plate VI.) They have what almost amounts to an affection for bees, referring to them as *hrela aWaĝa*, 'the warriors of God'. I have seen a man pick up a bee crawling on the ground and place it tenderly in the thatch out of harm's way. Honey, like butter, is not only a delicacy, but an auspicious substance, used in anointing.

The Konso are almost unique[1] in traditional Ethiopia for living in densely populated walled towns holding on average about 1,500 souls. Their sites are chosen for their defensive advantages, and generally they crown the summit of a hill, or are built on a spur, so that the terrain falls away steeply on three sides, leaving only the level ground of the fourth to be especially heavily defended. But they are not necessarily on the highest available ground, and sometimes better defensive sites have been neglected. Between the fields and the town walls there often intervenes a belt of dark and dense woodland, perhaps a hundred yards or more in depth, which was intended to deter enemies by the advantages of ambush it gave to the defenders. But the euphorbia and other succulent vegetation that were deliberately planted there have the additional function of being used to extinguish fires, by reason of their prolific sap; Konso towns are dangerously liable to fire, and when the alarm is given, the men rush to the *dina*, as these woods are called, and hack down the trees, which are thrown on the blaze. It is also often used for defecation: 'I am going to the *dina*' is a common euphemism. Landless people are buried there, especially the craftsmen. But it has no religious significance derived from or relating to these functions, and is regarded by the people as nothing more than a utilitarian device.

Within the belt of trees around the town stand the great walls.

---

[1] According to Helmut Straube (*Westkuschitische Völker Süd-Äthiopiens*) the Otschollo live in a single large town '. . . they are the only people of the Gamu Highland who do not live in single homesteads, but in a closed, fortress like village settlement lying on a prominent high summit on the Eastern slope of the Gamu Highland'. (Quoted from the English summary at the end of the volume, p. 383.)

Built of the ubiquitous basalt, without mortar, they are merely intended to deter the sudden attack of a massed enemy on foot armed
only with shields and spears, not to resist a siege. They are often
10–15 ft. high, and 7 or 8 ft. thick, with an allure (rampart walk)
in many cases. The Konso have never used the bow and arrow in
combat and their only missiles are spears, and stones, which they
can throw with great force and accuracy, a skill they have perfected
while scaring birds from the crops. Warfare between the towns in
the past was fairly common, but the warriors usually advanced to
meet each other in the open across the fields. Since the Amhara
conquest the walls have been allowed in many cases to be become
very ruinous.

It is not the case, as Azaïs and Jensen believe, that they are constructed in a double circle. The original settlement was surrounded
by a single massive wall, roughly circular in plan. The space within
this original wall must have been large enough to allow room for
succeeding generations to build their houses within its protected
limits, but inevitably an expanding population eventually out-
grew the original wall, and it became necessary to add further walls
from time to time. These however never extended the whole way
round the original wall, but were added to it in sections. The plan
of the walls of Idigle (Map IV) is an excellent example of how an
ancient town has extended itself piecemeal over the centuries.[1]

In most towns there are one or two principal gates (in size, that is),
which connect with the chief routes traversing Konso. There is
no truth in Jensen's assertion that there are always two, and only
two, main gates, facing north and east respectively. In the first
place, it is often hard to say which is a principal and which is
a secondary gate. Secondly, they are on paths which lead to the
town's sacred places or to the principal routes, and thus could not
have been orientated according to formal considerations; and
thirdly, there is little attention paid to the east in Konso thought,
and none at all to the north, so even if in a few cases gates do face
north and east, this has no religious significance, but is quite for-
tuitous. In the past, all gates, principal or secondary, were closed
and guarded at night by families retained and paid by the town for
doing so. With the coming of the *pax Amharica* this has now lapsed.

---

[1] I calculated the area of Gaho, a small town, as about 15 acres. Idigle is
about 25 acres, and Degato, the largest town in Konso, in the region of 35 acres.
Most towns would cover about 20 acres.

Konso towns make an overwhelming impression of antiquity and mystery upon the stranger; their russet walls, crude and massive, seem to have been forced out of the soil on which they stand, and the encircling woods, and the thin expanse of delicate foliage that

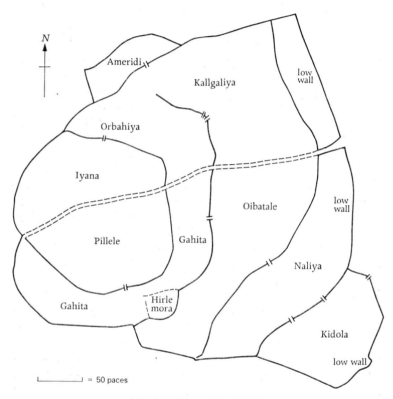

MAP IV. The walls of Idigle

hangs over them like a green mist blend them even more intimately with the surrounding fields. As one passes through their gates one is at once conscious of a genius for corporate life, for these towns are undoubtedly works of art. There could be no greater contrast than between the shapeless shanty-town of Bakaule, with its corrugated iron roofs and uninspired lines of whitewashed dwellings, and the Konso towns. The narrow lanes, turned into shadowy arcades by the tall palings of the homesteads that stand on either side, whose low arched gateways have an almost Gothic quality, open suddenly

into dancing places, the *moras*, often floored with grass, and en-
circled with low stone platforms on which numerous trees have
been planted for shade. Here the men sit gossiping and spinning
their cotton; the whole effect is often strikingly beautiful. They are
used for assemblies as well as dances, and lawsuits and religious
ceremonies, as well as more practical purposes like drying blankets
and hides, or laying out the parts of a new house. Adjoining them
are large men's houses (*magana* or *pafta*) with phallic roof-pots,
where the men, both married and unmarried sleep at night.[1] House
and dancing floor are collectively referred to as *mora*. The sense of
antiquity is heightened by the great monoliths, 'stones of manhood',
which sometimes stand there, testifying to the bravery of long-dead
warriors in victorious battles. In the most sacred *moras* are tall dead
juniper trees (*ulahitas*), stripped of their branches by the weather
of years and soaring into the air sometimes to a height of forty
feet or more. Most striking of all are their memorial statues to the
dead, *wagas*. They represent a dead man who has killed one or more
enemies in battle and perhaps a lion or leopard. The hero stands in
the centre flanked by his wives and victims; they are carved of wood
in a bleak and rigid style, and often line a great *mora* or the most
important paths into town, standing in small, severe groups.

The map of Būso (Map V) shows a typical distribution of *moras*
in a town. The size, contents, and social and religious significance
of *moras* vary considerably, so I include a table of Būso *moras* and
a table of Degato *moras* for comparison. In Būso it is said that there
must be no weaving-pits in sacred *moras*, but in Degato they
seemed unconcerned about this. *Ulahitas* are the sacred dead trees
erected for the warrior grade, and the stones of manhood commemorate victorious warriors. Towns are divided into wards, and
each ward will have one or more *moras* of its own. Some *moras*
belong to the town as a whole.

The Konso, being a gregarious people, are much given to holding ceremonies, most of which take place in the *moras*. While
women are excluded from some of the most important rites, they
may attend as spectators and they take part in many dances,
which are purely for entertainment. Women's dances tend to be

---

[1] I was told that it had been the custom for men to hang their shields in
some of these houses, and there were wooden hooks in the roof of the clubhouse
where I lived in Būso. Apparently the practice was discontinued when shields
began to be stolen.

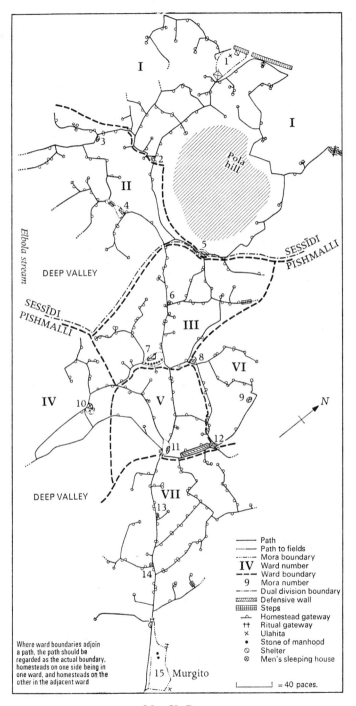

I

I

Pola hill

3

2

II

4

Elbola stream

SESSĪDI PISHMALLI

5

DEEP VALLEY

SESSĪDI PISHMALLI

6

III

7

8

VI

9

IV

10

V

N

12

11

DEEP VALLEY

VII

13

14

15 Murgito

Where ward boundaries adjoin
a path, the path should be
regarded as the actual boundary,
homesteads on one side being in
one ward, and homesteads on the
other in the adjacent ward

——	Path
....	Path to fields
—·—·—	Mora boundary
IV	Ward number
— — —	Ward boundary
9	Mora number
—··—··—	Dual division boundary
▨▨▨	Defensive wall
▦▦▦	Steps
⌐	Homestead gateway
✝	Ritual gateway
×	Ulahita
•	Stone of manhood
⌀	Shelter
⊗	Men's sleeping house

|———————| = 40 paces.

MAP V. BUSO

TABLE 1. *Būso* moras

No.	Name	Weaving-pits	*Ulahitas*	Stones of manhood	Clubhouse	Dancing-place	Town/ward
1	Kolalta	—	1	—	1	1	town
2	Tapata	—	—	—	1	—	ward
3	Kuile	—	—	—	1	—	ward
4	Tala'gamida	—	—	—	1	1	ward
5	Deemala	—	—	—	1	1	ward
6	Yalagâle	—	—	—	1	—	ward
7	Tara'jo	—	1	6	1	1	town
8	Ifada	—	—	—	1	—	ward
9	Palbala	—	—	—	1	1	ward
10	Gomïya	—	1	—	1	1	ward
11	Idigle	—	—	—	1	1	ward
12	Murōda	—	—	—	1	—	ward
13	Nalïya	1	—	—	1	—	ward
14	Pologâ	—	—	—	1	—	ward
15	Murgito	—	1	2	—	1	town

TABLE 2. *Degato* moras

Name	Weaving-pits	*Ulahitas*	Stones of manhood	Clubhouse	Dancing-place	Town/ward
Harale	2	1	—	1	—	ward
Pologê	—	2	—	1	1	town
Hangala	1	—	—	1	1	town
Murragâra	—	—	—	1	—	ward
A'gele	—	2	—	1	—	ward
Hoba	2	1	—	—	—	ward
Giyo	—	1	—	1	1	ward
Detati	—	1	1	1	1	town
Kobdale	—	2	1	1	1	town
Odïya	1	1	—	1	—	ward
Deele	—	1	1	1	1	ward
Kergo	—	1	—	1	—	ward
Lehïdi	—	1	—	1	—	ward
Gauda	—	1	—	1	—	ward
In the fields:						
Tōle	—	—	1	—	—	town
Nagïle	—	—	2	—	—	town
Halaudila	—	—	5	—	—	town

dull and monotonous, as they link arms and move slowly round in a circle singing a simple refrain, or parade in ranks up and down the length of the *mora*; then the men make their entrance for the *seega* dance, running round the arena, screaming and flinging their spears into the centre of the *mora*, while the women scatter like chickens to take shelter on the walls around the *mora* with cries of mock terror. The men face each other across the *mora* in two groups, screaming in simulated battle-fury, ringing bells, kicking their long shields and thrusting with spears and sticks, until the tumult reaches a climax and the groups rush together, passing through each other to reform on the opposite side, when the performance is repeated. During this display of martial ferocity the women set up a piercing ululation, like the crying of wild birds on a cliff-top, and the dust of the ground, threshed by the stamping feet of the men in their dance rises into the air, where it is turned to gold by the slanting sunbeams. If the social organization of the Konso is based on the towns, the life of the towns is inconceivable without the *moras*.

One of the most striking features of Konso towns is the manner in which the compounds are crowded tightly together. Each married man has his compound with a number of huts, from a minimum of three to a dozen or more. His junior wives, if he has any, each live in separate compounds, often at some distance from their husbands. Similarly, his sons will set up house after they marry in their own homesteads, with the exception of the eldest son, who lives with his father even after marriage, as he will inherit the principal homestead. Compounds are always divided into an upper level (*oida*) and a lower level (*arhata*). The family lives on the upper and the livestock is penned under cover on the lower. This distinction has an important religious significance. Homesteads are extremely cramped, the roofs of the huts touching and overlapping each other in many cases. The beehive sleeping huts are remarkable for their extremely low arched doorways, about 3 ft. high. Inside the hut is a short wooden tunnel, formed of two upright planks with a cross-piece on top. The effect of this is that anyone entering the hut has to crawl on hands and knees, and if he were an enemy would be at the mercy of the occupant, since he could not use a weapon in such a position, whereas the defender would be standing, able to spear or club him. There are, besides these beehive sleeping huts, separate kitchens, granaries which are raised on stilts and walled with cane, grinding houses, and cattle pens. Huts are often of massive construction, and may last, apart from being rethatched, for seventy or eighty years.[1] The courtyard around the huts is sometimes paved, but whatever its surface it will be hard,

---

[1] I was told that the men's club-house in which I first lived in Būso was two hundred years old.

and swept clean every few days. Rubbish is carried to dumps out-side the town walls. Manure is often shared between several home-steads, and there are many heaps throughout the towns. The whole compound is surrounded by a high fence of wooden palings. In many cases this is reinforced by planting small trees that are allowed to grow around the palings and intertwine with them so that a really dense mass of timber is created. These fences are partly to keep out thieves, but also the prying eyes of their neighbours. They have a strong sense of privacy and the phrase *tigalio*, 'someone else's house', is very commonly used among them. The fence is pierced by a single arched gate, in most cases not much more than 4 ft. high, and sometimes less. They are closed at night by piling logs held in place by upright timbers within the gate.

The compounds are in most cases adjacent to one another, with their fences acting as a party wall. They are divided into blocks by the lanes that wind between them. These lanes are barely wide enough for the cattle to walk along, and in the morning and at sunset, when they are returning from the grazing they block the ways completely. In the rains the ground underfoot is turned to ankle-deep mud and paths which are steeply inclined become rushing torrents. The householder naturally likes his compound to be as spacious as pos-sible and so encroaches on the paths until, for example, the women, who often carry great bundles of firewood or fodder on their backs, have to walk sideways to their homes, freeing their burdens at al-most every step from entanglement with the palisades. While people like their compounds to be as large as possible they have built their towns to take up as little room as possible.

An excessively large town wall in relation to the number of in-habitants would clearly be difficult to defend, and it was in their interest to compromise between the requirements of defence, and the needs of future expansion. It is understandable therefore that the towns should economize on space as much as possible. Land inside towns not used for housing or public assembly places is used for fields in the usual way.[1] The extremely cramped conditions are thus partly the product of the need for defence, and the need for land. But this is not a conclusive explanation. The southernmost town of the Turo region, Madara, is typical of the rest of Konso in the density of its settlement pattern; the only difference is that it

---

[1] Fields within the walls are called *enna*, as opposed to those outside, called *'dula*.

has no walls, and never seems to have had any. We must therefore recognize that there is a predisposition of the Konso to dense settlements, apart from the effects of having to fit their towns into walled enclosures. It is interesting to note that Madara is, of all the Turo settlements the closest to the main part of Konso, where walled towns are the norm, while further north in the rest of Turo settlements tend to be less dense. Karshalle, another settlement where I lived in Turo was fairly dense, and there used to be a walled town nearby called 'Dagatdēra, but otherwise settlement seems to become more scattered as one moves north. So possibly we are not dealing with a question of defence alone, but with an idea of how to live, which is not immediately related to the needs of warfare. I shall investigate the consequences of the Konso settlement pattern in the next chapter.

The day begins for the women an hour or more before dawn. In total darkness, unless there is some light from the waning moon, the silence only broken by the trees rustling in the chill breezes, they grope their way to the grindstones and begin preparing the day's supply of flour, often singing to themselves as they grind. The heavy stones send a muffled reverberation through the earth. In the twilight before dawn the men rise, and this is the time that everyone visits the latrines, on the outskirts of the towns. These are sometimes screened off if they are in exposed positions, but the faeces are kept together, and after they have dried, a very rapid process in the hot sun, they will eventually be collected and taken out to the fields for manure. Now the fires are blown into life, or a child is sent out to a neighbour with a potsherd to fetch fresh embers, and breakfast is eaten. A haze of smoke hangs over the homesteads in the first rays of the sun. Men sit about wrapped and still in their blankets, covering their heads against the chill of morning. When the sun is up the boys of each ward whose turn it is to herd the animals of their neighbours begin collecting the cattle and the sheep and goats at the town gates; when they have all arrived they move off along the paths to where there is some grazing land. The little children are sent out with their older brothers and sisters to play in the *moras*; one often sees a small child staggering along with a younger brother or sister of almost the same size on its back. The older girls by this time will often have made at least one journey to the well or water-hole with their mothers. They carry the water in gourds which are fixed between two flat light wooden frames and wedged with straw, and tied on their backs. A woman can carry as much as four or five gallons in a single load, but little girls begin to fetch water when they are about six or seven years of age, in small gourds and frames which are specially made for them. The fetching of water is essentially women's work, but a man will help out in an emergency, though he will not use the frame and carries the gourd on his head instead. Men always carry loads on their heads or shoulders; the bundle on the back is a mark of female status.

FIG. 1. A Konso hoe

Depending on the season some or all of the family will be going out into the fields when the water is in and breakfast finished. Men and women work together in the fields without distinction; the building of the walls, however, is men's work, as is house-building.

Before the great rains which come in the later part of February the ground must be dug over and cleared of weeds and stubble. As the rains begin the millet seed is sown broadcast and dug in. For uprooting and breaking the hardest soil they use single-pointed iron-tipped digging sticks. In weeding and general digging they use a double-tipped hoe which is perhaps related to the Ancient Egyptian model. When the rains have set in there is constant work in keeping down the weeds. As the crops begin to ripen the men often sleep out at night, in little shelters built in the fields, blowing horns and screaming at intervals to scare the animals which come in the hours of darkness to ravage the crops, while during the day at this time and during harvest months the young men are out with slings which they crack like whips and use to hurl stones with great force at the birds. There are many platforms in the fields on which they stand to keep guard. The women are out as well at this time, adding their screams to the general clamour. The same precautions are taken during the little rains.

When the day is well advanced the towns settle down to their habitual quiet—the distant murmur of voices, the lowing of cattle, sometimes the persistent tapping of a woman refacing a grindstone, with a stone maul, and the clinking of bells on a girl's ankle as she walks. When there is little work in the fields, the men sit around in the *moras* talking and spinning their cotton. In the heat of the day the older ones especially often lie enveloped in their blankets in the cool of the men's houses. The *shelagda* trees rustle in the wind, which blows the dust hither and thither, together with the bitter smell of drying faeces and dung.

As the sun goes down, about half past six, the cattle begin to come home from the fields, blocking the narrow lanes for a while. The screams of lust from the he-goats echo through the town again as they did in the morning. The women go again to the wells to fetch water for the evening meal and the fires spring to life. As twilight deepens, the leaves on the *shelagda* trees seem to glow a brilliant green, against the deep metallic blue of the sky, and by half-past seven darkness, apart from the stars, is almost complete. Blanket-robed figures are briefly illuminated in the light of fires in many kitchens, and people settle down for their evening meal. They hate going outside the town gates after dark, the time of ghosts and evil spirits which may meet them on the paths. Gradually the voices cease, and one hears the clatter of timber as the gateways of the homesteads are barred. In the old days the town gates were also barred at this time, and watchmen took up their positions to guard against intruders and wild beasts. The men go to the *mora* houses, where the sound of talk often goes on until midnight, accompanied by the strumming of their 'guitars'.

The towns have always been self-sufficient, inward-looking communities, often divided by bitter hostility from their neighbours, but they are joined by a network of paths, often filled with boulders and garden rubbish, or soil tossed over the walls from the fields. These paths, belonging to no-one and for the use of all travellers, are not now maintained by anyone. In the past it is likely that they were much better kept, especially where they led to the fields owned mainly by the townspeople themselves. While I was in Būso, the elders complained that the paths to the fields were becoming difficult to walk on, and all the young men with some adults to supervise them ran out one morning along a main route and stripped it of weeds, rocks and rubbish in a frenzy of energy. But such repair of the paths is now rare.

Fields are owned individually, and not held in common either by ward or lineage. Thus the land surrounding a town, while largely owned by the people of the town, is not 'town' property, and it is possible for members of other towns to buy such land. The people of Būso, who are very hardworking, are particularly rich, and have extended their land in this way to within sight of Degato and Kamole. But while the land of the people intermingles, their social life has always been concentrated in the towns. Apart from the rare regional generation-grading ceremonies, and some dances, to which friendly towns are invited, there is little contact between men of different towns. The only exceptions to this are the markets.

Scattered throughout the countryside there are a number of markets, which are invariably outside the towns, in some cases even quite isolated in the fields. Markets are rowdy affairs full of shouting and disputation, which is reason enough for them not to be held inside towns; in addition the presence of hordes of strangers could well lead to theft, or accusations of theft, especially if the offenders came from a hostile town. So the market sites are on conveniently neutral ground. On the day of the market people generally start assembling at about two in the afternoon, converging along the paths leading to the market place, some women bent double under bundles of pots twice their size, or loads of *shelaĝda* foliage, and the men with leather bags of grain on their heads, or leading in beasts for sale or slaughter. At Bakaule are tethered the camels of the Borana, who used to bring salt in the past when there were no lorries, and the Guji women, strikingly beautiful with long buttered ringlets, selling their half-curdled milk from large gourds, intricately embroidered with wire and beads. There are sometimes a few trees to give a little shade, but most traders, men and women, sit out in the sun until the market disperses at sunset.

Most people are self-sufficient in food, and so the markets naturally have a large section dealing with the products of craftsmen—pots, leatherwork, cloth and thread, and iron work—and other luxury items, and imported goods. There is a small group of despised craftsmen, whose sole source of income in the past, when they owned no fields, was derived from the articles they sold for grain in the markets, and so they are really essential for the existence of the craftsmen, since in the towns where they work individually there is not enough demand to give them a living.

Butter and honey are highly prized delicacies and command a good price, and the markets are also the principal occasion for slaughtering meat. Most Konso eat meat comparatively rarely;

cattle, sheep, and goats are too valuable for their manure to allow a larger quantity to be killed, though the Borana also bring a number of beasts of their own. In a Konso market, only craftsmen slaughter animals; it is forbidden for a cultivator to do so. Apparently in the past it was also thought to be wrong for cultivators to buy meat in the market.

I deal with the names and days of markets in the chapter on time-reckoning; suffice it to say here that it is likely that even before the Amhara a market was held almost every day in some part of Konso—a good opportunity for telling the news, and meeting people from other towns.

We have then a people already thick on the ground (perhaps 250 to the square mile) further concentrated into a number of towns of ancient date, with a long-standing tradition of intense loyalty among their members, and suspicion of or hostility to outsiders. Industrious, warlike, ingenious with their hands, gregarious, but without much common property and quick to assert their personal rights, they live close to famine if the rains fail, and prey to all the miseries of sickness, locusts, murrain, and violent death which beset primitive life. What have they made of their world?

III

SOCIAL ORGANIZATION

PART 1. POLITICAL ORGANIZATION

KONSO society is based on large autonomous towns, each governed by an elected council of elders, but subject to no effective authority in their external relations. In these respects they resemble some West African peoples such as the Yakö, Bwa, and Yoruba. While they also possess a generation-grading system, this does not, among the Konso, provide a framework of authority which can transcend the towns and serve to unite them in a wider nexus of co-operation. The functioning of the generation-grading system among the Konso is thus radically different from that of similar systems of other Galla peoples, as described by Knutsson, for example,[1] where it may provide the basis of a hierarchy of councils. Most studies of political organization in Africa have concentrated on centralized systems of government, under chiefs or kings, segmentary lineage systems, bands, or age-set societies. There is no comparative literature on systems of the Konso type.

1. THE REGIONS

Konso is divided into three regions, Garati in the east, Takadi in the west, and Turo in the north. Garati has the following towns:[2]

TABLE 3. *Garati towns*

1.	Kel'dime	10.	Ĥulme
2.	Idigle	11.	Poro'goda
3.	Lehīda	12.	Būso
4.	Tar̃a	13.	Ma'jella
5.	Kūile	14.	Kamōle
6.	Kandima.	15.	Kō'ja
7.	Patangaldo } Turīdi	16.	Nagule
8.	Ōlanda } Turīdi	17.	Tapata
9.	Degato		

[1] *Authority and Change* (1967).

[2] See Map III.

Ma'jella is anomalous, in that while its generation-grading system is that of Takadi, it owes ritual allegiance to the regional priest of Garati, and is considered to be a Garati town.

In Takadi the towns are as follows:

TABLE 4. *Takadi towns*

18. Foro ⎫ Iyēdi	28. Kunyara
19. Ḫormalle ⎭	29. Fāsha
20. Kābo	30. Modōne
21. Gahiti	31. Ḫamalle
22. Kēra	32. Kazargyo
23. Majeġe	33. Karshalle
24. Kūme	34. Oibale
25. Tēbana	35. Toĥa.
26. Gāho	36. Kunyara in Ḫolme
27. Saugame	

There are two further parts of Takadi, still owing religious allegiance to the 'Gūfa, the regional priest of Takadi, called Ḫolme and Elládi; Ḫolme is beyond Padigama mountain at Fāsha, extending westward, and Elládi is beyond Ḫolme again, going down to the Woito valley. There are far fewer people in these two parts, and no large settlements. It is an area of much more recent expansion than the main part of the Konso Highlands.

Turo has no walled towns now, and only one obvious one in the past, 'Dagatdera, now deserted. There are three quite large compact settlements, Karshalle, Arfīda, and Madara, and some other more scattered ones, such as Päïdi and Tishmalli, but there has never been the same development of urban life in Turo as we find in Takadi and Garati. Turo is, in this way and many others, less like the other two regions than they are to each other, and the reader should bear this constantly in mind. In Karshalle, in Turo, where I lived, which was a fairly large settlement of perhaps 200 people, there were no wards, and apparently no councils, nor any of the other town functionaries typical of Takadi and Garati which we shall examine later in the chapter. Turo was a difficult region for me to assess. Many Amhara have come to live there since the Italian war and have made far more impact than anywhere else in Konso. For example, the plough has entirely superseded hoe cultivation in Turo, and many of the Konso people came to the Coptic

Christmas festival at the local Amhara church, which they never
did at the other two churches in Garati and Takadi. But it is hard
to believe that even this degree of Amharicization could, in twenty
years, have obliterated not only the practice but also even the
memory of their urban institutions, if these had ever existed, especially as their daily life in its domestic details seems undisturbed—
women still do not cover their breasts in Karshalle, even though they
are aware that the Amhara regard this with deep aversion. The
French explorer Darragon passed through Turo in October 1897
in the wake of Menelik's army which had just subdued the Konso.
His route, which he illustrates in a map, did not go through Garati
and Takadi, but went to the north of these areas, so he never saw
the rest of Konso. He writes:

> Konso properly so-called is a curious little country recently con-
> quered by the Abyssinians and whose extent, in the part of which I wish
> to inform you, does not exceed 20 kilometres. This part, mountainous,
> is populated by completely black people, whose language and customs
> differ from those of the surrounding country. They are remarkable for
> their love of work. Their fields of coffee, cotton and maize are set out in
> terraces on the sides of hills, and are tended in irreproachable fashion.
> Their houses are symmetrically built on piles which keep out the
> damp.[1]

While we may contemplate these miserable scraps of information
and wasted opportunities with anguish, at least it seems clear that
even so superficial an observer as Darragon would not have passed
over in silence the existence of something so evident and unusual as
walled towns in Turo if there had been any such towns to be seen.
I conclude from this that the Amhara did not destroy any towns in
Turo, as their ruins would surely have caught Darragon's eye,
and that 'Dagaťdera, the one large and well-defended walled site,
was abandoned before the arrival of the Amhara.

While the towns in each region are autonomous, as I have said,
the regions possess, besides a rough geographical coherence, a moral
unity which is expressed in allegiance to a regional priest and the
possession of a generation-grading system which is common to all
the towns of the region, and which is only found within the region.
Garati and Takadi regions also each have a pair of sacred drums.

---

[1] This is clearly a reference to granaries, not dwellings.

There are three kinds of priest (*poĝalla*) in Konso: regional priests, *mora* priests, and lineage priests. Regional priests have certain ritual duties connected with the regional generation-grading ceremonies, *mora* priests are the guardians of particularly sacred places, and lineage priests are the heads of their lineages and bless them. These are not mutually exclusive offices however. The three regional priests and the *mora* priests are all lineage priests, but while the regional priests have small *moras* outside their homesteads these are not used during the regional grading ceremonies. Again, we find that many lineage priests are also the 'owners' of *moras*, both sacred and profane, within the towns, in the sense that the sites of the *moras* were provided by their ancestors, and there is some evidence that they have special ritual responsibilities for these *moras*. Thus the distinction between *mora* priests and lineage priests is inevitably less clear than between these categories of priest and the regional priests. The point of making it is that some *moras* are of such importance that the lineage priests who 'own' them derive additional status from this. Thus when I refer to *mora* priests I am referring to the guardians of particularly sacred *moras*. When referring to priests in general I shall speak simply of 'priests', and I shall only qualify this by 'regional', for example, when it is not clear from the context which category is intended. The Konso themselves make no terminological distinction between the priests except to refer to some as 'big priests' and others as 'little priests'; thus the regional priests, the *mora* priests, and the priests of large lineages in a town would all be referred to as 'big', while the priests of small lineages would be referred to as 'little' unless they were also *mora* priests, or their ancestors were considered to be among the founders of the town. There are, therefore, a number of criteria involved in the assessment of the status of priests; the three categories which I have designated are simply the most important. In Garati there are a few priests, apart from the regional priests, who wear a silver bracelet on their right wrists. (The normal insignia for a Garati priest are five iron bracelets on the right wrist.) It is said that the ancestors of these priests were born holding a gourd of milk, a bee, and a little cow.

The essential function of all priests is to bring Life and peace, and ideally they are forbidden to kill either in war or hunting, though this prohibition has lapsed for many lineage priests in Garati. The only blood they may shed is that of sacrifice. It would thus fundamentally contradict the nature of his office for a regional priest to have political power, or possess a private army which could enforce peace between warring towns, even if this were logistically possible in Konso circumstances. The regional priests live alone in the fields away from the towns. I shall discuss the reasons for this later.

Their functions are to bless their people, and I give details of these ceremonies in the chapters on the grading systems and ritual. They also act as peacemakers in their regions. When two towns are advancing to war they should send their representatives, *sara*, and the sacred drum-holders to intervene between the combatants, but they have no means of forcing peace on the opposing parties. In Garati there are some other peacemakers, from the small town of Lehida, who run between the combatants, and try to stop the fighting by mystical sanctions. Peacemakers are known as '*Nama Dawra*', 'people who forbid'. At most, however, they provide both parties with an excuse for honourable withdrawal.

The regional priests have not always lived in their present regions, and I shall give a short account of their family histories according to Konso tradition. The 'Gūfa[1] is the unquestioned regional priest of Takadi. His homestead is near Gāho. Of his origins it is said only that long ago his ancestors came from Ilota, the range of mountains a few miles to the north-east of Konso (see Map II). In Garati and Turo, however, the position is more complicated. The regional priest of Turo is the Kalla,[2] but although his permission and blessing are still necessary for the Turo generation-grading ceremony, he no longer lives there. According to the account given to me by the present Kalla, and supported by the other informants, his ancestors originally came from 'Kondare' in the province of Shoa, where Addis Ababa is now situated. In fact it is likely that this is a somewhat interpolated legend. In the first place, 'Kondare', which presumably means Gondar, is not in Shoa, but in Begemder, considerably to the north, and is of seventeenth-century foundation, and thus of rather too late a date to provide a plausible place of origin for the ancestors of the Kalla. Shoa, to the modern Konso, is the centre *par excellence* of the Amhara, and may be ascribed as the origin of the Kalla family simply to assert that they were originally

---

[1] For the means by which priests inherit their names see below, p. 100.

[2] It is possible, but not certain, that 'Kalla' is derived from the Borana name for their high priests, 'Kallu'.

Amhara. It is perhaps more likely that the first Kalla came to Konso in the fifteenth century when the Abyssinian Empire reached as far south as Lake Awasa, just over a hundred miles to the north of Konso.

When the first Kalla came to Turo his homestead was by the village of Karshalle, and the site of this homestead is still pointed out, now only a grove of trees.[1] From Karshalle in Turo his ancestors went to Karshalle in Takadi, where a large wood still belonging to the Kalla is yet to be seen. It is said that no-one was living in Takadi at this time, but this seems unlikely. From Karshalle they went to a hill overlooking Degato in Garati. This site, which is now a grove of trees, is less than a mile from the residence of another regional priest, the Bamalle. The quarrels which resulted led to the departure of the Kalla of that time to the site of the present homestead near Kamole. The Kalla is now regarded as the major priest of Garati, with the exception of the towns of Degato, Poro'goda, and Holme, which are generally acknowledged, even by the Kalla, to owe ritual allegiance to the Bamalle. There is still enmity between the Bamalle and the Kalla; the Bamalle says that before the Kalla came all Garati owed ritual allegiance to him. The fact that the Bamalle still anoints the sacred drums of Garati strongly supports this claim.

The ancestors of the Bamalle came from Liban in Borana, and after residing in Burji arrived at Kuile in Garati, whence they removed to Būso, where the old homestead, a grove of trees, can still be seen. Following an attack by armoured men about three hundred and fifty years ago (possibly soldiers from the Muslim state of Hadya, which reached almost to the site of the present Arba Minch) in which a Bamalle was killed, his successor moved his home to the top of the Honso hill, dominating Garati, where the Bamalle still lives.

In all regions these three priests have a close association with the generation-grading systems. These systems are based on a fixed cycle of years; eighteen in Garati, nine in Takadi, and five in Turo. On the completion of a cycle everyone moves up together into the next grade. Unlike true age-grading systems, in the Konso type one's position in the system at birth is determined by that of one's father. In the Garati region one is always two grades, no more

---

[1] I deal with the significance of priests' woods and old homesteads below, pp. 250 ff.

or less, behind one's father. The grades in Garati, from senior to junior, are:

Ukūda ⎫ Gulula ⎭	Dead or very old
Gurula	Beginning to leave active life
Orshāda ⎫ Kada ⎭	Nama Dawra. and main body of elders
Ĥrela	Warriors
Farīda	No marriage permitted

FIG. 2. Garati generation-grades

It will be observed from this table that one important function of the system is the prohibition of marriage to men in the most junior grade, for they say that it is bad for parents and their children to be procreating simultaneously. Still today a mother is not supposed to bear children after her first son has married.

In more general terms, the systems serve to divide the generations into four principal categories (though there are, of course, more than four grades). The first is that of the useless youngsters, who are forbidden to marry, claim a game animal if they kill it, take part in councils, or sacrifice, and are not held responsible for damage caused by negligence. Above them are the warriors, who can marry, take part in councils, sacrifice, and are in all other respects full members of society. Senior grades have primarily the responsibility of blessing the warrior grade, to ensure not only its fortitude and success in battle, but its very survival against sickness and death. They also curse pests which attack the crops. Besides their religious functions they represent the collective wisdom of society. Finally, in the fourth category, there are the oldest men, senile, who can do little but sit in the sun and spin cotton, and doze. Thus the generation systems provide an ideal hierarchy of functions for the main ages of man, which is also linked with the principal values and needs of the Konso. Associated with these systems are a number of ceremonies the purpose of which, broadly speaking, is to ensure rainfall, the fertility of the fields and crops, and of women and domestic animals, the absence of disease, internal peace, good hunting, and success in warfare.

Although the systems comprehend all the towns in each region, they play no part in moderating inter-town rivalries, because the members of each grade only form corporate groups within each town. The warrior grade, for example, cannot be mobilized as a whole to act as a police force within the region. Nor do the periodic ceremonies of the grading systems exert any obvious pacificatory influence. It would be thoroughly implausible to suggest that the grading systems have the effect of counterbalancing the tendency to fragmentation of Konso political organization, in view of the endemic warfare between the towns.

Garati and Takadi each has a pair of sacred drums,[1] which symbolize peace and harmony. They circulate between towns in a fixed cycle, being held for a number of years by the representative of an eminent family. In Garati the two drums are called Kadana and Dokona (Kadana means 'the great rains'; I am not aware that Dokona means anything in modern Konsiña). In Takadi they are called Kadana and Dopode. It was said by some that Kadana was the wife and Dokona the husband. Other people said this was absurd, as how could a drum, which was only wood and leather, have a sex? Associated with each pair of drums is a kudu horn, also named; kudu horns are used to summon people to assemblies.

The Kadana and Dokona drums are circulated in a fixed cycle among eight towns of Garati, as follows:

TABLE 5. *Garati drums*

	KADANA			DOKONA		
Order	Town	Family	No. of years	Town	Family	No. of years
Now	Kandima	?	2	Turīdi	Ogita	2
2	Idigle	Hirle	2	Degato	Gomba	2
3	Idigle	Panato	2	Būso	Kudyo	2
4	Tara	Omana	2	Kandima	Fulida	2
5	Kuile	Mareda	2	Kuile	Ampo	2
6	Kandima	Kalta	2	Idigle	Subeno	2
7	Kandima	Fulida	2	Idigle	Kado	2
8	Kandima	Haule	2	Kel'dime	Ogose	2
9	Kandima	Keda	2	Tařa	Kida	2
		TOTAL	18		TOTAL	18

There is also a similar cycle of sacred drums, in their case called Kadana and Dopode, among a nucleus of Takadi towns. The drums

---

[1] As we shall see, the towns in Garati and Takadi also have a pair of sacred drums each.

are held for nine years in each town (in Takadi the length of the grading cycle is only nine years), so that unlike Garati there is no theoretical limit to the number of towns which hold the drum.

TABLE 6. *Takadi drums*

KADANA

Town	Family	Ȟrelta[1]
Gaho	Karbite	Melgussa (now)
Majere	Guma	Hirba
Kera	Sholo	Galgussa
Iyedi (Hormalle)	Pisha	Melgussa
Saugame	Satale	Hirba
Majere	Jirero	Galgussa

DOPODE

Majere	Moye	Melgussa (now)
Gaho	Shalo	Hirba
Majere	Jirero	Galgussa
Kume	Dalda	Melgussa
?	?	?
?	?	?

(My informants were not clear as to whether there were any more towns in this cycle.)

As we have seen, in Garati the cycle of the generation-grading system is eighteen years, and this is also correlated with the drum cycle, which ends at the same time as the grading cycle.

Every year the two Garati drums are taken to the house of the Bamalle, who ceremonially anoints and blesses them (I describe this ceremony in chapter VII). There is a further ceremony concerning the Garati drums, when they are taken to a certain tree at Kandima. The drum-holders from the eight towns in the cycle, whether or not they have either drum in the year in question, all bring small gourds of beer. Together they drink some of the beer and pour the remainder onto the earth beside the tree. A member of the warrior grade (Ȟrela) climbs the tree in the evening, and prays 'May God send rain; may no bad person be seen in the land; may my voice bring unity; may I drink rain.' As he says these words the drum is beaten, and the kudu horn is blown.

The most striking feature of the sacred drums of the Konso is

[1] I explain this term below, p. 180.

that they must normally never be played, and not even touched or seen by women, craftsmen, or outsiders such as Amhara or white men.

While I was never allowed to examine any of the drums in Konso, I commissioned one from a woodworker. It was about 3 ft. long, and 15 in. in diameter, rather larger perhaps than the sacred drums. It consisted of a tree-trunk, hollowed into a tube, and round it a white cow-hide was wrapped, in the edges of which thongs and loops were cut so that it could be dragged tight around the wood, very little of which was visible when the drum was completed. There was thus no means of adjusting the tension of the diaphragms at each end, which were integrally related in the same hide. My drum was made of white hide, which in Konso symbolism is the colour of death, and, by extension, of cursing. My informant who made this drum told me that all drums were white—which may or may not be the case.

At the present time drums are beaten only on three basic occasions: (1) at the death of a priest, (2) at the end of a grading cycle, and (3) at the coming of the great rains. In a few cases they are used in the *iyanna* cult to summon spirits, but this is a recent alien importation (see below, p. 306). In Turo drums are beaten only at the death of a priest and have no place, I was told, at the grading ceremony of Osumada. Apparently the drums beaten for a priest are different from those used in the grading cycles. While it is symbolically appropriate that a mourning drum for a priest should be white, this would not be the case with the grading drums. Never having seen one of the latter, however, I am not in a position to say what colour they are.

Needham[1] draws attention to the very widespread use of percussive instruments in association with rites of passage, and transition in general. The use of drums in Konso to mark the death of priests, the change of year, and the succession of one grading cycle to another, is yet another example of this phenomenon.

But their association with transition is not emphasized at the conscious level of Konso thought. In their texts and conversation they are solely concerned with the drum as the symbol and focus of law and order:

When relations between two towns are bad, and they accuse each

---

[1] Rodney Needham, 'Percussion and Transition', *Man* (1967).

other to defeat each other, the one who wins between the two towns has a dance, and the town who has a stone erected for it, it is bad for that town. [The victorious town puts up a 'stone of manhood' to commemorate the defeat of its enemy.] In the past, when there were no Amhara, and no arresting of people, when two towns quarrelled together they took spears and flung them at each other, and killed each other, and on that day Lehīda makes its way among these people, and grabs them and argues with them. And the town which is in the wrong must pay compensation for killing.[1] If it refuses to pay compensation, Lehīda curses them; they say that by refusing to pay they have ignored Kadana [the great drum of Garati]. Now henceforth they have refused the Dawra. 'We do not want you; now you have nothing to do with Garati'. If two towns fight together in Garati, they bring one drum Kadana, and one drum Dokona between them; this Kadana is a drum of Garati, Dokona is a drum of Garati. The person who refuses its voice, it is bad for him. [The town is referred to here, not an individual person.] Now there is no Ĥrela [the warrior grade, as a result of ignoring the drum] and there are no children; they perish, and say 'We shall vanish away', for refusing Kadana, and for refusing Dokona; they do not have our drums of Garati, Kadana and Dokona, among them, and thus by Kadana and Dokona they perish.

In another text, which refers to the different pairs of drums held by each town, the theme of the drum as the preserver of peace, and law and order, is elaborated:

Long ago in the beginning the homesteads were scattered, and people said 'it is good to live together'. After this they cut down a tree and made a drum and said 'The person with this drum acquires office. The person with the drum, if there is quarrelling in the town, they pay a fine to him; the drum is like a person and may listen to people speaking together'. For this reason they made it. Quarrelling came and everyone went together to the house where the drum was and there debated. And when someone caused a quarrel in the town, at the place of the drum they said 'This person, let him pay a fine to the town.' And in the place of the drum together they remember that this person has quarrelled, and has paid the fine. When someone refused to pay the fine, the town rejected him, and said 'I will not give you my fire; I will not bring you

---

[1] I do not think this sort of fine bears any relationship to blood money. As we shall see, members of a town who disturb the peace by quarrelling are fined, and the proceeds go, as far as I can gather, to the Nama Dawra. In the same way, perhaps, towns which have broken the peace by fighting must pay a fine, which probably goes to the Nama Dawra—the sacred drum-holders—of the region. But I was unable to discover exactly who received fines exacted from towns.

my water,' then people will not work with him, and will not bury him; the voice of the town refuses him and he leaves there, and dwells among other people.

This text, of course, refers to the drums held inside each town, and not to the regional drums, but the ideas embodied in all drums are the same—those of peace and unity.

The association of drums with authority is a common African phenomenon, and among the Konso they are the symbols of reasoned discussion and consensus. By 'accepting Kadana' one acknowledges that one is, whether as a person or a town, part of the Konso moral order; it is said of the craftsmen, the despised outsiders who do not accept Konso values, that 'they refuse Kadana'. Nevertheless, however widespread a phenomenon may be, we may still meaningfully ask in any particular case 'Why should a drum, a wooden cylinder wrapped in leather, be the symbol not only of social harmony, but of rain?'

The concept which links the auspicious symbolism of the drum with its social significance must presumably lie in one of its physical characteristics. I would suggest that this link is a symbolic one between the sound of the drum when beaten, and the sound of thunder, the harbinger of rain. It seems plausible to suppose that in the past when quarrels and battles were being ritually composed, the ceremonial included, as well as sacrifice, the beating of a drum, thereby establishing ritually the relationship between peace and rain which had hopefully been achieved on the social level between men. The three potentially dangerous situations of transition—the change from one grading cycle to the next, from the dry season to the great rains, and from the death of a priest to the succession of his son—might also be regarded as occasions calling for auspicious ritual reinforcement, among other things by the beating of a drum.

Thus the regional priests, the grading systems, and the sacred drums can supply only a moral, and not a political unity. As I mentioned earlier, the nearest equivalent to a police force exists in Garati only, where the men of the little town of Lehīda in times past, when two towns were fighting, would all run between the combatants and cast down their staves to separate them. But even here the sanction invoked was essentially mystical, not physical. It was said that anyone stepping over them would die by mystical means but the threat clearly was often not enough. If the combatants refused to listen the men of Lehīda could do nothing. (Lehīda is supposed to have migrated from Takadi region, from the vicinity of the towns of Ĥormalle and Foro, to its present position below Idigle, and this slightly alien origin is a possible reason for its neutral status.) As we shall see, the institution of the peacemakers operates much more efficiently within towns. There are many accounts of fierce battles between towns, but I never heard of anything worse than stone-throwing between the different wards of towns. Of course, this might also be taken as an indication that inter-ward relationships are sufficiently peaceful not to provide a real test of the peacemaking capacities of the Nama Dawra.

2. POLITICAL RELATIONS BETWEEN THE TOWNS

There are thus no built-in safeguards in the over-all political system, if system we can call it. In the following text we are given a very clear picture of the dismal state of affairs which town enmities could produce before there was an Amhara police force to protect travellers and permit traders to move without fear of being murdered on the road.

In the past in the country of Garati the towns were full of people, and within the towns they cultivated the fields . . . In the past someone from another town did not leave it; God refused the rain, and people hungered thereby, and were finished. In the past people travelling on the road were robbed; then there was no government, and people were killed on the road. Someone going on the path to Ma'jella was killed; someone going to another territory like this was killed. Therefore in time of famine, when there was nothing to eat in the house, people died, so what to do? They could not go to buy crops as they were killed on the road, so they starved to death. . . . We heard this story of the past from the old men. Now, under the authority of the government, when men are hungry they go to Gidole, they go to Iavello [to buy millet.] In the past there was no government. In our country in some years the rain is little, and people lack anything to eat, and go for corn to another land, and buy millet. In the past there was no path; people were robbed on the path and died, so it was bad.

The battles between the towns often began over relatively minor incidents. I was told by one of my oldest informants in Takadi that a large dance was once held to which a number of towns came; there was a quarrel between the men of Ībale and Tēbana, at which presumably Ībale blood was shed. The next day the men of Ībale attacked Tēbana and fired it, almost totally destroying it. The survivors of Tēbana joined with their allies of Gaho and attacked Ibale, with the same methods and the same results. Tēbana today is but a shattered remnant of a once large town, and Ibale is totally destroyed; even its walls have been cast down, and its sacred places dug up and returned to fields. Gaho also quarrelled with Kunyara, a small town a couple of miles away, because their boys beat Gaho cattle which were straying on to their fields. Kunyara was burnt as a result and their stock taken. Before its destruction in about 1875 Ibale refused the use of a path leading to the lowlands to the people of Gaho; I understood that the men of Gaho successfully asserted their rights.

Būso and Ma'jella fought four battles over some fields between them, but these, of course, were owned by individuals; there is virtually no common ownership of anything in Konso. In this case the whole of Būso came to the assistance of a few of its members. It must have often happened that a quarrel between two towns was engendered by the conflicting interests of only a section of their members, but their loyalty to one another impelled them to act as a whole against the other town.

I never heard of any town fighting directly for the control of wells or reservoirs. The dispute between Degato, Būso, and Turīdi, which I discuss shortly, was rather a special case. Battles over land seem to have been more common on the borders of Konso than among the towns in the interior. Turo fought many times with the Gauwada and the Gidole, though not apparently with the Ala, an *ensete* people with whom they seem to have been on good terms. It is recorded that Turo once defeated some of the towns of Garati, including Būso, but when they arrived to collect their spoil after the truce the men of Garati treacherously murdered them—I was told this in Būso. I was also told in Gaho that an alliance of Garati towns had attacked Takadi, but had been repelled.

In the Mora Murgito in Būso there are two 'stones of manhood' commemorating the victories of sets (named subdivisions of grades) in battle. In Mora Tara'jo there are six such stones. It is possible to date these battles very roughly because they are associated with particular sets.

In explaining these battles, it was said that they were fought for control of various plots of fields.

In Degato there is also a number of 'stones of manhood' whose sets are also remembered, and which can therefore be dated.

TABLE 7. *Būso battles*

Mora	Set	Town fought against	Date (approx.)
Murgito	Orḣasha	Īyēdi (Foro and Ḣormalle)	1827–45
Tara'jo	Kīyala	Ma'jella	1845–63
Tara'jo	Karmōla	Ma'jella	1845–63
Murgito	Onīla	Īyēdi	1863–81
Tara'jo	Kandala	Kandima	1863–81
Tara'jo	Kīlōla	Kamōle	1881–99
Tara'jo	'Gawasha	Ma'jella	1899–1917
Tara'jo	Kamamurra Arabala	Ma'jella	1935–53

TABLE 8. *Degato battles*

Mora	Set	Town fought against	Date (approx.)
Detati	Onīla	Turidi (Patangaldo and Olanda) Gidole	1845–63
Kobdale 'Dīle	Turufa	Gidole Pa'idi (Turo)	1845–63
Ḣalaudila	Kīlōla	Amhara	1881–99
Ḣalaudila	Torumfada	Amhara	1899–1917
		Turīdi	1899–1917
Pazandeda	Kanama	Turīdi	1917–35
Nagīle	'Gawasha	Idigle	
'Gīrata	'Gīranguba	Many lions	1917–35
Ḣalaudila	Orguba	When the Italians had departed, and the Amhara had not yet returned	1935–53

There were two other stones at Ḣalaudila Mora which were so old that no-one could remember for which sets they had been erected. It is interesting that in both Būso and Degato battles are recorded as occurring since the Amhara conquest, shewing that especially in their early years they did not have full control in Konso.

It is clear from the stones in these two towns that most of their battles have occurred in the last 150 years or so. Gāho's three stones also relate to battles within this period. While it is possible that towns only started recording victories with stones at the beginning of the nineteenth century, so that battles of earlier times left no memorial, it is also possible that there has been a real increase in warfare between towns in the last 150 years. If this is so, it might be explained by the increasing pressures in population, but at this point we can do no more than speculate. The following list of the number of stones in various towns gives some idea of the frequency of battles. (Since I have used my photographs of *moras* to assemble these figures, and did not collect them on the spot, they should be treated as minimum estimates.)

TABLE 9. *Konso battle-stones*

Kandima	(Garati)	10	
Tēbana	(Takadi)	15	
Gāho	(Takadi)	3	
Saugame	(Takadi)	4	
Idigle	(Garati)	9	
Kamōle	(Garati)	5	
Kazargyo	(Takadi)	4	
Kūme	(Takadi)	2	
Poroĝoda	(Garati)	6	
Būso	(Garati)	8	
Degato	(Garati)	6	(excluding 2 stones which were not erected for victories.)

This gives an average of 6.5 stones. If we reduce this to 5.5, since Kandima and Tēbana are exceptional, and apply this to the thirty main towns in Konso, it gives a figure of 165 stones. On the assumption that the vast majority of these battles have taken place since 1800, it seems that there has been at least one battle a year somewhere in Konso during that period, whatever the frequency of battles may have been before then.

From what informants told me about the causes of battles, it does not seem that the density of population and its pressure on resources has been the sole cause of warfare. The Konso have a high regard for military valour, and when there has been bad blood with a neighbour for some time, a little incident has been enough to start a battle.

But they are certainly aware of conventions in warfare: there were supposed to be no night attacks, and no setting fire to towns. As we have seen, in the heat of battle, this latter prohibition was at times ignored. It is also considered disgraceful to kill women, children, and the aged. Many years ago they also imposed upon themselves a limitation of armaments which recalls Pope Innocent II's prohibition on the use of the cross-bow as an inhuman weapon. Their spears used to be barbed, with saw-teeth, as in the illustration (fig. 3), which undoubtedly would have inflicted frightful wounds,

not least when the time came to cut them out of the victim's flesh. Apparently it was decided that these spears, called *'jika*, were making warfare excessively unpleasant and it was generally agreed to ban them. *'Jika* are now used only for ritual purposes. Their present spears are of the familiar 'leaf' pattern, which inflict clean wounds and are easily withdrawn. I managed to obtain a *'jika*, but when I asked a smith to make me a copy from this, he was most embarrassed, and finally said that he dare not, as they were bad spears and forbidden.

A town which felt itself to be outnumbered might placate the enemy by offering them presents of cattle. Battles were followed by a peace-making ceremony—'to cleanse the land'—at which the central feature was a sacrifice and a feast, and the combatants all put pieces of the hide of the slaughtered beast on their right wrists. The priests and *shorugatas* of both towns would join in the blessing of both towns.

FIG. 3. *'Jika* spearhead

But unregulated violence is only one aspect of the relationships between the towns, for they are often united in long-standing alliances. There is frequently a senior town in the alliance, called *apa* (father) or *ĝarda* (eldest brother) to whom the rest stand as *ina* (son) or *kusita* (younger brother). The status of the senior town is based both on the supposition that it provided the original settlers of the junior town, and on the relative sizes of the towns. Let us consider one particularly close relationship in Garati, that between Degato, Poro'goda, and Ĥulme. These are linked in the *ĝarda- kusita* relationship, with Degato as *ĝarda*. Members of the same family change residence from one town to another with great facility. The Bamalle is their unquestioned chief priest, living on the great wooded hill called Ĥonso just above him. Poro'goda and Ĥulme are within a few hundred yards of one another, and they are both ten minutes' walk from Degato. The cycle of sacred drums, which I shall deal with later, is shared among all three towns, the only case I know where this happens, with the possible exception of Olanda and Patangaldo. Degato and Poro'goda and Ĥulme also hold a number of ceremonies together.

Traditionally the allies of these three were

Būso
Ma'jella
Kandima
Kuile

A few years ago Būso allowed Turīdi (a name for both Olanda and Patangaldo) to use its water supply when their wells ran dry in a severe drought. Turīdi are the particular enemies of Degato, who consequently broke with Būso over this, which they regarded as treacherous conduct, besides almost fighting a pitched battle against Turīdi, only being stopped by the police.

But long before this Būso was at enmity with Ma'jella, which has always been friends with Degato. Thus while two towns may be one another's allies, the enemies of one may be the allies of the other.

Map VI shows the relations between the towns, a continuous line denoting alliance, a broken line enmity. The map, however, is incomplete. I personally resided in towns 2, 9, 12, and 26, and while I was able to obtain most of the relations between these towns and their friends and enemies, it was often very difficult to obtain data on the relations between other towns where I was not residing. Thus it is not clear, for example, whether 22 and 6 are friends, enemies, or sufficiently distant to be neutral. Nevertheless, there is sufficient data to make the basic characteristics of the relationships between towns fairly clear. Some towns are united in specially close 'nuclear' alliances, which are ringed. In such cases the alliances are 'balanced'—that is, they have all friends and all enemies in common—and all mutual relationships are friendly. There are also other, looser, alliances which do not satisfy these conditions, in so far as they are unbalanced. That is, they are of the form

where town 2 is friends with 1 and 3, who are enemies. This puts 2 in the potential position of having to choose between 1 and 3 should they fight. Examples of balanced relationships are:

Since completing this monograph for the press I have shown in detail by simulation how the existing pattern of nuclear alliances and the chains of unbalanced relationships are the result of stochastic processes.[1] The demonstration of this is too lengthy and requires too many diagrams to be presented here. Briefly, the basic

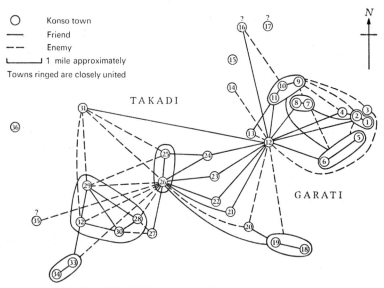

MAP VI. Political relations between the towns

assumptions of the model used in the simulation of Konso town relationships were: (1) that towns rate one another on a scale of preferences, (2) that such ratings can be asymmetrical, i.e. one town A may rate another town B higher than B rates A, and (3) that initially, in each simulation, there are many unbalanced relationships. A model network of 14 towns was constructed and initial evaluations distributed at random. Battles were originated between series of pairs of towns chosen at random, and the ultimate pattern of relationships between towns which resulted from three different

[1] C. R. Hallpike, 'The Principles of Alliance Formation between Konso Towns', *Man*, vol. 5, 1970.

simulations always bore a remarkable resemblance to those existing in reality in the following respects:

1. There were similar proportions of nuclear alliances.
2. The proportions of 2-, 3-, and 4-member alliances were also similar.
3. There were many unbalanced relationships.
4. There were long chains of alliances which were not nuclear.
5. Isolated towns (that is, with no allies) also occurred.

The significance of these results is that the pattern of relationships appears to be the result not of migration, nor of the attraction of larger towns for smaller, but rather that it is the product of stochastic processes and the basic structural principles outlined above. The rules by which town relations are governed are outside the conceptual grasp of the Konso and, given the fragmentation of power, beyond their capacity to alter from within the system. There is also no point in asking whether the characteristics are 'functional' or 'disfunctional'. In one sense, in relation to their society as a whole, they are clearly disfunctional, but, basically, the system has arisen as a result of certain historical processes in the course of which it has escaped from the power of the people to control it. This is a good example of what is likely to be a universal phenomenon—the capacity of certain relations-systems to develop characteristics of their own which are relatively independent of the norms and beliefs systems of the total society.

It is noteworthy that the distance between towns has very little to do with the relations between them; thus Būso and Ma'jella have been the bitterest of enemies, though they are only on opposite sides of a narrow valley, while Idigle and Taŕa, apart from one incident in the past, are on good terms, being separated by only about two hundred yards. Būso also made a pact of friendship with Ĥamalle, which is about three hours journey away in Takadi. The alliance was cemented by both towns cutting down a tree together, and dividing it into two; each town then made a drum from its own half of the trunk.

While, therefore, we can refer to the ritual organization of the regions, with a great priest, a distinctive generation-grading system embracing all the towns in the region, and an associated set of ceremonies, and a cycle of sacred drums, there is no organization within the region at the political level. By organization I mean a

nexus of relationships based on marital alliance, descent, or trade, or
which migh be provided by the generation-grading systems if each
grade were a corporate group cutting across town membership. In
this sense the regions have no political organization, and relations
between towns are anarchical and formless. As we shall see, it is the
very unity of the towns which makes any larger unity impossible.

3. SOCIAL INSTITUTIONS WITHIN THE TOWNS

As opposed to the generally anarchical and formless relationships
between the towns, within each town the organization of government and social relations is intricate. The lineages are represented
by their priests and the wards by their councils but there are other
functionaries such as the Nama Dawra, who stop fights between
the wards, the *Apa Timba*, who hold the sacred drums of the Ĥrela
and Kada grades, besides the *shorugata*, and the lineage priests.
While the lineage[1] priest is essentially responsible for blessing
his lineage, his beneficent powers can apparently extend also to
the town as a whole, especially in the case of the most important
lineage priests.

The priest is a man of peace, and this explains his frequent inclusion in the list of Nama Dawra. The *shorugata*, however, has
more obscure attributes. He inherits his status by primogeniture in
the male line, in the same way as the priest; but there are no clear
taboos associated with his person, or his home, or any of his actions.
Nor is he associated with any special social group. It is said that his
ancestor became a *shorugata* because he was rich, honest, and a
brave hunter, and in general was notably successful by the stan-
dards of Konso society. Like priests, they take a prominent place
in town rituals and sacrifices, and their homes are used as convening
places on such occasions. It seems probable that because they represent families which have been successful, they are seen as being
well qualified to bless others; while the priest has a primary responsibility to his lineage, the *shorugata* has no special status in his lineage, and therefore acts more as a sort of priest or at least 'auspicious
person' for the town as a whole. It was suggested to me in Būso that
shorugata had a pre-eminent claim to be councillors, but in practice
I found that of the 44 council members in Būso, only one was a

---

[1] Both clan and lineage are exogamous and patrilineal; the lineage is localized,
and a sub-division of the clan, which is dispersed.

shorugata; in Degato the proportion was 4 out of 21; and in Idigle, 3 out of 14.

Towns are divided into wards, *gandas*. This word *ganda* is also used to refer to an isolated homestead out in the fields or a group of them, which seems to be an almost contradictory sense of the word. In fact the usages are related historically, in this way. The Konso language, like many Cushitic languages, does not make much use of the plural form, in the Konso case, the suffix, *-da*. Where there are several homesteads in isolation, they will often be referred to collectively as *ganda*, but more properly as ganda*da*. When towns were being formed, each group of homesteads within them would have been called so-and-so *gandada*, with a name, but the *-da* would have been dropped, thus producing the usage by which *ganda* means a ward, as well as a single homestead. A homestead within a town is never referred to as *ganda*, but '*tiga*', home or house.

When the towns were formed, it is likely that there were at least two wards, never just one. We can see from the map of Idigle that the original settlement on the western side surrounded by the circular wall is divided into Iyana and Pillele, and that wards have been added successively on a dualistic axis, a path in fact running east–west. In the case of Idigle, this dualistic principle, while present, does not follow the north–south division that suggests itself from the ground plan, since in fact Iyana, Pillele, and Gahita are in one division, and all the remaining wards in the other. But in Būso, Degato, and Gāho there is also a dualistic division of the town above that of the wards. In all these cases except that of Idigle, these divisions have their own names, quite apart from ward names. In every town someone born in one division is not allowed to set up house in the other division, though he can marry a girl from either. The map of Gaho on p. 94 below supports this contention, in so far as lineages appear to keep entirely to their own divisions.

There is some evidence of mild hostility on occasions, and in the larger towns, such as Būso, which is almost cut in half by a cone-shaped hill, people in the division on one side of it were noticeably less familiar with the people in the other division on the far side. Būso originally was composed of six smaller towns, which came together to form Būso as it now is. Some of the old towns are still associated with existing wards, and the most prominent of the priests claim that they were once the chief priests of the original towns. A table will clarify this:

TABLE 10. *Original towns of Būso*

Original towns	Present ward	Priest
Tara'garada	Nalīya	Ĭdya
Tarakaldoda	—	Gĭya
Polada	Kolalta	'Gubale
Teshumalle	Kuile	Turumalle
Polo'godita	—	Ĥigo
Ifada	Ifada	Ku'jo

Ifada is a curious ward, in that its adult males function as peace-makers between the rest of the wards if they should fight, in addition to the regular Nama Dawra of the town, whom we shall consider later. They keep to themselves in the Sōla dances, and their perpetuation of their original town name in their ward name is a further intimation of their exclusiveness. There is still an important sacred place called Ifa (Ifada means 'the Ifa people') and a cattle pool of the same name a short distance from Būso.

The wards are divided into two sections as follows:[1]

Nalīya ⎫
Idigle ⎪
Gomīya ⎬ I Pishmalli
Tara'jo ⎪
(Ifada) ⎭

Kolalta ⎫ II Sessidi
Kuile ⎭

We see here, as in Idigle, that there is a marked imbalance in numbers between the wards of one division and the wards of another; in Idigle the proportion is 6: 3, in Būso, 5: 2. In Gaho, a smaller town in Takadi, it is 2: 1. Gaho is an interesting case, as it was devastated in the fighting with the Amhara, but while there are people left in the original town, substantial numbers moved out into the surrounding fields, and made their homes there, and are still affiliated to the original wards of their owners. The town itself is

---

[1] The number of homesteads in each ward is as follows:

Nalīya   81 ⎫
Idigle   27 ⎪
Gomīya   14 ⎬ *Pishmalli*
Tara'jo   58 ⎪
(Ifada)   19 ⎭

Kolalta   68 ⎫ *Sessīdi*
Kuile   42 ⎭

TOTAL 199   TOTAL 110

The average area of a homestead is 400 square yards. The average number of people in each homestead is five.

divided into Kelgeleda and Tapata, which are both the names of wards and sections; Kelgeleda is further divided into one other ward, Ĥĭleda. In spite of this subdivision, the two sections are of roughly equal size. The outlying groups of homesteads are affiliated as follows:

KELGELEDA	TAPATA
Kalga (a very big cluster)	Kushabo
	Eɪlada
Konshiti	Kagara
Ĥĭle	Korīdi
	Degato
	Kugo

Roughly speaking, this division seems to be geographical. In Gaho itself, the division between Kelgeleda and Tapata runs roughly north–south, and this is reflected in the division of the outlying homestead clusters, those of Tapata being on the east, and of Kelgeleda on the west.

It is said that the Tapata division was founded by a man from Turo, and Kelgeleda by a man from Fāsha called Tesho Kamaza and that there were many immigrants from Tebana nearby. People from Tebana are allocated to Kelgeleda or Tapata according to the ward in Tebana they come from;

Eebala ⎱ Kelgeleda   Degato ⎱
Marshina ⎰   Arfīda ⎰ Tapata
                          Nalīya ⎰

This again, if it is true (and I had no evidence to check it) also corresponds to a division of Tapata on the east and Kelgeleda on the west. (We should not assume that this is evidence for any orientation of the divisions in terms of the cardinal points of the compass; in Būso after all, Sessīdi is to the north of Pishmalli.)

In addition, the two basic divisions of Gaho have alternative names for ritual purposes; Tapata is Kardōda, and Kelgeleda is Kundateda. Kundateda and Kardōda each have a sacred drum, of the type discussed earlier.

Degato, in Garati, is an example of the extension of the dual division outside the single town. As we saw earlier, Degato is very closely linked with two other towns, Poro'goda and Ĥulme. Degato is itself divided into two divisions, Ilika and Paraguta, and these extend to the other two towns, so that Poro'goda is all included in

Ilika, and Ĥulme in Paraguta. Ĥulme is a very small settlement, without protecting walls, but Poro'goda is large. Within Degato, the wards were originally divided so that Ilika had six, and Paraguta five, but after Degato was badly damaged fighting the Amhara (it was the other town beside Gaho to resist Menelik's army) the wards were redivided, and now each division has only two large wards each. I was given the name of eight families which had been the founders of the two divisions, four families for each division. The consequences of the extension of the division to Poro'goda and Ĥulme is that a man from Poro'goda can come and live in a part of Degato which is barred to some born in Paraguta division in Degato itself.

The absence of any equality in the number of wards in the dual divisions, in all the towns we have examined, and the marked imbalance in some cases suggests that we ought not to seek for an explanation of this seemingly pointless exercise in social division in any enthusiasm for purely dualistic classification, of a cosmological nature. The fact that in Būso, Gaho, and Degato some stories of the founders of the towns were recollected in explanation of the divisions, and the strong suggestion that persons coming from one place went to live in one division, and persons from another place or area lived in a different division, suggests that the divisions were intended to demarcate diverse elements in the original population of the towns. As I have said, they are unlikely to reflect any cosmological concern with dualistic classification, which is not a dominant element of their culture, or, least of all, a special interest in the cardinal points of the compass. East and west, like right and left, have been given practically no attention in their symbolism. Since the dual divisions have no relationship to their symbolism, and are certainly highly disfunctional, it seems likely that they arose from the same kinds of stochastic processes as I described above in the case of the town relationships, only produced in this case by relations between wards or homesteads, and perhaps lineages. Whatever their ultimate explanation, it must be admitted that at present their origins are mysterious.

Membership of a ward is purely by residence, not related to any hereditary rights apart from those vested in a particular homestead or plot of land. There are a few exceptions, as when someone within the boundaries of one ward having quarrelled with his fellow ward-members announced that he was going to be a member of another ward henceforth. I also knew a man whose family had a long association with one ward and by reason of this was himself a councillor of his ancestral ward, though living in another, but these are exceptional cases. There are no ceremonies required for joining one, and I was referred to as *gandita*, ward-member, by the other residents in my ward wherever I settled. Sociability and mutual assistance, however, are required of members of one's ward. I was asked by a neighbour one day to come and drink beer in someone's house, since all the ward was invited. I tried to escape the invitation, since Konso beer is a sour alcoholic grain soup, with the millet floating in it unstrained, and not the most enjoyable means of becoming drunk, but he insisted, saying, jokingly, that it was obligatory for me, and that if I refused no one would speak to me. Unpopular people, who are unduly quarrelsome or mean are ostracized, and this is a sanction used against people who refuse to pay fines or tributes. In its most effective form it involves refusing to supply such a person with fire or water. Meanness, shewn in lack of hospitality, is particularly disliked, and someone who hides his beer when visitors call is a stock figure of fun. Everyone in a ward is supposed to turn out to help look for a neighbour's animals if they are lost, and fines are imposed on those who refuse, as they are on those who are persistently quarrelsome. Really obnoxious people, especially habitual drunkards, may eventually be expelled altogether. One case in Būso occurred not long before I came, when a man returning drunk from market tried to set fire to someone's house; the neighbours retaliated by demolishing his own huts and sending him into exile.

The mutual obligation of ward members is seen as counterbalancing those of the lineage. When I asked why wards were necessary, the standard reply was 'If we had no wards, who would bury us?' It is the duty of ward-members to bury their fellow members, something they regard as too painful for the relatives. The greatest disgrace for a man is for the ward to refuse to bury him, and for his relatives to have to pay a working-party to do the job. This is a revealing remark about the status of the lineage and other kin in relation to the ward as a whole. For a dead man's kin take no part in his burial, as they are conventionally expected to be incapacitated with grief. In Garati they never even attend the actual burial, but only the second mortuary ceremony some time later. The ward neighbours are therefore seen as performing certain essential functions, of which their assistance at burials is the paradigm case, which cannot be performed by a man's kin.

The wards, whose membership is not based on kinship, are not strictly necessary from a practical point of view. Life in the towns, with all it implies in the way of co-operation, could go on without them, as they could elect a council to govern the town as a whole.[1] The wards are necessary for them as conceptual devices to clarify the confusion of large numbers of people living together. They are familiar with the fact that ties with their neighbours tend to fade with the distance between homesteads; the arbitrary division of the towns into wards, members of which all have equal duties to one another, as opposed to the members of other wards, helps to overcome this problem of the indefiniteness of obligation, and of collective identity.

While, as I have said, there is no concept of chiefly rule among the Konso, the Amhara administrators have installed *balabbats* in each town, whose job is to communicate decisions and proclamations from the local governor, and to collect taxes. But these functions confer no power on the *balabbat* within Konso society except in so far as his responsibilities to the administration enable him to bring the police to arrest criminals and those who refuse to pay their taxes or attend court. Before 1897, however, when towns were sovereign entities, control in each case was vested in the councils of elders, called *hīyoda*,[2] which still function. The *hīyodas* could call on the support of the warrior grade, Ḥrela, to arrest criminals, and enforce their decisions. These councils both debated issues of general concern—without being able to violate public opinion— and acted as a court of justice. It was and still is the custom for councillors and other town officials to receive a tribute in cash or kind from the town as payment. The organization of the council varies from town to town; I take the case of Būso as an example of how they are organized in practice. In Būso each of the six wards has a council, generally of five men, with an apprentice council of three or four, who can replace their elders when they retire. Būso is the only town I know which has this type of apprentice council. I give it as an example because it shows very well the extent to which grades are correlated with conciliar status. There was, however,

---

[1] See Dyson-Hudson, *Karimojong Politics*, pp. 107 ff., for an example of a settlement pattern not demarcated by fixed boundaries.

[2] Cf. Galliña *haiyyu*, 'a leader'. The working parties, described below, also have one or two *hīyodas* to co-ordinate them. I think, therefore, that the word *hiyoda* can also mean "leader" in Konsiña. I shall translate it as 'councillor', however, where appropriate.

no over-all council of the whole town; I believe that when a matter concerning the whole town was to be discussed, all the councillors would sit together. While the names of the men concerned will naturally convey nothing to the reader, I use them, instead of giving lists of numbers, because this enables us to see which names recur in other contexts. The ward councils are composed as follows:

TABLE 11. *Councillors of Būso*

I. *Ifada Ward*

Name	Grade
1. Usati Telahīya[1]	'Gurula
2. Pazano Ku'jo[2]	Kada
3. Barisha Usati[1]	Kada
4. Pīyo Sora	Kada
5. Kuyita Ku'jo[2]	Kada (priest)

[1] Usati Telahīya was the father of Barisha Usati.
[2] Pazano and Kuyita Ku'jo are brothers. Kuyita is the eldest and a priest.

There is a junior, apprentice, or 'Hrela' council, as follows:

1. Kuyita Kombole	Kada
2. Parao Pano	Hrela
3. Kalgallo 'Gudade	Hrela

II. *Naliya Ward*

Name	Grade
1. Kalabo Hīyiso	Hrela
2. Gudado Gensho	'Gurula
3. Kirite Hoiro[1]	Orshāda
4. 'Jewa Sade	Orshāda

'Hrela' Council

1. Kalgallo Kazo	Kada
2. Harafo Sade	Hrela
3. Kapino Hoiro[2]	Hrela

[1, 2] Father and son.

III. *Idigle Ward*

Name	Grade
1. Kuyola Orgoshe	Kada
2. Killo Kalida	Kada
3. Kecho Kasambiya	Kada
4. Orhiya Gumsha	Orshāda (*shorugata*)

'Ĥrela' Council

1. Karo Tawisha   Ĥrela (priest)
2. Garmo Saldedo   Ĥrela
3. Iyano Gumsha   Ĥrela

IV. Tarajo Ward

Name	Grade
1. Kalgallo Läa	Orshāda
2. Kuyola Kolobo	'Gurula
3. Gusiya Kumano	Orshāda
4. Gusiya Tidiya	'Gurula

'Ĥrela' Council

1. Kuyita Onara	Orshāda (priest)
2. Kumodo Pasa	'Gurula
3. Gahano Gauwada	Orshāda

V. Kuile Ward

Name	Grade
1. Ialissa Panano	'Gurula
2. Sauwe Ĥambiro	'Gurula
3. Tubaro Palde	Kada (priest)

'Ĥrela' Council

1. Kadano Alīya	Ĥrela
2. Tubaro Kamala	Kada
3. Lamitta Gahano	Kada

VI. Kolalta Ward

Name	Grade
1. Tubaro Kula	'Gurula
2. Pasita Lumalle	'Gurula
3. Lamitta Kunina	'Gurula
4. Lamitta Pore	'Gurula
5. Sabo Turumalle	Kada (priest)

'Ĥrela' Council

1. Gusiya Korosho	Ĥrela
2. Killoya Kamande	Ĥrela
3. Kalabo Päīdo	Ĥrela
4. Iyano Koyala	Ĥrela

Some of the apparent anomalies in grade membership are due to the fact that the person in question is in an unusually high or low grade for his age.

It will be noticed that there is considerable correspondence between membership of senior councils and high grades, on one hand, and of junior councils and low grades on the other:

TABLE 12. *Grades of Būso councillors*

Senior councils	'Gurula	10	Junior councils	'Gurula	1
	Orshāda	5		Orshāda	2
	Kada	9		Kada	4
	Ĥrela	1		Ĥrela	12

I give the councillors of the towns of Idigle and Degato for comparison.

TABLE 13. *Councillors of Idigle*

Pillele Ward

1. Īyano Pode	Ĥrela		
2. — Hamsha	Ĥrela (*shorugata*)		
3. Garmo Torīya	Ĥrela	Kada	2
4. Rōbo 'Girando	Kada	Ĥrela	3
5. — Kalangalle	Kada (*shorugata*)		

Oibatale Ward

1. — Ilgo	Ĥrela	Kada	1
2. Kalabo Beesho	Kada	Ĥrela	1
(probably incomplete)			

Gahita Ward

Dubious data

Kalagalīya Ward

1. — Kalamalle	Kada (priest)		
2. — Busur'go	Ĥrela (priest)		
3. Garmo Kīge	Ĥrela	Orshāda	1
4. — Sakiti	Orshāda	Kada	2
5. Tuba 'Hōra	Kada	Ĥrela	2

	Total	'Gurula	0
		Orshāda	1
		Kada	5
		Ĥrela	6

TABLE 14. *Councillors of Degato*

Town Council

1. Kalabo Rōbo	Ĥrela (Otīya ward, Paragutīda division)
2. Kuyite 'Jolte	Ĥrela (Odandita ward)
3. Kazarta Hewla	Ĥrela (Otīya ward, Iligatīda division)
4. Urmala Deebo	Ĥrela (Lehīda ward)
	Ĥrela 4

Paragutīda Division

Otiya Ward

1. Kalabo Rōbo	Ĥrela		
2. Gazo Uluba	Kada		
3. Elīya Mata'ja	Kada (priest)		
4. Kuya Mere'ge	Kada	Kada	5
5. Lamitta Kumada	Kada	Ĥrela	1
6. Kalabo 'Jor'galle	Kada		

Odandita Ward

1. Garmo Sūgo	Ĥrela		
2. Kuyite 'Jolte	Ĥrela	Ĥrela	3
3. Lamitta Balate	Ĥrela		

Iligatīda Division

Lehīda Ward

1. Urmala Deebo	Ĥrela (priest)		
2. Gahano Biyashe	Ĥrela		
3. Kadano Fulīya	Kada	Kada	4
4. Kapino Harbora	Kada	Ĥrela	2
5. Kamea 'Jela	Kada		
6. Tubaro Shela	Kada		

Otiya Ward

1. Kazarta Hewla	Ĥrela (priest)		
2. Kalabo Ko'jano	Ĥrela		
3. Kalabo Mareda	Ĥrela		
4. Kalabo Olāda	Kada	Kada	3
5. Gahano Pitita	Kada (priest)	Ĥrela	3
6. Kuyande Bore	Kada		

Total	'Gurula	0
	Orshāda	0
	Kada	12
	Ĥrela	9

The councillors are elected by each ward, and retain office for life, or until they become too old and retire, when they are replaced by one of the members of the junior council. Though I was never able to establish the exact electoral procedure involved, it appeared from conversation that certain men, who were generally considered to have the necessary qualities—intelligence, knowledge of affairs, ability to keep one's temper, good judgement, bravery, and honesty—would be well known in the ward, so at the time for appointing a new councillor it would only fall to the ward to choose between a very few names.

In other towns the apprentice council does not seem to exist, and in Degato there was a supreme town council of four, selected from each of the four present wards. In Idigle, 3 or 4 was the usual number for a ward council, and all these, numbering 14 in all, sat as a town council when necessary. In Gaho, with only 2 ward councils, with 4 councillors each, they all sat together as a town council.

We can see from the list of council members in Būso, that there are only five lineage priests and one *shorugata*, in spite of the fact that these men are persons of great social eminence.

There are very few instances of fathers being succeeded by sons —only four in Būso, for example. Nor is great age a necessary criterion; rather, when they pass a certain stage of senility, they retire from active life. I would think that men between forty and sixty are the most influential. The fact that there are so few *shorugatas* and lineage priests on the councils is a clear indication that councillors are chosen on their merits, and not privileged in this respect by family status.

It is significant that the only office which has an obvious hereditary basis is that of the *balabbat*, the only one which is alien. In Būso it has been in the same family (Īdya) for three generations, and this is the rule for all the other *balabbats* I knew of in the rest of Konso. Even in this case they all said that if they did not like their *balabbat* they could always sack him and choose someone else. *Balabbat* families are always the most eminent priestly families in the towns, and clearly the Amhara administration has chosen them as the ones most likely to command respect.

In each town there is a body of men who are the peacemakers, Apa Dawra, or Nama Dawra. Apa means 'father', or more generally, 'adult male who has married and begotten children', and *Nama* means 'person'. Dawra is a contraction of *idawrani* 'he forbids'. It is the job of these men to run between the quarrelling factions—wards or divisions—and cast down their staves of office on the ground to separate them. With the staves they also throw down sprigs of *hansabita* (*Labiatae, Ocimum suave*) an auspicious plant. Anyone stepping over the staves is thought to incur death by mystical means, but on some occasions hot tempers were clearly impervious to such threats. It was said that spears were not used in these internal fights but only stones, or perhaps sticks. In keeping with the mystical nature of their power, the Nama Dawra are either priests or *shorugatas*. In Būso there are two groups, one from Kada grade, and one from Orshāda.

TABLE 15. *Būso Nama Dawra*

Orshāda Grade	Status	Kada Grade	Status
Gusiya Bukūdo	*Shorugata*	Kazo Īdya	Priest
Sūgo Tawīsha	Priest	Kuyita Ku'jo	Priest
Gondodo Kurago	*Shorugata*	Sabo Turumalle	Priest
Kazo Orano	*Shorugata*	Kalabo Nablo	Priest
Kando Ĥīgo	Priest	Shan'go 'Gubale	*Shorugata*
Orĥīya Gumsha	*Shorugata*	Iyano Gembo	*Shorugata*
Kalgallo Kende	*Shorugata*	Kuyita Palde	Priest
Koda Kumande	*Shorugata*	Killano Gīya	Priest
		(acting for Sagara, who likes to avoid his ritual responsibilities)	

There are thus two groups of Nama Dawra, eight each of Kada and Orshāda, the two grades above Ĥrela. When the present members of Orshāda enter 'Gurula, the next grade, their sons, now in Ĥrela, will become Kada, and the present members of Kada will move into Orshāda. Another important ritual office is that of the Apa Timba (Drum Father) or Apa Para (Father of the Year) or *Sūga*, as they are variously known. Just as the two drums of Garati and Takadi are circulated among the lineage priests of the oldest towns, there are also two town drums, which in Garati are circulated among the members of Kada and Ĥrela grades. Whereas the great drums of Garati are often held for two years at a time, and in Takadi for nine, the town drums of Garati change hands each year, following a regular cycle, except sometimes for the first holder, who may hold them for more than one year as a mark of distinction.

In Būso besides the two drums certain ritual paraphernalia is also handed on each year. With the Ĥrela drum, called Ibo, is a kudu horn, by name Ħarasha. Horns are blown to call the people to important assemblies, hence their significance in association with drums, as an instrument of social unity. Both in Garati and Takadi the great drums are associated with the horn. Horns are also used to scare animals away from crops, another point of significance in their symbolism. The paraphernalia also includes a club called Pinish, a knife, an ancient spear of the '*jika* type, and a staff with brass wound around it, of a type called *maramara*. The Kada drum, called Mazīya, is only accompanied by a thin stave, the mark of an elder.

The two groups of Apa Para, one of Kada, and the other of Ħrela, are composed as follows:

TABLE 16. *Būso Apa Timba*

Year	Kada (*Hirba*)		Ħrela (*Galqussa*)	
	Name	Status	Name	Status
1	Īdya	Priest	Maħo	Shorugata
2	,,	,,	,,	,,
3	,,	,,	,,	,,
4	Turumalle	Priest	Ħīgo	Priest
5	Ku'jo[1]	Priest	Bukudo	Shorugata
6	Palde[2]	Priest	Ħombolo	Priest
7	Nablo	Priest	Olahe	Shorugata
8	'Gomeri	Shorugata	Agija	Priest
9	Gembo	Shorugata	'Gudade[3]	Shorugata
10	Panano	Shorugata	Tarfalo	Shorugata
11	Kulile	Priest	Tawīsha	Priest
12	Gīya	Priest	Ō'ja	Shorugata
13	'Gubale	Shorugata	Kumande	Shorugata
14	'Jemola	Priest	Nguro	Shorugata
15	Ħoibo	Shorugata	Ħala	Shorugata
16	Gonīdo	Shorugata	Päīdo	Priest
17	Ku'jo	Priest	Onaĝa	Priest
18	Palde	Priest	'Gudade	Shorugata

[1, 2, 3] These have second years.

At the end of each cycle the Ħrela group of drum-holders move up to Kada and take over the Kada drum, while the sons of the present Kada holders will become Ħrela, and take over that drum.

The function of the Apa Paras of Ħrela and Kada is to pray for rain; they are blamed if the rains are bad in their year. They should also do nothing prejudicial to peace and social harmony in the town. The cycle of drum-holders is also a means of calculating the passage of the years in the eighteen-year cycle. As befits its primarily ritual status its members, like the Nama Dawra, are all either priests or *shorugata*.

There is also a town-crier, the *saleda*, conveying any important news or decisions to the people, going from *mora* to *mora* in the night.

TABLE 17. *Būso functionaries*

Name	Priest	Shorugata	Apa Para	Nama Dawra	Councillor
Ĭdya	×		×	×	
Turumalle	×		×	×	×
Ku'jo	×		×	×	×
Palde	×		×	×	×
Nablo	×		×	×	
Gomeri		×	×		
Gembo		×	×	×	
Panano		×	×		
Kulile	×		×		
Gĭya	×		×	×	
'Gubale		×	×	×	
'Jemola	×		×		
Ħoibo		×	×		
Gonido		×	×		
Maħo		×	×		
Ħĭgo	×		×	×	
Bukudo		×	×	×	
Ħombolo	×		×		
Olahe		×	×		
Agija	×		×		
'Gudade		×	×		×
Tarfalo		×	×		
Tawĭsha	×		×	×	×
Ō'ja		×	×		
Kumandi		×	×	×	
Nguro		×	×		
Päĭdo	×		×		×
Onara	×		×		×
Orano		×		×	
Kurago		×		×	
Gumsha		×		×	
Kende		×		×	

I summarize the data on Būso and Degato relating to the distribution of offices among the most eminent families, to show not only the sort of variation there is in different towns, but also that there is not a clear-cut nucleus of aristocratic families which hold all offices, but that there is a gradation from the very few eminent families in a town, to those which hold only one office, or are only priests or *shorugatas*, and are hardly distinguishable from 'commoners'. Unfortunately, I have had to exclude the Gaho data as it is rather unreliable. While it has the same functionaries as Būso and Degato, their proportions are different.

TABLE 18. *Degato functionaries*

Name	Priest	*Shorugata*	Apa Para	Nama Dawra	Councillor
Pada	×		×	×	
Kasima		×	×	×	
Pariyi		×	×	×	
Kato		×	×	×	
Koata		×	×	×	
Pori		×	×	×	
Gura		×	×	×	
'Jolta		×	×	×	×
Suguda		×	×	×	
Lasha		×	×	×	
Ga'ja		×	×	×	
'Jeeme		×	×	×	
Robo		×	×	×	×
Kergo		×	×	×	
Alaho		×	×	×	
Jalule		×	×	×	
Telīya		×	×	×	
Karbaro		×	×	×	
Palati		×	×	×	
Korne		×	×	×	
Pitita		×	×	×	
Tanda		×	×	×	
Kama		×	×	×	
Marēda		×	×	×	×
Ashuma		×	×	×	
Karshamo		×	×	×	
Pula		×	×	×	
Uluba		×	×	×	
Dinge		×	×	×	
Mīle	×		×	×	
Deebo		×	×	×	
Ĥewla		×	×	×	
Mata'ja		×	×	×	

I was not able to establish the exact recipients and distribution of fines, but it was clear that the Apa Dawra were entitled to regular contributions from householders throughout the year—I was asked to contribute after the Sōla—but it seems that the other office-holders are also entitled to contributions, and that they also share the fines that are levied. These officials would include the Apa Para, and the councillors—the latter especially where the ward was imposing fines. We shall see that as much as E$10 is sometimes levied for quarrelsomeness, and I have also seen gourds of millet, with axe-heads planted in them, paid as fines in Idigle. I was told in Gaho that every householder paid about five or six dollars in tribute to the town officials each year.

But besides councils, Nama Dawra, and Apa Timba, another essential group in the traditional Konso town is the warrior grade, which is seen as complementary to, rather than in conflict with the elders. In the past, when the Konso were independent, the decisions of the council regarding criminals or those who refused to pay tributes or fines were enforced by the men of Ḫrela, in the last resort, if the lesser sanctions of ostracism and non-co-operation against the recalcitrant neighbours were ineffective. Theft in particular was rigorously punished, and I was told in Būso that the worst thieves were flung to their deaths from a nearby cliff.

As we have seen, it is Ḫrela grade which holds one of the town drums, the symbol of authority and social cohesion.

In the town grandmothers, grandfathers, and boys, one has no eyes, one has no hands, one has no legs, so the Ḫrela drum guards the people of the town of Būso. So beer is made for Ḫrela, and after being given to Ḫrela in a big gourd, Ḫrela guard to see if sickness comes, the drum guards, the drum guards all, old men and old women, Ḫrela guards. These sleep in Būso, they are well, our people, as I have said, thus, the old men and the old women, and the boys and the husbands and wives and the lineages, thus our Ḫrela guards the people in this town. Thus this town has a wall around it. After taking office Ḫrela guard, thus they guard all the Būso people. The people collect beer. Our Ḫrela has the drum. The old men of Garati come and sit by the drum and discuss; after trouble they come, and sit before Ḫrela, with the drum among them, when there is trouble. Without the drum everything is spoilt, for they quarrel, the old men, the fathers, Ḫrela, they quarrel. The fine for people who quarrel with one another, the fine they bring is a *pireda* (E$ 1.50), for a serious quarrel, three *piredas*. . . . If Ḫrela do not have the drum the fathers and grandfathers are spoilt. They pay fines to it, both large and small. If someone refuses to pay a fine, the town says 'Go and live elsewhere, we want nothing of him, he is spoiling what is ours . . . we reject the son which we begot,

get out! he has defied our voice, so go away, get out!' They reject him and his works. Now, after someone dies, the ward together buries him. We are in Tara'jo, [a ward] and this is the *mora* Gomīya.[1] If someone defies us, we say 'Get out, go away! we reject your works'. If he refuses to co-operate, and he does not listen to us, he pays a fine. Fathers, grandfathers, and Ḥrela pay fines, this is so in all wards. When these people obey it is good, their people, their fathers, their children, their cattle, their goats, it is well with them all. When voices in this ward are united, it is good, all men laugh in these *moras* of Tara'jo and Gomīya.

Thus the warrior grade is seen as exercising 'authority', albeit under the direction of the elders, and its punishments are not simply the exercise of organized violence. There is a drum for the warriors as well as for the elders of Kada. As we shall see, peace not only affects immediate inter-personal relations, but also, ultimately, the whole well-being of their world, especially rainfall and the fertility of the women and animals.

The Konso have evolved an efficient organization to make decisions consistent with public opinion, and to enforce law and order. Let us reconsider them as a whole. Each town is split into two dual divisions, residents of one being forbidden to reside in the other. The dual divisions in turn are divided into wards. Each ward has its own council, and there may also be a town council, composed either of representatives from each ward, or of all the wards sitting together. Ḥrela grade provides the police force, and is thought of as the warrior grade. The Nama Dawra also act to prevent internal fighting, but by supernatural sanctions. The Apa Para, however, perform purely ritual tasks, the procuring of rain and the counting of the passage of years in the grade cycle.

We have seen in the lists of council members that while lineage priests and *shoruḡatas* are eminent personages this does not give them any rights of membership in these councils, where personal qualities are the only ones relevant. In this respect, at least, religious and secular functions are kept quite separate.

[1] There are so few people left in Gomīya ward that it has virtually been assimilated by Tara'jo ward.

PLATE IV. The town of Kūme

The warrior grade among the Konso, by contrast to the status of warriors among some other tribes in East Africa, is seen as an essential part of the social and moral order, and complementary to the elders rather than in conflict with them. This is a point which I shall take up again in the chapter on the generation-grading systems.

But besides these bodies and officials for the government of the town, there is another type of organization, the *parga* or *marbara*, which is a working party of friends, constituted on a permanent basis, which goes around the fields of those who have either no inclination, through age or sickness, or no time to cultivate them themselves, and receive quite a substantial payment for doing so. The *parga* is a small body of about ten, the *marbara* of about thirty. The word *marbara* is taken from the Amharic *mahibar* meaning a society.[1] It therefore seems likely that in pre-Amharic times the *parga* was the only type of working party, and for some reasons the larger *marbara* was introduced in relatively recent times. Unmarried girls in some towns are included in the men's *marbaras*, but married women always have their own. In some towns, such as Idigle, where there is no enthusiasm for work in the fields, there are now, whatever the case in the past, very few *pargas* or *marbaras*. In Būso, however, which is very hard-working, I was given the names of 18 men's *marbaras* which, if they each had an average membership of about 30, would comprise about 540 men. In a town of Būso's size, with about 1,600 people, this would be virtually the whole male population capable of doing the work.

Rich men are members of the working parties, as well as poor men; but it is likely that the basic purpose of the *parga* and *marbara* is to enable men who have inherited insufficient land to live on to supplement their crops with grain (or money at the present time) and perhaps even to save enough to buy more fields of their own. Opportunities for the redistribution of land must exist to account for the fact that there is no landless group as a result of the division of ancestral land among the sons of successive generations, and it seems clear that the working-parties provide precisely these opportunities.

---

[1] At least I assume it is taken from the Amharic; some of my informants said that this was the case. But there is none the less a possibility that it is not a borrowing at all, and is one of a small number of words common both to Amharic and Konsiña.

Friendship and the willingness to work hard are the sole criteria of membership. There are one or two *hīyodas* whose only function is to decide when and in whose fields the *marbara* should meet, but otherwise everyone is equal. I obtained details of three *marbaras* in Būso, which show clearly that wards or grades are not the relevant criteria of membership.

TABLE 19. *Working-party membership*

Orimfada Marbara

Ward		Grade	
Idigle	23	Orshāda	4
Tara'jo	4	Kada	7
Gomīya	1	Ĥrela	19
Nalīya	1		
Ifada	1		
	30		30

'Gadasha Marbara

Ward		Grade	
Idigle	11	'Gurula	1
Tara'jo	8	Orshāda	2
Nalīya	7	Kada	5
Gomīya	1	Ĥrela	11
		Farīda	8
	27		27

Ōlidida Marbara

Ward		Grade	
Idigle	20	'Gurula	1
Ifada	5	Orshāda	5
Tara'jo	4	Kada	20
Nalīya	3	Ĥrela	6
	32		32

The large numbers of Idigle members of the three *marbaras* is due to the fact that I collected these details while living in Idigle ward.

Harmony and friendship are the governing principles for the relations between members. This is why only very rarely do fathers and sons belong to the same *marbara*. There were no fathers and sons in Orimfada, one pair in 'Gadasha, and in Ōlidida two brothers and their uncle. It is understandable in view of the restraint between generations that fathers and sons should not as a rule work together in *marbaras*. It is more surprising that brothers should so seldom belong to the same *marbara*. In Ōlidida there were two brothers, in 'Gadasha two more, and in Orimfada, two pairs of brothers. The superior status of the eldest brother explains why he should not as a rule belong to the same *marbara* as his younger brothers, but it is hard to see why there should not be a more frequent association of younger brothers and half-brothers in *marbaras*. For example, Sagara Gīya's two younger brothers Killano and Iyano and his half-brother Gutchulo each belonged to a different *marbara*. I think this is good evidence that while members of the lineage and the family have certain mutual obligations, these do not necessarily imply a very close friendship.

Periodically, especially in the lull before the great rains which demand everyone's presence in the fields, each *marbara* collects money to purchase a bullock as a feast for its members and their families, after which a dance is held in the *mora*, and the *marbara* sings its song. Orimfada *marbara*, of which I had just become a member by paying E$1.50 (about 4s. 3d.) killed its bullock one morning. We all assembled between 7.30 and 9.00 a.m. as Sagara Gīya, in whose homestead the ceremony was taking place, stroked the animal from head to rump with a sprig of *pijipijata* (unidentified). Then the rest of us took some *pijipijata* and stroked it down our foreheads, and touched our left and right ankles with it. Some *kadikajeda* (unidentified) was then brought, and we touched our navels, foreheads, and ankles with it. We then drank beer together. When the beer was finished, *ifīya* (*Labiatae, Becium sp.*), *teemhada* (*Celastraceae, Catha edulis*), and salt were passed round in a bowl. We all ate a bit of each and spat it out. We also took some soot to anoint each temple. There were almost no blessings on this occasion. When everyone had finished with the plants, Sagara Gīya took the *pijipijata* and *kadikajeda* outside. The *pijipijata* he threw away, saying that it was now bad, but placed the *kadikajeda* under the logs in the gateway. The bull was then killed, and some of the meat cooked. All the meat, raw and cooked, was then shared out between us.

The object of this ceremony is to ensure the well-being of the *marbara*, and in particular that it should not be destroyed by quarrels.

Because social relations are intensely concentrated within the towns, and project only feebly beyond them, the preservation of solidarity within the towns is a matter of prime importance. The stability of residence and the lack of kin ties with other towns meant that, under the traditional order, it was hard for a body of persons who disagreed with their neighbours to move out and set up their homesteads elsewhere. Under the Amhara dispensation, this has occurred. Some of the people of Idigle, which I referred to in the Introduction as rent with quarrels, have departed and set up groups of homesteads some distance away in the bush.

The Konso are well aware of the necessity of social solidarity, not only for practical reasons, but because they believe that quarrelling within a town is visited with God's anger in the form of drought and sterility. In a later chapter I shall be giving some examples of Konso rituals whose object is to promote peace, fertility, and success in war and hunting. It is frequently argued, by Radcliffe-Brown and his followers, that an important social function of religious ritual is the maintenance of social solidarity. But this is not why the people perform such rituals, whose objects among the Konso are peace, fertility, and other material benefits. Nor is it useful, in most cases, to say that, whatever the purposes of a ritual, and the beliefs supporting it, its social effects are the increase of solidarity. For it is obvious that Konso rituals which are performed for the benefit of a town or lineage, and whose congregation will consist of that town or lineage, will have little effect in cementing solidarity within these groups, since the rituals occur comparatively rarely, compared with the solidarity resulting from the demands of day-to-day relations, and with the norms and values supporting solidarity between neighbours and kin. The participation in a ritual by a group of people is better evidence that some social solidarity already exists than that such solidarity is reinforced by the ritual. For example, the ceremony which I am about to describe was poorly attended by one of the dual divisions of Būso because they were angry with the other division. Again, every eighteen years in Garati a large ritual is held to mark the promotion of the members of the grades. Most of the towns in Garati send representatives, but a small group of towns which are on the fringe of Garati, while considered as Garati towns, are socially distant, and therefore do not send representatives. Moreover, there is little evidence that this ritual brings about any social solidarity between the towns which do attend, since they may begin fighting again soon afterwards. Such a ceremony therefore expresses, rather than creates, a feeling of basic moral unity, and has no more demonstrable social effect than this.

The ceremony which I now describe is explicitly devoted, however, to the maintenance of social order and solidarity, and the principal means to this end are hortatory speeches by the eminent men of the town. The name of the ceremony is *Ĥora Dehamda*, meaning literally 'Fining and Discussion', which I was lucky enough to observe in Būso.

It began by someone announcing that a wild animal was attacking the cattle in the grazing land a mile or so beyond Būso. This was really a trick, and those who did not realize ran off with their spears to help. This deception caused a great deal of annoyance among some, who said that crying 'Wolf!' in this way was self-defeating; but I was told that all *Ĥora Dehamdas* began in this way by a false call to arms.

In the afternoon I followed a group of men out to the cattle pool (then dry) called Sheebshe. They were carrying spears and bells. When we reached the pool there was a short dance, after which we turned back and entered some fields nearby. They all began cleaning and sharpening their spears. When enough people had assembled some elders took three or four groups away and lectured them privately on their duties as members of the town, and on recent cases of bad behaviour. Only the senior men of Ĥrela grades and above attended these lectures. Younger men even of Ĥrela were forbidden to listen, as I was. After this was over, in about half an hour, we all moved up to a higher knoll, where we sat in the shade and listened to speeches by some elders. (I give examples of these later.) During them we were interrupted by the arrival of some boys who had been hunting unsuccessfully for dik-dik in some nearby bush. When the speeches were over, we made our way back to Būso: on the path we found some evil medicines which an enemy of Būso had placed there to frustrate the ceremony.[1] It was decided to burn them as soon as possible. We arrived at Būso on the path leading through its most sacred *mora*, the Mora Murgito. Where the path entered the *mora* there was a ceremonial gate formed by a group of lineage priests and *shorugatas* holding some staves over the path. Everyone ran beneath them, and Īdya, the most important lineage priest of Būso aspersed each person with a mixture of water from a water-pipe (evil spirits are supposed to dislike the smell), water from the river Sagan, and milk, both of which are auspicious. He

[1] At least, this is what was said officially, but it is more likely that they were placed there by someone from Būso in order to give the impression of outside hostility, and thereby heighten the atmosphere of defensive solidarity within Būso. The chances of an enemy of Būso having placed such medicines on the path at such a psychological moment are remote, since the *Ĥora Dehamda* was only announced that morning.

used a sprig of *hansabita* which is also an auspicious plant. The purpose of the ritual gate and the aspersions was to take evil influences away from the men and boys as they ran beneath it, and prevent them from contaminating the town. Once inside the *mora* a number of *seega* dances were performed, while the women watched from a distance—the first part of the ceremony they had had the opportunity of seeing. Several elders made short speeches; while they were speaking their audience crouched on their haunches with their spears; as each speaker finished they all rose to their feet, stamping rhythmically and shouting, while the women set up their piercing ululation.

When these proceedings were completed in Murgito everyone went to the Mora Tara'jo, in the centre of the town. The same people (Gembo, Gumsha, and 'Gubale *shorugatas*, and Ku'jo a priest) held the staves again, and all the men passed under them, as they had done when entering Murgito. They arranged themselves in the *mora*, squatting expectantly, as the women watched from the surrounding walls.

It is important to realize that the whole *Ḥora Dehamda* ceremony is couched in very formal terms. Thus the speeches contain many blessings, for example—'May sickness go to a secret place, may the enemy weaken before you'—whose inclusion seems rather incongruous at first sight. There were many symbolic allusions, such as to 'the breasts of the seven families at which the whole town has ceased to suck'. This means that the town has ceased to depend on the spiritual powers and blessings of the seven most important priestly families. The speakers make a number of allusions to current problems and sources of discontent to emphasize the fundamental code of Konso life. They refer especially to the pernicious practice of selling thatching grass, *mida*, and fields, upon which the good and traditional life of the Konso depends, in Bakaule. 'You used to be farmers, but now you are becoming traders' is a fair summary of some parts of the speeches. As we shall see in the chapter on their values, they regard trade as essentially destructive of social harmony. At one point in the speeches, two men are called up to pay ten Konso dollars each as a fine for having been too quarrelsome. (1 Konso dollar is E\$ 1.50, and so the fine is roughly equivalent to two English guineas. At another *Ḥora Dehamda* I attended in Idigle fines were paid in the form of gourds of millet, with an axehead stuck in the top.) The idea of fining, and hence punishment is central for an understanding of this ceremony; many references are made to the necessity of punishment for keeping the town on the path of virtue and prosperity.

The speakers were as follows:

1. Ranguli, of uncertain status.
2. Sauwe Ĥambiro, a councillor of Kuile ward. Gurula
3. Kuyola Orgōshe, councillor of Idigle ward. Kada.
4. — Onaĝa, son of a priest. Ĥrela.
5. Kalabo Hīya, lion killer.
6. Ōlabo Īdya, the *balabbat*. Kada.
7. Kuyita Kū'jo, councillor and priest of Ifada. Kada.
8. Sābo Turumalle, councillor and priest of Kolalta. Kada.
9. Guberno 'Girale, man of Ĥrela.
10. Kalisho 'Jēmola, man who has paid a fine earlier.
11. Shango 'Gubale, Apa Para of Kada.
12. — 'Gudade, one of the Apa Para of Ĥrela, but of another year.

I was told that any adult man could speak (excluding Farīda, of course) who wanted to, and that on these occasions some Ĥrela men always do so. Apparently a Ĥrela man must conclude the speeches, and perhaps it is necessary that he should be one of the Ĥrela Apa Para.

These speeches are incompletely transcribed from the tapes on which they were recorded, largely due to the noise going on in the *mora* at the time. Their contents are in themselves rather incoherent, but their general import comes over quite clearly, I think. (Words which are in italic and followed by a question-mark in brackets are of rather unreliable translation.)

1. *Ranguli*

May sickness go to a secret place. May the enemy weaken before you. My children, . . . why is God punishing you? A little time ago the elders and the drum said 'Come and hear my speech' [referring presumably to the exhortations in the fields earlier]. That is now finished, it is done, the council in the fields is finished. 'May your crops ripen' they say, 'May there be nothing bad', they say, 'may the path leading to death be small, may the people be far from it' . . .

2. *Ĥambiro*

May God *bless* [?] you with milk gourds. Listen, why do your Ĥrela, your elders, fine you? It is like this, for your truthfulness, therefore they punish [literally, 'fine'] you, so that you may till the soil, therefore they punish you; and wherefore, consider this, that this person spills blood in the land, that one is full of drink and cannot find sleep on his mat, so that his strength is taken from him, and by day he *hides* [?] Ĥrela have seen this. Listen, wherefore [you are punished] consider this, that after this [assembly] here with Garfura [the river valley with many fields below Būso] it is well [literally 'sleeps']. So that we may suck at the breasts of the seven priests; when you suck them you prosper. This grass [for thatching] has grown tall for building houses, [yet] people are selling it at Bakaule, at Bakaule, and *fathers sell it for drink* [?], and tomorrow you will suffer, and the grandfathers will punish you, and the warriors will punish you. Because of this thing you cannot look at me. The *shelaĝda* is gone away, now there is no sucking the breasts of the seven families. The wives have gone away there [to Bakaule] taking thongs [to help them carry the bundles of *mida*, presumably] and after having gone they buy salt and the *mida* of the children [?] they give away. Now there is no sucking the breasts of the seven families [but] within them you will prosper. Take the hooks and hook down the *mida*, watch, like this [gesturing as though hooking down *mida*] and *Ĥrela watch me doing this* [?] wherefore because of these [faults] you are punished, and the father on his mat at night lacks sleep, and Ĥrela lack sleep. Let all this be far from me, and Ĥrela have observed me.

3. *Orgoshe*

Listen, O Būso, God give you gourds of milk God give you gourds of milk. What is the discussion for? Down there [in the fields] you discussed, and recounted the good and bad things together. You, Būso people, have been punished. Listen, the women and the men understand the discussion. Down there it is finished, *your Ĥrela have carried those things which were said, and what the fathers and the councillors said.* [?] Listen, millet is man, and man is millet. In how many years up here and down there does the harvest fail? . . . man eats millet, man is millet and millet is man. Prosperity is millet for you, *this is so here* [?] the hand of man in this way *profits* [?] man. Fathers and mothers you know and the babies [with] the fathers and mothers have heard. Of God may sickness go to a secret place, and what is bad be far from me. . . .

4. *Onaĝa*

Listen, Būso, may there be gentle rain, may the leats overflow, may the maize sprout in rows. In future, what, O Būso . . . [4 words] . . . Kalisho 'Jemola, ten dollars on the head of the bull, come here, I say, if you are present. Kalgallo Agaso, ten dollars on the head of the bull, come here, I say, if you are present. [The two men come forward and

pay their fines]. Now, listen, listen, Būso, why are you being punished?
So that] grandfathers the gentle rain may fall on you, and that the
maize may sprout in rows ... [3 words] ... for this you are punished ...

5. *Hīya*. (Largely unintelligible because of background noise.)

6. *Īdya (balabbat)*

The first part is indecipherable on the tape, except for the assertion
that the people of Būso were once farmers, and are now becoming
traders. He continues, Because of what, now there is no listening
together, moreover living together is ceasing . . . and what of the
shelaĝda? A short time ago they reproved and set out the right thing
to do, and recounted the way of duty, and told together then to collect
wood, thus they tell you, of the cutting down of trees, and the right way
of collecting *shelaĝda*. People give birth within the palisades of the
homesteads [probably a reference to the necessity of preserving wood
for making palisades, and not selling it.] *After this wood has been disposed
of the children suffer* [?]. . . . A boy says 'chéhé' with his goats in front,
and after driving them in this way they do not eat the crops in other
people's fields. [But if] the boy throws stones, he is just a fool for throwing stones, [i.e. see that you do not cause dissension by damaging
people's property as the result of reckless behaviour. Driving goats by
throwing stones frightens them, and makes them scatter.] . . . And after
enjoying yourselves in the *mora* you drink *yaĝa* and are full, and in the
night leave the gates of the paths open [apparently a reference to the
old custom of barring the town gates at night]. You go to Bakaule and
sell your fields, and going there is the path of tears. . . . The Amhara
want truth in you, and you told them lies in the past. And you seize
someone and tomorrow take him before the Amhara and accuse him,
and your money is lost and gone away. . . . [The Amhara courts
charge for hearing cases, and this is why the Konso lose their money
in taking each other to court. The *balabbat* apparently goes on to recommend that the traditional remedy of the expulsion of offenders should be
used instead.]

After the speeches, of which I have only transcribed half here,
some dances were performed, which concluded the ceremony.

This description of the *Hora Dehamda*, the ceremonial expression of social order and harmony, forms a fitting conclusion to a
description of Konso towns. But in order to understand them fully
it is necessary to supply another dimension to the picture—that of
kinship. I shall therefore defer a general analysis of the social significance of the towns until I have described the system of kinship
and marriage.

PART II. KINSHIP AND MARRIAGE

For the Konso, kinship is not an all-pervading mode of relationship. Obligations to fellow ward-members, and to one's town in general, are as important in daily life as kinship obligations, and, as we have seen, lineages have no part in determining the composition of elders' councils, or indeed any aspect of social organization in the towns as a whole. We shall see that property is held individually, not by the lineage, and that consequently, even in this area of social relationships, the role of the lineage is very much less than in societies where property is held in common by descent groups. The largest kinship category is the clan, *kaffa*.

1. THE CLANS

There are nine exogamous patrilineal clans, *kaffa*, which are found in all three regions, and their names are as follows:

Tigisīda	Eeshalīda
Saudata	Pazanda
Argamīda	Kerdita
Toĝmaleda	Elīda
Mahaleda	

In addition, in Takadi there are two other minor clans called Ogdomīda and Kudumīna.

The clans are dispersed throughout Konso, but not all the clans are represented in each town. It is possible to estimate the size of a clan population in a town by counting the number of lineage priests, though since lineages vary in size the results of the calculation can only be approximate. In Table 20 on page 88 I give the number of priests in each clan in Būso, Degato, and Idigle. In Gaho the numbers both of people and priests were too small to allow a reliable estimate; there only four clans were represented, and seemed to be of roughly equal size. In addition, I was also given a text containing a list of priests and their clans, which acted as a sort of random sample.

The Konso have some generally accepted traditions that their ancestors came originally from various parts of the surrounding territory, such as Liban, Borana, Gauwada, Ala, and Ilota (the range of mountains to the north-east), but it was not possible to find any correlation between the origins of the various priests and their clans, such that, for example, priests whose ancestors came from Borana were all Saudata, or from Ala were all Mahaleda, and so forth. The two lists of clan origins which obtained from different informants also show no significant correlation.

TABLE 20. *Relative clan sizes*

Clan	Idigle	Buso	Degato	Gaho	Text	Total	Order
Saudata	11	4	1	+	7	23	1st
Kerdita	2	2	4	+	9	17	2nd
Argamīda	0	5	6	+	4	15	3rd
Tigisīda	4	3	3	0	3	13	4th
Pazanda	6	1	4	0	2	13	4th
Eeshalīda	4	0	2	+	6	12	6th
Toĝmaleda	2	0	4	0	3	9	7th
Elīda	2	0	1	0	5	8	8th
Mahaleda	0	0	3	0	0	3	9th

Members of a clan are regarded as brothers and sisters, and for them to have sexual relations is incest, *manyera*. Related to this is the custom of addressing any male of one's mother's clan as '*abuya*' —'mother's brother'. He replies '*ashuma*'—'sister's son'. Even licentious talk is forbidden as between real brothers and sisters, and on the road men and women take care to discover each other's clans before indulging in such talk. A woman always retains membership of her father's clan and lineage after marriage, when it will become dormant, as it were. If she is divorced she may still not marry one of her own clansmen, although she may marry another man of her ex-husband's clan.

In Garati, but in no other region, there are some *moras* where the clans assemble if there has been serious quarrelling among their members. On these occasions the clans assemble as follows:

TABLE 21. *Clan alliances*

Elīda ⎫ Toĝmaleda ⎭	Murra Doho
Eeshalīda ⎫ Argamīda ⎭	Murra Rufi
Saudata ⎫ Mahaleda ⎭	'Dula Tongoya
Kerdita ⎫ Pazanda ⎭	Murra Ĥalipa
Tigisīda	Ĥangaladiya

Murra means 'a wood', and *dula* means 'a field'. We shall find these combinations of clans repeated when we consider the tripartite religious division of the clans.

In Turo I was told that at Tishmalli (a settlement area in Turo) there was no intermarriage between Pazanda, Ogdomīda, and Kerdita, and between Argamīda and Eeshalīda. In Takadi it was said that Kerdita and Ogdomīda were very close, and ideally there should be no intermarriage between them.

Apart from the peace ceremonies, which occur fairly seldom, and the prohibition on intermarriage between members of the same clan, the clans have no practical function in regulating the personal relations between their members. They are ritual and conceptual entities, rather than social groups with any sense of common identity. Considering that the total population of Konso is about 55,000 the average number in each clan would be around 6,000, spread over the whole of Konso, so it is not hard to understand why the clans should be such nebulous entities. They believe that all the surrounding peoples, Borana, Burji, Guji, Gidole, Ala, and Gauwada have the same basic nine clans, only with different names, which nevertheless have a one-one equivalence with those of Konso. They believe that the first people on earth were the founders of the clans, and according to one account the clans descended from nine brothers, but their traditions are rather confused on the exact way in which the clans were established, the only point that is emphasized being that the members of each all descend from common parents. Of course, there is no way in which they can prove what is an entirely figurative descent, since among the total Konso population a man would only know a small fraction of his clansmen by name, and fewer by sight. Moreover, there is no specially emphasized taboo on the killing or wounding of a fellow clansman, as must happen sometimes when there is a battle between towns. That it is thought bad to kill a member of one's own clan is undeniable, as we can see from the existence of the clan *moras* in Garati, but clearly town loyalty is more important than clan loyalty.

There is a tripartite division of the clans of a religious nature, as shown in Table 22.

As I have indicated, there is some doubt among informants as to the status of Tigisīda, Toǧmaleda, and Elīda, which is complicated by slight differences between the regions. Nevertheless, these three divisions exist in all three regions, and there is unanimity about

TABLE 22. *Ritual divisions of the clans*

Odīya[1] (God)	Teedibīya (Earth)	Käälo (the Wild)
Argamīda	Saudata	Pazanda
Eeshalīda	Mahaleda	Kerdita
(Tigisīda?)	(Toĝmaleda?)	
	(Elīda?)	

which division the six unambiguous clans belong to. This uniformity is clear evidence of the antiquity of these ritual divisions in Konso. In explaining them, my informants said that God listened to the prayers of the Odīya clans, and the earth listened to the prayers of the Teedibīya clans. In Būso they did not refer to 'Käälo', but 'Sagan', and said that the spirits of the Sagan listened to the prayers of Pazanda and Kerdita. In Idigle and all other places they said that Käälo represented wild animals. But, as we shall see, no prayers are made on ritual occasions, and there is certainly no evidence that the various clans pray to God, the earth, or the forces of the wild. These three divisions are in fact basic cosmological principles, and related to many of the characteristics of

TABLE 23. *Clan totems*

Clan	Totemic objects	Forbidden food	Oath word
Argamīda	Sun, kite, camel, *razotta* (small plant)	Camel	*Kala!* (camel)
Eeshalīda	Dik dik	—?	*Ishala!*
Tigisīda	Small stones, *Kunita* (a tree)	*Kunita* (fruit of)	Our stones! *Kunita!*
Saudata	Elephant, monkey, locust, baboon, *karsata* (plant)	*Karsata* (plant)	*Sauda!* *Karsata!*
Mahaleda	Hyena	—?	*Mahale!*
Pazanda	Fox, yam, kidney	Kidney	*Hala* (kidney)
Kerdita	*Kara* (burrowing animal) leopard, heart	Heart	*Sadada!* (heart) *Kerde!*
Elīda	Hyena, heart	Heart	*Sadada!* *Eliya!*
Toĝmaleda	Porcupine, sheep	*Mala* (part of viscera) and fat tails of sheep	*Garharta!* (sheep) *Togme*
Kudumīna	?	Lees of beer	?

[1] Also occasionally referred to as 'Ĥalibihiya'.

some of their most important social categories, but it is necessary to defer any detailed examination of their nature until the last chapter, when all the relevant evidence has been presented.

Each clan has its totem, forbidden food, and oath-word, which are often related. I shall take Garati as my example, and place the evidence from Turo and Takadi in a footnote,[1] as my Garati material is the most reliable. See Table 23.

Their own explanations of these totems is that their ancestors chose them arbitrarily as the symbols of their respective clans. It was emphasized that they were 'only a game'. Their attitude to the

[1] TAKADI

Clans	Totems	Forbidden food	Oath word
Argamīda	Sun, kite, porcupine	Camel	*Kala*
Eeshalīda	?	?	*Ishela hanno*
Tigisīda	*Gabaleda* (type of monkey?), *kunita*, *tibita* (plant),	*Kunita*	*Kunitino*
Saudata	*Razotta*, earth, elephant monkey, locust, *karsata*	*Karsata*	*Karsata*
Mahaleda	Fox, hyena	Hyena (don't kill blackbird)	*Mahale hanno*
Pazanda	Kidney	Kidney	*Halta*
Kerdita (and Ogdomīda)	*Kara*, sheep	Sheep	*Tum'ino*
Elīda	Salt	?	*Eliya hanno*
Toĝmaleda	?	?	*Togmale*

TURO

Clans	Totems	Forbidden food	Oath word
Argamīda	Camel	?	*Argama Kala*
Eeshalīda	?	?	*Eeshale*
Tigisīda	Small stones, *kunita*	*Kunita*	*Kunitino*
Saudata	Monkey	Heart	*Saude*
Mahaleda	?	?	*Mahaleeya*
Pazanda	Kidney	?	*Halda*
Kerdita	Heart	?	*Kerdiya*
Elīda	?	?	*Eliya*
Toĝmaleda	Sheep	Sheep from which tail has been cut	*Sunge Togmale*

Both these lists were collected in each case from only one informant, and they are likely to be defective.

forbidden foods was slightly more serious, it being said that if a man ate one of these his teeth would fall out. There is really no idea how these taboos originated, but one was that the people of Elīda long ago had eaten the heart of a beast and become sick, and the elders had decided that heart was bad for Elīda and should not be eaten. Some other clans have their own peculiar prohibitions and characteristics, such as Toĝmaleda, who never eat sheep from which the fat tail has been cut. The men of Ala are said to cut off this tail while the animal is still alive, and if a Toĝmaleda meets such an animal he casts earth at it and turns away. A Pazanda woman never gives birth during the first half of the month, during the waxing of the moon. These totems and the prohibitions surrounding them are certainly of very ancient origin in Konso, but since they are so arbitrary, lack any accompanying legends, and have little to do with the rest of their beliefs it is not possible to analyse their significance. The oath words are less of a problem, since they are accustomed to call on God to judge between disputants, when one man's word is pitted against another's, and these words are used on such occasions.

The members of each clan are not supposed, in general, to have any characteristics in common; the only exception to this is the belief that Tigisīda people are often mean.

In explaining the clans there are two distinct aspects to be considered. The first is historical. It is possible, for example, that these names were once the names of areas, not necessarily in Konso itself, where the people of that designation came from. But even if the clans were once identified with certain areas, from which they derived their names, this does not explain why, in a very different Konso, where these areas have long since disappeared, if they ever existed, and the clans based on them have also lost any corporate identity, the people should insist that all the members of a clan are like brother and sister, and regard any idea of intermarriage as out of the question. We come here to the second aspect of the clan, which is to understand why, whatever their origin, they have continued to exist although irrelevant to the basic institutions of the Konso society.

The idea of lineal descent groups is, as we shall see, basic to their culture. Common patrilineal descent for them is something which, ideally, can never die, even if the exact genealogical relationships are forgotten. Given the basic idea of patrilineal identity, I would suggest that their true function is somewhat similar to that of the wards, in that they help to reduce the complexity of the Konso population as a marrying and propagating group over time, to a simpler model, that is, of only nine basic patrilineal groups inter-marrying.

For example, when I was discussing clans with some Konso, they said 'How many clans do you have in England?' 'We don't have any clans in my country.' 'What! then how do you marry?' (i.e. 'How do you know whom you can marry?') The clans are thus re-tained to clarify the confusion of a multiplicity of lineages. This clarification is necessary even within the towns as there are many lineages even here—in the larger Garati towns there may be as many as thirty or so. Dyson-Hudson in *Karimojong Politics* makes the same point that clans can serve as a conceptual model. 'The nineteen clans are, indeed, essentially guide lines for ordering the vast multiplicity of small-scale, short-lived, ever proliferating groups that Karimojong have in mind when they speak of people interacting with each other because they are related'.[1]

2. THE LINEAGE

The members of a lineage (known as *kaffa*, like the clan, and occasionally as *kōza*, granary, a term also used for the clan) all tend, with few exceptions, to live in the same town; they are also bound together by their allegiance to a common lineage priest. A man's greatest obligations are to his lineage on one hand, and to his ward on the other. But while residence in one's father's town is the norm, the high concentration of settlement in towns means that while an eldest son inherits his father's homestead, and lives with him after marriage, a younger son will not normally be able to live next to his father's homestead when he comes to marry and will set up home on his own. Nor, at least in Garati, is this regarded as a bad thing. It was said to me that there was much witchcraft and magic within the lineage, and so it was better not to live too close to them. In Būso it was clear that on the whole families were scattered among the wards, if not wholly at random, then at least with considerable disregard for lineage ties. The only exceptions were the members of the Ku'jo lineage, who all seemed to live in Ifa ward, and there was also the prohibition on a man born in one of the dual divisions living in the other.

The map of Gaho (Map VII) shows the dispersal of lineages on

[1] Dyson-Hudson, op. cit., p. 90.

the ground. It should be remembered that Gaho was devastated
by the Amhara, and while people are now moving back into the
town, there is still a large area which is used as fields. But the old

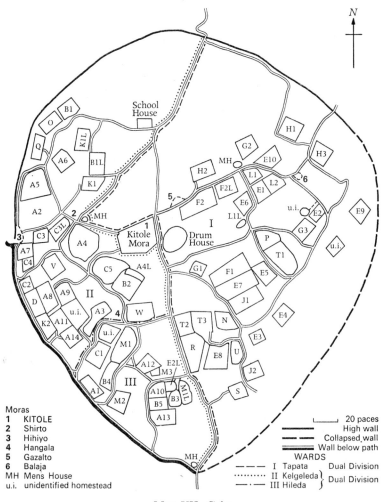

MAP VII. Gaho

homestead sites are still known and retained by the original owners,
and not freely available for purchase. It was said that it was forbidden to sell them at all, but this seems unlikely, since several
families have come to Gaho since the Amhara conquest. It seems

probable, however, in view of the tendency to return to the town, that families would be unwilling to part with sites they might wish to reoccupy later. To this extent, therefore, while Gaho is partially uninhabited, the open land is not free for unrestrained expansion in response to demand.

In making this map it was necessary to work in secret, for reasons I have already given in the Introduction. I could only spare a short time each day on the work, but luckily the people had no idea what my compass was for, and pacing is an unobtrusive as well as a surprisingly accurate means of measuring. But these circuitous forms of mapping are time-consuming, and a large part of my three months in Gaho had been spent before I could set about establishing the ownership of the compounds. I had to rely on only two informants for the genealogical data; I would wander through the town with one, and when we had passed a homestead whose owner I wanted to know I would question him in a whisper, and then, if no one was looking, quickly write the name on a scrap of paper and slip it in my pocket. As it was I was angrily threatened (by a man I barely knew) with legal proceedings for having written down his name and where he lived.

I have given the circumstances in which this map was made in some detail not only to allow the reader to estimate its reliability, but also as some sort of excuse for the shortcomings of my data.

Because a large part of the original Gaho inhabitants are still living outside the town, in the scattered settlements, a father, for example, may still remain there while his sons move into the town, or, on the other hand, sons may leave the town and live outside. This explains why some lineages as shown on the map do not contain any cases of fathers and sons having homesteads in the town. Eldest sons live with their fathers.

The meaning of the notation on the map is as follows. A letter denotes a lineage, and the numeral following is that which I have arbitrarily assigned to each lineage member. The letter 'L' following a letter and number means *lamiteda*, second wife, of the man designated by letter and number. There are several letters which stand alone, without numbers; this is because I could not find out to which lineage they were attached. If I had been able to, it is very likely that most of them would be found to belong to the four or five lineages into which each half of the town is divided. My data are not sufficiently reliable to allow me to indicate precise relationships within the lineage beyond those of F, FB, B, S, D. These relationships are shown in the tables below in the following manner:

A   2   B ⌐   F ⌐
    3   B ⌐   ⌐
    4   S ⌐

A2 and A3 are brothers; A2 and A4 are also father and son—the notation is sufficiently simple to need no further elucidation.

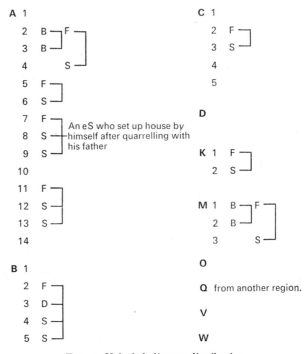

FIG. 4. Kelgeleda lineage distribution

Because Gaho is divided into only three wards, the dispersal of lineages among wards is less obvious here than it was in Būso, for example.

The lineage makes certain demands on its members. As one of my informants said, 'After a member of the lineage pays a fine, the lineage will compensate him, so a man is afraid of his lineage', the implication being that he will be unwilling to incur obligation, and with the responsibilities of repaying him his lineage will expect him to behave himself. It is expected that if a lineage member is poor or down on his luck, he will be helped with a loan of grain by another man of his lineage, and especially by the lineage priest, but he will have to repay this when times are better. When I was in Gaho I encountered a good example of the type of loyalty which

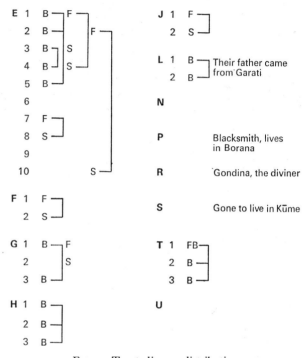

FIG. 5. Tapata lineage distribution

is expected within the lineage. Kudagude Kewdallo, the landlord of the homestead I rented, was a member of the lineage priest Sīyto's lineage. I was asking him one day for the names of some of my neighbours, which he gave without demur. But he refused to speak about one of them, or even utter his name. I discovered that this man and his father—they were also members of Sīyto's lineage—had had a dispute with another of the lineage members over the boundaries of some fields. As is usual in these cases they both appealed to God to strike the other dead for lying. The man in question and his son were victorious, in that their opponent died shortly afterwards. In consequence the victors were excluded from all contact with the rest of their lineage, who now refuse to mention their names. Although the man who died had been proved to be in the wrong (in their eyes), they still held that the winner was in a sense guilty of his death, since if he had never been a party to the dispute in the first place the other man would still be alive.

Other significant indications of lineage solidarity are to be found in vengeance and mourning obligations, and property inheritance. Vengeance does not comprehend the whole lineage. The Konso reject the pusillanimous and mercenary expedient of blood-money, and demand the life of the murderer as the only possible recompense. They may kill the murderer's brother, father, or son if they cannot find the person himself, but they said that to take vengeance on old men or boys was not right, nor would female relatives be killed—though they might be beaten up, their beads ripped off, and their water-gourds smashed. I was also told that a member merely of the murderer's lineage was not liable to be killed in vengeance. In relation to vengeance it is interesting to note that it does not establish a feud. The killing of the murderer seems to settle the matter, at least as regards further violence. But the sons of the two concerned never eat or speak together nor, in Garati, their grandsons. Only their great-grandsons may be reconciled, and in Garati there is a special ceremony at a sacred stone, called the 'Daga Shé where reconciliation is made, and where the two parties afterwards eat together. In Takadi the grandsons may eat together at a reconciliation ceremony, but there is no equivalent to the 'Daga Shé. If one member of the lineage killed another there would be no vengeance, but the man would be ostracized by the rest of the lineage.

On the death of a man, the ward has equal responsibilities with the lineage. At such an occasion the whole lineage assembles at his home, even if they hear of his death after the burial. One often meets a file of men on a path warbling their chant of mourning as they go to the home of a dead kinsman. But the whole town will also come to his home, and the ward will also bring small presents of money (one or two dollars) to show their sympathy. The ward is also responsible for the burial, in which the kin, agnatic or cognatic, take no part. The unmarried children of the dead person will shave their heads. So within the general context of mourning obligations the lineage plays no greater part than the ward, and in some ways less.

Property is only inheritable within the lineage; if a man dies without heirs, the nearest male relative of the lineage according to his seniority, will inherit. Women cannot inherit any form of property, nor be the means by which property is inherited. But there is no corporate property of the lineage; fields are owned individually and can be disposed of at will by the owner. The lineage, therefore, has no common economic interests which could provide a focus of unity.

Members of the lineage are not always sure of how their collateral kinsmen are related to them, especially if the relationship is distant. One of the more extensive genealogies I was given contained seventy-two names, but it only reached back four generations from my informant, and the fourth generation was dubious. Links in the genealogical chain are often forgotten, I think, and men are said to be brothers who were really father and son, or even grandfather and grandson. It is the lineage priest, and the knowledge of descent from him, simply as a tradition, and the custom for each new generation of men to set up house in the same town as their fathers, that gives some sort of cohesiveness to the lineage. Descent through women is only remembered for about seventy years. A man will know the family from which his grandmother came, but not, I think, his great-grandmother. For when his children are sufficiently grown up to take an interest, his grandmother—their great-grandmother—will almost certainly be dead. Nor in general will he know to whom his grandfather's sisters were married.

The priest is the focus of the lineage, since his essential duty is to bring Life—health, fertility, and peace—to its members. This he does in two ways, by preventing the outbreak of serious quarrels among its members by mediating in their disputes, and by officiating at two ceremonies at the beginning of the great rains, called the *Arhata Īla* and the *Logīda* (which I describe in full in Chapter VII). His status was concisely summed up for me at the beginning of my stay in Būso, when someone, talking of Sagara Gīya, said 'He is a priest, a great person; God encircles him; there is no quarrelling in front of him.' They say that if a lineage has no priest it will suffer disease, its crops will fail, its women and cattle will become sterile, and it will die out. A blacksmith in Degato complained to me that the priest of his lineage had gone to live in Borana, which was why the lineage was suffering so much. When the priest sacrifices he distributes the meat to the lineage, and they in turn bring to the priest the leg from any beast they slaughter at any time during the year. Men who have killed a leopard, lion, or python bring the skins to the priest, who hangs them in his homestead.

One of the most important distinguishing features of the priests is that they alone have retained their family names unchanged down the generations—a most important factor in preserving their social identities. To understand how this is so we must consider the Konso system of name inheritance. We may take the Gīya family as an example.

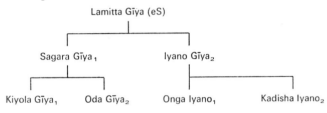

More abstractly we can represent the inheritance pattern of names as follows:-

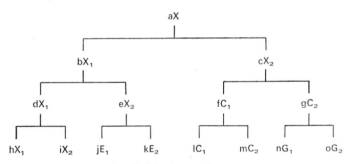

FIG. 6. Inheritance of names

The rules are as follows:

1. All siblings have the same second name; this includes half-siblings.

2. In the second generation the sons of *eldest* sons alone keep their father's second names, while all the sons of younger sons take their father's first name.

3. Half-brothers are counted as younger brothers in the inheritance of names, whether or not they are the first-born sons of their mothers.

The system of name inheritance thus unites two principles, the unity of the sibling group, and the precedence of eldest sons. Thus as the office of head of the lineage is inherited by male primogeniture, the family name of the priestly line will never change. Families which are related to the priestly line through a younger son will also, of course, preserve the same name in each of their senior lines, which may in time acquire local fame. In Garati it is permitted for the descendants of a priest's eldest son by a junior wife (*lamitta*) also to become priests after the lapse of several generations. The rule is that the first generation of the junior line takes one ring (a Garati lineage priest wears five iron rings on his right wrist) the second two, the third three, the fourth four, and the fifth becomes a full priest. But this smooth progression can only take place with the consent of the priest himself, who may not wish the junior branch to split off, as this may leave him with a much reduced lineage. For the junior branch has to give presents to the lineage priest who is asked on his death-bed to allow the aspirant to take the next ring, and, if he agrees, having been sufficiently propitiated with presents, he will say '*insage*', 'I have blessed'. If the aspirant is in the fourth generation, the priest will give him the sacred knife with which to sacrifice, as a symbol that he is now a priest. He will previously have bought a *hallasha* (a phallic head-piece; for details see below, p. 149), which the priest anoints at the Logīda each year, and also the rhinoceros horn (*gaza orshīda*), and the red beads (*furoda*).

In Būso there are about fifteen lineage priests, five of whom have become priests in the manner indicated. There are at least three more families holding three rings. Since the population of Būso is about 1,600, it follows that the average membership of a lineage is about 100, including wives and children. Degato is about 2,800 in population, and has a proportionally greater number of lineage priests. In Turo and Takadi, however, the junior branches cannot become priests.

I was given the following text by a blacksmith in Degato on the ceremonies accompanying the assumption of the five iron rings by a lineage priest when he succeeds to the office. Since the smith has to make the rings for the occasion he has a good knowledge of the details.

On the occasion of the priest's taking the five rings, he provides three rams. The first one, the smallest, is killed by the priest in the gateway of his house. He rubs his right wrist with the blood, and leaves the carcase there for the ward to take and share. The second one is bigger, and for his lineage. This one he kills on his *oida*. Again he puts its blood on his right wrist. In both cases the priest does not eat of the meat. The third one, the biggest of all, he kills inside his house. This is for his own family, and he eats of its meat, and puts its blood on his right wrist. On a second occasion he provides two rams, one for his lineage and one for his family. The first one is for the family, and is killed inside his house; the second one is killed on the *oida*. It is cut in half, one side going to the family, and the other to the lineage. On a third occasion he provides a single ram, which is only for his family. It seems that although he always puts the blood of each ram on his right wrist, he does not make a wrist band from the skin. On each occasion his wife makes dough balls of *pagana*, and adds to it liver, stomach, and red meat, in small morsels. The lineage take three balls each, and the priest gives three to each house of the ward. The priest's mother's brother puts on the five rings, all on the same occasion. His sister gives the iron, and takes the head of the ram killed to her own house. His grandmother (which one?) gives beer.

This text was not dictated to me verbatim; but is reconstructed from an interview.

If a family dies out, the next of kin with the lineage inherit the property, and if the priests' direct line becomes extinct, the lineage will supply a successor to carry it on, from the next most senior line. But the original name of the priestly line will be preserved. While it is true that accurate genealogical knowledge does not extend further back than about four generations, it is extremely unlikely that a priestly line would not have produced collateral lines and potential successors within that period.

While residence within the town is fairly free and not governed by ward boundaries, it is nevertheless customary for a man to live in the same town as his father, but we find that there has been rather a high incidence of mobility among priests in the past. Out of a list of forty-two priestly families, which is only a small sample, but on which I was given sufficient information, twenty-four were reported to have moved at some time in the past from some other place to their present homes. Of course, objectively speaking, since the Konso people as a whole are not autochthonous, mobility has been an integral part of their history. But the point is that they do not regard a priestly line which is reputed to have come from some other town or area as lacking any authority or spiritual efficacy on that account. Two priestly families, the Aloboha and the Shirto, are

V. Women fetching water

said to have been born from a black gourd, which became bigger and bigger, and finally burst, releasing the ancestors of these families. But such ascriptions of autochthony are quite exceptional. We have seen how the Bamalle and the Kalla have moved from place to place, and even the 'Gūfa, the most stable of the three, is supposed to have come originally from Ilota to his present home near Gaho. It is said that a priest liked to move in order to make himself great. There seems to be no mobility among priests at the present time. We shall consider the significance of the mobility of priests in the last chapter.

3. THE FAMILY

Within the lineage is the family, *tōla*. The word has roughly the same range of application as our word 'family'. It can refer to a particular line of descent, as in *tōla* Bamalle, 'the Bamalle family', in the same way as we might talk of 'the Percy family'. More usually, however, it means the nuclear family, father, mother, and their children; in another context it can also mean the father's co-wives and their children. Again it can mean a group of brothers and their children; but their married sisters would definitely not be included here in this use of the word *tōla*. People would say they were *tōla abila*, another family. In their early years, while their fathers were still alive the children of a group of brothers, who would probably be closely associated in play, would be said to be *olini tōla*, a family together. When they grew up and married, and their fathers died off, they would gradually cease to be *tōla*, and become *kaffa*, part of the lineage. Within the family the father, as one might expect, is the head and master, but his wife is not unduly subservient. The husband is often out in the fields or sitting in one of the *moras*, while his wife is at home preparing the food. It is natural in these circumstances that she should be mainly responsible for looking after the children. But though she is regarded with more warmth than the father, as in all societies, the Konso could never be said to suffer, as a culture, from an Oedipus complex. Most of the children I saw crying, if they had not been hit by another child, had been beaten by their mothers. They say that a man is 'afraid of both his father and his mother'. When a woman beats a child—which may be for some minor disobedience—she takes a thin withy and flicks it over the head and body. I never saw or heard of a child which suffered any serious injury as a result of parental cruelty, though no doubt there are a few instances. Sagara Gīya's little son, Kīyola, who was the apple of his parent's eyes was allowed, although more than two years old, to defecate in the homestead, and even in the kitchen; the normal practice with a child of this age, who can understand correction, is to beat him, and I asked my servant why his parents were so lenient. 'They are afraid that if they were often angry with him he might die', he replied. He was the first of their sons who had survived (by Sagara's first wife) and so the mother especially, as well as his father, was particularly anxious for him not to die. We may infer that if parents treat their children harshly and they afterwards become sick and die, the parents blame themselves for the death by attributing it to their punishment. The punishment of the child is reserved for the parents; a co-wife cannot punish the child of another wife, and even when one of the parents is angry with a child, the other will go to its defence. The *abuya* (MB), however, is allowed to punish his sister's child; this applies to all her brothers, not just the eldest. One afternoon Kalgallo Läa's wife was attacked by her small son Iyano, of about eight or nine years of age. In a fit of temper he tried to stab her with a spear. Someone wrested the weapon away from the boy, and his mother called her brother, Mamo Guisa, since her husband was out at the time. He went up to her house and fetched away his nephew, who by this time was blubbering with terror. Mamo brought him down to his own house and tied him up to a post, with his arms behind his back. He then beat him for some minutes with a thin stick, while the boy screamed for mercy. He was an obnoxious brat and his offence was a very severe one, and it was the general opinion that he thoroughly deserved his beating, but eventually some of the neighbours told Mamo to desist as he had suffered enough. Grandparents do not chastise their grandchildren. It is the custom of old women in rich families to wear heavy brass bracelets; when I asked if it was forbidden for young women to wear them I was told 'No, not forbidden, but mothers often have to beat their children, and if they were wearing these bracelets they might kill them. So only grandmothers wear them, as they never hit their grandchildren.' The relationship between grandparents and grandchildren is more friendly and relaxed than between parents and children, but there is still great respect for the grandfather especially, and he is said to be like God.

So far I have not considered the problem of the polygynous

family. In fact only about one man in ten or more can afford the expense of a second wife, and fewer still have married three. Sagara Gīya was the only man I knew who had married four. Relations between co-wives are conventionally hostile, but in practice they depend on the personalities of the women involved. Whatever the relations, it is the custom for each wife to have her separate homestead, with a few cattle, sheep, and goats for her own use, and some of her husband's fields. As in the case of sons who are setting up their own homes for the first time, it is often difficult to find homesteads for extra wives which are close at hand, and in any case they say it is good for them to live some distance apart. So it often happens that the homesteads of co-wives are in different wards. If the wives get on amicably together they may visit each other, and while I was in Sagara Gīya's homestead they were often coming in and out during the day. Normally a wife is given a separate homestead when she marries, but when there is not one immediately available, she may stay in that of the senior wife—if the latter agrees, of course. Sagara Gīya married his fourth wife, Kasse, a couple of months after I left Būso. She was still living in his ancestral home when I finally left Konso seven months later. But this arrangement is only possible when the senior wife, as Koyite was, is acquiescent. The husband still tends to sleep in his chief homestead, or in the *mora* house, and take his food also in his main home. It is said that the junior wives often complain that they are sexually neglected. This is especially true if the second or third wives continue to live in the towns of their birth after they marry a man of a different town, as sometimes happens, perhaps through a shortage of land. But this sexual advantage of the senior wife tends to disappear as she becomes older and less physically attractive when the husband's desire will become diverted to his younger wives—it is largely for this reason, after all, that he marries them.

The children of the various wives will all play together, irrespective of the relations, good or bad, between their respective mothers—they have the same father and this is the important fact. A junior wife is called *lamiteda*, from *lamata* meaning 'second', and -*da*, the feminine ending. The son of a *lamiteda* is called a *lamita*.

4. KINSHIP TERMINOLOGY

It will help the reader to understand the working of kinship relations among the Konso if I now set out their terminology.

TABLE 24. *Kinship terminology*

(Vocative terms are in parenthesis)

1.	*aka*	FF, MF
2.	*okoyoda (okoyo)*	FM, MM
3.	*apa (apo)*[2]	F, FB
4.	*ahada (īye)*[2]	M, MZ
	īya	
5.	*mamada (mama)*	FZ
6.	*abuya*	MB
7.	*alaua*[3]	B (w.s.)[1]
8.	*alauda*[3]	Z (m.s.)[1]
9.	*ina*	S
10.	*inanda*	D
11.	*inano*[4]	FBS, BS (B (m.s.))
12.	*inandīno*[4]	FBD, BD (Z (w.s.))
13.	*ashuma*	FZS, ZS
14.	*ashumda*	FZD, ZD
15.	*ina abuya*	MBS
16.	*inanda abuya*	MBD
17.	*apula*	MZS
18.	*apulīda*	MZD
19.	*oba*	SS, DS
20.	*ofta*	SD, DD
21.	*handōda*	W (See note 2, especially in relation to 'husband'.)

1. w.s. = woman speaking; m.s. = man speaking.

2. There is no referential term for 'mother' in common use. *īya* means mother, but has mostly been displaced by the word *ahada* meaning married woman, plus the suffix *-īno* 'our' which being the plural of the possessive denotes that she belongs to the family as a whole. *Ahadīo* means '*my* married woman', i.e. 'my wife'. *Handōda* means wife, strictly speaking, but, like '*īya*' is very seldom used. Similarly, there is no word at all meaning only 'husband'. 'Apa' means not only father, but more generally 'adult male who has married and become a father' and in this sense it comes closest to 'husband' of any word. If one wants to ask a woman if her husband is at home, one would say something like '*Apa tiga arēja?*' 'Is the master of the house here?'

3. A girl cannot refer to her sister as *alauda* but would have to say *inandīno*, 'our girl'. The word *alauda* can only be used by the brother to refer to his sisters; he too cannot refer to his brother as *alaua* as he is of the same sex—the word *alaua* can only be used by the sister.

4. *ina'no* means 'our boy', and *inand'ino* means 'our girl'. Thus usage denotes that the person referred to is of the same family or lineage as the speaker, and of the same or a junior generation. One would not refer to someone of a senior generation as 'our boy' or 'our girl'; nor does one ever address anyone of a senior generation, whether related or not, by their name.

22. *ĝarda*[5]   eB
23. *kusita*   yB
24. *ĝariteda*   eZ
25. *koyiteda*   yZ

5. *ĝarda* also means "edge", as of a knife. Of course, this may only be a case of homonyms, but it still presents interesting speculative possibilities.

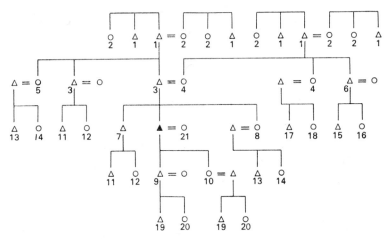

FIG. 7. Kinship terminology

There are two other important terms, *daldīda* and *sargata*, (*sargateda* for a woman) which cut across our concepts of 'affine' and 'cognate'. It is difficult to give precise rules of membership for either category, and it should be emphasized that the Konso themselves are sometimes unsure. It is said that *sargata* is derived from the Amharic *sark*, a wedding, but this is possibly a folk etymology. The allocation of relatives between the categories of *kaffa*, *daldīda*, and *sargata* reflects the fact that the wife is never a full member of her husband's lineage—she can marry his brother if he dies—and similarly, that female members of the lineage are partly dissociated from it at marriage.

The following features of their terminology are worthy of note in relation to the rest of their society.

1. The terminology is not a wide-ranging one, either in time, where one cannot even tell if an *aka* is a member of the speaker's lineage or not, or in scope of relationship, where it does not extend referentially beyond first cousins. Nor can the terms be used in

combination; to say, for example, '*abuya oba mamada*', 'Father's sister's mother's brother', would be impossible.

2. It distinguishes in particular some close cognatic kin, viz. ZS, ZD, FZS, FZD, MB, MBS, MBD, MZS, MZD, and this is relevant to the fact that these close cognates retain important ties with ego, and in almost all cases subject to marriage prohibitions. It is also interesting that the closest relatives within the lineage are not distinguished clearly by referential terms, and in this respect there is a marked contrast with the usage obtaining in the case of close cognates. It is as though the fact that these relatives are not of the same lineage as ego, but are nevertheless thought to be very closely related, necessitates their being especially precisely demarcated.

3. The vagueness of the terms for 'husband' and 'wife' is an indication of the fact that they pay more regard to the status of being a father and a mother.

4. The terminology places great emphasis on seniority—the four terms to distinguish eldest and younger siblings, and a different set of terms for each generation indicate this.

TABLE 25. Daldīda *and* sargata

Kaffa	Daldīda		Sargata	No relationship
W	WF, WM	WZ	WB, WZ,	
	WMB	WS	WD, WS	
	HF, HM,			
	HMB			
	HB, HZ.			
	BW			BWF, BWM,
				BWB, BWZ
Z	ZD		ZH	ZHF, ZHM,
				ZHB, ZHZ
FW	FBW			
FZ	FZH			
	FZS, FZD			
M	MF, MFB, MM		MZH	
	MB, MBW, MBS, MBD			
	MZ, MZS, MZD			

5. COGNATIC AND AFFINAL TIES

Cognatic ties, as we have seen, are of much less importance than lineage ties. As I have said before, they are forgotten after about seventy years, or three generations. There is, however, one cognatic relative who is of great importance—the *abuya*, mother's brother.

The significance of the *abuya* derives from the fact that he is the mother's closest male relative. Her role as father's wife is irrelevant, because the *abuya* does not have any special relationship to his sister's husband, nor acts as the representative of his lineage, or as her 'provider'. It is for this reason that the mother's father is not of such importance, as brothers and sisters are regarded as being more closely related than father and daughter. They have the same parents and were born from the same womb. Moreover, they are of the same generation, a factor of great importance in Konso thought. I was discussing the *abuya* problem once in Takadi, and said that I had no *abuya*, since my mother was an only child. I asked who would act as my *abuya* if I were a Konso. There was a good deal of thought about it, since it is an unusual dilemma, though not, of course, unknown. The solution offered was that my mother's father's brother's son should act as my *abuya*. The idea of my mother's father acting as my *abuya* was definitely rejected. It was generally agreed by all my informants that the mother's brother always took precedence over the mother's father in rituals of blessing in the family, even if the mother's father could bless as well. It is not perhaps entirely fanciful to suggest that the word *abuya* is a contraction of *apa-iya*, 'father–mother', or male mother.

What is the conventional pattern of relations between the rest of the kinship categories outside the family? Relations between the lineage as we have seen should be loyal and helpful. Cognatic kin should also be treated as friends—we recall that cognatic kin are much more restricted than agnates. Relations between affines are more difficult. They laughed when I told them that in England men were supposed not to get on with their mothers-in-law, and said that the same thing was true in Konso. A man respects his mother and father-in-law, but there is often hostility with the mother-in-law. With his father-in-law on the other hand he is said to be on generally good terms. A woman is on equally bad terms with her mother-in-law especially if she is the senior wife of the eldest son, when she will be living in the same homestead as her husband's mother. In these circumstances it is not surprising that there should be friction between the two women. The relations between the husband and his wife's brother can also be strained because after the death of her father her brother is the person to whom above all she turns for protection if she is quarrelling with her husband.

6. THE STATUS OF THE ELDEST SON

Primogeniture is a phenomenon which has received little attention in studies of kinship, yet it is widespread, and is often not only a basic rule for the inheritance of status and property, but also has important religious associations, especially among the Hebrews of the Old Testament, for example.

We shall see in Chapter VI that sibling seniority is not confined to the descent system, but is an integral part of the generation-grading systems, so I shall try to give an explanation here of its basic significance, and of the relationship between sibling and generational seniority. I shall first recapitulate the relevant details of Konso primogeniture, and then consider the unity of the sibling group and generational seniority, with which the status of the eS is closely connected.

The naming system is based, as we have seen, on the principles of primogeniture and the unity of the sibling group.[1] Its effect is to distinguish the component lines of the lineage according to two related criteria—the number of eS there are in ego's direct line of ascent, and the number of yS who interpose between the first eS in this line of ascent and the priestly line. Thus lines which have a long descent through eS, as indicated by the continuity of their second name, have more status than lines descended through several yS, and lines at only one or two removes, through a yS, from the priestly line also have status on this account. In accordance with the principle of primogeniture, priests, as we have seen, are the eS of an unbroken line of eS. This is a fact of the greatest importance in understanding the status of the eS among the Konso, and I shall refer to it again shortly. The eS of a lineage or regional priest, on the death of his father, ceremonially curses his ghost; he is explicitly regarded as replacing his father. A number of conversations I had while living in the homestead of Sagara Gīya, a lineage priest and one of my best informants, made this very clear. His eldest son was forbidden to sit on a certain stone outside the homestead gate which was reserved for Sagara alone. If the eldest son had sat there he would have been wishing for the death of his father. Other indications of the status of the eS are that he lives in his father's

[1] My reference to the 'unity of the sibling group' is not intended as an endorsement of Radcliffe-Brown's theoretical position on this matter. Whether the 'unity of the sibling group' is a universal principle of descent systems or not, my use of the term here is simply a recognition of the ethnographic facts among the Konso.

homestead, and, when his father dies, receives twice the share of the patrimony inherited by each younger brother. For ritual purposes the *abuya* is always the MeB, not MyB. The eS is also supposed to marry before his younger brothers.

As we have seen, the unity of the sibling group is expressed in the naming system, whereby all siblings take the same second name, irrespective of the order of birth. We also saw that the MB is regarded as more closely related to her than the MF, and that if no MB is available for ritual purposes his place should be taken by the MFBS. Clearly, generational equality is a highly significant principle, and the sibling group is, *par excellence*, a group exemplifying this principle.

The separation of the generations is the converse of the unity of the sibling group. One calls all males of the FF's generation *aka*, and all females *okoyo*, all males of the F's generation *apo*, and all females *iye*. The FF's generation are seen as exerting essentially moral authority, and the F's generation as using physical chastisement—the grandmother never beats her grandchildren, and it is said that the grandfather 'is like God'. In Konso society generally, as we shall see, the sequence of the generations, and their respective roles, are of paramount social and ritual significance.

In the context of these facts, why then is the category of eS of such significance, and why is it vested with sanctity in the role of the lineage priest? We have seen that the Konso are highly generation conscious, that within each generation siblings are regarded as closer than parents or children, and that the eS is regarded as replacing his father. Thus the position of the eS is pivotal in the descent system, as we may see in the following diagram:

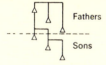

The eS forms a bridge between the generations, and his status is thereby marginal or liminal. By being born, the eS transforms the status of his father from *ina* to *apa*, and when his father dies, the eS is the medium by which the status of the father is transferred to the sibling group in the succeeding generation. He is the means by which generational seniority is created in the first place and the means by which it is ultimately transmitted. Now, as I remarked above, we often find that eS have a sacred status, and I suggest that, in common with many other forms of sanctity or spiritual power, this is closely allied with their marginal or liminal status. This may seem a trifle far-fetched, but let us take another look at the diagram. There is one other liminal category there—that of the youngest sibling of the father's generation, who is the most junior member of the senior generation, as opposed to the eS, the most senior member of the junior generation. Thus, if my explanation of the status of the eS among the Konso is correct, it is also a plausible explanation of the rare and puzzling phenomenon of ultimogeniture, since the youngest son can be seen as having as much affinity with the junior generation as with his own senior generation—in short, as being a sort of very senior eB in relation to the generation below his own. We may press the comparison between ultimogeniture and primogeniture a stage further. Among the Konso we find that the sanctity of the priest is defined by his being the eS of a line of eS; there are also a number of references in ethnographic literature generally to the special sanctity or supernatural powers of the scion of a line of youngest sons. Specifically, in our own culture, we are familiar, for example, with the reputation of the seventh son of a seventh son for having psychic powers, but structurally, the seventh son of a seventh son is really the mirror image of the lineage priest of the Konso. The priest is descended from a line of eS, the psychic person ideally from a line of youngest sons. The only difficulty about comparing primo- and ultimogeniture is that while the status of the eS is fixed, barring death, that of youngest son is relative and fluid; hence the necessity of specifying some particular category of junior sibling, such as 'seventh'. But structurally the analogy between eS and youngest son seems quite clear, and provides considerable support for the hypothesis that the social and ritual status of the eS among the Konso derives from his liminal position. We shall take up the status of the eS again in the chapter on the generation-grading systems.

7. MARRIAGE AND MARRIAGE PROHIBITIONS

Marriages among the Konso are not arranged by the parents of the couple irrespective of their children's wishes; while the girl's father may have definite preferences about her future husband, with which she is expected to comply, if she is determined to marry someone else she can do so, and her father is powerless to stop her. Young men have considerably more initiative in choosing their wives.

The only forms of obligatory alliance apply to the three regional priests: the Kalla only marries girls from Päidi in Turo. The Bamalle must marry a Takadi girl as his first wife, but his subsequent wives may be from any part of Konso. The 'Gūfa only marries a Päidi girl as his first wife, but his subsequent wives likewise may be from any part of Konso. Marriage is supposed to result from the affections of the couple concerned; it is said that at first husband and wife love each other, but as time goes on their affection often cools; a more enduring link between the husband and wife is the birth of children.

I shall have more to say on the question of sex in the next chapter, but it is relevant here to note that they disapprove of sexual relations before marriage, although unofficially it is apparently frequent, and value virginity in women. There never seems to have been any prostitution for money among them, but I was told of certain women, called *arabalīda*, who offer their bodies to men, but without taking payment. As I have no personal knowledge of this I cannot add any further details.

In Garati and Takadi the wedding feast takes place in the home of the groom's father. The bride brings with her only three of her girl friends, who sleep with her for three nights before she sleeps with her husband on the fourth. In Takadi the girl sleeps with her husband on the first night. None of the bride's family comes, and the reason I was given for this was, as they tersely express it '*sūda mala*' 'because of the sexual intercourse'. It seems more likely to be a ceremonial expression of hostility. No ritual takes place at the ceremony, which is simply a feast.

The question of bridewealth in Konso in obscure. The Amhara are said to make payments to the bride's family and this was given as the reason for the increase in marriage payments among the Konso. In Garati I was told that the custom had grown up in the last ten years or so; in Gaho it was said that it was older than this. It seems likely that fathers have decided that it is a useful source of income, and decided to copy the Amhara in this respect. In Būso the chief present to the father of the bride is a cotton blanket, and in some cases about E$10 (30s.) though it is said that some families refuse this money. Whatever is given, it is stressed that it is only to establish friendship between the groom and his new father-in-law. The husband also gives his wife butter and honey for three months after the marriage, and this is considerably more expensive than the presents given to her father. As will appear in the text quoted below, the girl is at first regarded as a stranger by her husband's family. Commensality among the Konso is one of the chief ceremonial expressions of social harmony. It seems likely therefore that the luxurious food given to the bride by the groom is a formal process of incorporation. Fathers have to pay these costs in most cases, as the sons would not be able to afford them, or to set up homes for themselves either. In Takadi it seems that bridewealth is more elaborate; nowadays the money may vary between E$50 and 100 (E$7=£1), which represents in real terms a fair-sized bullock. The *abuya* of the bride takes about E$3, the bride's mother is given butter, as are both her grandmothers, and the lineages eat honey together. After the marriage in Takadi the couple visit the houses of the groom's lineage and sleep the night there, although I understand that sexual intercourse does not take place on these occasions. There is a good deal of uncertainty about the amount of bridewealth in Takadi, and often about which relatives take what, which makes it unreliable as a guide to the relative status of the various kin, but it seems that in Takadi there is more emphasis placed on the interest of the groom's lineage in the marriage than there is in Garati.

I obtained the following text from Garide, my servant, which brings out many aspects of Konso marriage very well.

A girl and a boy like each other; the family [of the girl] forbids it. The girl says 'I like him and will marry him'. She hides from her family and marries him. The family of the girl go and accuse the man she married, at the *balabbat's* house. And the girl says 'I like this boy; you were giving me to another, but I will not take that boy, so I will marry this one.' And her parents say 'Why will you marry this fool?' She says 'My womb and my belly desire him, you are giving me someone whom my belly does not like, I will not take him, so I will marry [the one I like]. Her parents bring an accusation at the *balabbat's*. The *balabbat* says 'We will go to the elders to ask about this and decide it together.' The elders say 'The girl has married, and has not come back to your house, and has not done your work [i.e. obeyed you]. Her belly desired [another] and she married him. You indeed have begotten this girl, and this being so let there be no quarrelling, because of kinship [my paraphrase] and so bless the girl'. And if the parents refuse to listen, and continue to accuse, they go together to the government, and the girl says 'I liked him and married him.' The government asks 'Girl, you and your family came here together, will you go with the man you married?' She says 'I will go with my husband, my belly desires him, I do not want my family, I will go with my husband.'

Now he speaks of different circumstances, when the daughter is obedient to her parents:

Children grow up, and the daughter hears the voice of her parents, and where they give her in marriage, there she marries. When the girl is about to marry and come to the home into which she will marry, her parents say [to her] 'We have been asking among our kinsmen and our friends there [at her future husband's home] if the girl will like it', and they ask the girl there 'Girl, will you accept this [new] home?' The girl says 'You are my father, you are my mother, if you are giving me this thing of yours is good . . . [3 lines obscure] . . . Now you are giving me to their house my belly has liked you; I have seen what my parents want, you are giving me, and so I will marry, you have given me. So call the *mamada* (FZ) and the neighbours, and the *daldīda*, and bless me then. The *mamada* and the *daldīda* come and bless the girl, and say to her 'Work hard, and bear sons and daughters for us, and as your [new] family sleep, so you sleep with them, then wake, when they go out to the fields, and work hard, and till the fields', and with *gompeda*, and with salt and with *ifiya* they bless her, and say 'Bear many sons.' [actual words untranslatable; this was a paraphrase they gave me].

He now talks about how the young man asks the girl to marry him:

When a family has a daughter, and a boy asks for her on the path, and her womb is good [i.e. she likes him] he sends an old man to her family, and this old man goes and asks her parents, and they say 'These things which the boy asks, we do not know if the girl is willing, we will ask her, and then give a decision.' The girls sleep in the sleeping house [the '*tiga mugdoda*', used by many unmarried girls in the ward] at night, and the boy and the girl are playing there in the sleeping house [there is not supposed to be any impropriety there] and the boy says 'a little while ago I sent an old man to your parent's house; have you heard anything between your parents?' She says 'These things of my parents, if we like one another, and you like me, [so] work on my family so that in a few days my parents will not be angry with me. You make the old man speak with them, and when he has done his work, it will be good with us.' . . . [8 words obscure] . . . Then after this the boy sends the old man, and the family give [the girl]. Then they [the girl's parents] receive the bride wealth [literally 'compensation'] and after they have it the girl marries in return for it, the boy marries her. When the girl is married she calls three girls . . . [obscure, 'to give her courage' was their paraphrase] . . . and they stay three days at the house where the marriage is. And on the fourth day at night the three girls go to their own home and they say 'As we sleep in our own homes, we will leave you' thus they say, and go away. And she remains in the bosom of the family. And they say that the girl is a stranger. After this she eats there for three months, and in the fourth month she starts working; then an old woman comes from the house of a friend [presumably a friend of the husband's family] and the old woman takes her to the fields, and from this time on she does all the work [that she should as a wife] and becomes a wife.

Divorce is easy, for men and women. The man may expel his wife from the home, and as she brings nothing to the marriage she can take nothing away. There are thus no problems about the division of joint property. Equally, the wife may decide to leave her husband, if she prefers another man, or thinks she is being cruelly treated, or sexually neglected. In this case she will go back to her father's or brother's house, if her father is dead, and either live there and help in the daily work, or be given some fields to support her. It is possible for single women to survive; if they are of *hauda* (craftsman) stock they can prepare skins or make pots; their families may give them fields, or as in the case of a female diviner I knew they may make a living by divination, though this is much rarer. In most divorces, however, the woman wishes to marry another man and the problem of how she is to support herself does not arise. While divorce is quite easy, in practice my Gaho figures suggest that only about 2 per cent of women actually have been divorced. Adultery is regarded as a very serious offence, and the husband is held to be justified in killing both the wife and her seducer if he finds them in the act, and her family would not avenge her. Husbands do beat their wives on occasions, but it is known for strong women to beat their husbands, deplorable though this is felt to be!

The marriage prohibitions are as follows. In Garati a man may not marry any daughter of his FB or MZ. He may marry the younger daughters of his FZ or MB, but never the eldest daughter of either category. In Takadi, not only are all the daughters of FB and MZ forbidden in marriage, but also all daughters of FZ and MB. Cross-cousins whom one is forbidden to marry are in both regions referred to as *īya* 'mother'. What are the reasons for this prohibition? We have already seen that marriage within the lineage (which is a subdivision of the clan) is incestuous, and so naturally marriage with the FBD is forbidden; she will be referred to as *inand'īno* 'our girl', just as a sister may be. The MZ is not a member of ego's lineage but of his MF's, and his MZD will be still further removed as a member of his MZH's lineage. Therefore there is no question of a lineage affiliation preventing marriage with the MZD. We have seen that the FB is addressed as *apo*, father, and MZ as *īye*, mother, and of course this does not mean that they are thought of as real fathers and mothers (children call all men of their father's generation *apo*, and all women of their mother's generation *īye*). What is significant, however, is that in a system of terminology which embraces such relatives as MZD the term for a closer relation such as FB or MZ should not be differentiated in referential usage. I think we are justified in concluding that since the term for FB is the same as for F, they are thought of as having important similarities, quite apart from the respectful usage which would lead a boy to address his FB as *apo* and his MZ as *īye*. Thus, as the M and MZ are so closely associated, we have a possible reason for an objection to their children marrying—they are thought of as being almost brothers and sisters. A similar objection to marriage between cross-cousins as well as between parallel cousins can be seen in the prohibition in Garati upon marrying the eldest daughter of the MB or FZ, and in Takadi upon marrying any daughter of these relations—indeed, they are referred to in Garati and Takadi as *īya*, and someone remarked too when telling me this that a man could not marry his mother—a possible reason for applying the term to the MBD and FZD. Thus in Takadi, and Garati to a slightly lesser extent, there is a belief that children of siblings should not intermarry and, where they are allowed to marry, the siblings are of different sex. In Takadi they also told me that the MZDD and FZDD could not be married. On whether or not the MBDD could be married there was considerable doubt. In Garati I was told that the MBDD was distant, and that ego's son might marry her, but that the FZDD was still too close and should not be married. The reason for allowing marriage with the MByD but not MBeD, and FZyD but not FZeD is surely related to the general status of eldest child in relation to younger child, and this applies to girls as well as boys. The daughters should marry in order of seniority, the eldest first, and so on; the same rule applies to the marriage of eldest sons before their younger brothers. How far the prohibitions on marrying cognatic kin extend in theory is not of much practical relevance, since such ties are forgotten after about seventy years.

Siblings are also subject to other marital prohibitions; a man cannot marry his wife's sister, while she is still alive. Nor can two brothers marry two sisters. But after a husband's death one of his brothers may offer to marry her if she has not borne a son. If her husband was a younger son one of his brothers will offer to marry her, whether he had a son or not; if she refused she might be turned out of the homestead, but this was not inevitable. The wife of a deceased eS, however, would be expected to bear children in his name (by one of his surviving brothers), if he had died without issue. If he were survived by a son, his wife would not be expected to bear other sons by his brothers. The wife of a priest is not allowed to marry again, whether she is divorced from her husband or widowed, though I know of at least one case where this happened.

Just as kin ties are mitigated by the general claim on loyalties made by the town, so marriage lacks much of the importance it has in other primitive societies as the means of binding kin groups together.

When I was in Gaho I obtained the marriage data for a number of lineages, and it was clear from these that not only do members of the same family marry women from quite different lineages, but also often from quite different towns. Their rules of marriage therefore are structurally defined only in their negative aspect; the choice whom to marry is determined by other considerations, but chiefly by having grown up in the same town as one's future wife. As we might expect, when boys and girls grow up together in a Konso town it is predictable that they should frequently intermarry.

In some cases, where there is no suitable girl available at the time when a young man wishes to marry, or the choice of women is particularly repulsive to him, he will have to seek elsewhere. I collected the figures in Table 26 from Gaho to show the frequencies of marriage within the man's home town, and with other towns. Tēbana is the closest town to Gaho, with which it has a long tradition of friendly relations. In view of this it is understandable that Tēbana should come second on the list, albeit with less than a third of the Gaho marriages recorded. Kūme is rather further, about half an hour's walk, like Majeġe, and both these towns have a tradition of friendship with Gaho. The rest of the towns are either enemies of Gaho, with whom there would have been no marriages at all before the Amhara, for obvious reasons, or are too far away to make marriage a practical possibility in most cases. The marriage statistics therefore have a pattern which is predictable from what we already know of their social organization—the relations between the towns, and the relative lack of importance of marriage in forming social links between the kin of the man and woman concerned. (It would have been interesting to compare these figures with those of the other towns where I lived, but Gaho, having a population of less than 500 was the only one where the collection of data of this sort was a practical possibility. Degato, for example, has a population of nearly 3,000.) Since I knew only a few people well wherever I lived, I could not have gathered a statistically reliable sample either.

TABLE 26. *Marriage frequencies*

	Name of town	Number of marriages
1	Gaho	60
2	Tēbana	18
3	Kūme	7
4	Karshalle	5
5	Majeĝe	3
6	Kēra	2
7	Kunyara	2
8	Ḥolme	2
9	Fāsha	1
10	Modone	1
11	Iyēdi	1
12	Saugame	1
13	Garati	1
14	Turo	1
	Total	105

8. CONCLUSIONS

Konso society is not based primarily on kinship ties. While the lineage makes important claims on its members in terms of friendship and co-operation, it does not provide the basis of the other social institutions. Even within the lineage, we have seen that its claims on its members stop short at property, which is as free from the claims of kin as it is from the claims of neighbours. We noted also that within the lineage the sibling group was more closely united than cousins of the same lineage, and that vengence only comprehended the family, not the lineage as a whole. Against this background of relatively weak lineage ties, in relation to the other demands of town, ward, and *marbara* loyalties, it is not surprising that marriage should produce such small changes in the structure of affinal relations. In comparison with the other rites of passage—the emerging of the child into society in the third month (the *sogeda*) the entry into the Ḫrela (or warrior grade), from the childhood grade of Farīda, and death—marriage is the least important, both in its personal implications and in its ceremonial, of which there is hardly any.

But while the lineages are not the basis of co-operation among the Konso, certain of the principles upon which all descent systems are based are of fundamental significance in their society, especially in the working of the generation-grading systems, for these systems are based on generational and sibling seniority, and the special status of the eS.

Again, the lineages are male by definition. The lineage endures, theoretically, for ever, just as the name of the priest endures, while women move from one to another in a state of fluidity. In the same way, women are thought of as leaving the towns at marriage and living elsewhere with their husbands (though this belief is an exaggeration). The lineages remain in the towns, the women move between them. This social mobility of women is of great importance in determining Konso attitudes towards them, especially in their scheme of values, as we shall see in the next chapter.

PART III. GENERAL CONCLUSIONS

We are now in a position to assess some of the general characteristics of Konso social organization. The reasons for the evolution of the towns are obscure, and undoubtedly manifold, but the ecological circumstances provide little clue. To be sure, if they had to subsist on a slash-and-burn agriculture, then such large and long-established towns would not be possible, at least in their present numbers. But the converse of this, that *because* they have a stable form of agriculture based on manure their towns have grown up as a result, is a *non sequitur*. The cultivation of crops such as *ensete* and *tef* has enabled many of the peoples of Ethiopia to settle permanently in one place, but they show in general no tendency to develop towns, or even large villages; on the contrary, their settlement pattern is very scattered. In many cases, as among the Amhara, gregariousness is positively repulsive to them. It might be argued that the peculiar requirements of stone-terraced fields, in terms of the co-operation of labour needed in their construction and maintenance, would tend to favour the creation of towns. But this argument is not supported by the facts, since one region of Konso, the Turo, which in the past had as much terracing as the Garati and Takadi regions, has never developed towns to the same extent. The Gauwada tribe, who also have terraces or had them in the past, have not developed towns either.

The Konso themselves say that originally their ancestors used to live in scattered homesteads, but there was so much fighting and murder that they formed towns for mutual protection. This may or may not be so, but it does not explain why towns were the solution finally adopted. Many other peoples have problems about internal law and order, but very few have chosen the Konso remedy.

Relations between the Konso and the Borana have apparently always been hostile. But it seems unlikely that Borana raids were the reason for the Konso forming towns, for the following reasons: the Borana do not raid in large groups, but in small parties, or singly; their purpose in doing so is not for plunder and certainly not to encroach on the Konso Highlands, which would be useless for their herds, but to gain the prestige of killing a male. The Konso do not fear the Borana, but despise them for what they consider their cowardly tactics in shooting from ambush instead of coming out into the open and fighting like men. It is likely that if the Borana attempted a mass assault on Konso territory they would be given a severe drubbing, and this would have been true in historical times as well. Moreover, the Galla peoples are widespread in Ethiopia; is it likely that only in one area the fear of them would have caused the aboriginal population to form walled towns of Konso type? So while the towns do have some practical advantages for co-operation and self-protection (and we must not overlook the greater danger of really devastating battles they produced), they could only have arisen because the people were willing to live together in dense groups, a mode of life which is intolerable to many other peoples. This, of course, while a necessary condition of their existence, cannot by itself explain it; in fact a full understanding of the genesis of their towns could only come from a knowledge of the historical circumstances in which they arose.

The towns have now existed for several centuries, and we can assume that such adjustments, if any, that occurred in the rest of their social organization as a result, have now been completed. Certainly, some features of their urban organization, such as the dual divisions and the wards, are closely related to urban life, in the sense that they would be of little use to a people dwelling scattered over the land. But there is no demonstrable relationship between towns and conciliar government, or the relative weakness of descent groups in ordering social relations. Town life is quite compatible with government by chiefs, which would render councils unnecessary. The lack of chiefs has nothing to do with the existence of towns, but is based on their dislike of the idea of being ruled by one man, and this dislike is as basic an element of the values of their society as their gregariousness, or their martial spirit.

It is certainly possible that the relatively narrow range of lineage ties, and the insignificance of marriage as an instrument of social cohesion, has been brought about by the circumstances of their urban life. But among the Gurage, for example, the population of their large villages is ideally composed only of patrilineal kinsmen.[1] There is in fact nothing in the nature of urban life which is incompatible with strong kin ties. And we may equally go on to ask why, even if there is a connection between Konso urban life and the minor role of kinship, there are any lineages at all, and not just sets of nuclear families.

Let us now consider the interrelationships of the other offices and groups within the towns—the lineage priests, the councils, the Nama Dawra, the Apa Timba, the *shorugata*, and the warriors. The institutions of the towns are organized on the basis of three distinct principles—those of descent, residence, and seniority. The descent groups are the lineages, residence groups are towns, dual divisions, and wards, and the generation system provides the three basic categories of elders, warriors, and boys. The chart (fig. 8) illustrates the relationship between these three categories of seniority on the one hand, and to the town offices on the other. It also shows how these offices are related to the residence groups, descent groups, and the grading system. The chart may be read from right to left, so that we see first how the criteria of membership of offices in the centre derive from the grading system, then how the offices are related among themselves, so that the Nama Dawra, Apa Timba, *shorugata*, and lineage priests are loosely connected, and

[1] Shack, *The Gurage*, pp. 91 ff.

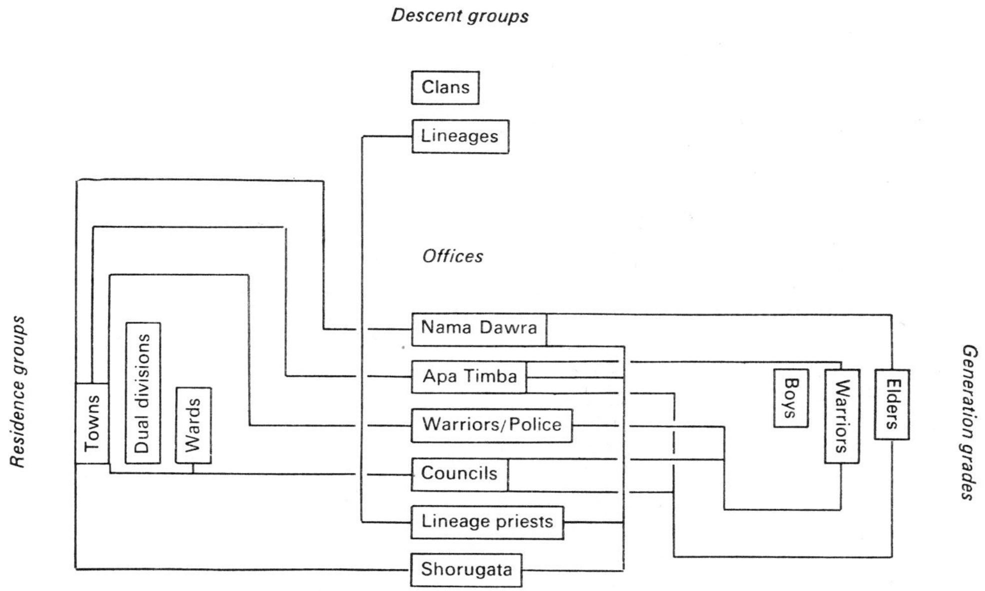

Generation grades

Elders

Warriors

Boys

Descent groups

Clans

Lineages

Offices

Nama Dawra

Apa Timba

Warriors/Police

Councils

Lineage priests

Shorugata

Wards

Dual divisions

Towns

Residence groups

Fig. 8. Town organization

finally to what areas of town organizations the various offices are related. But these offices are mainly operative at the level of town and ward organization; moreover, four out of the six are of a ritual nature. It is clear from the chart that dual divisions, wards, councils, lineages, and working parties have little connection with them, and it is after all these types of group which govern face-to-face relations within the town. Moreover, wards, lineages, and working parties are not themselves integrated into a structure, that is, a system of discrete parts linked by rules in a network of relationships. A ward cannot confront a lineage, nor a working party confront either.

The social relations within a town cannot therefore be said to be dominated by any particular institution or principle of organization. On the face-to-face level, relations are governed by the norms of the ward, ward-council, lineage, and working-party. At this level the system of generation-grades is only effective in distinguishing boys from adults. On the level of town relations, offices are filled on the basis of the generation grades, ritual status, and, in the case of councillors, on the basis of personal attributes. Again, descent groups and the grading systems each have their own rationale, which is independent of the other two. There is thus no over-all structure in town organization, which is in many ways simply a heterogeneous conglomeration of institutions.

The concept of a 'structure' implies that its component parts are interdependent, that is, that they are governed by a set of rules. An organization has a structure to the extent that the removal of a component institution, or the alteration of the rules, will produce changes in its mode of operation. In our own society the business corporation is an obvious example of an organization which has a structure; the breakdown of a component institution in this structure, such as the accounts department, will have far-reaching effects, as will a change in a rule, such as recruitment policy. Among the Konso the generation-grading systems have a very definite structure. They are composed of a number of institutions, the grades, governed by a set of rules, and, as we shall see, changes in these grades or rules have empirically demonstrable effects. There is clearly a basic correlation between structure and purpose. Business corporations have a structure because their operations are determined by certain clear objectives; similarly, the generation-grading systems are also designed to fulfil specific purposes. But the towns, unlike the grading systems, or business corporations, are not 'for' anything in particular, and consequently it is not surprising to find that their component institutions lack any specific body of co-ordinating rules. This is not to say that their institutions are meaningless, but that in order to understand their significance we must view them in the context of the people's total world-view. We cannot explain the town institutions in terms of their mutual interactions, for, as I have tried to show, their interrelationship is, for the most part, of the loosest kind, and cannot be reduced to a general body of rules.

There is one feature of the town organization, however, which calls for further analysis—the overlapping membership of lineages, wards, and working-parties. The concept of 'cross-cutting ties' is frequently used in social anthropological analysis to explain a congeries of institutions whose membership overlaps as increasing social cohesion. Such an explanation might be offered for the overlap of wards, lineages, and working-parties. It seems to me, however, that too much stress may be laid on the contribution of institutions to the maintenance of social cohesion, as though this were a satisfactory explanation for their existence, and, moreover, that an analysis in terms of cross-cutting ties is often hard to correlate with any conceivable purposes, explicit or implicit, that one can imagine as existing in the minds of the natives. The Konso are quite well aware of the necessity for social cohesion, which is maintained by their mode of town life and their values. Are we to suppose that they deliberately interwove their wards, lineages, and working-parties to reinforce the cohesion of their towns still further? It is quite possible that some of their institutions—the grading-systems, the sacred drums, the Nama Dawra, and the towns themselves, or their prototypes—were established after a process of deliberation with particular ends in view. But it is verging upon fantasy to suppose that some mute intuition of social harmony led to the overlapping membership of wards, lineages, and working-parties as a means of reinforcing social cohesion. I am not saying, of course, that they do not have this effect; I am only concerned to deny that they have this intention. I would also concede that the notably large degree of overlap between the membership of these institutions is socially significant, but I suggest that the concept of 'cross-cutting ties' is not the best one to explain what this significance is. It seems to me that the reason is quite different.

The Konso are aware that dependence on kin and neighbours creates reciprocal obligations, which are felt to be burdensome; one 'fears' one's actual or potential benefactors, in the sense that one is made uneasy by having received favours, and made aware of that person's or group's superior power. The following text makes their attitude to benefactors, especially the ward and the lineage, very clear.

Once girls and their brothers have grown up together and married, the sons call their fathers' sisters '*mama*'. All the lineage which begot her [their mother] all these the sons of one generation call '*abuya*' . . . and they create *daldīda*, and there is respect [literally, 'fear'] between people. And when someone goes to the house of a big person in the lineage, they are given food, and it is said that he is a big man, and so what he has he gives them, and they are afraid of him for he is important. And when someone is in trouble he goes to the house of the big man who has many fields, and the poor man asks for the loan of some of them, when the year is small, for their millet, and he gives some. He is a man of whom people are afraid, because he gives a little help. Therefore people are afraid among one another, because they live together. After someone has had bad luck and *lost his money* [?] they give to one another, and together create *daldīda*, and create them a ward, and create them a town, and create them a lineage. And thus, after someone has died, because of these ties they are afraid among one another, and after someone dies, who is a member of the ward, the ward takes the corpse of the dead person to his ancestral fields, and buries him there. They go to the place of his family where they bury him. When the ward has finished the grave they go to the house of the dead man, and after the *daldīda* have made food, they give it to the people of the ward, who after coming to the house eat it, this food of the *daldīda*. Then the friends of the family come to the house, and comfort them, and run errands for them, and fetch fodder for their cattle, and fetch them water. Therefore they are afraid of the town and afraid of the ward. The ward goes to this house at night to sleep. The family is afraid of what the *daldīda* has done. They come every morning for weeping and sit with the family.

In this text it is made abundantly clear that obligation is not only felt to be a powerful sanction for co-operation and social order, but is also felt to be oppressive.[1] They 'fear' those who have helped them, or who are in a position to do so. The word for 'fear' is *fura*,

[1] The Japanese conception of *on* is a very good example of the way in which obligations are felt to be burdensome and oppressive. See Ruth Benedict's *The Chrysanthemum and the Sword* (1946).

and while it is clear that it is not used in the same way about benefactors as it is about lions, it is sufficient for my purpose to show
that their words for, and hence concepts of, 'fear' and 'respect' are
basically the same.

In Garati I was often told that people did not like to live close
to their kin within the towns. When I asked if in the beginning
before the towns were formed men built their homesteads around
that of the lineage priest this was emphatically denied. 'Men do not
like to live close to their kinsmen', they said. I was also told that
witchcraft was most prevalent between kinsmen and friends,
a statement which puzzled me greatly at the time. In view of this
attitude to obligation, which is markedly individualistic, we can
see why they should display such a strong preference for living in
groups which are not based solely on kinship. It is a means of es-
caping from the tyranny of exclusive allegiance. Aid and assistance
can be obtained from quite different sources, with the result that
neither ward nor lineage can exercise the same control as it would
be able to if it were the sole object of allegiance. We have seen that
the working-parties too are not based either upon the lineage or
the ward. While it seems likely that the basic reason for men joining the working-parties is economic, this does not in itself explain
why they should not be based either on the lineage or the ward.
Both are large enough to supply sufficient manpower, and the relationship between members of the working party is consonant
with lineage loyalty, and with neighbourliness. But if we accept
that the Konso are reluctant to allow any group to gain too great
a control over their loyalty and allegiance, it seems very likely that
they prefer their working-parties not to have any specific relation
either to lineage or ward, but to be *ad hoc* collections of friends.

It might be argued that their towns, on the other hand, are pre-
eminently groups which do claim exclusive allegiance. But the
towns are, in the first place, very large in comparison with wards
and lineages, and provide social mobility for the formation of
private groups, friendships, and contractual relationships so that
they are not so potentially oppressive as the wards and lineages. Secondly, and equally important, one's obligations to one's town are
vaguer than those either to ward or lineage. In practice the only
important expressions of this loyalty are in time of war, and customary prestations to the town officers. I am not in any case sug-
gesting that the Konso try to avoid all forms of obligation (they are

only too well aware that it is the concomitant of any kind of assistance), merely that by having a number of groups with overlapping membership they considerably mitigate the degree of its concentration.

So, within the town, the life of a man is not dominated by obligations and ties to any one group. The absence of corporate groups with common property rights to land, or blood-money, or bridewealth, which might be the basis for competing interests within the towns, means that social relations with regard to property and marriage alliances are essentially private, and not the concern of lineages or wards.

Within the town there is no power structure which can give rise to organized competition. The ward and town councils seem to be filled by men on the basis of personal qualities which are acknowledged by consensus. Certainly my informants never hinted that the election to a council could be the focus of factional dispute, and since the councils are not authoritarian bodies with perquisites in the form of power or wealth, this is not perhaps surprising.

We may say therefore that the dispersal of ties within the towns so that there is no type of group which is dominant over the individual, and no real power structure, property-owning group, or even ritual leader of the whole town in many cases, makes it possible to reconcile a high degree of individualism with a basic social harmony, since there is no clear-cut group structure on which factions could be based. In confirmation of this I would quote the single exception to these general characteristics of the towns I have just described—the dual divisions. In Būso there was considerable friction between Sessīdi and Pishmalli, and in Degato Paragutīda and Ilgatīda had fought battles in the recent past. The dual divisions, of course, as we have seen, do isolate whole groups of lineages, unlike the wards, and also seem to have a tendency to isolate working-parties. But I know of no instance where friction between dual divisions has ever destroyed a town.

I have emphasized the stability of male membership of towns, and this is clearly an important element in the maintenance of bonds of loyalty and solidarity. But the very stability of the town populations, and their internal cohesion, such that almost all a man's important personal relationships tend to be with fellow townsmen, make it so much the harder to form coherent systems of relationships between the towns. It is significant that in the case of Degato, Poro'goda, and

Ħulme, there appears to be very considerable mobility of population between them, a state of affairs which the people thought normal and proper. But apart from towns grouped as closely as these, alliances are more temporary affairs, and inter-town relationships as a whole can only be described as anarchical. This is the price which they pay for a disproportionate degree of cohesion within the towns. Excessive solidarity at one level therefore produces anarchy in the society as a whole. Neither the grading systems nor the regional priests can be said to be compensatory mechanisms to mitigate this anarchy. At least, if they are such mechanisms they work very badly. They are, in my view, more properly related to Konso values and their world-view as a whole, and not to their political relations.

IV

KONSO VALUES

I WOULD define values as 'those qualities, characteristics, or objectives which the people consider as estimable for the individual or for
communal life'. Some values are not immediately applicable to
actions, as for example the qualities of masculinity in relation to
femininity, or maturity in relation to youth, or, again, a people's
feelings about death. Especially in the last instance we are not
dealing with any sort of action but with a fundamental characteristic of the human condition, and the people's feelings and beliefs
about it. In fact, it is not necessary for the purposes of my argument to provide a formally satisfactory definition of 'value'. It is
sufficient to show that the 'values' which I describe in this chapter
have an analogous position in Konso life to the rules of a game—in
short, that one cannot go 'behind' them, and must accept them as
the basic principles of their society. It is with these criteria in mind
that I talk, for example, of Konso egalitarianism, and their attitudes to Life and Death; my selection of Konso 'values' is not,
therefore, ultimately determined by semantic considerations.

In this chapter I consider the quality of their social relations,
their ideals of friendliness, co-operation, neighbourliness, peace,
honesty, telling the truth, and manliness. I consider also their beliefs
in the worth of the individual, freedom, seniority, and the essential
rightness of the ancestors. These values are of so general a nature
that they would be relevant in any primitive society, irrespective of
its social organization. But every society selects for special emphasis a small sample of the almost infinite range of possible values open
to society and works upon them in its isolation, to give them in
each case a unique blend and force, which creates, especially in the
mind of the foreign observer, a sense of the special personality of
each culture.

I. SOCIABILITY

The Konso could never be described as a ceremonious people.
The tone of their social relations is predominantly rough and

hearty good fellowship, expressing itself in a profusion of hand-shakes and greetings. In the finer points of manners, such as rising in the presence of their elders, they are notably lacking. This rather uncouth deportment is very noticeable in comparison with the Amhara, who are a people pre-eminently endowed with style. The Konso have no style. One of the first things which struck my atten-tion was the refusal of the young lads who were sitting around me in my early days in Būso to get up and allow old men to sit, leaving them to squeeze in as best they could. I deduced from this, wrongly, that the elderly were not respected among the Konso. They are, but respect is seldom shown in such formalized terms. Among the Borana, on the other hand, each time a man of status joins a group, it will rise and reseat itself in the new order of precedence. Shack records that among the Gurage 'women always turn their backs to a noble, and take cover in a nearby bush when he passes'.[1] The Konso would regard such behaviour with astonishment.

They place more emphasis on co-operation and friendliness than on formal manners. The householder has important obligations to the ward in which he dwells; if a neighbour's beast is lost he is ex-pected to turn out and help look for it, on pain of a fine for refusal. Persistent quarrelling may lead to a fine being imposed by the elders on the culprit. Collections of grain or money are often made within the ward for beer, and each house in turn may make the beer, which all the ward is expected to come to drink. People who con-sistently refuse such invitations without good reasons are eventually ostracized. They may simply be refused the loan of fire and water, which makes life very inconvenient, as fires often go out during the day, and the common practice is to send a child round to one of the neighbours for some more, running with the embers on a broken piece of pot. If a man is really unpopular, neither his kin nor any-one else will come to mourn at his house when he dies, and the ward will refuse to dig the grave, forcing the family to pay a working-party to dig it. A town is liable to expel its most obnoxious members altogether, as I mentioned earlier.

Their dislike of the *hauda*, the craftsmen, is often explained by the hard bargains these drive in the markets and their constant

[1] Op. cit., p. 106.

PLATE VI. Cattle pool

quarrelling over petty sums. Poor people seldom have more than beer to offer the casual visitor when he calls, if indeed they have that, but a rich household prides itself on its hospitality, and when I called on such people as the Kalla or the Bamalle, or the greater lineage priests, I was always offered beer and food.

2. PEACE

Konso boys play roughly among themselves, a favourite game when they were sitting around my chair in the evening lamplight being for one to reach behind someone's back and clout another boy on the head; often the night resounded to the ensuing blows. But these tussles seldom developed into serious fights, and boys concerned were quite friendly afterwards. Wrestling is another favourite sport among boys, and a cry-baby will be ridiculed. But serious fights will cause adult intervention, and sometimes quarrels between the parents.

Fighting, as opposed to horse-play, conflicts with their ideal of peace. Baxter (op. cit., p. 65) says of the Borana:

> Even wrestling is considered a dangerous sport after childhood for fear tempers will be strained and real hurt or anger ensue. It is thought more proper to display strength and skill by individual feats at hunting, dancing, or watering stock at a dangerous slippery well. Indeed Boran in the Government Station even shunned football for fear of hurting other Boran and thereby engendering ill-feeling between their respective families.

In this connection it is significant that there is no institutionalized fighting between mature men, nor, indeed, any competitive sports, with the exception of the *kurīla*, where a lump of cloth is tossed in the air and scrambled for in the *mora*. '*Afa pisa ōlini ɗagīni*', when 'all voices are heard together', or social harmony, as we should express it, is the guiding ideal of their social relations. '*Nagīd 'awe*' 'Peace today', and '*nagīdanōla*' 'Peace remain with you' are two of the commonest salutations. '*Tōla nagīda irĝaba?*' 'Does your family have peace?' was the question they asked me when I received a letter from home. In this context *nagīda* means more than just the absence of violence or quarrelling, and implies prosperity and contentment. If there is quarrelling and dissension in a town, God punishes them by withholding the rain.

Their clearly manifested suspicion of unbridled emotion is, I think, an essential aspect of their ideal of *nagīda*. It is interesting that in the past fermented beer was the prerogative of the old men. They know only too well what disruptive effects drunkenness can have on social relations, and for this reason we should not be too ready to assume that the reservation of alcohol for the old men was merely the perquisite of gerontocracy. Old men are supposed to be milder in their passions than the young, and more self-controlled, and it is likely that alcohol was confined to them for this reason. Beer is also used in libations, which are performed by elders. Perhaps for the same reason only old people, both men and women, smoke pipes; they are aware that tobacco can have intoxicating effects. Similarly, spirit possession, which is manifested in behaviour of an hysterical type, is also greatly feared. It is likely that this fear derives from the uncontrollable behaviour of the victim, who is not regarded as amenable to social restraint.

A second aspect of their ideal of *nagīda* is the emphasis they place on discussion, *dehamda*. Difference of opinion should be settled by discussion, not violence, though they recognize that if one person is really intransigent, force may be the only solution. Within the lineage, the priest should be asked to settle disputes, but people of different lineage either go to the *hīyoda* council themselves or ask their respective lineage priests to speak for them at a private meeting or before the *hīyoda*. Speeches such as those at the *Ĥora Dehamda* are also the occasion for disciplining unruly neighbours, who are quarrelsome or refuse to pay their tribute to the town officials, and for general exhortations to behave properly by the leading members of the town.

But as I have mentioned before, litigation is not only fairly rare, but definitely discouraged among them. Throughout my stay in Konso I very seldom saw lawsuits in the *moras*.

So while the Konso can be said to value *dehamda*, 'discussion', they value it in the sense of preferring it to violence, but ideally there should be harmony, and no necessity for fighting or argument. It is in discussion that *dugāda* manifests itself.

'*Dugāda*, truth, in a rough translation, is a very important quality among the Konso. It has the connotation of honesty, and impartiality, and absence of self-seeking. They know that most of the time men fall below this standard and ironically refer to the grave as the *porra dugāda*, the 'road of truth', because only the dead tell no lies. Closely allied with this virtue is honesty in relation to property. Theft is abhorred among them. I personally found them extremely honest and trustworthy. I often left my house or tent unlocked without fear that anything would be stolen.

3. SENIORITY

Respect for seniority is a very basic principle of Konso society, and finds its expression in reverence for the ancestral traditions as well as for generational status.

To leave the teachings of the ancestors is bad. Thus long ago the old men, the boys and the wives lived contentedly in their homes. Their people were good, their cows were good, their children were good, their speech was good. For the family to talk [reasonably] together at home is good.

Now, after the coming of the Amhara, and the taxes which they impose, everything has gone bad.

The Amhara came, and are devouring the wealth from among the people. Our ancestors never seized money; people gave money, but never took it by force. Now people have become bad, not listening to one another. Without God people have spoilt the land, there is only quarrelling.

In the beginning God was close to the earth, and the world was good. At that time, so they think, the order of society was laid down, and the elders charged by God with preserving the social order, but as time has passed, men have become more corrupt. They say that the ancestors were more truthful and reasonable in their conduct than they are, and the presence of the *ďaga ďeeruma*, the phallic stones in the *moras*, is a constant reminder of past achievements in battle which should be emulated today.

Their high evaluation of the past does not mean, however, that they believe the present is in consequence inevitably bad, and that the future will be even worse. In our culture we are familiar with the attitude that in the past men were backward, and that they are progressing towards a millennial future. But even if we have a tendency to believe in progress, the Konso do not believe in regress. The order of Konso society established by Waĝa (not the grading-systems or the towns, but the moral law and the authority of the elders) is not comparable to a clock wound up at the beginning of time and which is slowly but irreversibly running down. Rather, this order is immanent in the actual state of society, and can be made manifest by listening to the elders and the priests, preserving the grading-systems, as essential pillars of the social order, and performing the necessary sacrifices and rituals.

It seems that senior men are respected not only for the personal qualities of wisdom and restraint which they have developed, but because they are at the same time the repository of morality and right conduct, and to this extent their status is analogous to God's. I was told for example that one's grandfather 'is like God', and their concept of God's authority is explicitly paternalistic. It is thus appropriate that it is the elders who should have the prime responsibility for blessing.

4. THE VALUE OF THE INDIVIDUAL

A high regard for *dehamda*, 'discussion', and *dugāda*, 'truth', or the rule of law, implies a rejection of arbitrary authority, for which they have a strong distaste. Within the family the father can beat his children or wife, but only within reason. He would be restrained if he used too great violence on any of them, and while, as we have seen, he can put pressure on his daughter to marry a man of whom he approves, his will in such a matter is not decisive. Similarly, a wife can leave her husband and return to her family if he ill-treats her, and count on their support. The priest has no power to compel a member of his lineage to do anything, although from respect they bring him tributes of meat or game trophies.

While they have a definite concept of status, such that a rich or senior person, or a priest can be referred to as a *namaguta*, 'big person', and a poor or young person as *namashaka*, 'little person', they would only make such distinctions within limits. The greatest priest is still only a man, who must observe the same rules of conduct as his fellows, and can only request, not command; and there are no means by which a poor man can be exploited or robbed by organized violence.

They have a very strong belief that people should not have a monetary value placed on them or be treated as commodities. One of the chief reasons they give for hating the craftsmen is that in times of famine they sold their children to the Borana in exchange for food. In Garati I was told that dogs were not bought and sold among the cultivators, because dogs are like people. A good dog will be buried like a human being when it dies, wrapped in a skin, with a little stone to mark the grave, and the same is often done for monkeys. It is interesting to note that all their animals, even chickens, have personal names, often human ones. Compensation is never accepted for murder; blood must be avenged with blood, either of the murderer or of a near male relative. The explicit reason for this is that to accept money for a dead kinsman would be the equivalent of selling him. While at marriage presents are given to the father of the bride, this does not establish a claim on the girl, nor is it the *sine qua non* of a valid marriage. It is simply for the sake of friendship.

The circumstances of their life in towns encourage dances and ceremonies, for which the *moras* are admirable arenas. But in spite of their enjoyment of gregarious occasions, and their emphasis on sociability and co-operation, they still recognize the right of the individual to advance himself economically. Besides the *dina* and some of the wells, there is really no other common property among them. Even the *moras*, which used once upon a time to be the fields of a particular family, while given over to the town's use, are still associated with the original owners—almost invariably priests—and said to be in a sense 'theirs', though they could never plough them up or reconvert them to their own use. Each man's house is his own, as are his fields, and he may do as he likes with them. There is no common lineage property in anything, though there would no doubt be problems for a lineage priest who wanted to dispose of his ancestral home. Nor is there any sort of entailment on land or houses, to ensure a patrimony for a man's sons. Even among the lineage, especially in Garati, those who are poor or down on their luck are only assisted within reason, and loans of grain are expected to be repaid. In Takadi, it was said that the lineage priest would relieve his kinsmen, and it seems that there is less selfishness here than in Garati. In times of famine, I was told in Garati, rich men were known to exploit their poorer neighbours mercilessly, selling half a gourd of grain for a plot of land. It says much for the strength of law and order within the towns that rich men's granaries were not simply smashed open by their starving neighbours, but I never heard of this happening.

Both fields and homesteads can be rented. In Garati, and possibly the other regions, the contract is deemed always to begin in the month of Pardubota, when it can be terminated at the wish of either party. If the landlord does not give notice to quit in Pardubota he has to wait another year. Contracts, *firma*, are nowadays made in writing, in the presence of witnesses, *makita*. In the past, of course, they had to rely on witnesses alone to support contracts. While women cannot inherit land or homesteads, they are not forbidden to rent them. Rent, *peealada* or *kira*, is paid for fields either in money or service. If the latter is chosen, the tenant, *tēgolīda* (literally, 'poor man') will work in the fields of the landlord, *tēandolīda* (literally 'rich man') three times in the year, at sowing, weeding, and harvesting. When a homestead is rented, rent can be paid in beer. The tenant is expected to keep the property in good repair. Fields and homesteads may be bought collectively by two or three friends, as an investment, when they would share the rent, or the use of the property in the case of fields.

Property, both land and homesteads, can be bought and sold, and contracts are made in the same way; the purchaser is given a piece of stick or grass as a token of the property he is buying. Often a go-between, *turoĝabdita*, will be used to make the preliminary overtures. They are familiar with payment by instalments, and with interest, *ðalða* ('fruit', or 'that which is begotten'). This may be very high. Thus the creditor who advances two dollars now may demand three in return six months hence. But one should beware of striving for a false precision in such matters; doubtless there is a great variation in these transactions.

Damages, *adanða*, are an important aspect of their law of property. Thus, one would be liable for someone injured while helping one to build a house. When a cow is being herded by someone else, and is eaten by a hyena, for example, the herder is only liable for half the value of the beast. A special type of damages, *māza*, is paid to a husband for the seduction or enticement of his wife. They distinguish between damages and a fine, *hōra*. Thus, in the case of rape the culprit would not only be liable to a beating from the husband, and perhaps close members of his lineage also, or damages, but also have to pay a fine to the town officers.

While they value harmony, there is thus ample scope for individual achievement in their way of life. The *waga* statues erected to the memory of a hero present to the public view the sum total of a man's achievements. (The word *waga* has nothing to do with that for God, Waĝa. It is a contraction of *wa aka*, 'something of the grandfathers'. People in Takadi still refer to them as *wa aka*.) In the statues are displayed the man, his wives, and his slaughtered enemies. If he has killed a game animal there will also be a carved representation of that. Occasionally one will find a carving of a monkey; rich families often keep monkeys as pets, and the appearance of one in the *waga* group, besides being for fun, also denotes that the family was wealthy. In front of the group there may be a cluster of small stones. These indicate the number of fields the man has bought, showing that he was hard-working and thrifty. I once counted about 150 in front of one man's *wagas*, but this was exceptional. Moreover, while these stones are themselves a good indication of wealth, the fact that a man's family has been able to afford to pay a craftsman to carve the *wagas* (a skill confined to very few) is also an indication of wealth. The *waga* statues are the symbols of individual achievement.

5. DEVIANT BEHAVIOUR

Inevitably there is a proportion of lunatics, imbeciles, eccentrics, and other deviants among them. The principle categories are *tarīda*, madman, *sagōda*, effeminate man, and *nama saytana*, someone possessed by an evil spirit. Madmen are tolerated, unless they are vicious, when they receive the same treatment in retaliation. Often a relative will give them a little plot of land where they can build a hovel and they often do small jobs for food. Begging is not an institution among the Konso as it is with the Christian Amhara, but people will often give scraps of food to the needy, or allow them to share their beer. Imbeciles, *ēba*, being less able to take care of themselves than madmen, whose disability may be only periodic, or not affect their ability to work, tend to fare more hardly. There was an imbecile girl in Būso when I was there, repellently ugly, incontinent, and perpetually crying, because of the teasing of the boys, who would run behind her and flip her skirts up, or pelt her with dung. Her parents, reasonably enough, regarded her as a tiresome liability, and barely gave her enough food to support life. She died shortly after I left Būso. Imbeciles who are jolly and laugh are not tormented, though they may be made to perform antics like dancing bears for the onlookers' amusement, but sad and wretched imbeciles like the girl receive far rougher treatment.

Sagōdas, especially if they are effeminate in manner, tend to be bullied and ridiculed, but they are allowed to live inside the towns, and are not expelled. But I shall have more to say about *sagōdas* when I come to discuss Konso attitudes to masculinity.

Nama saytana are men possessed by an evil spirit. There is another sort of possession, by a type of spirit called by the Galliña name of *īyanna*; this is supposed to be a beneficial spirit, and those whom it possesses act as diviners. *Saytana* is an Amharic word, meaning a demon, as well as Satan, but there always seems to have been a belief in evil spirits, *oritta*, before the Amhara. It is likely that the Konso have simply adopted the word *saytana* for its convenience. The *iyanna* is clearly a Galla importation, and not indigenous to Konso. I shall discuss its significance in another place. The *nama saytana* seem to coexist fairly amicably with their neighbours. They are not possessed all the time, and have long periods of normality, in most cases. But some of them do seem to exude a miasma of evil. Such a man used to live just below the men's house in Būso where I first lodged. When he died the people were too afraid to touch his homestead themselves, and asked some Christians to burn it for them. Only the kitchen was left, and it had been made into a sort of shrine for the evil spirit, which might become angry if it were driven away entirely. When *nama saytana* are possessed they run about wildly, or sit shaking their heads from side to side; it is said that some climb into trees and eat glowing coals. As we shall see in the case of *īyanna* possession, the diviner behaves in a similar fashion; but all such behaviour is greatly feared. But this very fear prevents any drastic action being taken against the *nama saytana*, since they are believed to be able to set their devils on their enemies.

6. THE STATUS OF THE CRAFTSMEN.[1]

The conflict between legitimate self-interest and social responsibility is most clearly demonstrated by the status of the craftsmen.

In most of the towns some *ḥauda* are to be found, comprising blacksmiths, weavers, potters, and tanners. When I was discussing the craftsmen one day with some cultivators, someone said: 'The *ḥauda* live *ḥauwe* (alone or separate), so that is why they are called *ḥauda*.' This is not only linguistically speaking a plausible etymology, but in sociological terms it exactly expresses their status. They are not a submerged class, but a separate class, not fully integrated into the religious and social life of the cultivators. Whatever the case in the distant past, their separation has never, within the limits of

---

[1] See also my article, 'The status of craftsmen among the Konso of south-west Ethiopia', *Africa* (July 1968).

memory or tradition, been physical. One never finds, for example, that any ward is exclusively populated by craftsmen, though some wards may have more craftsmen than others. Nor do they ever form distinct settlements away from the towns. Besides their crafts they have no cultural features that set them apart from their cultivator neighbours. Their dress, mode of speech, and houses are identical with those of other Konso, and in some cases their ancestors have lived in the same town for generations.

All craftsmen work individually, selling their products in the markets to anyone who wishes to buy. They also accept commissions, especially from people who provide the raw materials, when they only charge for their labour. But in the normal way they buy their own raw materials.

One can certainly dismiss the suggestion that they are of a more negroid origin than the cultivators, and that they are the remnants of a conquered aboriginal population. Their physical characteristics, in so far as one can generalize about something which varies greatly among them, tend on the whole to be less negroid than the rest of the Konso, and more to resemble the Borana.

Before 1897 they owned little or no land, and cultivators would not eat or drink with them, and certainly not marry them. This situation has slowly changed over the years, and many craftsmen now have land, and eat and drink with cultivators, but cultivators still regard marriage with them as disgraceful. Thus the rigidity of the distinction between cultivators and craftsmen has become softened, like that between the sexes and the generations. The loss of independence after the Amhara conquest has, I think, ultimately been responsible for this process. Moreover, many men who are cultivators by birth have taken up weaving. In one town three of the four most prominent weavers were close relatives of one of the most prominent lineage priests. This would have been unthinkable a hundred years ago, and is still disapproved of. I have never heard of any cultivator who learned the blacksmith's, potter's, or tanner's arts, however. There is certainly less prejudice against weaving than against these three arts, but this is quite possibly the result of the money that can be made from weaving. It would be interesting to see if cultivators would take up ironworking or pottery if there were a similar demand for them.

Among the craftsmen themselves I could not discover any hierarchy of crafts. Smiths in particular may take up weaving when they become too old to use their hammers, and in general, while crafts are handed down from father to son, mother to daughter, there were no prohibitions against a man or woman *hauda* learning a different one.

But in spite of the entry of cultivators into the ranks of the craftsmen, and the increasing number of craftsmen who are buying fields, if one is born a cultivator one can never become a *haudīda* (sing. of *hauda*) merely by taking up weaving, and a craftsman does not become a cultivator by acquiring fields. Status is conferred by birth and nothing can ever alter it. It is said that even if a craftsman has fields, he still has no skill in cultivating them, and can only grow weeds. In popular imagination they prefer to spend their money on drink and meat, rather than invest it in land.

But in some respects craftsmen are not excluded from cultivator life. Hunting game animals and killing enemies in battle are the most highly respected achievements among the Konso, and the craftsmen are allowed their *wagas* (those illustrated in Plate X are in memory of a blacksmith) and some have been notable hunters and warriors. As we have seen, it is the duty of ward members to bury their neighbours, and this service is performed by and for craftsmen without distinction, and similarly they have the *shilleda*. They also have their own lineage priests. But they have not been in the past, and as far as I know, are not today, admitted to the ward or town councils. One reason I was given for this was that if a raid or other hostile activity against another town were being planned, the craftsmen would go over and warn them from no other motive than spite and disloyalty. The significance of this accusation will become apparent shortly.

Perhaps the most significant area of Konso life from which the craftsmen are excluded is the grading systems. In Garati this exclusion is total, but even in Takadi, where the craftsmen do join the grades, they would not be allowed to touch the drums. It is above all in Garati, where there is the longest delay on average before marriage, and where girls below the authorized grade for marriage who conceive children are compelled to have abortions, that the craftsmen have least part in the grading system. They themselves say that abortions are impious, since God created the human body at conception, and this is why they refuse to take part in the Garati grading system. In the other regions of Konso, girls who become pregnant before the authorized grade are merely exiled to another town until they enter it, when they are allowed back. In these regions abortions are strongly disapproved of by everyone. Here the craftsmen take part in the ceremonies, and regulate their marriages by the grades in the same way as the cultivators. This integration seems to be of long standing, since even my oldest informants assured me it had always been like this. In the town of Gaho in Takadi, where I lived, one of the craftsmen families has sacrificial responsibilities, the most interesting of which is at the end of the nine-year cycle, when it is the custom to make an incision on the penis of two men of a senior grade, which symbolizes the cutting off of the whole organ, because after the ceremony the men so treated are not supposed to beget any more children.

The craftsman operator stands on a sacred stone '*Shila*', which is afterwards purified with the blood of a goat, since at other times a craftsman is supposed not to stand there, but to walk round it. The members of the most junior grade, those prohibited from marrying, and who are in other ways not full members of society, are likewise forbidden to walk across it. Craftsmen are also prohibited from touching the sacred drums, which in such a case must be purified. As an outsider I was equally forbidden, as were the Amhara. There is thus no doubt that, while the craftsman family in question has ritual responsibilities, its representative performs them in the capacity of an outsider; it is extremely likely that 'circumcision' is regarded as religiously defiling for the operator, since it is the case that in Garati a man from another tribe is brought in to perform it. 'Outsiders' who perform religiously defiling tasks occur in other contexts as in Takadi at the same time as the circumcision, when a man is hired from Garati to 'cleanse' the land; he never returns to Takadi. In Turo, which is much poorer in ritual formalities than the other two regions, I could find no occasions on which the craftsmen had any such specific roles at religious ceremonies. We can thus say that while in both these regions craftsmen are allowed to participate in the purely social organization they are still regarded as outsiders, even though they have ritual responsibilities. In Garati, where there is an institution which is repugnant, abortion, the craftsmen say that they want no part in the grading system, but there is also the fact that the cultivators of Garati have a more rigorous attitude to craftsmen, preferring to exclude them totally from all participation in the distinctive features of their society. I was certainly far more conscious of the dislike, and even disgust, which the cultivators felt for the craftsmen as a class in Garati than anywhere else in Konso.

It is a basic feature of Konso culture to give symbolic value to various tasks and materials, which are associated with groups, men and women, craftsmen and cultivators. And we cannot fully understand the status of the craftsmen without realizing that the crafts of weaving, pottery, ironworking, and tanning themselves have symbolic values. Cotton is an inauspicious substance for the Konso. It ripens in the hot months, when the land is parched and water scarce, and it is white, the colour of bone and death. For these reasons, which were explicitly stated to me, it is often forbidden even to spin it in the most sacred places. Like bone or white stones, it is, in the form of threads, a weapon against the evil eye, operating as a destructive medicine against the evildoer. I think it is, therefore, likely that when weaving was introduced into Konso the people were prejudiced against it for this reason.

In the case of pottery, someone once said to me that it was 'bad' to treat earth as food, grinding it, mixing water with it, and kneading it, like flour, instead of tilling it and sowing seed in it, the right way. While ideas of the natural and the unnatural are not prominent in Konso thought, in this case I think it is a genuine basis for their dislike of making pottery.

That there should be any religious prejudice against ironworking and tanning is harder to demonstrate. Fire among the Konso is closely associated with the production of food. I would suggest that for them the use of it to 'cook' earth as was done in the past when iron came to Konso in the form of ore that had to be smelted, is unnatural. Moreover fire, though useful, is regarded with aversion on most occasions as a hostile and destructive force; dreams of fire are evil portents. Earth on the other hand is regarded as the source of life. So besides the unnatural use of fire to cook earth in smelting, and also iron, an inedible substance, in the later stages of work at the anvil, there is the religious opposition of earth and fire. In the case of tanning we encounter the Konso horror of death. While the drying of skins in the sun is done by everyone, the lengthy treatment of skins is relegated to the craftsmen, in all probability because of their association with death.

One possible objection to this analysis is: if it is 'bad' to make or process these articles, why are the cultivators prepared to use the finished products? I would suggest that they differentiate between the finished article and the process of manufacture. In the course of making something the artisan is associated with it in a peculiarly close relationship, which the mere owner or purchaser does not have. Moreover, where only the actual process of manufacture is held to be unnatural—as with ironworking or pottery, this stigma will not affect the finished goods. In the case of cotton, where the material itself is inauspicious, I think it likely that, by being made into something of totally different appearance, the nature of the material itself is felt to be different.

The notable exception of woodworking, as the only craft habitually practised by cultivators, can be explained as the only craft that is indigenous to the cultivators. It is possible to carve with stone tools, and iron ones may have been imported before any smiths came to reside in Konso. The carving of wood is necessary in housebuilding in particular, and also bowls and other simple utensils are made of it. Wood is an inoffensive substance that is not subject to any taboos in their religion.

However, I do not think that religious prejudices of the sort I have just discussed are the sole or even the main factors which have been responsible for the status of the craftsmen in Konso.

When I first began asking why the craftsmen were disliked, I was often told that in times of famine they used to sell their children to the Borana, in exchange for meat, and because of this monstrous behaviour the cultivators ostracized them. There is no doubt that the Borana have bought Konso children, since Dr. Paul Baxter records meeting some Konso sold in this way while he was working among the Borana,[1] though we are not told if they were *hauda* children.

I was given a text as follows:

In the past when everyone knew only hunger the *hauda* sold their sons for dollars, the sons which they had begotten they sold, therefore the *edanda* hate the *hauda*. To sell one of your own is forbidden among the *edanda*. So when the *hauda* die, their graves are in another place, and they do not bury them near the *edanda*. This is because these people do not recognise Kadana [the drum] and so the *edanda* hate the *hauda*.

The remark about craftsmen's graves being in a different place from cultivators' graves puzzled me for some time. For it is Konso custom to bury a man in his ancestral fields, and so everyone's grave is of necessity separate from that of anyone of a different lineage. But

---

[1] Ernesta Cerulli, op. cit., p. 62, quotes a personal communication from Baxter.

in the past, when the craftsmen had no fields, they were of necessity buried in the *dina* (the wood around the town). My informant, however, interpreted this as a symbolic segregation of the graves of the craftsmen from the cultivators.

Now the Konso, as we saw earlier, have a deep dislike of putting a monetary value on a person, so this behaviour of the craftsmen violated one of the basic values of the cultivators. But it is also characteristic of the craftsman's general attitude towards his fellow men: an attitude which looks on them merely as means to his own selfish ends, objects to be exploited, not people to whom loyalty is due. In the past, as I have mentioned before, they owned no land, partly because they had no wish to own it, and partly because the cultivators would not sell it to them, and they relied on their crafts to support them, exchanging their products for grain and other necessities in the markets. It is easy to see that under these conditions their survival depended on being able to drive a hard bargain, and they still have a not undeserved reputation for being mean and mercenary, trying to squeeze the last cent out of customers, and giving as little as possible in return.

As a further consequence of their dependence on manufacture and trade, they are also considered to be quarrelsome, as a result of their obsession over money. When I was asking some cultivators whether a particular town would be a nice place for me to live in, they said, 'Oh no, don't go there. It's full of *hauda*, and all they do is quarrel and shout at each other all day long.' Here again, the craftsmen are seen as people not properly integrated in society, pursuing their legitimate self-interest to the point of social disintegration.

The Konso often refer to the moon as a craftsman because, unlike the sun, the moon rises and sets at different times each night, and is sometimes visible during the day, generally behaving in an irregular and unsettled way. In the same way the craftsmen are thought of as having no settled abode, moving from place to place as they feel inclined. This is certainly a correct impression, particularly with regard to blacksmiths. In one lineage of smiths which I investigated, out of its ten adult male members no less than five were resident either in other parts of Konso, or in Borana. The cultivators, who have always had the ties of land to keep them in one place, naturally tend almost invariably to remain in the place of their birth, and since towns are permanent settlements one finds that cultivator families have resided there for several centuries in many cases. It is not difficult to see that the lack of opportunities for smiths as well as other craftsmen in Konso is largely responsible for this mobility of craftsmen, which was facilitated in the past by the lack of land. The lack of opportunity for craftsmen can be seen by the fact that in Garati and Takadi regions there are probably no more than twenty smiths out of a total population of over 50,000. In Turo there are perhaps as many as ten smiths out of only about 3,000 population. No pots are made in Turo, and in Garati and Takadi there are even fewer potters and tanners than smiths. The number of weavers is vastly greater, including as it does cultivators as well as craftsmen, and may be as many as 700.

The image of the craftsmen among cultivators is then one of mercenary quarrelsome individualists who pay less attention to the norms of friendliness, co-operation, and the common good than they ought to in their pursuit of private well-being. But it is recognized that craftsmen quarrel among themselves as much as they do with the cultivators. There is no idea of the craftsmen ranged collectively against the cultivators in some kind of conspiracy. Nor should it be thought that in ordinary contacts there is any obvious bitterness or animosity. Day-to-day relations in the *moras* are perfectly friendly, and some craftsmen may be well-liked and have many friends among the cultivators. To this extent the image of the craftsmen I have presented is a caricature of the cultivators' imagination, rather in the style of Fagin and Shylock in English literature.

It seems clear that the arts of ironworking, pottery-making, and weaving have been introduced from outside Konso, and the more specialized techniques of tanning are probably also of alien origin. Iron ore for smelting came from Gofa in the north, and there is a greater concentration of smiths in Turo, to the north of Garati and Takadi; many of the smiths in Degato said their forebears came from Turo. It seems highly likely that ironworkers came to Konso from this direction. Potters are supposed to have come originally from Burji, and still today all the women potters I met had been born there and came to Konso as the wives of Konso craftsmen. Weaving has no place of reputed origin among the Konso, but the fact that the style of their looms is identical with those of other parts of Ethiopia, while the practice of weaving in Konso long antedates the Amhara conquest, points to an origin outside Konso, and many of them say that the craftsmen brought the art, before which skins alone were worn. But the fact that these arts were of immigrant origin is not in itself reason why the Konso should stigmatize their practitioners. According to their own traditions the origins of the cultivators are as diverse as those of the craftsmen, some having come from Borana, and others from all the neighbouring tribal areas. So a pure descent from autochthonous forebears is not a necessary criterion for being a cultivator, yet paradoxically craftsman and cultivator status is determined solely by descent. It seems likely that the elements of cultivator stock, diverse though their origins undoubtedly were, by reason of their agricultural pursuits were able to fuse easily into a homogeneous pattern of life. But in the case of the *hauda* crafts, the exigencies of making a living by manufacture and trade, rather than agriculture, produced those craftsmen qualities I have described, partly in reality and partly in the imagination of the cultivators.

I would say then that the reasons for the present and traditional status of the craftsmen are as follows. The number of *hauda* who brought these crafts would have been small, and the level of demand would not have encouraged any cultivator to learn them. In any case, the materials and mode of processing them used in *hauda* crafts violated the religious prejudices of the cultivators, who would have had no inclination to learn them, but rather an incentive to ostracize them on these grounds alone. Having to depend solely on selling their products, the craftsmen were naturally put in the position of being mercenary and hard bargainers, and their lack of land, and the necessity of living where demand was greatest would have produced more mobility among them than the cultivators. They were thus forced to remain as outsiders among their agricultural neighbours.

But the hostility between the cultivators and the craftsmen was not produced by simple resentment alone. Basically, it was the result of a clash of values. The craftsmen were considered to ignore the canons of social harmony, loyalty, and co-operation so deeply valued by the cultivators, thereby putting themselves outside the pale of true Konso society.

7. MASCULINITY

Contrasted with their ideal of peace is that of masculinity, which plays an important part in Konso thought. What we may call 'phallicism' is rife throughout pagan Ethiopia, finding its most notorious expression in the custom of cutting off the genitals of enemies as trophies. (The extent to which the testicles or the penis are most desired by different tribes is obscure.) Phallic stones are distributed over a large part of southern and eastern Ethiopia, and are found abundantly in Konso, where they are called *daga deeruma*, 'stones of manhood'.

They are placed on the graves of men who have killed an enemy in battle. Every great *mora* in a Konso town has one or more of these stones, which commemorate the victory in battle of a past *harriyāda*, or set, of Ĥrela, the warrior grade. The following text describes the circumstances and sentiments which lead to the stones of manhood being erected.

> In the past they put up *daga deeruma* (in the *mora* Murgito) for the following reasons. One group of people were Ĥrela, their *harriyāda* being called Kīlōla; this *harriyāda* was many and big. After they had gone to war, and slaughtered, and returned, their spears victorious, for the sake of renown [they put up the stone] in another year when the fighting was finished. They danced, and said, 'We were *men*, all our spears were victorious, and we will put up a stone of manhood. After putting it up everyone will tell of us, and will say, 'This grade long ago was called Kīlōla, and in the past were fierce men', thus they will talk of the victors'. After this they made beer [presumably their women actually made it] and went and told their friends, and drank the beer, and gave of it, and slaughtered he-goats, and ate of them, and danced the *seega* in the *moras*. Then the town-crier called, and sounded upon his horn, to tell that Ĥrela were going and labouring, and that all virile men were going to carry in the stone, and they go and lay hold of this stone, and carry it [to the town] and as it arrives the girls begin to ululate, and the men coming with it scream, and the women ululate to the men carrying the stone, and they put it down in the *mora*, and call the *Apa Dawra*. They come, and plant the stone in the ground, and bless the stone of Kīlōla.'

The men's clubhouses also have phallic clay roof-pots. The men sleep in these houses at night to preserve their strength, which they believe is dissipated by too much indulgence in sexual intercourse. Each ward has at least one of these clubhouses, which are quite capacious inside. Sometimes the men, especially the older ones, will sleep at home, and there are some men who do not use them. The phalluses on the pots are not only, I think, a sign that the house

is exclusively male in occupancy, but are also symbols of its fundamental purpose.

The priest also has a similar pot on his largest huts. We recall
that the priest is the bringer of fertility to his lineage; with this in
mind it is clear why he should have a phallus represented on his
roof. The priests also have another representation of the phallus,
called the *hallasha*. They obtain these from the Borana. They are in
two parts, a pointed metal phallus (of cast
zinc) and the base of a large white conus
shell, into which the metal piece slots, as in
Fig. 9. This *hallasha* is bound to the priest's
forehead during a ritual. Its purpose is to
destroy evil influences, and in the symbolism of the *hallasha* we see another aspect
of the erect penis, in which it is regarded
not only as an instrument of impregnation,
but as a weapon. In ritual the *hallasha* is
used in conjunction with a rhinoceros horn;
when the priest's eldest son curses his
father's ghost to prevent it returning and
when the priest curses a thief, the *hallasha*
and the rhinoceros horn are used in conjunction. It is said that the blast of malefic

FIG. 9. The *hallasha*

force from the *hallasha* and the rhinoceros horn on these occasions
makes it unsafe to live near a priest's homestead, which is why
the priest usually lives outside the towns. The penis is therefore
associated with the penetrating horn of the rhinoceros, which
explains why the *hallasha* is bound to the priest's forehead. As
we know, rhinoceros horn is widely supposed to be an aphro-
disiac; in the case of the *hallasha* an opposite symbolic process
takes place, whereby 'penis' becomes 'horn'. The aggressive
symbolism is not exhausted, however, by representing the penis as
an analogue to the rhinoceros horn. The name '*hallasha*' also means
'canine tooth' and the white shell and the white metal use the
colour of death (white for the Konso) as an aggressive medicine to
keep away or to kill hostile forces.

In the past the Konso used to cut off the genitals of their dead
enemies; the *waga* statues of a man's victims have no sexual parts
—the only figure in the group to have them is that which represents
the hero himself, which bears an ostentatious penis. The enemy's

penis would be slit and put on the killer's right wrist, just as the strips of hide from a sacrificial beast are slit and put on the wrists of the congregation.

A brave man is called *horma*, 'a bull'. This refers, I think, not only to sexual powers and ferocity, but to strength. One of their virtues which they were always stressing to me was their ability to carry heavy loads of timber, to build walls in the hot sun, and to walk and run great distances. In some of the *moras* there are large boulders, weighing between 100 and 150 pounds, which the young men use to demonstrate their strength.

Warfare is the traditional means for displaying martial ferocity but hunting is another occasion for the display of manliness. Konso flocks are only rarely endangered by the depredations of wild animals. The terraced hills in which they are grazed have no cover for lion or leopards, who prefer the jungles of the Sagan River, or the bush of Gomīda plain. During my two years in Konso I never saw a lion or leopard. Hyenas, the greatest danger to stock, are trapped, not hunted and have no prestige as a game animal. But hunting for the Konso is not just an occasional necessity to protect their stock, but, with warfare, the most prestigious activity for a man. Only three animals are counted as game animals, the lion, the leopard, and more rarely the boa-constrictor. Rhinoceros and elephant have been extinct in the areas apparently for at least fifty years.[1] Many animals of the antelope variety are hunted for meat, but their killing confers no prestige. The game animals *par excellence* therefore are lions and leopards. To reach them the hunting parties have to make the long journey, about five or six hours, to the Sagan, nowadays often supplementing their spears with rifles. The killer and his associates (five people altogether may claim a share of the honour, in Būso at least) perform a ceremony of triumph in the chief *moras* on their return, at which the lineage priest of the principal killer presides. They parade through the town ringing bells, and the killer is kissed by the women, who call him 'our bull'.

In the context of this high estimation of masculinity, I was interested to see if they had any marked attitudes towards effeminacy and homosexuality. I found two words each for penis, vagina, and sexual intercourse, but no less than four for 'effeminate man'—*sagōda*,

---

[1] Donaldson Smith described the Sagan region as full of game, especially elephant and rhinoceros, in 1895. In 1901, according to Harrison, the Amhara were rapidly wiping them out for ivory.

miteeza, palandeza, and one other which I omitted to record. This
suggests a rather special interest in the topic, but one must be careful about translating these as 'homosexual'. They denote a wide
range of effeminate behaviour; a man who never marries, a weak
or cowardly man, and a man who wears skirts, will all be called
sagōda, or one of the other words. Men who actually wear skirts are
very few, and those who do are clearly incapable of acting as men.
I knew one in Gaho, who earned his living curing skins, a female
occupation. He was very effeminate in voice and manner, and clearly
the victim of some bullying. It was said for example that 'He won't
hit you back if you take his meat away, or knock him down.' I was
told that these *sagōda* liked to play the passive role in sodomy, and
the description I was given of the manner in which a *sagōda* would
induce a man to perform this upon him in the night was so detailed
that it could never have been invented. The question is whether
normal men only practise sodomy with *sagōda*, or among themselves.
I am strongly inclined to think that it is not confined to relations
with *sagōda*. They were generally very reluctant to talk about
sexual matters with me, and, while they may make coarse remarks
on occasions, are reserved among themselves, except in the men's
sleeping houses at night. When I was at Būso there was much
laughter one night outside my hut at supper-time. On inquiring
what it was about I was told that they were joking with one elderly
man, who had the reputation of being something of a *sagōda*, and
saying that they would take him out into the fields and rape him.
This sort of occasion, the conduct of the transvestites, and the
sexual strains put on men by society, lead one to suppose that they
seek relief among themselves in homosexual intercourse on occasion.
But this is not to say it is approved of. I deal in Chapter VII with
the significance of the number six in ritual, and its homosexual
significance, and there can be little doubt that for them such a
form of sexual relationship would be sterile, unnatural, and hence
deplorable.

Relationships between men and women are not subject to the
sort of formal etiquette one finds in many primitive societies. In
assessing the status of women among the Konso it is essential to
remember that they are an informal people, and without much
social stratification. Thus there are none of the elaborate forms of
greeting, such as kissing the feet, which are found in more formal
societies, and no deep sense of society as a series of hierarchies

by which a more rigid differentiation of the sexes could be maintained.

The *moras* are exclusively for men, where they may sit for hours during the day, while women only pass through them. Women only come to the *moras* to watch ceremonies or participate in dances. Relations between men and women in groups tend to be restrained. One night I was sitting in a *mora* with some men, and we were all talking freely together; then a complete hush fell on us as a file of women passed silently through us in the moonlight. No one spoke until they had gone, when the conversation began again. Relations between individual men and women are less restrained, and on a number of occasions I have seen them shout abuse at one another. But there is no open display of affection between the sexes.

Before the Amhara enforced the wearing of trousers the only male garment was the blanket worn as a toga, but in any hard manual labour the blanket is an encumbrance, and men used to go completely naked when working. No stigma was traditionally attached to the display of the male genitals. Today they wear trousers because the law demands it, and because they are beginning to adopt the Amhara attitude that nakedness is shameful. Women, however, have always worn skirts. The different attitude to male and female nakedness is shown by the fact that young boys are often still without trousers at the age of seven or eight, but little girls are put into skirts as soon as they are able to crawl about, or even while still in their mothers' arms. Women's skirts are traditionally made of leather, in three pieces, a short flap hanging down in front above the knees, a broad skirt behind falling to the back of the knees, and swept up to the belt in front so that the thighs are exposed when walking. The third piece is worn underneath the large skirt at the back, and its effect is to hide the curve of the buttocks, making the area completely flat. The general impression is that women's dress is designed to conceal any anatomical detail which suggests the female genitalia. We would rightly conclude from all this that whereas the penis is admired, the vagina is feared, and these deductions have been born out by various statements made to me. For example a man said to me: 'Some girls' vaginas are so strong that they can snap off a man's penis.' More generally it is held that sexual intercourse weakens men, both for warfare and for carrying heavy loads and other strenuous work in the fields, and should not be indulged in very often. A young man who has recently married will be reproved by his father if he sees that he is sleeping with his wife on too many nights. Traditionally, at least in Garati and Takadi, the men, both married and unmarried, slept in the clubhouses at the *moras*. Unmarried girls who are sexually mature in many cases sleep in houses called *tiga mugdoda* or sleeping house, under the supervision of an elderly couple.

While the Konso value manhood so highly, they therefore deprecate sexual relations, in the sense that while they are admittedly enjoyable, they are supposed to be bad for men. There should, officially, be no premarital intercourse, no intercourse while a wife is pregnant or suckling a child (and this can go on until the child is nearly three), and no intercourse for a woman after her first son has married. Within marriage itself intercourse should not be too frequent, because of its weakening effects. The prohibition on men of Farida grade marrying can also delay marriage for them until they are over thirty. While these are theoretical limitations, in the sense that, for example, it was said to me that a man who wanted to marry a girl should more or less force her to have intercourse to show his intentions were serious, this was strictly unofficial, and would have been denounced by the elders if said publicly. No doubt men do have intercourse with their wives more frequently than they should, and at times when they are pregnant or suckling. Nevertheless, the existence of the men's sleeping houses shows that more than lip service is paid to these ideals.

In Degato and Idigle there is a hunting festival every few years, the Kara. Unmarried girls who are sexually mature have to leave the town during the hunt itself, which may go on during the day for eight or nine days, the men returning to sleep in the town at night. Men who are married may not sleep with their wives during this time, nor do any marriages take place. These restrictions are, of course, imposed because they believe that women make men soft. One of the justifications most commonly advanced for the prohibition of marriage by young men in the Farida grade is that men become soft and useless as warriors if they have wives and families to think about. In fact Farida are not warriors, but this explanation nevertheless expresses their belief that women have an emotionally as well as a physically deleterious influence on men.

It is significant that women are excluded from the ceremonies at which *ulahitas* (the sacred juniper trees specially associated with the warrior grade) are erected, though they can watch; nor are they allowed into the most sacred *moras, miskata*. I was given a number of reasons for this prohibition: that God did not like women, and therefore did not want them at his ceremonies; that women might give away the secrets of the ceremonies to people in their future husbands' towns (there are no secrets in these ceremonies, and women can watch them anyway); and that the *moras* are only for men. I deal below with the more fundamental implications of these statements, but at the level of immediate observation the reason that women are not allowed to watch the *ulahita* ceremonies, which are for the benefit of the warrior grade, is derived from the weakening effect which women are supposed to have on men. Women who are sexually mature, and still able to bear children are not allowed to sit near an *ulahita*, but little girls and old women may. This shows that it is not the nature of women as such which makes them antipathetic to the *ulahita*, but only a part of them—their sexual capacities.

There is a close association between men and iron, and a corresponding prohibition against women making iron objects. But it might seem to my readers that women would not, in any case, have the strength for this work. Konso smiths, however, are not noticeably muscular, and the larger hammers familiar to those who envisage an English blacksmith are not used. Their women are extremely strong, working as they do for several hours a day at the grindstone, and frequently carrying half a hundredweight of water up steep slopes. Thus the prohibition against women making iron objects does not seem to derive from their physical incapacity. The chief objects made by the smiths have traditionally been spearheads, knives, axe-heads, and digging-stick heads. Now spears are obviously purely masculine objects and symbolic of virile courage and warfare. Knives traditionally have always been closely linked with sacrifice, which only men may perform. Axes are used solely in male occupations, such as house-building and tree-felling, though digging-sticks and hoes are admittedly used by both sexes. Women take no part in warfare, are forbidden to slaughter for meat, and also to sacrifice, and on the basis of these facts it seems almost certain that iron is thought of as a male symbol, and consequently for a woman to manufacture it would be quite inappropriate.

8. LIFE AND DEATH

The death of the body is associated in Konso thought with all

VII. Gahanna

the other ills of the human condition—famine, drought, sickness, sterility, and social disorder—and Death in this wider sense is thought to be averted by the well-ordered society.

For the Konso the proper order of things is well summed up in the following text:

I listened to the elders of long ago. They said 'Let people listen to one another. If they listen God will send rain, and ripen the millet, people will be born. . . . After people have listened to one another, God likes it and then rains, and the millet ripens. . . . They bring back a woman from a strange house [lineage] and when she is established she hears the voice of her husband and tills the family fields, and brings fodder for the cattle, the cows give birth, they drink the milk, and the children bring fodder; after the bull that has been born drinks the milk it becomes fat, and the family sells it, and with the money the family is well-off. They hear the voice of the head of the household (*apa*) the millet ripens . . . they laugh, there are no running noses and colds . . . God is good to them. Their children are well-off. Thus when things are established in this way[1] there is no sickness in the land, and this family is well-off. Their women bear men-children. And families and the people who listen to one another in this way, it is good with them. Their men and their old women, and their wives, are well-off together, when they listen to each other, thus they prosper and buy fields. God is thus good to them, and thus their children are well-off.'

This then is Life, and it is fitting to discuss death, as the total opposition to it, at the conclusion of a chapter on Konso values.

Death is very horrible to the Konso. But they are quite ready to talk about it, and the ceremonies surrounding it, at times almost as though fascinated. Sagara Gīya, my diviner friend, one evening gave me a minute description of the ritual that his eldest son would perform when he died; I think he relished the idea of having so striking a ceremony performed in his honour, but he was an unusual man. The after-life for them is the usual drab and bat-like existence envisaged by so many pagan peoples. Death is the end of human existence as they think of it. I was sitting by the open grave in which an old informant of mine was shortly to be buried. Someone turned to me and said 'He was your friend, and told you stories; now he is just flesh.'

There is a short myth which also expresses their attitude to death concisely.

At the time of Creation God said to the turtle [which lives in wells

---

[1] '*mugini*', literally, 'sleeping'.

and is associated with water spirits] 'Go and say to Man "Man dies and comes back again; the moon dies and is lost forever." So the turtle went with his message and came to Man and said 'Man dies and is lost for ever; the moon dies but returns'. When the turtle had done this God asked him saying 'When you went there what did you say?' The turtle said 'Man dies and is lost for ever; the moon dies but returns'. God said 'Why did you speak thus? This is not the message I sent you with'. Then the turtle said 'I will go again and deliver the right message'. 'You won't' said God, and cut him in two. (This is why the turtle is so short to this day.) Thus God cursed the turtle. Then God went far away.

When a person dies, he or she is carried out into the fields and buried the same day. A young person when dead is terrible to them, and even if he expires during the night the neighbours will be roused and his corpse carried outside the town. The relatives take no part in the burial itself. It is the responsibility of the ward to do all this work, and relieve the kin of the suffering involved. Only men do the digging, partly because it is very strenuous work, partly because 'Women would only sit here crying, and never do any digging'. When my old informant Usati Telaẖīya died, during the night, the fact was announced to everyone by the wailing of the family. Neighbours from the ward went to the house and prepared the corpse. In this case, since he had been a grandfather, his head was covered in butter. This is an honour given only to grandfathers and grandmothers. He was then placed in a crouching position and tied, first in his cotton blanket, then in his sleeping-skin. He was left there in his house during the morning and early afternoon while the grave-digging was in progress. Relatives and neighbours congregated in his house to weep with the family. When the grave was well advanced we returned to the house from his fields where he was to be buried, about a quarter of an hour's walk away. The men of the ward brought him out of his hut and carried him to the gate of the homestead, now filled with the shrieks of the women, and the sobbing of the men. Once he was on the shoulders of the first man who was to carry him we all set off at a fast jog for the grave, to a rhythmic funeral chant whose words were meaningless as far as I could discover. As we passed through the Mora Murgito the chanting ceased. This chant is used solely on funeral occasions, and it is forbidden to sing it or conduct any dance associated with death within the precincts of this, the most sacred *mora* of all.

Earlier, on the way back from the grave to collect the body, there had been an angry scene between the older men and some rather drunken youths, who had been banging their *kaula* sticks and singing when they passed through the Mora Murgito. At the graveside itself there is no professional undertakers' solemnity. The family provide large quantities of beer, and the fact that it is of the alcoholic variety, *yaĝa*, not the unfermented variety, *erorda*, which is usually drunk in the fields, suggests that a degree of drunkenness is intended. There is often quarrelling among the grave-diggers, and even without this the conversation is thoroughly casual and profane. The graves are about 5 ft. deep, and of oblong plan, about 3 ft. by 1½ ft. At the bottom is a lateral niche, cut in the long side of the hole, in which the body is placed. This is done specifically to prevent the earth falling on the corpse itself. In some areas a smaller hole is made at the bottom of the shaft, in which the corpse lies covered with timbers.

When Usati's grave was ready, after great exertions, since most of it was cut out of the soft rock which underlies the top soil, the body was unwrapped, and the anus inspected to see if any faeces had exuded and if necessary to wipe them away. The body was placed firmly in a crouching position, with the hands clasped on the breast. In Garati only grandfathers and grandmothers are supposed to be buried in this position, other people being interred in the extended position. It was explicitly stated to me that the reason for burying old people in this position is that it is the same as that of babies. They can hardly be supposed to think of it as the 'foetal' position, since they have no means of knowing the position that the foetus adopts within the womb. The crouching position is roughly that which the young infant adopts in its mother's arms, or sleeping at her side, and it is surely this position which is imitated at burial in the case of old people, because it is realized that they are childlike in their weakness and general impotence. Usati's body was lifted up by the sleeping-skin when the blanket had been replaced around him, and by its corners lowered into the grave. In his case he was buried roughly facing towards the west, on his right side. The west and the right side are, of course, at once familiar to anthropologists as conventional symbols in burial rites. But it is important to note that the west has no special association with death for the Konso, nor the east with life. Indeed, when I asked them in Garati which way a corpse faced at burial, they said it depended on where his

ancestors had originally come from, Ala or Ilota. Ala is roughly
north-west of Garati, and Ilota is north-east, and people are said to
be buried facing either of these two directions. I was told that I
would be buried facing England, since I would be thinking about
my home. In Takadi I was told that people were buried facing their
actual homes where they lived at the time of their deaths. Only in
Turo was it explicitly said that they were all buried facing west, or
the sunset, the two meanings having only one word *dumateta*.

After the body was placed in position, a wall of stones was built
across the niche, and then the earth poured back. Nothing is usually
buried with corpses, except, perhaps, as in this case, the old man's
fly-whisk. His eldest son inherits his pipe and his eating bowl,
which curiously enough is employed in lifting the soil out of the
grave.[1] When the last of the soil was ready to be heaped in, silence
was called for, and we ranged ourselves around the hole. We pushed
the remnants of the soil back in three movements, saying each time
in a low voice *'inegnade'*, 'you have gone bad'. Finally the earth is
pounded down with a heavy rock. This is ostensibly to prevent
hyenas catching the scent of corruption and digging up the corpse.

There are no further ceremonies associated with the grave, except
the killing of a bull some weeks or months later, and the placing of
two or three sticks on it to indicate whether it is that of a man or
woman. *Wagas* will also be erected at this time. For this ceremony
all the relatives, including the immediate family, will come.

For the Konso to bury people in the fields, which is their normal
practice, creates a symbolic conflict with the use of those fields for
agricultural purposes. (Graves themselves are not avoided, and one
often sees millet sprouting from them where it has been sown.)
But the coincidence that what provides life also receives corpses has
not escaped them, and will be discussed in Chapter VII.

The death of a priest is even more dreadful than the death of an
ordinary man. There is no mourning, the body is eviscerated and
covered in butter and honey (auspicious substances), and left un-
buried for nine days. After this it is buried in a basket in a temporary grave, with the viscera in a jar beneath the corpse. After three
years it is exhumed and placed in a grave of the usual type, which
is to be its permanent resting place. A great priest is buried in the
ancestral juniper wood adjoining his home. At Turo is was said that

---

[1] This is perhaps a symbolic expression of the fact that the eldest son only
inherits his father's goods and status by the death of his parent.

priests were buried at the end of tunnels, which led off from the bottom of deep pits. These are all indications that the physical dissolution of the priest, the bringer of Life, is something even worse than the dissolution of ordinary men. For the priest is the antithesis of death and when it comes to him its effects must be mitigated as much as possible.

The custom of having dances in memory of grandfathers who have died is at first sight inconsistent with their horror of death, and with their grief for the departed. The *shilleda*, as it is called, is only held for grandmothers and grandfathers, and is performed either in a *mora* (not the most sacred *mora*) or else in a field within the town walls, depending on local custom. Despite the fact that it is called *poyda*, or 'weeping', it is a very jolly affair, and a stranger would never guess that it had any connection with death. The only outward indication of its purpose is the use of white clay to daub the bodies of the dancers; white is the colour of death in Konso symbolism. When I asked them why they had a dance for such a sad occasion (it may be held weeks or months after the burial, when the bull is killed and the grave adorned) they either said simply that it was their way of mourning, which is untrue, or that it was to cheer up the relatives. But as it is not performed for young people, whose death creates far more grief, and is often held some time after the death of the person concerned, this is clearly not the right answer. The missionary informed me that he had been told that it was performed because they were glad the old man or woman was dead. But they are not glad at the time, and death is always in my experience greeted by very genuine sorrow, whether it is of an old man or a child. At one *shilleda* I attended, two men performed an extremely obscene dance, where one of them extended his right arm holding a club stiffly in front of him, and his partner leant over backwards with his mouth open. As they danced about the man with the outstretched arm tried to put his club into the mouth of his partner amidst hilarious laughter. It was, of course, a burlesque representing sexual intercourse. Such a dance would never be performed in the usual way. I would suggest, in view of this sort of licence, that the *shilleda* expresses their relief at the lifting of restraint imposed by the older members of society. They are not exactly glad that the old person is dead, but now that he is they feel relieved of the burden of his moral authority and censoriousness.

Once a person has died, however, his ghost is of little significance.

The body is simply flesh, *soa*, which is buried at death. *Soa* is also the word used for animal meat, which one buys in the market. The breath is *nesa*, and at death this is taken by God. Vitality, which is in practice the pulse, especially as seen beating below the ribs, is *lupoda*, and this simply disappears when a man dies. The soul is *kelelīda*, or *katilīda*, which is also the word for shadow. *Katilīda* is really a compound of the word *kata* meaning 'shade', and the suffix *-olida*, meaning 'a person'; thus the whole word means 'shade person'. *Kelelīda* means 'inside person'. At death the soul finally leaves the body and pursues an independent existence as a ghost, *kareeya*. The only difference between a *katilīda* and a *kareeya* is that the *katilīda* still belongs to a living body, which it leaves at night in dreams, but to which it finally returns, while a *kareeya* has no body any longer. We are not to suppose that the soul and the shadow are thought of as the same thing. For there are no beliefs about shadows in relation to magical practices; the shadow is never referred to as having any mystical properties, while it is said that some diviners can see the souls of men in the daytime and talk with them. The relationship between shadow and soul is in fact an analogical one. The shadow, and for that matter the reflection, *gawada*, which is sometimes used to refer to the soul in a similar way to 'shadow', are both similar to the soul in these three ways: they are insubstantial; they are unique to the person himself; and they have a peculiarly intimate bond with that person. There is thus no question of the reflection or the shadow *being* the soul under different aspects; they are simply related to the body in a fashion which is analogous to the soul's relation.

Ghosts can sometimes be seen and heard. My servant used to hear them talking together in a *mora* on the path from Būso to Degato at night, so he said, and would rub his legs with paraffin before he set out for home, because 'They smell it and think it is a *ferenji* coming, and they are afraid'. Sometimes, people say, one will be walking alone in the fields in broad daylight, and suddenly one will come upon the ghost of an old man, with white hair, sitting on his grave and spinning cotton. This is very bad and one will die soon afterwards. Ghosts are also supposed to move about at night with a loud flapping noise. I was sitting outside my hut at Būso one night, on a high spur of land overlooking the gorge of the Elbola stream below, talking to some neighbours. The moon was three-quarters full, high on my left hand. Suddenly, from the right there came a loud flapping noise that moved towards the river, and died away as quickly as it had begun. They all immediately said it was a ghost, going down to the river to drink. Unfortunately the moon was not in the right place to illuminate the source of the noise. I should mention that there are no large birds that flap in Konso, except a few vultures over near Bakaule, which are not in any case nocturnal. All the large birds glide noiselessly, especially around the Elbola gorge. During their centuries in Konso the people have accumulated a great body of knowledge of the local fauna, so if they have never found the bird, if bird it is, which makes this noise, they have good reason to give it supernatural significance.

They have little idea of the kind of life that the ghosts lead; but certainly there is no belief in any separate abode or punishments for evildoers, and rewards for the good. Sinners are punished by sickness or death in this life; after death there is just a common bat-like existence for all. The ghosts have some influence on the living; in particular, they may cause the deaths of nice people, because they decide that such a person would be pleasant company for them, while they postpone the death of a vicious quarrelsome person as long as they can. This is a restatement of our own saying that 'the good die young'. They are thought still to be in contact with their surviving relatives and descendants, returning in dreams either to the lineage priest or their immediate surviving relatives. When a man or woman dies, he or she will return a short time after death, in a dream, to demand the sacrifice of a bull, which will be carried out. When drinking beer, a man will spit out the first mouthful on to the ground, saying '*nagīda*'; this is called a *logīda*. Sometimes a man will put offerings of food for them in the *aleda*[1]. They may cause sickness in men, and dreams about the dead are mystically dangerous encounters with their ghosts. Principally, however, they come to visit the lineage priest in dreams, which is why certain lineage priests are expert dream diviners. Ghosts have no moral influence, and even sickness or death is very seldom attributed to them.

Their deep horror and repugnance towards death is vividly illustrated in their interpretation of dreams. Dreams are the real experiences of the soul, 'on the astral plane', as we ourselves might express it. Their symbols of death in dreams are a gloomy forest of

---

[1] A thatched repository for valuables supported by a single wooden pillar which is intended to be too slippery for rats to climb.

the imagination. What in the waking world are harmless and even pleasant activities become transformed in dreams into an army of morbid fantasies.

Dancing, even if it is not a *shilleda*, in a dream signifies death. People going to the fields are not going, as in real life, to weed and reap, but to dig a grave; if they are building a wall, it is not a terrace wall, but the circular wall around a grave. Stones in dreams are the stones of these grave walls, and a *'daga 'deeruma* portends the death of strong men. A hole is always a grave, and even for a weaver to dream that he is putting his feet into the small pit beneath his loom is to dream of his own grave. To cut wood is to cut it for one purpose only—to make the *wagas* for a dead man. If a man is shaving his head, it is only because one of his parents has died. In real life women often butter their hair; to dream of doing so is to dream of death, because the corpses of grandfathers and grand-mothers have their heads buttered. Bells, in a dream, mean death, because they are rung, among other occasions, on the death of a priest; so does the cry of the town crier, for this is a voice at night, and the kin of the dead person also cry out in the night. Many gourds of beer in a house at night are there for the guests to drink at a funeral. A bull is killed, in a dream, not for meat, but at the mortuary ceremony for a dead man. A hide drying in the sun is a portent of death, because a man is wrapped in hide when he is buried, and a broken pot stands for the death of a woman. A falling *ulahita* means the death of Ĥrela, and a man who dreams of smok-ing a pipe in the fields will die; in real life no one smokes a pipe in the fields, which in a dream are the place of death, and only the aged smoke at all. To be alone in a *mora* means that all one's neigh-bours have died, and to be walking along a path when the sun sets is to dream of one's own death. To dream of spinning cotton is to dream of drought and famine; white cattle being driven together, and women bringing in dry grass symbolize the same thing. Dreams of fire are always bad, and signify death and destruction; ashes signify poverty. Smoke and mist are alike bad and are signs of sickness. Birds are the symbols of famine, and high winds mean death. For one's cotton blanket to be blown away by the wind is a sign that one's son will die.

Not every dream however has such gloomy connotations. To be driving red or black cattle in a dream is a good omen and signifies meat. Climbing a tree or hill is a good sign associated with food.

All dreams to do with food or water are good, and even the dream of a man falling into a well is good. Curiously, to dream of honey is a portent of sickness. Fetching water is an auspicious sign, and so is a snake, which symbolizes water. Soot is a good omen for women, and picking up iron on the path symbolizes money. It is good to dream of houses and palisades being built, and, perhaps the strangest of all, it is auspicious to dream of one's own death, which will never happen after such a dream. It will be seen that the bad dreams strongly outweigh the good, and this reveals yet again the Konso pre-occupation with death.

The death symbols, with the exception of an *ulahita* falling, are not bad in real life, when they have no significance whatever beyond themselves. The symbols of death abstract one particular association from a thing or activity—as for instance fields and agricultural work—and make it the only relevant characteristic. In waking life the fields have no inauspicious associations, and to make a wall or to dig are only connected with the work in hand. One might suppose that since their fields are the source of life for them they would have an auspicious significance in dreams; the area occupied by graves is very small in comparison with the whole area of the fields, and the amount of time spent in digging graves in comparison with that spent in agricultural pursuits is similarly minute. Yet in dreams the auspicious association of the fields with food is ignored, and only the fact that men are buried there is remembered. The same process of excluding all the neutral or auspicious associations, and concentrating solely on the inauspicious is applied to the other symbols—hides drying in the sun, broken pots, a man carrying human faeces (this is an omen of death, as the faeces represent a man, who is being carried to the grave), and so on. In the case of the auspicious symbols there is a slight difference, in so far as many do not have any bad associations in real life. For the Konso death is the ultimate negation of all that they hold worthwhile. Their religion is devoted to the maintenance of Life, in the fullest sense of the word, meaning prosperity, health, full bellies, the fertility of humans, animals, and crops, and success in hunting and warfare.

9. OUTSIDERS

The categories of insider and outsider are extremely important in understanding Konso society. While they cannot be classed, strictly speaking, as values, since the people themselves have no concept of insiders and outsiders as such, we have already found that a large number of social categories are opposed to one another on the basis of the insider/outsider dichotomy, as follows:

TABLE 27. *Outsiders and insiders*

Outsiders	Insiders
women	men
Farīda	adults
craftsmen	cultivators
criminals	law-abiding citizens
madmen	the sane
foreigners	Konso

We have seen that the drum is the symbol of social order and the acceptance of the values of society. Consistently with this drums must never be touched or seen by women, craftsmen, or foreigners. It is very likely that criminals and madmen would also be forbidden to touch or see them, but I did not question them specifically on this. We have seen that the craftsmen are regarded as outside society, and in Chapter VII below I shall discuss the evidence that women are also regarded as outside society in some important respects. In the section on deviants in this chapter we saw that criminals are liable to expulsion, a sanction which extends to quarrelsome persons, while madmen as such are incapable of taking part in society. In Chapter VII I shall show how madmen are related to evil spirits, the symbols of anomy and disorder, and the polar opposites of God, the source of social order.

But there are several different types of outsiders, and we must leave an analysis of these until the last chapter.

10. CONCLUSIONS

It is a truism that every society must maintain a certain level of internal harmony and order if it is to survive at all as a society. But above this minimum level, it is plain from many descriptions of primitive peoples that disputation and even violence are frequently an accepted part of social life. The Konso's ideal of peace and harmony is in fact not the expression of a universal desire, but a cultural trait as particular as generation-grades or terraced agriculture. The same is true of their high estimation of the worth of the individual and seniority, their devotion to masculinity and the phallus, and their all-pervading concern with Life and Death. While all these values are found among many other peoples, at their level of development among the Konso they have become cultural obsessions. In fact it is probably inevitable for every society to develop its obsessions, which may be transmitted across time and space without much regard to the circumambient ecological and social circumstances. The mode of life of the Konso and the Borana could hardly be more different, but in their values they appear to exhibit remarkable similarities, so that one feels they both share a common moral universe.

Konso values, of course, are, as the people themselves realize, only ideals. Nowhere is this clearer than in their estimation of peace and truth. They know how easy it is to quarrel and to lie, and say that only in the grave is a man free from either of these vices. Their most important social institutions—the drums, the priests, the Nama Dawra, and the grading systems—are the fruits of their conscious efforts to establish an ideal social order, of which their actions often fall far short.

Moreover, within the body of their values there are some inherent and deep-rooted tensions. These are between peace and the admirable nature of military prowess, between the female as necessary to society and as weakening men and being outside the basic social institutions, and between the right of the individual to advance himself economically and the strongly egalitarian and gregarious quality of their society as a whole.

Even where their values do not conflict, they do not, of course, form anything like a logically coherent system. Do the values of any society? There is no necessary relationship between their concern for peace, the value of the individual, bravery, or Life. But there is no necessity for them to try to work out the application of their ideals in theory; they have a set of institutions in which these are given customary expression, and which command their respect. The chief of these are the grading systems, which I shall shortly consider.

V

KONSO TIME-RECKONING

THE Konso resemble most primitive peoples in lacking a unified mode of time-reckoning. That is, they use a number of different units of measurement, based on the sun, the moon, the stars, and the seasons and related agricultural activities, and on a cycle of market days, which are not interrelated either astronomically or numerically.

There is no word for 'time' in Konsiña. In English we use the word 'time' in many different senses, which combine to give it a false aspect of concreteness and mystery. For example, 'it is *time* to go to bed' is *'mugita igide'*, 'sleeping has arrived, is ready'. 'What *time* is it?' is *'sadeda meğa'*, literally, 'hours how many?' (*Sadeda* is derived from the Amharic *sat*, meaning in this context 'an hour'.) 'He has been a long *time*' is *'iōlade'*, 'he has delayed'.

In reality they are concerned not merely with the measurement of time, but with grasping intellectually, and so regulating, the experience of duration. As we shall see in the next chapter, change is one of their cultural obsessions, especially as it manifests itself in human society. In this connection it is an interesting fact that my watch was a constant source of fascination for them, not only because of the rapid motion of its second hand, but because it could tell the time. They were always asking me 'What is the time now?'

Their calendar is based on a cycle of twelve lunar months which, according to the Konso, all have thirty days. In 1966 the sequence of months in relation to the European calendar is shown in Table 28.

Each month begins with the new moon, and the month is divided into two halves, corresponding to the waxing and waning of the moon. The first night of the month is called *ḥoita*, the second *sewrata* or *koatōda*, and the third *kōbanda*. These are also the names of the night of the full moon and the two succeeding nights. But while the synodic month is not exactly 30 days long, but about 29½ days, and, therefore, some months have only 29 days, the Konso nevertheless always insisted that each month was 30 days long. It seemed to me that at the end of the month their reckoning simply tailed off and started again with the new moon.

TABLE 28. *Konso months*

	Garati	Takadi	Turo	Work
Jan.–Feb.	Oiba	Oiba	Oiba	Dry. Preparation of ground.
Feb.–Mar.	Saganogama	Saganogama	Saganogama	Rains begin, sowing.
Mar.–Apr.	Murano	Murano	Murano	Wet, sowing, weeding.
Apr.–May	Pillelo	Pellelta	Pillele	Wet, weeding.
May–June	Hari	Harda	Hari	Little rain, bird-scaring.
June–July	Tôla	Tela	Tellele	Dry. Bird-scaring.
July–Aug.	Orĥolasha	Orĥolasha	Oĥonolisha	Dry. Harvest.
Aug.–Sept.	Sessīsha	Sessīsha	Sessīsha	Dry. Harvest.
Sept.–Oct.	Pardubota	Pardubota	Pardubota	Little rains. Preparing ground cutting stalks off old millet. Sowing maize.
Oct.–Nov.	Keesha	Keesha	Keesho	Little rains. Weeding.
Nov.–Dec.	Olindela	Olindela	Olindela	Little rains. Harvest begins.
Dec.–Jan.	Poringa	Poringa	Poringa	Harvest.

The failure of the calendar to synchronize with nature is far more apparent in the case of the lunar year in relation to the solar year, which is approximately 11 days longer than the lunar year. Thus the lunar year advances about a month in relation to the solar year every three solar years. I could find no evidence that months were ever omitted or inserted to take account of this, nor were there any intercalary days at the end of the year. Indeed, strictly speaking, there is no first or last month in a Konso year which is generally accepted as such. The regional drums of Garati change hands in the month of Murano, but the town drums are often changed in other months. If a new year began at any one time, it would be the onset of the great rains.

But the Konso insisted to me that the seasons always fell in the same months every year, yet why they should believe that their calendar remains synchronized with the seasons I never discovered. This slipping of the calendar is not obvious, however, within the space of only five or six years, because the seasons do not come and go with any regularity. In my first year in Konso, 1965, the little rains continued until the end of December, but in 1966 they stopped in the middle of November. They thus provide no clear point of reference with which to correct the Konso calendar.

Nevertheless they are aware of the changes in the orientation of the Milky Way in the course of the year, and correlate this with the coming of the rains, as they do with the changes of the rising position of the sun in relation to features of the local landscape. They also use the evening star, Moha, to estimate the arrival of the rains, noting its movements along a particular ridge of hills at the time of its setting and saying that the rains will come when it reaches a certain point. Moha is referred to figuratively as a *poĝalla*, and the rain is said to be his urine. The Pleiades, Pūza, are also used to indicate the coming of the rains. So their knowledge of celestial predictors for the seasons means that the calendar is not essential, but at most a convenient service.

The months are not simply periods based on the appearance of the new moon. Certain months are auspicious, and others inauspicious, and some of the most important ceremonies are only performed in one particular month (Table 29). Other ceremonies depend for their

TABLE 29. *Months and ceremonies*

Ceremony	Month
Garati	
Kadabaha	Pillelo, Tola
Kařa	Pardubota
'Ganōda	Olindela
Takadi	
Timba Tula	Pardubota
Oibatale	Oiba
Tūda	Pillelo
Turo	
Osumada	Oiba, Saganogama

performance on the seasons. As we have seen, fertility of crops and animals, and plentiful rain, are the chief desires of the Konso. It is therefore extremely likely that long ago it was decided to hold all the ceremonies in some relation to the seasons. How else can we explain the attribution of auspicious and inauspicious qualities to the months?

TABLE 30. *Auspicious and inauspicious months*

	Garati	Takadi	Turo
Oiba	Sōla at Idigle	Oibatale ceremony	
Saganogama	Drums changed at Degato	Good month	
Murano	Bad month, especially for Tigisida		
Pillelo	Kadabaha, Good.	No *killana*,[1] bad	
Hari	Bad		No *killana*, no marrying
Tōla	Good		
Orholasha		Good month, time for *killana*	
Sessīsha	Bad	Bad, no marrying, no *killana*	
Pardubota	Good	Good	
Keesha	Bad	No big *killana*	No *killana*, no marrying
Olindela	Good	Good	
Poringa	Bad		

In Table 30 there is only one month, Pillelo, which seems to have a completely opposite status in different regions. This apart, there is surprising agreement between the regions on the ritual status of the months, especially on the months which are inauspicious. But the whole question of auspicious and inauspicious months is thrown into confusion by the fact that two of the most important ceremonies I witnessed in Būso were held in inauspicious months, namely the erection of the new *ulahita* at the Mora Gomiya, which was put up in Hari (13 June 1965), and the Sola in Būso which was performed on days in Keesha. Yet in spite of this apparent contradiction between what actually happened and what was supposed not to happen, there is no doubt whatever that there is an idea in all three regions, and in every town where I lived, that certain months are auspicious, and others inauspicious. It is possible to relate the ritual status of the months to the seasons by considering the calendar as it would operate in other years. At this time the correlation would be as shown in Table 31. This explains the bad months Hari and Keesha as falling at the ends of the little and the great rains respectively. Similarly, Tōla and Orholasha are at the beginning of the great rains, the Kadana, and Oiba is at the beginning of the Hagida, the little rains, and these are good months. But Olindela, rated as good,

[1] *Killana* means 'religious ceremony'.

TABLE 31. *Auspicious and inauspicious months in relation
to the seasons*

		Garati	Takadi	Turo	Season
Dec.–Jan.	Hari	Bad		No *killana* no marrying	Dry 1
Jan.–Feb.	Tōla	Good			Dry 2
Feb.–Mar.	Orĥolasha		Good		Wet 1
Mar.–Apr.	Sessīsha	Bad	Bad, no *killana* no marrying		Wet 2
Apr.–May	Pardubota	Good	Good		Wet 3
May–June	Keesha	Bad	Bad	Bad, no *killana* no marrying	Dry 1
June–July	Olindela	Good	Good		Dry 2
July–Aug.	Poringa	Bad			Dry 3
Aug.–Sept.	Oiba	Good	Good		Dry 4
Sept.–Oct.	Saganogama	Good	Good		Wet 1
Oct.–Nov.	Murano	Good			Wet 2
Nov.–Dec.	Pillelo	Good	Bad		Wet 3

falls in the rainless months, just before Poringa, rated as bad. Sessīsha, also rated as bad, falls in the middle of Kadana. While therefore we can explain the ritual status of some months according to
whether they fall at the beginning or the end of the rains, Sessīsha,
in the middle of Kadana, has to be explained by some other principle. Falling as it does in the middle of the rains, its ritual status
may be due to this being the crucial period for the crops, when the
amount of rain received will decide whether or not they will live
or die. Since crop failure and famine is a common experience it
is not surprising that the Konso at the initiation of the calendar
regarded this month as dangerous. Olindela, in this revised calendar, would be the month in which harvesting begins, and therefore
auspicious. Poringa is more difficult to explain, coming also in the
harvest period, immediately after Olindela. If it is considered as
the ninth month of the year, (the drums of Garati are changed in
Murano, the last month of the year) this would be a reason for its
bad ritual status. It is said that no *killana* should be performed on
the ninth day of any month; as I have said before, nine is considered
a very bad number.

The seasons and their related activities form yet another mode of
time-reckoning. The great rains are Kadana. They are followed by
the dry season called Mazana, and then by the little rains, Hagida.
The hottest and dryest months, from about December to the

middle or end of February are Bona. But besides these seasonal terms, and the months, there are also words for the times in the agricultural year when a particular activity is going on (Table 32).

TABLE 32. *The cycle of agricultural activities*

Ḥīshima	The preparation of the ground, especially the uprooting of the old millet stalks, and the burning of rubbish, and the breaking up of the hard earth
Ïla	The sowing of the seed
Arma	The first weeding
Ŏlaba	The interval between the first weeding and the next
Arma	The second weeding
Ebalda	The cool season after the rains, when the millet is beginning to ripen, and the bird-scaring begins in earnest
Fera	Harvest time
Mazana	When people rest after the harvest
Ḥīshima	The preparation of the ground for the second sprouting of the millet, and the next sowing of the maize, at the little rains

In all regions there are weeks, *torba*, of seven days. *Torba* is Galliña for 'seven', not Amhariña—the Konsiña for 'seven' is *tapa*. The days are named in Table 33. The word for 'day' is *guiada*, 'light', but sometimes *tukanda*, 'darkness', is used instead.

TABLE 33. *The days of the week*

	Garati	Takadi	Turo
Sunday	Sambatta	Sambatta	Sambatta
Monday	Omboko/Ajajo	Omboko	Omboko
Tuesday	Omboko barīda/ Ajajo barīda	Langīya	Langīya
Wednesday	'Gomosa	'Gomosa	Robe
Thursday	Bakaule/Dibapa	Bakaule	Bakaule
Friday	Bakaule barīda/ Maramari	Hardile	Arba
Saturday	Idigle	Palauwa	'Gidama

There are two interrelated problems here; the original number of the days, and the meanings of the days. The number 'seven' has no other place in Konso numerology; moreover it does not divide evenly into thirty, the number of days in their month. While the Amhara have a seven-day week there is no reason to expect it to appear among the Konso, short of a very striking coincidence. It is clear in fact that the present seven-day week is the result of Amhara influence. The most obvious evidence of this is the day 'Sambatta' which is clearly derived from the Amharic 'Sanbat', meaning Sabbath, which falls on the same day. Omboko is an Amhara settlement about two miles from Bakaule. But there has always been a Konso market here under the name of Ajajo. This was also called 'Urmala Kalla', 'Market of the Kalla', since the Kalla's house used to be on a prominent hill not far away. Langīya is a market about an hour on foot before one reaches Turo, out in the bush, and now adjacent to the motor track from the main part of Konso to Turo. There is also a smaller Langīya market near Hamalle in Takadi, that has been closed down by the administration because of disorderly conduct. 'Gomosa was a market near the Gufa's wood in Takadi. This has been abolished by the Amhara, since an earlier governor who lived at Fasha wanted a market nearer his own house. The equivalent day in Turo, Robe, may have been a market, but I was unable to locate it. Bakaule is now the chief market in Konso, on Thursday. This too is an Amhara innovation, since Bakaule is the chief government town. But I have been told that this day long ago was known as 'Maramari'. I know of no market by this name. Friday in Garati is supposed once to have been called Dibapa, but here also I never found the site of a market with this name. Arba, the name for Friday in Turo, and Hardile, Friday in Takadi, equally have no ascertainable origins. Idigle, the Garati name for Saturday, refers to the small meat market outside the walls of the town Idigle which is still functioning. Palauwa is the name of the Fasha market, introduced by the Amhara, and 'Gidama that of the main Turo market, which is of considerable antiquity. Clearly then, before the Amhara, markets were held at Ajajo (now Omboko), Langīya, 'Gomosa, Idigle, and Turo. Since the Amhara administration has interfered with the organization of markets it is hard to establish on which days they originally fell. For example, 'Gidama might have been on Monday instead of Saturday, and changed by government decree. Also, in different regions, there were and are different names for the same day, because people prefer to go to the nearest market, unless they have something special to buy or sell. Thus on Saturday many people in Garati will go to Idigle, and hence Saturday here is called Idigle, while in Takadi it is called by the name of the market of Palauwa, and in Turo it is called 'Gidama.

Since there could, therefore, have been two important markets on the same day, before the Amhara took over, it is very hard to establish the old cycle. I was, however, given a cycle of market days by a very old informant, in Takadi, as follows:

Langīya ⎱ Deho ⎰	Turo
'Gomosa	Takadi
Ajajo	Garati
Idigle	Garati

It is noteworthy that four of these are outside Takadi, and the whole list is spread out well among the three regions. This suggests that other regions as well as Takadi had these same principal market days. The other names such as Hardile, and Dibapa, could either have been smaller markets, with a more localized clientele, or names invented to fill in gaps caused by the introduction of the Amhara seven-day week. I think it highly probable that the number of market days in the old system had no mystical numerological significance, but was purely utilitarian.

Each day is divided into a number of periods, which were expressed by my informants in terms of the Amharic clock; I have translated this into the European method of time reckoning.

TABLE 34. *Divisions of the day*

Night	*halgeta*
First light	*parāë*
Just before sunrise	*janjamīda*
Sunrise	*birtōta*
Sunrise until 9 a.m.	*tēganda*
9 a.m. until 11 a.m.	*gudada*
11 a.m. to 2 p.m.	*guiada'guta*, or *tagalida*
2 p.m. to 4 p.m.	*kalagalla*
4 p.m. to 5 p.m.	*harsheda akalagalla*
5 p.m. to 6 p.m.	*kakalseema* (when the cattle return home)
6 p.m. to 7 p.m.	*shisheeba* (twilight and sunset)
Sunset	*dumateta*
7 p.m. to 8 p.m.	*shisheeba'aguta* (when it becomes quite dark)
8 p.m. and for a time after	*edowa* (suppertime)
Night	*halgeta*

Most of these words refer to natural conditions, as for instance, *guiada 'guta*; *guiada* means 'day', or 'light', and *aguta* means 'big';

thus the expression means 'great light', for the time of day during which the sun reaches its zenith. *Kakalseema*, whose etymology is obscure, was linked on the other hand with the coming home of the cattle (in the minds of my informants), which is not a celestial event, but a social one; this also is true of another division of time, *edowa*, or suppertime. But clearly most of their divisions of the day are related to the sun, and the degree of light it is producing, and its position in the sky. Their time-classification is not exhausted by these divisions of the day.

Both years and days immediately preceding the present can be referred to by precise expressions:

Day before day before yesterday	*ĥata kalla*
Day before yesterday	*ĥala kalle*
Yesterday	*ĥala*
Today	*awe*
Tomorrow	*pari*
Day after tomorrow	*pardani*
Day after day after tomorrow	*namaguli*
Day after day after day after tomorrow	*sedaguli*

In ordinary conversation *ĥata kalla* is very rarely used, *ĥala kalle* being preferred instead; its general meaning, besides 'the day before yesterday' is 'the other day'. *Namaguli* and *sedaguli* are not often used either.

There is also a series of terms for the years immediately preceding and succeeding the present.

Year before last	*paratura*
Last year	*paraballe*
This year	*parama*
Next year	*paraua*
Year after next	*paragedo*

It will be obvious from the preceding descriptions of the various units of time-reckoning that they are not the reflection of social activities, but constitute a separate scale of reference, based on the movement of celestial bodies. Nevertheless, since these units of measurement are not only correlated with social activities, but also can be projected into the future or the past, they raise the problem of the extent to which the possiblity of making precise references to future or past events affects Konso ideas about the relation of the past and future to the present.

It is particularly noteworthy that many Konsiña words for time and movement can be used for space and movement. *Ĥata isegi* means 'Long ago, it is far'. *Porra isegi* means 'the path is far'. In the same way *idehi*, 'it is near', can be used of a place or an event, or a month or a day. Words of movement can also be used in spatial and temporal contexts, e.g. *loalla ideni*, 'the cattle are coming', and *Sambatta ideni*, 'Sunday is coming'. *Mackina paleda itarbe*, 'the car has passed the town', and *Pardubota itarbe*, 'Pardubota (month of) has passed'. *Kodasede ibiramde*, 'this work has been finished', and *parama ibiramde*, 'this year has been finished'.

They have sufficiently clear a concept of a month, for example, so that as one day succeeds another they can conceptualize the month as beginning with thirty days and ending with none, so that when it ends they can say '*ibiramde*' which means literally 'it has been exhausted, used up'.

I think they do conceive the sequence of years, months, and days as analogous to points on a journey, landmarks on a path along which they are going. This is clearly shown in their parallel usages for movement in space and time. The word for 'future', *turoba*, is a good illustration of this, as it can also be used in the sense of 'beyond', spatially—*iĩōda turoba*, 'beyond the hill'. It might be argued, however, that they conceive spatial distance in terms of temporal distance, as exemplified by such expressions as 'a journey of two days' distance'. But it seems more plausible to treat spatial and topographical distance as the model for temporal distance because of its concreteness and the simplicity of apprehending it.

But we should not conclude from this that they regard the future as in any sense pre-ordained. The fact that they can project the cycle of months or drum-holders indefinitely into the past or future does not imply that they believe these units of measurement to be 'attached' in any way to concrete events, except perhaps the outline pattern of the seasons. It may be objected that their belief in divination must imply a belief in a pre-ordained future. But they believe that in dreams, which are the principal instrument of divination, the soul leaves the body and has mystical experiences of its own. It is of the greatest importance to realize that good or bad dreams are not merely portents, but the actual experiences of the soul 'on the astral plane'. So while such dreams are held to foretell the future this is no reason to suppose that for them such a future already exists. If they did believe in a predestined future, how would this square with the use of magic by the threatened person, either to nullify the impending evil, or to get rid of it on to someone else? Since a predestined future that can be altered is a concept which is meaningless to us, it would be unjust to atttribute it to the Konso. The 'future' which the diviner foresees is nothing more than the ultimate consequences of the present dream experiences of the soul. These experiences can be compared to diseases. Just as a doctor can truly say to a person seriously bitten by a rabid dog 'In two to three weeks time you will begin to show the first signs of rabies', the diviner can say 'as a consequence of dreaming that you fell into the Sagan river and were carried away, you will soon develop sickness'; the consequences both of the dream and the disease may be avoided if the appropriate remedial action is taken. The dream is thus a mystical disease of the soul, with inevitable consequences unless appropriate magical remedies are applied, not a glimpse of a predestined future.

I am bound to mention one aspect of divination here which does not square with my argument. It was said that Sagara Gīya had successfully predicted the deaths of two people in Būso by haruspication, and as a result had been asked not to make any more such prophecies. This suggests that the act of prophecy itself may be thought of almost as a spell with maleficent force; indeed, we frequently find in the literature on divination that the acceptance of a prophecy by those to whom it refers is a necessary condition of its efficacy. The implications of this are too complex to pursue here, but it is at least clear that the force of Sagara Gīya's prophecies could not derive from a belief in a predestined future, since his neighbours, by asking him to refrain from publishing such prophecies any more, seem to believe that his silence is in itself sufficient to prevent such misfortunes. But, of course, if they were truly pre-ordained they would happen whether he publicly predicted them or not.

If one asks 'Does God know all the future?' meaning by this, for example, whether the next rains will be good, they would certainly answer 'yes', but this is simply because God himself sends the rain; and His knowledge of the future is nothing more than His awareness of His own intentions.

There is a general belief that there are a few people who can foretell the character of the coming year by observing the stars. As the following text makes clear, the knowledge of the future which is supposed to be obtained in this way is closely associated with God. My informants talked of 'looking up at God' as they observed the stars, with the implication that the characteristics of the stars in some way reflect the dispositions of the Almighty.

We look at the moon, up at God, and we look at Pūza [the Pleiades] [to see if] this year will be good or bad. We look up at the moon and the stars; in one year there will be a battle, we see it in the sky, in one year the millet will flourish, and a year may come when there is no millet, thus we see in the sky. There were battles in the past; they looked up at God and saw which town was to be defeated and burned. In the coming year they see a great sickness in the sky, they who know how to observe, and tell it to the people and say 'This year is bad', and 'This year is good'. People who thus look up at God are the diviners of Garati. They see the coming year, how the gourd plant will flourish, how the finger-millet will fare, how it will ripen, this they see in the sky. As the stars form their configurations [Literally, 'set up house'] the observers watch their configurations. Thus the observers watch, and in the month of Keesha they watch for the future year to see if there will be a bad year, and how the millet will ripen . . . Hunger destroys people, our old people, so they look up at God, and say 'This year will be good, prepare your fields, work hard, the millet will ripen' thus the watcher informs the people. In another year he says 'This year will be bad with no rain' thus he tells them. At this time [when the informant is speaking] in Garati the sun is fierce in the face. In this month the sun is fierce in the face, in this month of Poringa, and they look at the sun to see the path of sowing, so that there will be no sowing before the strength of the sun has waned, and when its strength has gone away they sow, after the rains have begun. Now this month is Poringa, and the month which is coming is Oiba, and in the dark half [i.e. the second half] of Oiba they begin to sow, and prepare the fields for the coming year. . . .

This text makes it clear that the future which is supposed to be foreseeable in the dispositions of the celestial bodies is of two different sorts, the recurring future of the seasons, where the only element of doubt is when they will come, and much more definite events, such as epidemics and battles. I had a long discussion with an old man of Degato who was a star-gazer, and asked him if he could tell which town would be burned in the coming year, or if sickness would come. It appeared that the popular claims for the powers of the seers are much exaggerated compared with their own estimate of their capabilities. Apo Tonīda, the old man in question, said that one could not tell precisely which town would be burnt, but if there was a very dry year, it would not only make it much easier for a town to catch fire, but the social tensions generated by famine would make battles all the more likely. He said that sickness came in the form of night mist after the rains, and implied that this mist, *'giya*, 'smoke', was the direct cause of sickness. (*'Giya* is another word for sickness.)

There are apparently a few stars whose positions are believed to determine some events in the coming year, such as rainfall, and murrain, but these can be interpreted as signs of the intentions of God. Waĝa is so emphatically associated with the heavens that it seems quite proper to interpret celestial signs as indications of His intentions. We may conclude that their beliefs in star-divination do not rest on any assumptions of a predestined future.

They have a clear conception of large distances of time in the past. I have a text in which my informant calculates the number of years since the arrival of the Amhara, by using the drum cycles in Būso. His answer is correct to the very year. Again, I was told for example that about 360 years ago some men in armour had raided Konso, and killed the Bamalle, but were defeated by the walled defences, and had gone quickly back to their own land. The person who told me this said he knew how long ago it was because it had happened at the time when the first stone had been put in Bakasha wood,[1] which makes his figure of 360 years quite accurate.

Ĥata, 'ago, in the past', has a very relative significance, depending on the scale being used. It can relate to a man's lifetime, or to a long sequence of sets; my best informant in Degato knew the sets back to a distance of 150 years from the present day. Remoter still, family events such as the story that the ancestors of the Bamalle family came from Liban, in Borana, and lived in various different places on their journey to Konso, are told as matters of fact, and probably are factual, at least in part. Even further back in time are the events which led to the foundation of Konso—the establishment of the grading systems which were supposedly copied from the Burji. Yet while they may be very unsure of the actual number of years which have elapsed since such events took place, they have no doubt that the events were of exactly the same kind as are happening to them in their own lives. The founding fathers of their society were no mythical 'culture heroes'.

[1] See below, p. 192 n. 1.

But when we come to legends about how things began we are on more difficult ground. For there are legends about the ancestors of real families, whose descendants are alive today; the story for example that the first lineage priest Shirto was born from a black gourd, or that when a Bamalle died childless a snake begot a child on his wife to continue the line. There are other stories which relate to legendary events (legendary in that they could not possibly have happened), which clearly are supposed to have happened in the last two or three hundred years—the story of the well of Ħambara, on p. 294, for example. While they have a good sense of history, therefore, they include in their annals stories which we should consider legendary, but which to them, with a more lively belief in the working of supernatural forces in their world than we have, would also appear as factually true. It would not be justifiable to conclude that as the period of their stories recedes in time, the nature of the action becomes more 'supernatural'.

Their calendar certainly has important practical uses, but it seems clear that it has been elaborated beyond the demands of simple agricultural necessity. After all, activity in the fields goes on in relation to the climatic conditions, and to celestial events which, in a lunar calendar, can have no permanent relationship to the names of the months.

Nor is the concept of a year of any use in the computation of personal ages without a sequence of years anchored at some fixed point in the past, as the Christian, Jewish, and Muslim systems are. The eighteen-year cycle is the longest sequence of years of this type, and of course it is far too short for keeping the reckoning of a human lifetime. In any case, they are not really interested in their exact ages.

Market days are of course very important social occasions, and it is natural that each day in question should bear the name of its market, but a sequence of market days does not constitute a calendar.

It seems that their concern with categorizing duration is not just a matter of practical convenience, but a cultural obsession. This belief is supported by the nature of the grading systems, part of whose appeal, I will suggest, is that they regulate the experience of one type of social change—the process by which a person advances in status from infancy to senility. The generation-grades are, among other things, a form of social calendar.

VI
THE GENERATION-GRADING SYSTEMS

THE Konso generation-grading systems are their most complex institutions. They differ from age-grading systems in that one's position in the system at birth depends on that occupied by one's father, and by the automatic promotion of everyone at the end of a fixed number of years. But because the Konso systems are based upon generational status and upon a fixed cycle of years, there is an inherent difficulty in maintaining some sort of correlation between the grades and the average age of their occupants, which does not arise in true age-grading systems.

I use the term 'generation-grade', or more briefly, 'grade' to refer to the fixed categories in the hierarchies through which men are promoted. Within each grade there may be one or two groups called *harriyāda*, which possess a distinctive name which they retain throughout the lives of the members, and which does not recur. I call these groups 'sets', and they are structurally analogous to age-sets in true age-grading systems. Unlike the grades, which are the same throughout a region, the names of sets are peculiar to each town. There is a third type of group which has no counterpart among age-grading systems, but which in one region bears a superficial resemblance to the dual division of the Masai age-sets into 'Stones' and 'Leopards', or the Karimojong age-sets into 'Brass' and 'Copper'. Since this type of group is unique to the Konso I use their own word *ḥrelta*.

There are three grading systems in Konso, and I shall first consider the one which operates in Garati.

I. THE GARATI SYSTEM

The grades are as in Table 35.

In fact these names really designate the *people* who occupy the grades. The grades themselves are Farīyūma, Ḥrelūma, Kadūma, etc. The *-ūma* suffix corresponds to the English '-hood', meaning 'quality of', as in 'fatherhood', so 'Fariyūma', for example, can be translated as 'Farīdahood'. This is a refinement, however, which having been mentioned can well be ignored. I shall defer a descrip-

PLATE VIII. Men's house

TABLE 35. *Garati grades*

Ukūda	
'Gulula	
'Gurula	
Orshāda	*shēnita* (adults)
Kada	
Ĥrela	
Farīda	

tion of the social function of each grade until I have analysed the principles underlying the operation of the whole system.

Everyone, as soon as he[1] is born, is placed in a grade whose rank is solely dependent on the grade of his father. This is the first and most important rule. Secondly, the interval between the father and all his sons is always two grades and nothing else. Thirdly, no one may marry before he reaches Ĥrela grade. Fourthly, every eighteen years there is a great festival called Kadabaha. At this time everyone in Garati moves up one grade, simultaneously. No movements between grades can take place at any other time.

Let us suppose that a man enters Ĥrela at the age of twenty, an age when he is sufficiently mature to marry if he wishes, though no one is compelled to marry when he enters Ĥrela. After a year his first son is born. This child will not be in Farīda, but what we may term for convenience 'Farīda-1'. Children in this category are sometimes referred to as 'Little Farīda', but it is not an official grade. One year of the cycle has now passed, and there are another seventeen still to go before the next Kadabaha. At the end of this time the son will move up to Farīda, and his father will move up to Kada. The son will remain another eighteen years in Farīda, after which he will enter Ĥrela, and be allowed to marry. At this time he will be thirty-five years old. This is the maximum age at which anyone can enter Ĥrela, since the son could not have been born earlier than one year after his father entered Ĥrela himself.[2] His father will have further sons, but they will not have to wait as long as first-born sons before entering Ĥrela, as can be seen from Fig. 10. Let us suppose that the father has another son two years before the end of the cycle in which the eldest son was born. This younger son will only spend

[1] In the Garati system women as well as men are included in the grading system. But since all these systems focus upon the role of men in society, for brevity's sake I refer to sons only.

[2] In rare cases irregular unions between men and women below Ĥrela are tolerated, but all children conceived as a result must be aborted.

two years in Farīda-1, instead of seventeen like his elder brother. At the age of two he will enter Farīda, and, eighteen years later Ĥrela, at the age of twenty. Succeeding brothers, if born when their father is in Kada, will start life in Farīda, not Farīda-1, because of the rule that all children are two and only two grades behind their father. The sons of a father in Orshāda will start in Ĥrela at birth. The consequence of this will be that eldest sons will have a longer

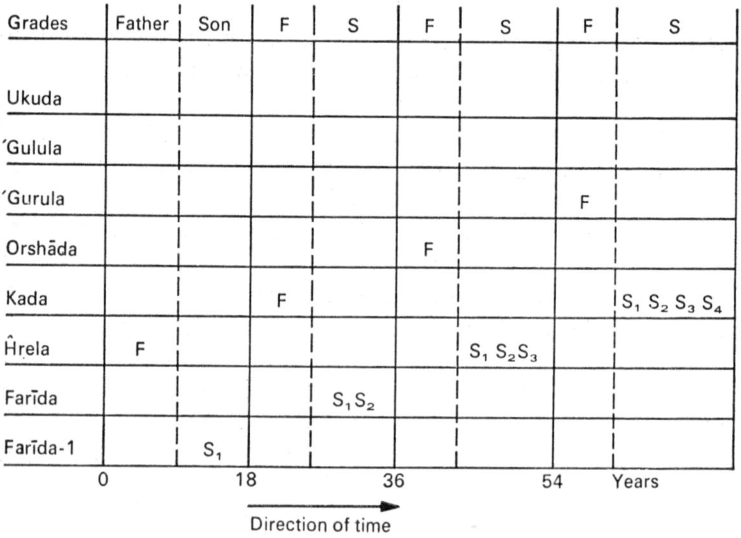

Grades	Father	Son	F	S	F	S	F	S
Ukuda								
'Gulula								
'Gurula							F	
Orshāda					F			
Kada			F					S₁ S₂ S₃ S₄
Ĥrela	F					S₁ S₂S₃		
Farīda				S₁ S₂				
Farīda-1		S₁						

0   18   36   54   Years

→ Direction of time

S₁ = eldest son, S₂ = second son, etc.

FIG. 10. The progress of fathers and sons through the Garati system

obligatory delay before marriage than their brothers. All will enter Ĥrela together whatever their ages. So also the children of younger sons will be in higher grades than the children of elder sons, on the average, because their fathers, being younger at the age of marriage will still be having children when their elder brothers have ceased to do so.

The problem of the excessive promotion of younger sons is aggravated by polygyny, which extends the fertile period of a man's life. We saw in the section on kinship in Chapter III that a woman was not supposed to bear children after her first son had married, and this would also prevent her husband begetting further children of his own at the same time as his son. But by marrying more wives a man can avoid this restriction, and there are thus a few men who manage to extend their fertile years over more than thirty years, and whose youngest children are the same age as their grandchildren. The result of this is that while they are of the same age they are of different generations, and will be graded accordingly, and will, if their father is in 'Gurula, for example, start life in Kada. Let us take an instance of this sort to see how the grading system deals with it.

A boy whose father is in 'Gurula is born in Kada after one year of the cycle has elapsed. He will enter Orshāda when he is seventeen, and may perhaps marry when he is twenty in three years time. His first son may be born a year later, and will enter Ĥrela, with another fourteen years of the cycle to go. If this boy in turn married when he was twenty, that is, having been in Kada for six years, and produced a son a year later, this boy, the grandson of the boy born into Kada originally, will be born into Farīda and remain in it eleven years. We can see, therefore, that if a man has sons when he is in the high grades, normally occupied by grandfathers, while these sons too will be in unusually high grades, in two generations this deviation will be almost obliterated. The examples I gave were all eldest sons, of course, and the 'upgrading effect' will still increase for the younger sons as they will be born when their fathers are higher up the grade system, and when there are fewer years to elapse in the cycle. But ultimately this deviation will disappear for younger sons as well. It should be remembered that very few men (between 5 and 10 per cent) have two wives, and there is a high level of infant mortality, which means that this disturbing element in the grading systems is quite small.

I found that the grades did roughly correlate with the apparent average ages of their members, and the reasons for this are as follows:

(1) Men cannot marry when they are in Farīda. If they could it would mean that men who only entered Ĥrela when they were thirty might already have a ten-year-old son, who would enter Farīda-1, and if this boy himself married in ten years time, his son would be in Farīda-3, by the two-grade rule, and would have to wait another seven years until he entered Farīda-2, where he would spend eighteen years, another eighteen in Farīda-1, and another eighteen in Farīda, making sixty-one years in all before he entered Ĥrela. This would gradually erode the whole system, as some men would never reach the higher grades at all, a disability which would spread to all their progeny.

(2) The rule that all sons are two grades behind their fathers means that sons of upgraded fathers are pushed down two grades, and their start in the system is largely wiped out.

(3) A further important consideration is that the rule forbidding marriage only applies to men in Farīda. Men who are born into higher grades are not affected by it, and will tend to marry earlier, and their sons are born lower down in the system than if their fathers had had to wait longer before marriage, and in consequence had advanced further up the system. This factor operates in conjunction with (2) above to help nullify the deviation of upgraded fathers.

The system therefore stratifies the generations into three blocks of two grades each, for grandfathers, fathers, and sons respectively, in the following manner:[1]

TABLE 36. *Grades and generations*

'Gurula	grandfathers
Orshāda	
Kada	fathers
Ĥrela	
Farīda	sons
Farīda–1	

Ĥrela and Kada are both composed of fathers (in the sense that they are formally capable of begetting sons—they are, of course, sons themselves in relation to *their* fathers), and Orshāda and 'Gurula are composed of grandfathers. Ĥrela is the first grade in which men are allowed to marry, and the sons of Kada are still in Farīda, so this is why neither Ĥrela nor Kada can contain grandfathers, whatever the actual age of their members. When a man enters Orshāda his sons enter Ĥrela, and are allowed to marry. Thus Orshāda men are potentially grandfathers, even if some individuals may be too young to be of marrying age. 'Gurula men, *a fortiori*, are grandfathers as well. The stratification of grade members into their generational status is, however, only one way of considering the grading system. We can also think of it as regulating the speed and order in which the generations pass the dividing line

---

[1] The two upper grades, 'Gulula and Ukuda, which should contain great-grandfathers, are in practice unfilled. I never found anyone in Ukuda, and only two men in 'Gulula. I shall deal with the historical reasons for their existence later.

between Farīda and Ḣrela. The operation of the system is designed
to delay the opportunities of marriage to the younger generation
until their parents have finished begetting. As an informant put it,
'A family produces a son, and he grows up, and his father and
mother are still fertile; so they say that it is good that the boy should
be in Farīda for a time. It is bad for the son and the father to be begetting at the same time. When the father and the son are begetting
together God does not send rain.' I shall consider the religious
implications of this text later, but in social terms it is clear that the
system is seen as separating the generations sequentially, so that
they beget in order of seniority, and assume the rights and duties
of each grade in due order.

A man is forbidden to marry a woman in his father's grade, as
she is, in terms of the system, his mother—this rule applying irrespective of the actual grade of his own mother. The same rule applies
reciprocally to women. I could find no other marriage restrictions
in Garati deriving from the grading system, apart, of course, from
that relating to Farīda.

But the grades are only part of the system. In Garati the members
of each grade are either Galgussa or Hirba, as follows:

TABLE 37. *Grades and ḣrelta*

Ukuda	Hirba
'Gulula	Galgussa
'Gurula	Hirba
Orshāda	Galgussa
Kada	Hirba
Ḣrela	Galgussa
Farīda	Hirba
Farīda-1	Galgussa

A man is a member of Galgussa or Hirba, as he is a member of
Farīda or Ḣrela, by inheritance from his father, but the difference
is that he stays in Galgussa or Hirba all his life. Galgussa and Hirba
are both referred to as *ḣrelta*. If a man is Galgussa all his sons are
Galgussa, and if he is Hirba, all his sons are Hirba. It is said that
Ḣrela is Galgussa at the moment (1966), and at the end of the
eighteen-year cycle Ḣrela will be Hirba, and Kada will be Galgussa.
At the present time the function of the Galgussa/Hirba division
seems only to clarify the operation of the grading system by separating the generational sequences Farīda–Kada–'Gurula, who are

related as S–F–FF, and Ḥrela–Orshāda–'Gulula, who are also related S–F–FF. But the Galgussa/Hirba division is not just for purposes of clarification. It is said that in the long past Galgussa contained only eldest sons, and Hirba only younger sons. While there is, of course, now no direct means of verifying whether or not this account of the origin of Galgussa and Hirba is true, there is overwhelming evidence to support it. Galgussa/Hirba are integrally related to the grading system, and to no other part of their social organization. In Takadi a similar division, into Galgussa, Melgussa, and Hirba is also operating, related in the same way to the grading system, and it is said there that Galgussa was originally composed of eldest sons, Melgussa of second-born sons, and Hirba of younger sons. Finally, in Turo where the corresponding divisions are called Barbihīda and Ḥalibihīda, Barbihīda is still today composed of eldest sons, and Ḥalibihīda of younger sons, in precisely the same way as the Garati system is said once to have worked. I do not think, therefore, that there is any reasonable doubt that Konso tradition on the origin of these divisions is correct. But grading systems which operated on the principle of sibling seniority as well as generational seniority would clearly have worked differently from the contemporary systems, and I shall consider this problem in section 4 of this chapter when I analyse the grading systems in their demographic context.

We have still not exhausted the complexities of the Garati system, however, as there is yet a third group related to the grading system, the *harriyāda*. The *harriyāda* are what we may call 'sets'; that is, they are named groups whose members remain in these groups throughout their lives, the names being non-recurring, and dying out with the last member of the group. The operation of this system will become clear if I give an example, from Būso, of how the sets operate at present (Table 38).

These sets are not established until the men enter Ḥrela. While the grades themselves contain women as well as men, it was emphasized to me that the sets are only for men. This is understandable since the sets are closely associated with warfare, and the victorious sets are commemorated by phallic stones, the *'daga 'deerūma*, in the *moras*. Although the word *harriyāda* means 'age-mate', in the sense of children who have grown up and played together and is explicitly said to have been borrowed from the Borana it can be seen from the chart that they are not only perfectly integrated with the grades, but the senior and junior sets are not recruited on the basis of age at all, but of sibling seniority, eldest sons preceding younger sons, and it seems likely that this organization of the sets is a survival of the arrangement of the grades when the *ḥrelta* distinguished between eS and yS.

TABLE 38. *Grades, ḥrelta, and sets*

Grades	Ḥrelta	Sets		
		Orḥasha	eS	dead
		Kīyala	yS	
Ukuda	H	Onīla	eS	dead
		Kandala	yS	
'Gulula	G	'Gaḍasha	eS	dead
		Kīlōla	yS	
'Gurula	H	'Gawasha	eS	
		Torumfada	yS	
Orshāda	G	'Gasha	eS	
		Tirkyēda	yS	
Kada	H	Arabala	eS	
		Kamamura	yS	
Ḥrela	G	Fulasi	eS	
		Tinīla	yS	
Farīda	H	··················		

When the men enter Ḥrela they are not all immediately divided into sets. For the first nine years only the eS have a set, and the younger brothers are nameless. In the tenth year (nine is inauspicious) these, too, are given a name. These names are traditional, and while formally speaking they are not recurring, over a long period of time some will be used again. I was told that originally they were the names of men who had been famous warriors; the same names constantly appear not only in other towns of Garati, but also in Takadi and Turo. The sets do not appear to have any corporate duties nowadays, but this is presumably the result of the cessation of warfare brought about by the Amhara.

So far I have concentrated on a purely technical exposition of the working of the system. Let us now consider the social functions of each grade.

Farīda is essentially the grade of childhood, and its members have a number of privileges and restrictions connected with this. The chief restriction on boys and girls is that they may not marry. Temporary liaisons are occasionally permitted, but these must be childless, and if any girl becomes pregnant she is made to have an abortion. A Farīda boy may not claim the honours of killing a game animal, nor sacrifice, if he is a priest, nor take part in a council. On the other hand, since they are not considered as fully responsible agents, they are not held strictly to account for accidental damage to property; if a Farīda boy threw a stone and by mistake killed a domestic animal it would be said that he did not realize what he was doing. This indulgence, however, does not extend to outright delinquency.

The entry into Ħrela is the greatest step in a man's life. For now he can marry, hold a triumph for killing a lion or leopard, join a council, and sacrifice. Moreover, he is now considered as pre-eminently a warrior, with the primary responsibility for defending the town against invaders. Ħrela also used to be the police force of each town, apprehending and punishing criminals on the orders of the councils.

Kada's functions are different. They bless Ħrela, and curse the grubs, ants, birds, and other pests that infest the crops. At the conclusion of the Sōla festival in Būso they were carried round the *mora* on the shoulders of the men of Ħrela.

Orshāda are seen as very similar in function to Kada. When the lineage priest reaches this grade he has the right to wear the *hallasha*, the phallic head ornament, at religious ceremonies.

'Gurula marks the period of decline in a man's influence and faculties, when he withdraws from active life. They have no particular duties to the members of other grades, though they retain their capacity to bless.

As I mentioned earlier, there are scarcely any men in 'Gulula or Ukuda. Of 'Gulula it is said *etaninjo*, 'they are incapable', and of Ukuda *itawde*, 'they have gone away'. I show below that originally the Garati system was based on a nine-year cycle, and it was the change from the nine- to the eighteen-year cycle which left these two grades almost functionless; nevertheless, under the old system they would still have contained the oldest members of society, and represented senility and useless dependence in the ideal hierarchy of the grades. For the grades cannot, by the rules of the system, be anything more than ideal types. Certainly, the average age of their members is correlated with grade status, such that in all systems the youngest men are in the bottom grades, and the oldest men in the top, but generation grades can never attain the degree of correlation in this respect which occurs in true age-grading systems.

It is possible to suggest interpretations of the names of the first four grades. 'Farīda' may be derived from *farada*, a type of locust, only eaten by children, not even by adolescents, and hence a symbol of infantile status. 'Ĥrela' may be derived from *ĥrēla*, meaning boundary, the implication being that they are the men who guard the territory of a particular town. 'Kada' may be related to *Kadana*, the great rains, as the primary function of Kada is to bless and bring the prosperity of nature. The name 'Kada' is found in Galla generation-grading systems in Ethiopia, and these people also use the word *Kadana* to refer to the great rains. 'Orshāda' may be derived from *orshīda*, rhinoceros; it is the rhinoceros horn which is used to curse, and this may imply that the essential function of Orshāda is to curse pests. I cannot suggest any interpretation for the last three grades.

The status of women in the grading systems varies. In Garati they are said to belong to the same grades as their brothers, and in this region the women of Kada take part in a ceremony (described in Chapter VII) in which they bless their sons in Farīda. But while in Garati the women of Farīda are subject to the same prohibition on marriage as their brothers, as soon as Kadabaha is over they, unlike their brothers, are free to marry. The boys are expected to wait at least another two years (and sometimes four or five) so that their first child will be born in the auspicious third year of the cycle, I was told. The following text expresses their different attitudes to the marriage of women and men once they have entered Ĥrela. (In rare instances a Farīda boy and girl are allowed to live together, but any pregnancy resulting from the union must be aborted.)

Two Farīda marry, but there is no bearing of children; if there is a child in the womb it is got rid of. When Kadabaha has come, the [late] Farīda girl says 'I will not have any more abortions with you; you have five more years yet. But my years are finished. I am a *shēnita* [adult] and I will marry someone else.'

Thus while it is necessary to impose such restraint on girls marrying as is provided by Farīda (to prevent them being married by older men, I was told, and their male contemporaries thus being deprived of potential wives when the time came for them to marry) it is clearly regarded as less important to delay the marriage of girls than of boys. Indeed, as we shall see in examining the Takadi system, the girls are actually promoted a grade above their brothers to reduce the delay before their marriage. In Takadi and Turo, moreover, women are not said to have any grades once they have become *shēnita*. It seems likely therefore that, since the grades above Farīda are basically concerned with the social categories of warriorhood and elderhood, from which women are excluded, it is regarded as socially beneficial not to restrict the numbers of marriageable women beyond the limit imposed by the Farīda rule. The application of the Farīda rule to women as well as men is probably dictated not only by the need to preserve a supply of wives for the young men, but also because it is considered bad for the fecundity of daughters to overlap that of their mothers, though less serious than for the fecundity of sons to overlap that of their fathers. In Garati, as I have mentioned, women do have grades beyond Farīda, but this is because in this region the social role of motherhood is given more official recognition than in the other two regions.

In Garati the end of the eighteen-year cycle is marked by the most important ceremony of all, called the Kadabaha. If this word has any connection with the Kada grade, it could be roughly translated as the 'becoming Kada'. The ceremony is held in the month of Pillello but the exact day is decide by the holders of the two sacred drums, and announced to those towns in Garati which come to the ceremony. There is some doubt as to whether Kō'ja, Nagule, Tapata, and Kamole come to the same *mora* as the rest of Garati, as they are something of outsiders. It seems likely that they hold ceremonies of their own at the same time. Among the population of the central towns of Garati there is a small element which goes to its own *mora* out in the fields, called Mirig,[1] because they have a tradition of a separate ancestral origin in Ilota, the hills just to the northeast of Konso. Beyond the fact that the *mora* priest Luko presides over their ceremony, I was unable to discover any more about this ritual. An informant gave me the following text:

Long ago the Ilota or Monorĝda people came, and their ceremony

[1] Phonetically, the word 'Mirig' is, by ending in *-ig*, quite untypical of Konsiña.

took place at the Mora Mirig. There was no Mora Damalle then. Another people came from Ala and these were the Garati people. Their *mora* was Damalle, and at all ceremonies no Monorĝda person came to Damalle; their priests were different. One was called Luko, his house is at Patangaldo, and he is a ceremonial official, and of Galgussa, and is the chief priest of Mirig. At Degato there is a priest called Argashe who is of Hirba, and performs the ceremonies at Mirig for Hirba.

I shall ignore this deviation, which only concerns a small minority of the population, and concentrate on the ritual at Damalle, and its associated *moras*.

Damalle is a dense thicket of trees and cacti about three-quarters of an hour's walk from Idigle in the country to the east. It covers about two acres. Within it is a small enclosure entered by two narrow paths through the vegetation. This enclosure is almost on the edge of the thicket, and is dominated by an *ulahita*, beside which is a fireplace.

On the appointed day, if the members of Ĥrela grade are Galgussa, they go to the *mora* at Olanda called Kidoma, whose priest is Doho. The Kidoma is a small slab of stone, said by some to have been put there by God.[1] Others say that when their ancestors first came to Konso they found it there already, so how can men know its origin? It is possible that it is a relic of the mysterious predecessors of the Konso who are supposed to have dug some of the wells —the Mādo people. It is often referred to as 'the navel of Garati'.

If the men of Ĥrela grade are Hirba they go to the Mora Hirle in Idigle, whose *mora* priest is Hirle. Whichever *mora* they go to, they have to sit in silence, with a small black cloth over their heads (called a *talboyada*; such a cloth is supposed to be thrust into the jaws of a lion when it is killed). Nor can they eat, except for chewing the leaves of the *khat* plant; this grows in many parts of Ethiopia, and when chewed can allay the pangs of hunger. They are allowed only to drink milk. While the men of Ĥrela have gone to one or other of these *moras*, those of Farīda who are old enough to do so have gone out to hunt for the dik-dik, a small antelope. If they are unlucky this may take them two or three days, and I was told that Ĥrela must remain in their *mora* throughout this time. It is possible however that everyone returns home at night, and continues the next day. Only an eye-witness account could definitely establish

[1] The typical *daga deeruma* is a pillar, and much taller than the Kidoma, which only stands about 3 ft. high.

this. The little boys of Farīda, who are too young to hunt, remain in their towns. When Farīda catch their dik-dik, they take it still alive to the *mora* Damalle, where the priest of the *mora*, Kallala of Lehīda, kills it. When it is dead, the assembled Farīda give a great shout, which is heard from the Hirle or Kidoma *moras* on the hills above, and the men of Ĥrela there know that they are now Kada. In Damalle, Kallala cuts the skin of the dik-dik into tiny pieces, and each boy is given one. The Bamalle also comes to the Mora Damalle, accompanied by a virgin of the Ĥolo family in Lehīda. They both bless the boys of Farīda, who have now become Ĥrela, and the Bamalle is said to receive a black substance called *irgeda* from God, or the sky, with which he anoints the eyes of the boys.

Each boy who attends the ceremony in the Mora Damalle wears over his (right?) shoulder the skin of a dik-dik, cut into strips, to the ends of which are sewn bundles of the wing-cases of a large reddish-brown beetle, called *takita*. Cowrie shells are also sewn on to the skin. These skins are preserved and handed down in families. It would not be possible for them to be freshly prepared before each Kadabaha, in view of the scarcity of dik-diks. In Takadi the young men entering Ĥrela there carry bundles of thick plaited threads with numerous red seeds sewn to the ends.

A bull is also killed, and a new *ulahita* erected. At this time the ritual fire will be lighted, and watched for three nights. A new stone is brought and erected in the Bakasha wood just below Damalle, to mark the beginning of a new cycle.[1]

[1] There are now twenty-one of these stones in two rows, one row for Galgussa, one row for Hirba. As Galgussa enters Ĥrela, a stone is placed in its row, and the same is done for Hirba when it enters Ĥrela. Now in the days when Galgussa and Hirba were not hereditary there would have been less point in distinguishing them so clearly; moreover, it is likely that, in the event of so drastic a revolution in the grading system as changing its basis from nine to eighteen years, and making Galgussa/Hirba hereditary there would be a break in the lines of stones, but there is none. This being so, we can assume that the first stone marked the beginning of the new system, and calculate that, since in 1966 there were five years to the end of the cycle, the number of *lunar* years (the Konso do not calculate by solar years) since the first stone was put in is 373 years. Making allowance for leap years and the extra days of the solar year, it follows that the first stone was erected 361½ years before 1966, i.e. in A.D. 1604½. Moreover, this was clearly a late development in the evolution of the grading system. Neither of the other regions registers the passage of the cycles by stones and it is clear that the whole Garati system is the result of a long period of evolution, since while it has a marked resemblance to the Takadi, there are important divergences, which have occurred over a long period of time. (The present cycle in Takadi ends in the same year as that in Garati, which shows that there was a very strong tie in the past.)

At the other two *moras* the two sacred drums, Kadana and Dokona, have been brought, and are beaten by the priest of the *mora*. At the Hirle *mora* there is a little ritual 'house' of stones set in the ground where the priest Hirle sits with the drums.

During the Kadabaha, probably after the killing of the dik-dik, there occurs the 'circumcision' of three old men in Damalle. They are selected from priestly families—there is some doubt about exactly which ones. They are from Hirba, if Ḥrela is composed of Hirba men before the ceremony begins, or from Galgussa if Ḥrela is Galgussa. They will be from Orshāda grade, i.e., just before Orshāda is promoted to 'Gurula. The 'circumcision' actually consists of nicking the tip of the foreskin, so that blood flows; the whole foreskin is not removed. During the ceremony they wear skirts, and after it are not supposed to have children, or even sexual intercourse. It is said that they become women. If the representatives of the families in question do not wish to undergo this ordeal they can hire another man with similar qualifications, i.e., who is in the same grade and is a grandfather. The operator is a man from Ala who comes especially for the ceremony.[1] As we have seen, when a man in 'Gurula has a child it disturbs the working of the grading system by placing the baby in a high grade at birth, but even more important is the fact that it makes it almost inevitable that fathers and sons will be propagating simultaneously, only in this case it will not be F and S, but FF and F, whose fecundity periods are overlapping. It is possible that at one time all men entering 'Gurula were prohibited from begetting any more children, and this rule would have been analogous to that preventing procreation by Farīda.

When the ceremonies in the chief *moras* have ended the men return to their towns. Looking out from the walls to see the return of the new Ḥrela and Kada is forbidden, and anyone caught doing so will low like a cow, and say 'Umbaaa. I am a cow. I don't know what I am doing.' When they arrive in the towns the new Ḥrela grade run around the walls, kicking their shields, and then go to the *moras*, while they dance the *seega*. The Kada dance the Heemasha, in which they are carried round on the shoulders of Ḥrela, announcing that they are now Kada. The women take no

---

[1] A similar ceremony takes place in Takadi. In Turo, all the men entering the senior grade wear skirts, of a ceremonial pattern, but there is no circumcision, and, as far as I can gather, no prohibition on the procreation of children in any grade above Farīda.

part in the ceremonies, except the girls of Farīda, who are due to enter Ĥrela, have their heads shaved, and when the men of the new grades return to the towns they dance in the *moras* with their feather head-dresses.

Before I consider the nature of the grading systems as a whole I shall complete the description of the Takadi and Turo systems. This will bring out the common characteristics of all the systems, and show us which elements are confined only to one or two regions.

2. THE TAKADI SYSTEM

The Takadi system has the following grades:

TABLE 39. *Takadi grades*

Ulula
Orshāda
Apada (Kada)
Akoda
Sūga
Ĥrelita
Forita
Farīda

There are thus eight grades, as opposed to seven in Garati. These grades have rather different names from those of Garati, and there are two other major differences in the rest of its organization. The cycle is based on nine years instead of eighteen, and there are three hereditary divisions, Galgussa, Melgussa, and Hirba, instead of the two divisions, Galgussa and Hirba, in Garati. Galgussa, Melgussa, and Hirba are associated with the grades in the same way as in Garati. Basing the system on nine years means that it will take someone entering Farīda sixty-three years to reach Ulula, as opposed to the 108 years it would take someone to reach Ukuda in Garati.

There are therefore a considerable number of men in Ulula. After remaining in it for nine years, however, they do not pass beyond it and leave the grading system; they remain permanently in Ulula as long as they live.

But I found that the Takadi system was as well correlated with the apparent ages of the grade members as the Garati system, so that the youngest boys are on the whole in Farīda, and the oldest men in Orshāda or Ulula.

To understand why this is so we must now examine the way in

which the hereditary divisions of Galgussa, Melgussa, and Hirba are integrated with the grades.

At the present time the system is as follows:

TABLE 40. *Grades and ḥrelta*

Ulula	Galgussa, Melgussa, Hirba
Orshāda	Galgussa
Apada (Kada)	Melgussa
Akoda	Hirba
Sūga	Galgussa
Ḥrelita	Melgussa
Forita	Hirba
Farīda	Galgussa
Farīda–1	Melgussa

It is easy to see that this is a much more complicated system than the Garati, but the mastery of its intricacies by the people was remarkable; while I had considerable difficulty in elucidating it, this was largely my fault, not theirs. I was able to ask them the *ḥrelta* of any grade at random, and out of their fifty-four responses there were only two errors.

The movements of the G/M/H divisions through the grading system can be seen most clearly in this diagram:

	I	II	III	IV	V
Ulula	G,M,H, ...				
Orshāda	G	M	H	G	M
Apada	M	H	G	M	H
Akoda	H	G	M	H	G
Sūga	G	M	H	G	M
Ḥrelita	M	H	G	M	H
Forita	H	G	M	H	G
Farīda	G	M	H	G	M
Farīda - 1	M	H	G	M	H

Direction of time ⟶

FIG. 11. Takḥadi *relta* sequences

The column I represents the present arrangements of the grades in relation to the G/M/H division. Column II represents the arrangements which will come into being at the end of the present cycle, and III the arrangements in the next cycle. It will be seen that in IV the arrangement has returned to I again, and that V is a repetition of II.

Because the G/M/H divisions are now hereditary in the same way as the Garati ones, all sons will be three grades behind their fathers, instead of two as in Garati. While in Garati it takes a man thirty-six years to move into the grade his father was in at the time of his birth, minus the number of years already elapsed in the cycle before he was born, in Takadi it will take a man twenty-seven years to move into the grade his father was in at the time of his birth, minus the number of years already elapsed in the cycle before he was born. The halving of the length of the cycle has thus been partially nullified by the inclusion of an extra hereditary division, Melgussa, so that the time lapse between the generations is actually three-quarters that of the Garati cycle, not half, which is not sufficient to make a significant difference in the correlation between the grades and the average age of their members.

The same restrictions as in Garati on marriage by Farīda boys exists; it is said that Forita can marry, but in spite of this the ceremony at the end of the cycle, the Timba Tula, emphasizes, as in Garati, the importance of entering Ḫrela. It is said that Forita boys and girls who have married must not go near the 'Gūfa's house, and in Gaho neither Farīda nor Forita are allowed to go up on to Irbata *mora* where the ceremony of changing the grades will take place, or to mount the sacred stone where the 'circumcision' will be performed. This suggests that Forita is closer to Farīda than to Ḫrelita (indeed, many of the boys in Forita were far too young to be married), and that if they are allowed to marry, it is a concession rather like that in Garati, where if Farīda boys and girls marry they are not allowed to have children. In Takadi, however, abortions are strongly disapproved of; the girl has to leave her home town and live elsewhere until she enters the grade when she can lawfully have children. But I was told in Gaho that people in Forita are allowed to have children. One can only speculate here that over a period of time concessions may have been made allowing Forita to marry, while in the past they were only allowed to form childless liaisons.

As in Garati each grade also has a set, a *harriyāda*, attached to it, although as the cycle is only nine years there is only one *harriyāda* to each grade, and not two as in Garati.

It is said that a man should not marry into his own *ĥrelta*, a prohibition which is perhaps analogous to the Garati rule against a man marrying a woman of his mother's grade. But in Takadi, unlike Garati, women above Forita cease to have grades. As I have mentioned, the grading systems are primarily masculine institutions, and women's place in them is peripheral; once they have passed through Farīda (or, in Takadi, Forita) there are advantages in enabling them to marry without further delay. Indeed, in Takadi girls are advanced a grade in front of their brothers, by the following rule: the daughter of a Galgussa man is ranked as Hirba, the daughter of a Melgussa man is ranked as Galgussa, and the daughter of a Hirba man is ranked as Melgussa. The effect of this is to advance the girls one grade, as follows:

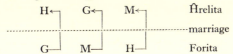

The rule can also be clearly observed in the following diagram:

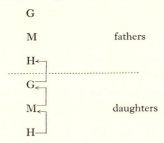

The reader may agree that the equations G = H, M = G, and H = M for the grade advances of the girls are a very elegant way of stating the rule that daughters are advanced one grade over their brothers, and show a remarkable mastery of the system.

It is said that each lineage must have representatives of Galgussa, Melgussa, and Hirba, and that if a Hirba family, for example, dies out, so that the lineage has no more Hirba members, the lineage priest will designate a member of Galgussa or Melgussa to take the place of the defunct family. My genealogical evidence supported this assertion.

The grades have the same sort of idealized characteristics as are found in the Garati system. Farīda are thought of in this scheme as useless little boys, who are allowed to play as they wish, for no one wants them. Forita work in the fields with Ḟrelita. Ḟrelita 'guard the land', and their functions are the same as those of their counterparts in Garati. Sūga have the two sacred town drums, in Gaho. I cannot speak for other towns, though I was told that the same was true for them also. The word *sūga* also means 'holder of the sacred drum' in Konsiña generally. Sūga grade is regarded as closely associated in a junior capacity with Akoda, just as Forita are the junior associates of Ḟrelita. Above Sūga the grades assume the function of blessing that I described for the Garati grades. These senior grades curse the pests which threaten the crops, and evil-doers, that they may all go far away. If one man injures another their representatives sprinkle the land with the chyme of a goat, saying 'Peace, peace, may the crops ripen'. They bless the flocks and the land, and pray that people may have many children. (The above descriptions of the functions of the grades are almost direct quotations from informants; it will be seen that the characteristics of the grades in Takadi are very close to those of Garati.)

The grades are also related to the cycle of sacred drums. There are, as I mentioned in Chapter III, two sacred drums of the region, Kadana and Dopode, which circulate separately through a fixed series of towns, and are held for nine years at a time. In Gaho and, I am told, in every other town in Takadi, there are also two sacred drums, called in Gaho Dopode and Marmede, which are held by the two ritual divisions, Kundateda and Kardōda.

TABLE 41. *Gaho drum-holders*

	Kundateda Dopode drum	Kardōda Marmede drum
Galgussa	Tapīyo family	'Danasha family
Melgussa	Surīle family	Kaldawa family
Hirba	Sāsa family	Nir'goda family

There are thus two drum-holders at any one time, both of whom are in the Sūga grade. The representatives of the family concerned will hold the drum for nine years. The retention of the drum by one family throughout the cycle means that the passing of the years has to be measured by some other means. This is done by breaking off a head of millet every year at the main harvest and putting it in a gourd kept for the purpose.

The ceremonies to mark the end of the cycle are less elaborate than in Garati, and mostly take place within the towns themselves.

I heard independently from two reliable informants that while the cycle ends in the ninth year, and the members of each grade are promoted at this time, the actual ceremony is not held until the next year. Nine is a very bad number, which is why the ceremony is postponed. Both in Takadi and Garati no ceremonies are held on the ninth day of any month.

In the ninth year all the towns send representatives to the 'Gūfa, who kills a bull and puts up an *ulahita* outside his house. At this time also the circumcision takes place, before the main ceremony called the Timba Tula in the following year. In each town there is a traditional representative of Galgussa, Melgussa, and Hirba who is cut. He should be a member of Apada about to be promoted into Orshāda and a grandfather. He stands on a special sacred rock near the Irbata *mora* of Gaho, and wears a skirt for the occasion. The operation is performed by a *hauda*. The old man concerned is not supposed to beget children afterwards.

In the tenth year the Timba Tula (the Travelling of the Drums) is celebrated in the month of Pardubota. At this time a turtle is killed, and its shell is filled with earth from a dead man's grave. This is given to a man from some other part of Konso, who travels slowly through all of Takadi, taking about three months, 'to purify the land'. He does not enter any of the towns, but lives near them, in a shelter of blankets in the fields. It is very important that he is not seen by women and children. Food is brought out to him from the towns where he is resting. When he moves from town to town a horn is sounded, and all married women hide. Eventually, when the three months have elapsed he takes the shell down to the Sagan river and throws it in. He is not supposed ever to return to Takadi, which is why he is not a native of the region. For his services he is not only well fed throughout the three months, but also paid something in the range E$20–30 (£3–4) and a goat, with its neck cut open at the back, and its tongue pulled through the aperture.

While this purification is going on (it is referred to as the 'cleansing of the land'), a man in each town goes into peoples' homesteads in the night and steps over them while they are asleep. It is bad for anyone to look up at him while he is doing this. If this rite is not performed married women may die in each town.

When the two drums of the region are being taken to their new town, married women also have to hide so as not to see them. We may conclude from this that women are thought of as having a mystically deleterious effect on the drums, as they have on the *ulahita*.

When the land has been cleansed, a ceremony is held in each town to mark the entry of Forita into Ĥrela. At Gaho it takes place at a *mora* outside and above the town, called Irbata. This is bounded on two sides by a low red cliff. Before the arrival of the 'Gufa the two drum-holders have run naked from their houses covered by the blankets of the men who are accompanying them, in a sort of moving tent. They run about a quarter of a mile beyond the *mora*, past two large trees, and return to the *mora* again. Here they meet the 'Gūfa, and ask his permission to begin the ceremony, which he gives. The drum-holders go and sit within the ritual house in the *mora*, composed of a circle of boulders, to which palings are added for the ceremony. The *shorugata* bring nine goats and sacrifice them nearby. When this has been completed and the intestines haruspicated, the 'Gūfa gives his blessing. At some time during the ceremony the boys of Forita come up on to the *mora*. Here they all take a collective set name, which they will retain throughout their lives in the grading system; also, each man on becoming a member of Ĥrela is given a new personal name by his mates. But neither here nor in any other region did I find that the members of a grade or a set were supposed to be bound together by any ties of loyalty or special friendship.

In the month of Oiba the 'Gūfa goes to the Mora Oibatale, in the fields below Majeĝe, where he sacrifices a bull and erects an *ulahita*. He is accompanied by the Apa Timba of Takadi, among other people.

3. THE TURO SYSTEM

The Turo system differs from the two systems I have already described in more respects than they differ from each other. This is consistent with the greater isolation of Turo from Garati and

PLATE IX. Women buying *shelaĝda* at the market

Takadi; I also found that Turo lacked many other features of ritual and social organization found in the other two regions, especially any system of ritually important numbers. We shall see that while the Turo grading system is complex, it has less associated ritual than the Garati and Takadi systems.

In Turo there are only four grades:

> Raga (or Shabalta)
> Pulada
> - - - - - - - - - - - - - - - Marriage allowed
> Dalda
> Farīda

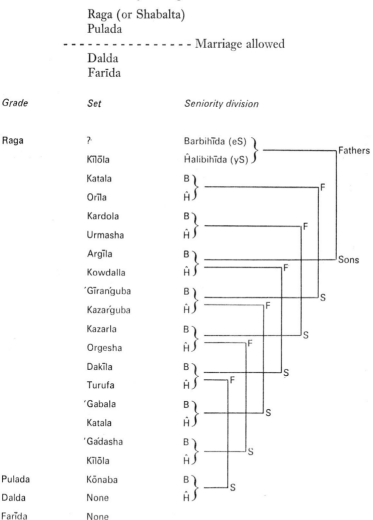

Grade	Set	Seniority division

FIG. 12. Turo grading system

The length of the cycle here, moreover, is only five years. We should expect, therefore, that it would only take twenty years to pass through the whole system, and that it would in consequence be useless for practical purposes. In fact the grades do have the same sort of correlation with the ages of their members as the grades in the other systems, a fact which puzzled me greatly when I first went there. One reason is that they have retained the principle of sibling seniority grading to the present time—eS are classified as Barbihīda, yS as Ḥalibihīda[1]—thus younger sons can be further removed from their fathers' grades than eldest sons, but even more importantly, the generations are separated by sets as well as by the B/H divisions. The system operates as shown how in Fig. 12.

It will be seen that Raga grade is composed of a series of pairs of sets. In the junior set are the younger brothers, and in the senior set the eldest brothers. The sets of the fathers and the sons, moreover, are separated by three pairs of sets—the fathers of the bottom two sets in Raga, 'Gaḍasha, and Kīlōla, are Orgesha and Kazarla. Because of the presence of sibling seniority grading in this system the exact number of sets between fathers and sons will vary as follows:

$$eS \rightarrow eS \qquad 6 \text{ sets}$$
$$eS \rightarrow yS \qquad 7 \text{ sets}$$
$$yS \rightarrow eS \qquad 5 \text{ sets}$$
$$yS \rightarrow yS \qquad 6 \text{ sets}$$

The number of years between the time that fathers enter Pulada —the grade in which marriage is first allowed—and their sons do so will thus range from $7 \times 5 = 35$ years, minus the number of years since the father first entered Pulada, for yS of eS, to $6 \times 5 = 30$ years, minus the number of years since the father first entered Pulada, for eS of eS and yS of yS, to $5 \times 5 = 25$ years, minus the number of years since the father first entered Pulada, for eS of yS. These delays are therefore comparable with those of Garati, which has a maximum delay of thirty-six years, minus the number of years since the father entered Ḥrela, and Takadi, which has a maximum delay of twenty-seven years minus the number of years since the father first entered Ḥrelita. However, I shall defer further

[1] It will be noticed that this term is the same as the alternative name, Ḥalibihīya, of the Odīya group of clans. This cannot be a coincidence; unfortunately, in view of the complete absence of any historical evidence, even speculation on this point would be useless.

discussion of the complications of sibling seniority grading until the next section.

But besides the rather subtle interrelation of the sets, the Turo system as a whole is less complex than the other two. The grades are only four in number, and since Pulada, in which marriage is first allowed, is the penultimate grade, all the rest of a man's life, which in the other systems would be divided among at least five more grades, in Turo is spent in one grade, Raga, only. This term means 'old woman'[1] and as far as I can tell is the only grade name to have any special significance. Raga are said to have the power of blessing, but clearly no differentiation is made between the active elders and those who have become senile. The Turo system concentrates on the period of transition from boyhood to warriorhood, and from warriorhood to elderhood, but makes no further distinction between the elders.

The ceremony to mark the end of the five-year cycle in Turo is even simpler than in Takadi. Some of the Turo lineage priests go to the Kalla's house and ask his permission to begin the ceremonies, which are known as the Osumada. Here, as in Takadi, the craftsmen take part in them. There is no central *mora*, such as Damalle or Oibatale. The most important one is Teera, in the fields about half an hour's walk from the Kalla's ancient homestead near Karshalle. The men from Madara, and two other settlements called Orba and Kazarguba, come here and erect an *ulahita*, which has been given by the Kalla from his sacred wood (regional and lineage priests who have juniper woods often make presents of trees to their lineage members for house-building or ritual). All the men dress in skirts for this occasion, and dance with long staves to the ends of which are attached bells.

Other settlements have their own *moras*. There is a general prohibition against sleeping with women on this occasion, and I was also told that members of Raga grade were not allowed to climb up on to the *oida* during the Osumada.

We may summarize the basic characteristics of the three systems as follows. All are based upon generational seniority, and all at one time also made sibling seniority an integral part of their operation. The consequence of making generational seniority the basis of the systems, rather than age, is that it is necessary that the fecundity of children and that of their parents should not overlap, and we find

---

[1] In Galliña it also means 'elder' and 'diviner'.

that all systems make strict rules preventing procreation until a certain grade is reached. In Takadi and Garati generational intervals are provided by the *ĥreltas*, and Turo is an exception in making the distance between fathers and sons in the system depend on sets. All systems have grades as well as *ĥreltas*, but the roles of these grades are essentially ideal, since while all the systems preserve a correlation between the average age of grade members and their grade status, the range of the age-span of each grade is too great to allow them to function as true age-grades. Moreover, while the systems are regional, and are all associated with regional priests, the grades do not cut across town boundaries so as to form a network of ties of a different nature from those obtaining between townsfellows. Women are excluded from the Takadi and the Turo systems once they have reached the grade in which marriage is allowed. In Garati they retain the same grades as men, but only in relation to their maternal role, for all the systems are concerned to articulate the relationship between elders and warriors, which are two crucial social categories in Konso, and with which women have nothing to do. Finally, it is clear that all these systems have little connection with social control or government, which is provided by other institutions. Their purpose is essentially ritual and moral.

4. THE DEMOGRAPHIC ASPECTS OF THE SYSTEMS

In this section I propose doing three things. The first is to analyse the problem of sibling seniority grading as it must once have worked in Garati and Takadi, and as it works now in Turo. The second is to give a computer analysis of the past and present systems; and the third is to decide, on the basis of this analysis, which criteria are basic to the present Konso systems.

TABLE 42. *The Garati system with sibling grading*

Ukuda	G	eS		
'Gulula	H	yS		
'Gurula	G	eS	Brothers	G-fathers
Orshāda	H	yS		
Kada	G	eS	Brothers	Fathers
Ĥrela	H	yS		
Farīda	G	eS	Brothers	Sons
(F–1)	H	yS		
(F–2)	G	eS		

An immediate consequence of sibling seniority is that sons are no longer a fixed number of grades behind their fathers. Table 42 of the Garati system, as it once operated with sibling grading, illustrates this.

Thus the fathers' generation will be divided into two grades, for eS and yS respectively, and the same will be true for the sons' grades, which will determine the following variations in the intervals between fathers and sons:

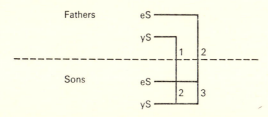

The maximum grade interval will be between yS in the sons' generation and eS in the fathers' generation, which will be three grades. eS in the fathers' generation will be two grades from eS in the sons' generation, and the same will apply to the interval separating yS in both generations. The shortest interval between the generations will be that between yS in the fathers' generation and eS in the sons'. In this earlier system the principle of sibling seniority worked in conjunction with that of generational seniority; it could counter-balance it or emphasize it, making the interval between the fathers' and sons' grades vary between one and three grades.

A second consequence of sibling seniority grading is that the delay before marriage would have varied very considerably. For example, if the Garati system had operated on its present eighteen-year basis, with sibling grading, the eS of an eS, born when his father had been one year in Ḥrela, would be thirty-five years waiting to enter Ḥrela. A second son, born three years later, would enter F–2 at birth, and would therefore wait 14+18+18 = 50 years to enter Ḥrela. The eS of a yS, on the contrary, would only have to wait for seventeen years, assuming he were born after his father had been in Ḥrela one year. His younger brother, born only three years later, would have to wait thirty-two years. In fact, there is good reason to believe that when the Garati system had sibling seniority grading it worked on a nine-year cycle. The evidence is first that still today the eighteen-year cycle is also referred to as the 'twice-nine years' instead of 'the eighteen years', that a nine-year cycle would have allowed the top grades of 'Gulula and Ukuda to be filled, whereas now they are empty, and that according to Garati tradition the cycle was once nine years. Nine is also symbolically important, as we shall see in Chapter VII. Let us see what the results would have been if the system had operated on a nine-year cycle:

eS of an eS, born after father has been 1 year in Ĥrela,
waits   .   .   .   . 17 years
yS of an eS, born after father has been 1 year in Ĥrela,
waits   .   .   .   . 23 years
eS of a yS, born after father has been 1 year in Ĥrela,
waits   .   .   .   . 8 years
yS of a yS, born after father has been 1 year in Ĥrela,
waits   .   .   .   . 14 years

Thus the maximum delay before marriage would only be twenty-three years for the yS of an eS, as opposed to fifty years if the system had been based on an eighteen-year cycle. While sibling seniority grading necessarily creates variability in the delay before marriage for different categories of sibling, it seems likely that variations in the delay before marriage which approached the difference in years between generations, as opposed to that between brothers, would have been regarded as unacceptable for this reason. We may therefore conclude that the Garati system with sibling seniority grading, and a cycle based on an eighteen-year period, would have been unworkable, but this objection would not have applied if the system had been based on a nine-year cycle, and I shall therefore consider what other defects the original Garati system would have had when I discuss the results of the computer analysis which Dr. Elliott and I performed.

Just as the Galgussa/Hirba division of Garati once distinguished eS from yS, the same was once true for the divisions in Takadi. Here Galgussa once contained eS, Melgussa second sons, and Hirba yS. This system would have worked in the following manner:

TABLE 43. *The Takadi system with sibling grading*

Ulula	G M H	
Orshāda	H	
Apada	G	eS
Akoda	M	2S } Fathers
Sūga	H	yS

Ĥrelita	G	eS	
Forita	M	2S	Sons
Farīda	H	yS	
Farīda–1	G		

The intervals between fathers and sons would thus have been as
follows:

eS → eS	3 grades
eS → 2S	4 grades
eS → yS	5 grades
2S → eS	2 grades
2S → 2S	3 grades
2S → yS	4 grades
yS → eS	1 grade
yS → 2S	2 grades
yS → yS	3 grades

While in Garati the original system would only have produced a
variation of one to three grades between fathers and sons, this one
would have produced one of one to five grades. This discrimina-
tion is likely to have caused much dissatisfaction.

The consequent variations in the delay before marriage of the
various categories of siblings would have been as follows:

Ĥrelita	G		Father
Forita	M		
Farīda	H		
Farīda–1	G	1s 'x'	
Farīda–2	M	2s 'y'	Sons
Farīda–3	H	3s 'z'	

Suppose a young man of Galgussa is in Ĥrelita, as the above
table depicts. His eldest son will be in Farīda–1. Let us suppose
this child 'x' is born a year after his father enters Ĥrelita. In three
years time (we must allow for the long weaning period) a second
child 'y' is born, and will go into Farīda–2. In another three years
child 'z' might be born, and would go into Farīda–3. The time
each child will have to wait before entering Ĥrelita will be as follows:

	(F–3)	(F–2)	(F–1)	Farīda	Forita	Total
1s 'x'	0	0	8	9	9	26
2s 'y'	0	5	9	9	9	32
3s 'z'	2	9	9	9	9	38

His eldest son must therefore wait twenty-six years before marriage, his youngest thirty-eight years. (It makes no difference for our purposes if marriage occurred in Forita or Ḥrelita. It is the intervals between the grades which cause the delay.)

Contrast these delays with those incurred by the sons of yS:

Ḥrelita	H		Father
Forita	G	1s 'x'	
Farīda	M	2s 'y'	Sons
Farīda–1	H	3s 'z'	
Farīda–2			
Farīda–3			

If the yS in Ḥrelita (a Hirba) is born one year after his father enters Ḥrelita, this child 'x' will enter Forita. His father has a second child 'y' who goes into Farīda. His third child 'z' goes into Farīda–1.

If we prepare a table for the delays of these three sons before they enter Ḥrelita we obtain the following figures:

	(F–1)	Farīda	Forita	Total
1s 'x'	0	0	8	8
2s 'y'	0	5	9	14
3s 'z'	2	9	9	20

A system which allows a *maximum* delay before marriage of between eight and thirty-eight years is clearly unsatisfactory. The original intention of the system is clear. It was supposed to differentiate between the generations, and also between the siblings in each generation on the basis of their seniority of birth, and for these purposes it is an ingenious system. But the great variations in marriage delay between the categories of son, and the very long delays imposed on some categories, such that sibling differences almost become generational differences, were probably found oppressive.

The Turo system, however, while retaining sibling seniority grading, does not entail such variability in the maximum delays imposed before marriage.

Pulada is the first grade in which marriage is allowed. From the following table we can see what is the maximum delay imposed on a boy before marriage.

Pulada	eS	'A'	Fathers
Dalda	yS	'B'	
Farīda			

Farīda–1
Farīda–2
Farīda–3
Farīda–4   eS   'a'⎫
Farīda–5   yS   'b'⎬ Sons

If an eldest son 'A' marries and has a son 'a' a year after he has entered Pulada, this son 'a', as an eS, will enter Farīda–4, because of the fixed interval between the generations. If 'A' has another son 'b' in three years time, 'b' as a yS will enter Farīda–5. In one more year the five-year cycle will end, and A's younger brother 'B' will enter Pulada and be eligible to marry.

The situation will then be as follows:

Raga	'A'		Fathers
Pulada		'B'	
Dalda			
Farīda			
Farīda–1			
Farīda–2			
Farīda–3	'a'	'x'	Sons
Farīda–4	'b'	'y'	
Farīda–5			

yS 'B' now has a son 'x' a year after entering Pulada and this son 'x' enters Farīda–3 with A's eS 'a'. Three years later, 'B' has another son 'y' who will enter Farīda–4 with A's yS 'b'.

We can now calculate the delay which will occur before 'a', 'b', 'x', and 'y' are allowed to marry:

		F–5	F–4	F–3	F–2	F–1	Farīda	Dalda	Total
Sons of eS 'A'	'a'	0	4	5	5	5	5	5	29
	'b'	1	5	5	5	5	5	5	31
Sons of yS 'B'	'x'	0	0	4	5	5	5	5	24
	'y'	0	1	5	5	5	5	5	26

Under this system the variation in the *maximum* delay before marriage is only between twenty-four and thirty-one years, a difference of only seven years. The discarded Takadi system would have had a variation in the maximum delay before marriage of from eight to thirty-eight years, a difference of thirty years, and in the old Garati system the variation would have been from eight to twenty-three years, a difference of fifteen years. In this respect of variation, therefore, the present Turo system is greatly superior to the old Garati and Takadi systems. The maximum delay before marriage in the present Garati system, for any son, is thirty-five years, and in Takadi it is twenty-six years. So the Turo system is quite comparable with these two in this respect, with a maximum delay of thirty-one years.

From the description given so far of the manner in which the Garati and Takadi systems operated with sibling seniority grading, it is clear that there would have been far more variability in the maximum delay before marriage for the various categories of sibling than there is in the Turo system. But this is not in itself conclusive evidence as to why the old Garati and Takadi systems were abolished, and the sibling grades made hereditary. The variability is inherent in the allocation of priority to eS, and considerable inequalities may have been tolerated for this reason. These systems, however, also have important demographic consequences, in so far as they regulate the age of marriage, and must, even if they are not primarily age-grading systems, maintain some sort of correlation between the grades and the average age of their members, if the ideal characteristics of the grades are to be meaningful at all.

Normally it would not be possible to estimate how such systems would operate over several centuries, since the sheer number of computations involved would be insuperably large, but the computer[1] is a tool which is ideally suited to operations of this sort, and accordingly Dr. Elliott and I devised a demographic model based on the following assumptions:

1. The minimum chronological age for marriage is twenty years (since people below this age are not in general considered mature enough to marry even if they are in a suitable grade).

2. All males marry within a year of being permitted, i.e. of attaining the age of twenty years in a grade where marriage is allowed. This also assumes an adequate supply of females, but my own information was clear that such a supply existed.

3. The maximum age for fathering children is fifty-five years. This is based on my own estimates, the level of polygyny, and the fertile span of females. There are, of course, a few men with young second or third wives who have children after this age, but they are too few to affect the calculations.

4. The maximum chronological age is seventy-five. The excep-

---

[1] An IBM/360 model 50, using Fortran IV language.

tions to this are very few in real life, and they would no longer be begetting children in any case.

5. It was assumed that exactly half of all live births are male. While sex ratios at birth vary considerably in different populations, the ratio of males to females at birth is lowest in populations which are most inbred, and so, in the absence of precise data, and in the empirical certainty that there is a sufficiency of women to allow all men to marry, it was therefore decided to make sex ratios at birth equal. The exact ratio is not in any case crucial.

6. The average number of children surviving to fecundity was assumed to be six (three boys and three girls), based on my genealogical data, with eS therefore one-third of the total male population.

7. The infant mortality rate[1] was assumed to be 25 per thousand, based on U.N. data, my own estimates, and on the fact that such societies in their traditional state almost certainly have a very slow growth rate, of the order of 0·02 per cent per annum.

8. Three years must elapse between live births, based on the prohibition on begetting another child while the previous child is mainly dependent on breast milk.

9. The distribution of population according to age-groups is as follows:

Age	Number of males	%
1–10	294	21
11–20	252	18
21–30	210	15
31–40	196	14
41–50	168	12
51–60	154	11
61–70	112	8
71–75	14	1
Total	1,400	100

The number and distribution of females is the same.

10. The average age of the society at the beginning of the first cycle of the projection was set at thirty years. This is an assumption made for the purposes of calculation, but experiment showed that five years' variation in either direction does not affect the outcome significantly.

11. The society contains 1,400 males at the beginning of the projection, and an equal number of females. This again is an arbitrary

[1] That is, deaths in the first year of life.

number chosen for convenience, and has no bearing on the validity of the results.

12. The probabilities of death are distributed equally over all ages, except for infant and prenatal mortality. It might be assumed that warfare between towns would produce significant periodic depletion, especially of Ḥrela grade. But I was told that when many fathers in a lineage were killed, the survivors of the lineage would sleep with the widows, and beget children in the name of the deceased. It was therefore concluded that countervailing factors of this sort would cancel out over the whole population.

13. It was assumed that there would be a slow rate of population growth, of around 0·02 per cent per annum, with oscillations. However, such determinants of population expansion or contraction as war, epidemics, and famine, were excluded from the model. Thus while the factors of infant mortality, the fecundity span, and general mortality rates are clearly the basic determinants of population increases and decreases over time, the particular grading systems will also have important consequences in this respect. The Garati system, which is known to work successfully, was taken as the control case, and the basic demographic assumptions were adjusted to give the required level of population increase for that system. It was found that some other systems were less satisfactory in this respect, and showed considerable fluctuation. This does not mean that such fluctuations and increases in population would actually have taken place (since the model specifically excludes the effects of famine, war, and disease), but merely that, given the rules of each system, and the basic demographic assumptions, some systems are inherently more stable than others.

14. It has been assumed, in the absence of any indications to the contrary, that the premises of this model are equally applicable to all regions.

It should be remembered that it is only a model, and not an attempt to reconstruct history, and consequently has to be based on a narrower range of assumptions than those which would obtain in real life. But it should also be remembered that, while the model clearly suffers from a deficiency of demographic data, even if this were as plentiful in relation to the Konso as it would be for an industrial society, this would not entitle us to conclude that such factors as infant mortality were the same in the distant past, or that they had been constant over time. There is, however, a good check on the reliability of the model's demographic assumptions. From my own experience it is certain that the present Garati, Takadi, and Turo systems are in equilibrium; that is, they maintain as high a correlation between the average ages of the grade members and the order of the grades as the rules of the system allow; we find, on average, the youngest people in the bottom grades, and the oldest in the top, and the numbers of people in each grade are in accordance with the population distribution according to age. The Garati system, at least, has been working for more than 350 years, and if there were any basic deficiencies in it they would have caused it to break down long ago. Since the results of the computer analysis showed that the present Garati, Takadi, and Turo systems were all in equilibrium, and superior to the discarded systems in a number of ways, it is reasonable to conclude that the assumptions of the model are basically correct.

On the basis of this model programmes were written for the following systems: I, the present Garati system; II, the Garati system with eS/yS grading and an eighteen-year cycle (it is very unlikely that such a system was ever used, but it is included here for comparative illustration); III, the Garati system with eS/yS grading and a nine-year cycle;[1] IV, the present Takadi system; V, the old Takadi system with eS/2S/yS grading and a nine-year cycle; and VI, the Turo system.

The results are set out in Table 44. Columns 2, 3, and 4 merely recapitulate the main characteristics of the various systems. Column 5 shows the changes in population from the initial 1,400 at 90 and 180 years after the beginning of the projection. Ninety was chosen since it is a multiple of 5, 9, and 18. It will be seen that there is an oscillation and a small rate of growth, which is almost identical for the present Garati, Takadi, and Turo systems. Column 6 shows the average age of the population in each system after 90 and 180 years, and we see here that again the fluctuations in the discarded systems were considerable. Column 7 sets out the average period of fecundity allowed by the system in relation to the maximum of thirty-five years, and column 8 deals with a very important aspect of the systems—the overlap of father–son fecundity. Column 12 deals with the ratios of grade populations over 180 years; that is,

---

[1] The present Garati system with a nine-year cycle is quite unworkable, since people would pass through the system much too rapidly and cluster in the top grades, and consequently it is not considered here.

TABLE 44. *A comparison of the grading systems*

System	No. of grades (excluding negative grades)	Period of cycle in years	Presence or absence of sibling grading	Total population size at T_0, T_{90} and T_{180}			Average age of population at T_0, T_{90} and T_{180}			Average period of fecundity (max = 35 years) to nearest 5 years	Father/son fecundity overlap	Range of variation in age of permitted marriage	Stability of mean ages—rank order	Age stability within grades over 180 years	Stability in ratios of grade populations over 180 years	Grade skew; S = some; M = much; T = top; B = bottom	Correlation between grades and average age of members	Stability of size and proportions of grades—rank order	General merit of system—rank order
				T_0	T_{90}	T_{180}	T_0	T_{90}	T_{180}										
	2	3	4	5			6			7	8	9	10	11	12	13	14	15	16
I. Present Garati	7	18	—	1,400	1,571	1,480	30·0	31·7	29·8	25	Low	Low	3rd	High	High	SB	V. High	1st	1st
II. Old Garati, 18-year cycle	7	18	+	1,400	1,609	1,513	30·0	41·7	22·3	20	Med. for yS of eS	High	5th	Med.	Low	MB	Low	6th	5th
III. Old Garati, 9-year cycle	7	9	+	1,400	1,456	1,512	30·0	32·6	33·2	30	High for yS of eS	Med.	4th	Low	Med.	ST	Med.	4th	4th
IV. Present Takadi	8	9	—	1,400	1,515	1,478	30·0	32·1	31·9	30	Low	Med.	2nd	High	High	ST	V. high	2nd	2nd
V. Old Takadi	8	9	+	1,400	1,793	1,686	30·0	21·9	50·8	20	High for yS of eS	V. high	6th	Low	Low	MT MB	Low	5th	6th
VI. Turo	4	5	÷	1,400	1,510	1,480	30·0	31·3	30·5	25	Low	V. low	1st	High	High	ST	High	3rd	3rd

with the extent to which there are expansions and contractions in the numbers of one grade in relation to the others. In column 13 the tendencies of systems to accumulate more members in the top or bottom grades than were there initially is described more precisely. The remaining columns are self-explanatory.

On the basis of the information on all the present and past systems given in the table, we can now compare Garati systems I and III, and Takadi IV and V, to see in what respects the discarded systems were superior or inferior to the present systems. Let us first consider Garati I, the present system, and Garati III, which had sibling seniority grading and a nine-year cycle. Predictably, there would have been a high level of overlap between the fecundity periods of the eS of yS, and a greater range of variation in the age of permitted marriage than in the present system. More noticeable defects in the old system would have been the considerably greater instability in the average age of grade members, and in the ratios of the populations of each grade. Thus, as we see in column 14, the correlation between grades and the average age of the members would have been much poorer. With regard to the average period of fecundity permitted to men, however, the old system would have been superior (thirty years as opposed to the twenty-five years of the present system) and in skewing both systems are somewhat defective, there being a tendency for men to be retarded in Garati I, and promoted too rapidly in Garati II.

Comparing the present Takadi system IV with the old Takadi V (having the three sibling seniority grades) we again find a high degree of overlap between the eS of yS in the old system compared with the present one, and, again predictably, a much higher degree of variability in the age at which marriage is permitted. There would have been an even greater instability in the average age of grade members, and in the ratios of grade populations, than in III. The correlation between men's chronological ages and their grade status would have been very much worse than in the old Garati system. In addition, the old Takadi system developed a much greater tendency to skew than the present one, and we find a polarization of people into the top and bottom grades. Finally, the average period of fertility would have been low—twenty years in relation to the theoretical maximum of thirty-five years. It seems therefore to have been a very bad system, and is unlikely to have lasted more than about 200 years. But since it was defective in all respects in comparison to the present system, we are given no clue as to which defects in particular led to its abandonment. But rather more can be learned in this respect by comparing the present and past Garati systems. In the old Garati system the average period of fecundity was actually greater than in the present system, so that we may assume that, provided it is not reduced too much, this factor is of secondary importance in deciding between two systems. Again, all systems have a tendency to skew to some extent, the only difference between the old and the present Garati systems in this respect being that the old system was skewed to the top, and the present system is skewed to the bottom. The most noticeable differences between the past and present Garati systems is that the old system was much inferior in maintaining age stability within the grades, and a correlation between the chronological ages of its members and their grade status. It will also be noted that these latter requirements are met very successfully by all the existing systems. All the present systems are also successful in preventing much overlap in the fecundity of fathers and sons, a requirement which was given to me as one of the basic desiderata of the systems by an informant.

We may therefore say that the basic purposes of the systems are as follows:

1. To grade society in terms of generational/sibling seniority,

2. and, in consequence, to prevent the periods of fecundity of fathers and sons overlapping, but at the same time preventing wide variation in the age at which marriage is permitted.

3. To keep the grades correlated with the average age of their members.

4. To ensure that such grading remains stable over time.

5. THE PURPOSES OF THE SYSTEMS

In view of the emphasis which the Konso seem to place on preserving a correlation between chronological age and grade status, it might be argued that the grading systems are as much age-grading systems as generation-grading systems. But an age-grading system is by definition a system in which the grades are recruited on the basis of age, while we have seen that the Konso grades are recruited by the criteria of generational/sibling seniority, which is a quite distinct method of recruitment. In practice there is a correlation between the seniority of grades, and the average age of their members, and, as I shall suggest, since the grades serve among other things as a conceptual map, an ideal hierarchy of roles, it is necessary to maintain such a correlation, but it is nevertheless a result of the rules of the system, not a rule in itself.

The complexity of such systems as those of the Konso makes it certain that historically they were based on some simpler system of an age-grading type, especially in view of the proximity of the Galla peoples to the other tribes of East Africa which have age-grades. Consequently, if we are to understand the reasons for these elaborate systems, we must first compare them with ordinary age-grading systems, which must have been discarded as in some way unsatisfactory.

Now age-grading systems divide societies into the categories of elders, warriors, and boys, and serve as systems of social control by allotting various duties to each of these categories. In these respects they are superior to generation-grading systems, which by introducing the element of hereditary status as a determinant of one's grade inevitably blur the clear-cut divisions by age which occur automatically in age-grading systems. We have seen that the Konso are concerned to maintain a correlation between the average age of the grade members and the position of their grade in the hierarchy, but since this would be better achieved by an age-grading system this is clearly not the reason for the choice of the generation-grading systems. Again, unlike age-grading systems, those of the Konso type are not designed to be systems of social control, that is, they do not order society into a series of action groups; their grades are ideal types. While I shall argue that the Konso systems also serve as conceptual maps of their society, hierarchies of ideal roles, an age-grade system can serve this purpose just as well.

We have seen that a central feature of all three systems is the prohibition of marriage to Farīda, yet this concern would be meaningless unless they were interested in generational difference *per se*, and it is the emphasis upon generational status which gives the Konso systems their peculiar form. We saw in the discussion of the status of the eS that sibling seniority is integrally related to generational seniority for the Konso, and in the discussion which follows I shall consequently refer to the principle of generational/sibling seniority.

I would not wish to deny that generational seniority is very closely related to the hierarchy of elders–warriors–boys, but it is important to recognize that these are conceptually distinct hierarchies. For sibling seniority is an integral part of generational seniority, but it has no relationship to the elder–warrior–boy hierarchy, being expressed in the relationship of the lineage priest to the lineage. Thus generational/sibling seniority represents a fundamental principle of order in its own right, but it is more than a principle of order, for the Konso realize that it is the sequence of the generations, and, within each generation, the sequence of siblings, which directly determines the age groups which compose society. Thus the grading systems are not merely creating an arbitrary abstract scheme, but expressing, a fundamental scientific truth about the way things are. They do not just categorize and classify, they reveal.

The Konso are looking for the bones, the basic skeleton which determines the form of society, as the geologist seeks for the rock strata which underly a landscape, or the metallurgist for the crystalline structures which define the characteristics of a metal. The Konso have seen society as based on the sequence of the generations, and the order of birth of siblings, of which the age-groups in society, and their roles, are but reflections. They discarded age-grading systems because they do not reach to the heart of matters; chronological age-groups are only the flesh which hides the underlying bones—the sequence of the generations. In their generation-grading systems they have articulated a principle of order which can be expressed with mathematical exactitude, and which underlies the changing face of the maturation cycle in society and the individual man.

The grades are a series of discrete roles; what knits them into a unit is the principle of generational/sibling seniority by which movement through the hierarchy is governed. But while the grades are secondary to generational status, as defined by the *ḥrelta*, they nevertheless add a vital dimension to the systems. For they relate the generations to their ideal roles in society, as the Konso conceive them. Farīda corresponds to the idea of irresponsible childishness, when the person is not a full member of society, a dependant, the recipient of orders, an apprentice. The end of Farīda, and the entry into Ḥrela, accompanied by the most important rites of passage in a man's life, marks the emergence of the individual as a full adult, the defender of his society against criminals and enemies, and the founder of a family himself. Membership of Kada exemplifies a third stage in a man's life, when he passes beyond the performance of simple physical duties to those of a maturer kind, as a councillor and blesser, leaving behind him the simple virile passions so suitable for a warrior, and developing the no less important capacities of wisdom and good judgement. Associated with this growth in seniority is the power to bless his juniors in Ĥrela, and to curse the enemies of his society, especially pests. Blessing is an inherent function of elders. In Orshāda grade these duties are continued. 'Gurula marks the last stages in a man's life, when he begins to retire from active life, into senile dependence, and he becomes again like a child (think of the infantile position of old people's corpses).

We have seen that two of the most important social categories among the Konso, and many other East African peoples, are the elders and the warriors. In the case of the Konso their relationship is ideally harmonious and complementary, and is expressed in the relations between Kada and Ĥrela. The elders are the repository of social wisdom, God's delegates charged with the maintenance of the social order, and as such are one of the prime sources of blessing for society as a whole. While the elders support society by their wisdom and blessing, the warriors support it by physical defence against enemies from without and criminals from within. But, as we saw in Chapter III, the authority of Ĥrela is not that of naked force, but legitimated by the possession of their own drum—the symbol of moral order and the acceptance of the basic rules of society. Both grades defend the social order and the moral law by performing the functions proper to their nature. It seems reasonable to say therefore that the ideal characteristics of youth and age are articulated and brought into a symbiosis by the grading systems and their associated ritual.

Besides stratifying society in terms of generational/sibling seniority, and of a hierarchy of ideal roles, the systems can also be regarded as conceptualizing the stages through which a man can expect to pass in the course of a normal life span; they delineate the 'seven ages of man'.

But there is still a basic question to be answered. Why do the Konso believe that their grading systems make the crops grow? My informant from Garati enlarged as follows on the reasons for setting up the Farīda system.

Long ago the people said 'We do not want the Farīda system. The

9 [sic] years' cycle is something the Ħoira people like', and they refused it. After this God withheld the rain for 9 years, and the people were hungry, and ready to die. Then they said 'Why refuse the Farīda system? It is because of this that Waĝa has not sent rain.' Because of this they made the Farīda system.[1]

We have seen from the text just quoted that it is thought that their ancestors adopted the system in order to ensure a plentiful rainfall. There is now, of course, no evidence why in that remote epoch the elders of the time actually did set up the system, but there is no doubt that at present there is a strong belief in the association of social order, peace, and harmony with that general well-being of men which derives from the physical world—health, fertility, rain, and success in war and hunting. And a well-ordered society is one which is not only without quarrelling but which is also organized on the right principles of order. The belief that a well-ordered society will also be right with the ambient world of nature is, I think, a basic reason in their minds for regarding their grading systems, together with the existence of the priests and elders, as the foundation of their prosperity.

I read Knutsson's study of the Macha Galla some time after I had completed most of the thesis on which this monograph is based, and it has not therefore influenced my interpretation of the Konso systems. He quotes a remarkable text to illustrate the central importance which the *gada* system once had for the Galla. Apart from the frequent allusions to monstrous progeny, a feature not found in Konso symbolism, it reproduces strikingly, and independently, from a related people, an account of the significance of the generation-grading system which is essentially similar to that which I was given by my informants in Konso.

When *gada* was destroyed, they left *gada*. The bull refused to mount the cow, men no longer respected justice. There was no one who could be given the office of *abba biya*, father of the land. There was no

---

[1] It is said that originally the system was adopted from the Ħoira (or Burji) people, as the following text makes clear: 'The Garati people left Ilota for the country here. The clans were established in Ilota. There were Ħoira (Burji) people here. They went to Ħoira. The Garati people then settled here. They established the Farīyuma here. The Ħoira people who used to be here had Farīyuma but they went away to Ħoira. The Garati people left Ilota and came here and used the Farīyuma of Ħoira which the Ħoira people had, retaining it in Garati. In this Farīyuma system they made one division into Galgussa and one into Hirba, and dug them both in together. Galgussa started first, and then Hirba followed; in this way they work together. . . . '

X. Waĝas

one who could take the office of capturing criminals. There were no longer any real elders, and few children were born. The cows gave birth to deformed calves. Pregnant women gave birth to their children at the wrong time. They bore children without hands. Lambs were born without forelegs and without tails. And calves were born which had no tails.

When the *gada* customs were destroyed, everything else was also destroyed. When *gada* no longer existed there was no justice. The crops that were cultivated no longer grew. And the oxen refused to fatten. The man who had formerly respected truth and justice abandoned them . . .[1]

If the grading systems in Konso were to be destroyed, they might well lament their loss in similar terms.

These systems thus stand at the centre of Konso life. They believe that a society which is rent by dissension will suffer drought and death, and for them peace is violated not only by quarrels, but also by confusion in the ordering of their society. The grading systems provide this order, by expressing the basic principle of generational/sibling seniority, by providing a hierarchy of ideal roles through which the generations pass in sequence, and in so doing also articulate the relationship between the categories of elders and warriors.

[1] Knutsson, op. cit., p. 180.

VII

GOD AND EARTH

THIS chapter is a study of Konso cosmology, and I have chosen one aspect of this—their apprehension of God and earth—which seems to me of central significance, for these two elements are closely related to masculinity and femininity, and to their conceptions of the social and the moral order.

As we have seen, Konso society is composed of institutions whose membership is essentially male. The lineages, the wards, the grading-systems, and the various offices associated with them, and the priests and *shorugatas*, are all institutions based on men, while women float, as it were, between them. I shall argue that God is seen as the author of social order, but that the responsibility of maintaining this is thought to have been delegated to men, and especially the elders. Thus blessing is essentially a male function and vested accordingly in the hands of elders, priests, *shorugatas*, and other ritual officers; on rare occasions women may bless as well, but this apparent contradiction must be left for the time being.

Women, on the other hand, are seen as in some ways outside society, in terms of their peripheral association with its basic institutions; and in terms of their closer association with physical nature, in their role as the preparers of food, and the bearers of children, they are symbolically linked with the earth. The Konso say that women do not bless.

Women's status is therefore ambivalent; on the one hand they are outsiders in relation to the basic social institutions, and because of their debilitating effect on men sexually, but on the other hand they are seen as necessary to the perpetuation of society through their fertility, and the nursing of children, and the preparation of food.

In the first part of this chapter I shall consider God, Waĝa, and describe some basic rituals and the symbolism associated with them. In the second part I shall consider the earth, and its symbolic associations with women.

PART I. GOD

I. GOD AND THE SOCIAL ORDER

God (Waĝa) for the Konso is primarily a God of rain and of justice; indeed, these two functions are interrelated, for He punishes towns which are guilty of too much internal quarrelling and bad feeling by withholding the rain from their fields. The following text gives a good idea of the manner in which the Konso apprehend their Deity. I append some notes on symbolic elements which will be of recurring importance in this chapter.

Long ago God was close to the earth. A woman was hooking down *mida* from a tree.[1] The hook struck God, and God bled upon the woman. She ran away into the house and wrapped herself in a cloth and a skin. God bleeds[2] for a day and a night upon the woman, who wrapped a cloth[3] around herself. After this God said 'Everybody on earth come here. I would give them a proclamation.' All the people, the animals, the birds, came to God, and the time was the third hour. And God gave names for the animals and for all the rest.[4] And He said 'I would go far away, I would go far away'. Because of this God went far away from earth; he was afraid of the hook, he was afraid, and he went far away. He said 'I hear when people have quarrelled together; the elders shall judge between you. I am present among you. I forbid whatever is evil among you. I would send rain for you. Let it be that you listen to one another, and do not quarrel together. In the fields let there be no quarrelling, and in the towns let there be no quarrelling. Let no one quarrel. And I, when people are quarrelling together, I will not give rain for you, when people are quarrelling together. And when people are doing wrong, I will let fall something bad among you.' This is a story about God.

A man disputes over the boundary of another man's field, and after a man has disputed another man's boundary, they curse each other together between the boundaries, and God hears, He hears, and the man of sin (him who is the liar) He kills, He strikes with the thunderstroke. This one He kills with sickness, and because of this the liar fears God; He may kill a person, He knows these things, the quarrel about a boundary, and what evil is being done, and the quarrelling that is being done. He hears, and kills them and destroys them, and consumes them, and strikes the family, and there is no son and no daughter,

---

[1] The woman, in the course of collecting food, strikes God.
[2] A clear association of women and blood.
[3] Women are traditionally associated with skins, so the reference to cloth here is obscure.
[4] God is the basis of conceptual order.

and He strikes the family, even their fields, and He takes the lineage, their lineage, them He strikes. Because of this, God's declaration of long ago, since then people are afraid of quarrels every day. Those living in our country of Garati, the lineages and their priests, and towns and wards, all together are afraid. All people hear what God has said, and are afraid together.

One man may say 'I am tough, what does God say?', and he kills people in the way, and robs them, and beats children in the way, and brings quarrels and accusations into the ward, and has no fear of God. While this person is behaving in this way, and may be killing and robbing, God is watching him, and his evil. He begets little, and his offspring die and he has no son, the evil-doer. Everyone says of him, 'the sinner is dead. God in truth has killed him; this person sinned and he killed him', and everyone thus reviles him, 'thus he did and he dies'. The evil-doer brought quarrelling into the town, and after God saw him He seized him. 'The sinner killed people', they say, and God seized this sinner; this evil that he did killed him. God hears what is going on among people, thus He seizes them. This is justice.[1]

God is thus seen as the original author of morality and social order, but He has withdrawn from the world He established, and made the elders His deputies. The Konso feel that their society is upheld by the principles of morality and the traditions handed down from their forefathers, of whom the elders are the surviving representatives. God is certainly seen as a father-figure, not so much in the sense of the begetter of the human race, but as the source of morality. I once asked them if a dream in which a son struck his father was a bad omen. I expected to hear a panegyric on social order, and the necessity of the young listening to the voice of the elders, concluding with the statement that indeed such a dream was a very bad omen. But I was mistaken. 'Oh no,' they said, 'such a dream wouldn't mean anything. What would be really bad would be to dream of the father striking the son. For this would mean God punishing a man.' This shows as clearly as anything can how God is identified with right conduct, and paternal authority; while this authority is burdensome (as I suggested was shown in the *shilleda*), it is nevertheless the basis of society. While he is remote, God still intervenes to punish sinners, and to judge between those who have called on Him by oath in a dispute. Traditionally there was only one word for actions which we should distinguish as crimes and sins—*dupoda*. Since the coming of the Amhara and their courts, however,

---

[1] *Milikida*, literally, 'measurement'.

criminals who are punishable under the new Ethiopian laws (and which, where they are offences against the person or property, were also punished in traditional Konso society) are called *wen'jeleda*, from the Amharic *wanjal*, a crime. *'Dupoda* does not comprehend all forms of anti-social behaviour. An *alimalita*, someone who ignores his social responsibilities, especially those of helping and respecting his parents, or his lineage if he is a priest, would not be considered a *dupolida*, a sinner, nor would a coward. (I was told that I was an *alimalita*, for, as they said, 'How will your parents till their fields, if you are an only son, for they will have no one else to help them?') Sin is essentially a fault of commission, not omission. Telling lies, for example would certainly be considered a sin, as would persistent drunkenness.

There are, however, no 'ritual' sins, involving sacred objects or taboos, which bring the offender under God's wrath. For a young woman to approach an *ulahita* would be very dangerous for Ĥrela, and when some Christian Konso girls, working at the mission, decided to flout this taboo in Patangaldo, they were arrested by the infuriated elders, but there is no question of God being offended in such cases; women are dangerous to the *ulahita*, as we have seen, because of the harmful effect of their sexuality on the symbol of the warrior grade.

It was said, in justification of the taboo in Garati on marriage with FZeD and MBeD, that it had been found that such marriages were cursed with the death of the children, and poverty, so they were forbidden, but I was never told that God punished incest (*manyera*) of this sort. It was repeatedly emphasized that it was totally forbidden for boys and girls of the same clan to marry, but there was never any suggestion that *God* would kill them if they did; it was merely stated that they would be expelled from Konso and that they or their children would die. A priest's old homestead, and his wood, if he has one, are sacred, and it is forbidden to cut them; someone who did so would be liable to go mad, but there is no idea of this affliction as a punishment; it is simply a mystical consequence.

Nor is He usually thought of as present in relationships between men. True, such expressions as 'Waĝa *ke dashew*', 'May God give to you, too', when thanking someone for a gift or some special service, or 'Waĝa *ke dinsho*', 'May God cure you', said to a sick person, suggest the contrary. But these are the only such expressions

I can think of, and even these are not heard with great frequency.
'Waĝa ke dashew' especially is not the equivalent of our 'Thank
you', but is reserved for much more solemn occasions.

Nor is Waĝa regarded as basically the Creator. While He is
responsible for the life in the foetus, and for successful conception,
there is much less certainty about how Man was created in the
beginning. According to one account the first man and woman
were born of snakes, and according to another they were born
from a gourd.

God is, however, closely associated with breath:

> When the first man was born, he had the same body, and fingers
> and hands and feet and toes and head and nose and ears and everything
> that we have. But he was as though paralysed. He did not move, or till
> the ground, or eat or speak or breathe. (But he was not unconscious;
> he could see what was happening.) God's wife[1] appealed to God, and
> said, 'The man cannot speak, have you some speech medicine?' God
> said, 'I have no such medicine, but I will bring some breath'. God
> brought breath, and then the man began to speak, and move about, and
> till the ground, and also was subject to death. When the man died,
> God took the breath back again.

God is therefore seen as sustaining Konso morally, and with rain,
and as the creator of each person at conception. But they do not display any awareness of God as immanent in the physical world, and
are content to allow the fundamental mysteries of the origin of
things to remain mysteries. Waĝa is far away, and they have no
experiential relationship with Him, feeling that He is present in
all things, though certain events, such as rainbows or thunderstorms, are regarded as manifestations of His power. There is,
about three miles from Idigle, a blow-hole in the side of a hill that
emits a strong draught of air during the day, and sucks in air after
sunset. The air rushing in and out of this hole, called *Kūmisso*, 'the
roarer', is described as the 'breath of God'. There is on Mount
Padigama at the other end of Konso a hole (which I never visited),
at the bottom of which it is said there is some supernatural water,
'the water of God', which ordinary people cannot see, but only
diviners. But these are rare curiosities; as we have seen, breath is
associated with God, and it is natural to describe invisible water
as God's water being something otherwise inexplicable. Normally,

---

[1] I have never heard any other reference to God's wife.

however, the Konso do not constantly refer to God as the author of the physical world around them, or even of its most curious features.

God is thus largely dissociated from the earth, the physical sustainer of society, and is regarded as the basis of the moral and social order. He is also contrasted in their cosmology with evil spirits, *oritta*. These are in some cases thought to be the ghosts of strangers who have been buried in the Gomīda plain, far from their native home. They roam the lowlands, looking for men to destroy. It is said that men travelling through Gomīda are often struck with agonizing pains in the side, and a bloody flux from the mouth and nose (which is perhaps pneumonia). Other evil spirits were never human beings at all, and some say that God created them. But there is no doubt of His hostility towards them; one reason for the frequency with which God causes large trees to be struck by lightning is that evil spirits like to sit in the shade beneath them. Some hills are said to have evil spirits upon them; there is a large conical mound in the centre of Būso called 'Pōla', which no one ever climbs because it is said that the evil spirits will blow a person down from the top. Evil spirits are also associated with wind in the form of 'dust-devils'.

Generally, like the ghosts, evil spirits only come out after dark, when they may perhaps be seen as bright lights moving out in the fields. Sometimes one will hear the sound of *sangura*, the bells on unmarried girls' ankles, approaching along a path, but no one is there; that is an evil spirit. It is said of ghosts and evil spirits that night is their special time, and that they fear cock-crow, as a warning of the coming of the light. The Konso have great fear of the dark, and hate travelling outside the towns during the night. But evil spirits can also make their influence felt during the day. One of Sagara Gīya's wives complained that an evil spirit was in the habit of sitting just outside her grinding-house, giving her severe back-ache as she worked the stones. (Normally, of course, women feel no aches and pains when working the grind-stones, as they are used to it.) She pointed out the spot where it would sit. Although he was a famous diviner, Sagara asked me to get rid of it. I composed a suitably elaborate ceremony of exorcism, and I was told later that it had gone. Burning the faeces of a dog or a hyena is a favourite method of exorcising spirits among the Konso, and garlic is also used.

Evil spirits are strongly associated with the condition of insanity, and possession is attributed to them, and them only. Gomīda, the great plain below Konso, which is *par excellence* the place of law-lessness, and where homeless strangers are buried, is particularly thought of as the home of evil spirits. We may therefore consider the possibility that the characteristics commonly attributed to mad-men are related to the characteristics they ascribe to evil spirits, and, more generally, to anti-social forces symbolized by darkness, the ghosts of strangers, and lawless places like Gomīda.

Now the madman, unlike the imbecile, refuses to associate normally in society. Typically, he lives outside the town in a hovel, or wanders the paths eating whatever roots and carrion he can pick up. He thus personifies the antinomian forces which the Konso see as the opposite of the beneficent forces of law and order, repre-sented by God. Moreover, as an individual, the madman is also the personification of motiveless, gibbering animosity. Some madmen, it is true, are genial, but many are full of curses and hatred. This aimless spite against humanity is also, of course, one of the chief characteristics of the evil spirits. It is said that some evil spirits were strangers who died in Konso, and were buried in Gomīda, where, angry and resentful at being separated from their own people in death, they roam for ever seeking men to kill. Gomīda, in its lawlessness, standing as the antithesis of the orderly life of Konso itself, is the fitting home of the antinomian and anti-human evil spirits. Perhaps the madman, as the personification of anti-social characteristics, is therefore the model for evil spirits.

2. THE NATURE OF KONSO RITUAL

There is no private prayer to God or supernatural beings among the Konso, and personal hardships, whether of a physical nature—such as disease, or the attack of pests on one's own particular fields —or of a spiritual nature—such as finding evil medicine in one's homestead, or having a dream with a sinister portent—are taken to the *suaita*, or diviner, for help.

Not only is there no private prayer; the rites themselves are not addressed to any spiritual beings either. Before the reconsecration of the *ulahita* in the Mora Murgito which had been spoilt by a bull climbing up beside it, some said that the ghosts were angry, others that God was angry. But these were clearly not the real justifications for them in performing the ceremony; the fear most clearly and definitely expressed was that if the ceremony were not performed the men of Ḣrela would be likely to die (because of the mystical effect of the bull's virility on their symbol—the *ulahita*).

Again, we find that speeches, blessings, and exhortations on ritual occasions are also almost entirely devoid of references either to God or earth. True, the Nama Dawra at the beginning of the ceremony at which the *ulahita* is reconsecrated say 'Wago *ga peedo*' 'O God, O Earth', but this is a very common ejaculation, not confined to ritual occasions; a man may say this in the course of an argument to stress his sincerity, for example, or his exasperation. Apart from this, there is only one other instance, apart from a solitary mention of God, by Turumalle, in which Ḣalibahīya is asked 'to cure us'. All these speeches are in fact *saga*, 'blessing', which simply express the hope that the good things mentioned will come about. *Saga* is not the same as *eĝinsata* which means 'requesting' in general, and in a ritual context 'prayer'. Yet while at the ritual level we can say that there is no prayer, they do have the concept of asking God for things, especially for rain. I was told, for example, that the Apa Timba would 'pray' for rain to God—'Waga *eĝinsani*' —although in fact at any ritual for rain he would almost certainly bless, not pray.

It seems reasonable to suppose that God is felt to be too remote to enter into the sort of personal relations implied by prayer, and for this reason at rituals there are no invocations, but only expressions of hope—blessings, in other words. Nevertheless, in total scheme of things rituals can be seen as a form of prayer, of requesting, because, like a request, they do not produce an automatic response. They are the occasions for the expression of hopes, which may or may not come true, depending, I think they would say, ultimately on the will of God. But this does not affect my point that at the level of ritual performance no spiritual beings, whether God, ghosts, the earth, or spirits, are addressed. God is far away; and we must analyse Konso rituals in terms of symbolism, not of theology.

For the Konso, as we shall see, the object of their rites is to build up an auspicious array of symbols, and any supernatural beings which may be mentioned in connection with their rites always seem to come very much as afterthoughts. Unlike the Nuer, for example, the Konso do not hold their religious ceremonies whenever they fear that mystical danger threatens, but at fairly fixed intervals throughout the year, and during the grading cycles, which is another indication that their rites have no direct relationship to the demands or intentions of spiritual beings.

One does not find any particular emotion displayed by a Konso 'congregation', let alone that 'thrill' or 'awe' earlier writers like Marett regarded as characteristic of primitive religion. Solemnity is the only noticeable feature of their attention to religious rites. During the blessings at the end of the ritual of reconsecrating the *ulahita* at Mora Murgito, the last man to speak, Shan'go 'Gubale, forgot his words, and walked up and down stammering in the most ludicrous fashion as he tried to think of something to say. The congregation shook with suppressed laughter, which only escaped in the form of a few titters during the blessing, but as soon as he had finished it burst out unrestrainedly. During a Sōla dance at Mora Tara'jo in Būso, one of the elders thought there was too much talking, and jumped down from the wall where he had been sitting, beating his blanket angrily on the ground, shouting, 'Be quiet, be quiet, do you think this is a market?' But solemnity apart, I could detect no other overt behaviour which suggested that those present at any of the rites were experiencing any kind of religious emotions.

There are prohibitions on speech during certain rituals, in processions to and from the fields at the Logīda, and for the women as they walk to the *mora* where they are holding a dance during the Sōla, or at the first sowing of the main millet crop when the family should not speak until they are returning from the fields. When we were going to the fields at the Logīda, I asked why we should not speak, and I was told that somebody might start a quarrel. This is patently unlikely; in fact the silence is symbolic. Knowing how easy it is to quarrel, and having the deep belief that social disorder is related to natural calamities, they choose to forbid speech as a ritual token of peace on occasions when the future of their crops and well-being is most sensitive to mystical threats engendered by quarrelling. I was told that notably quarrelsome persons were expelled from the towns during the crucial period of the great rains, but I have no empirical verification of this. It is also believed that if a child's parents quarrel during the first three days after his birth, the child will die. This is, therefore, a different matter from the solemnity proper to a religious occasion. But even during a ceremony the attention of those present will vary greatly. The women outside the barriers—they are not allowed into a *mora* when a religious ceremony is taking place there—will be talking most of the time, and children tend to rush about shrieking without much restraint. The congregation itself seems to fix its attention on the religious purpose in hand only at the crucial moments of the ceremony, and for the rest of the time chats as it feels inclined. C. G. Coulton's description of mass-goers in the Middle Ages is to me strongly reminiscent of the Konso attitude to their ceremonies:

> At King's College, Cambridge, a special home of orthodoxy in the fifteenth century, the royal founder prescribed by statute that, in chapel, the students should not 'in any wise make murmur, babblings, scoffing laughter, confabulations or indiscreet noises, lest, through their inordinate tumult and the various sounds of voices and other talk among themselves, the devotion and exercise of those singing psalms in the choir may be in any wise impeded'.[1] . . . For the Mass, according to Church teaching in our period, was an *opus operatum*, a ceremony which affected the congregation quite apart from their attention to the service, or their state of mind.[2]

For the Konso, too, their ceremonies are efficacious without any reference to the emotions or other states of mind of their observers or performers.

We may therefore consider Konso ritual from a number of aspects—its objectives, its relation to supernatural beings, its symbolic content, the occasions on which it is held, its sacred places, the status of those who officiate, and what may loosely be called the congregation, that is, those for whose benefit the rite is intended, even if they do not actually attend the ritual. In some of these respects their ritual is clearly related to their social organization. Rituals are chiefly performed for the benefit of the lineage, the ward, the town, and in relation to the generation systems, and some of the officials have a socially prescribed status. In so far as their rituals are intended to confer the universally esteemed benefits of Life on society as a whole, and are not, as in the case of Christianity, seen simply as acts of worship or at most as conferring solely individual benefits such as 'grace', it is not surprising that congregations are composed of persons united by especially powerful social ties, or, as in the case of Ḥrela grade, composed of persons whose corporate existence is deemed socially essential. If a particular group is important to the members of society, it is natural that they will wish to sustain it by ritual means, among others, and may be soley concerned with the well-being of their own group to the

[1] *Mediaeval Panorama*, p. 219.   [2] Ibid., p. 188.

exclusion of others. But it would clearly be fallacious to conclude from this that Konso rituals reflect in any significant way their social organization, beyond the mere coincidence of their congregations with important social groups. Their theological and symbolic content, and the occasions on which they are held can only be explained by treating them as part of a system of ideas in its own right, and in relation to Konso values.

3. THE SETTING FOR RITUAL—THE MORA

The focal point of Konso ritual for most purposes is the *mora*. In each town certain *moras* have a special sanctity, and there are in addition *moras* located in open country which are used for more important ceremonies concerning the region as a whole. Of the *moras* within the towns, some are wholly profane in their function. At the smallest, they may even have no dancing-floor, and comprise only a sleeping-hut and some stone platforms for sitting on during the day. Even larger *moras*, with dancing-floors, may not always have sacred functions as well. We can estimate sanctity in empirical terms by asking (*a*) whether access to a *mora* is forbidden to any class of person, (*b*) what its functions are, (*c*) what ritual objects it contains.

In the case of (*a*) we find that women are always forbidden to enter the most sacred enclosures, as are the craftsmen. Nor are women allowed to come near the *ulahitas* of the town, which are devoted to the well-being of Ḫrela grade, although they are not prohibited from the vicinity of lineage priests' *ulahitas*. In the towns, however, the prohibitions only apply to women of child-bearing years. Little girls and old women can sometimes be seen sitting beside *ulahitas* at dances and other ceremonies. At the Irbata *mora* outside Gaho, which is raised like a small plateau above the surrounding fields, Farīda and Forita boys are supposed not to pass through it, but to go along the path below it. It is said that no one at all should enter the Mora Damalle, in the normal way; it is a dense thicket of trees and sharp cacti, so entry is in any case difficult.

(*b*) Some *moras* are only used for religious ceremonies, while others have mundane activities performed in them, such as meetings and dances, as well as rituals. In the most sacred *moras* spinning cotton is forbidden, as well as the performance of *shilledas*, or mourning chants, and anything else to do with death.

(*c*) The chief ritual objects in sacred *moras* are: an *ulahita*

XI. Kalisso going to the fields

(always); perhaps some stones of manhood; an especially sacred enclosure, the *miskata*, in the form of a ring of stones, with perhaps some palings as well. Some sacred *moras* also have a number of groups of *waĝa* statues.

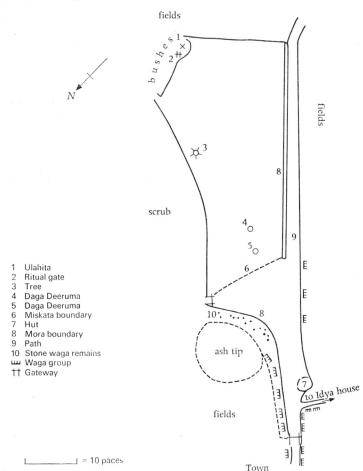

1 Ulahita
2 Ritual gate
3 Tree
4 Daga Deeruma
5 Daga Deeruma
6 Miskata boundary
7 Hut
8 Mora boundary
9 Path
10 Stone waga remains
ᚄ Waga group
†† Gateway

⌐_____⌐ = 10 paces

MAP VIII. Mora Murgito

A good example of such a sacred *mora* belonging to a particular town is the Mora Murgito at Būso.

The outer boundaries, (see Map VIII), are composed of stone walls or of a simple border of stones. At the northern end, by the gate leading into the town, are groups of wooden statues, the *waĝas*. The graves of these are not in the *mora* itself, but elsewhere in their fields; the presence of corpses in a sacred place would be fundamentally inconsistent with its sanctity. There is a low stone wall that marks off the real area of the *mora*[1] where the ceremony actually takes place, from the path which runs along this side. Women are banned from entering the *mora*, itself, although they can use the path here and go through the gate. On the occasion of a ceremony a pole, called a *miskata*, is placed across the entrance to this part of the *mora*, shown on Map VIII by a dotted line, to demarcate the forbidden area more emphatically. The most prominent objects in this area are two monoliths, about 5 ft. tall, which commemorate the victories of two sets. There are six more such monoliths in another *mora*, but these two are in Murgito because the *hariyādes* in question were particularly good warriors. (3) represents a tree, quite small, in which bones of animals killed in hunting are placed. In other parts of Konso the bones of such animals are normally attached to the *ulahitas*, not to separate trees. In Gidole one also finds *ulahitas* with the bones of animals attached to them, and the same standing stones nearby.

(1) represents the *ulahita*, which is the focus of the whole *mora*. It stands on a raised platform, faced with stone, which juts into the *mora* from the bank of earth behind, almost surrounded with bushes. The dead juniper trees which compose the *ulahita* in this case are about 12 ft. high, and bound together with *ĥalala*, a plant which, as we shall see, provides the garland for the sacrificial animal and the triumphal wreath for the killer of a lion or leopard. A new juniper tree is added every eighteen years, and the old ones are left to rot away. Beside the *ulahita* is a ritual gate, made of two uprights and a cross-piece of wood, through which the bull is made to pass when it is sacrificed at the ceremony of erecting a new *ulahita*.

This then is the stage on which the major ceremonies of Būso are acted. Nor is the word 'stage' an idle metaphor. The sacred *moras* such as these can in a real sense be called religious theatres, where the drama of the victory of Life over Death is acted out in the form of their ancient rituals. A theatre is a place where the actors assume a *persona* that is not their own, and behave according to rules which are prescribed for the occasion. A church is a place where the priest and his assistants act, not in their personal capacities, but according to the rules, in the same way as in a theatre. It is interesting that at

Kunyara in Ĥolme the principal *mora* is in the form of an amphi-
theatre: a flat open space, bounded along one side by a curving
set of tiered stone seats, where the women can sit and watch the
performance.

Their *moras* are precisely demarcated with boundary stones, with
the entrances formed in many cases by wooden gateways. Within the
most sacred *moras* we often find a smaller enclosure, sometimes
fenced with palings, called the *miskata* (meaning 'without women')
and which can correctly be described as a *tiga killana*, or ritual
house. This will be the most sacred part of the *mora*. But there is
no obvious need, in the absence of any natural feature of the landscape with sacred status, such as a tree or a rock, why their rituals
should be carried out within a specially demarcated area. Are we
justified in taking the existence of the sacred places for granted?

Examination of a number of *moras*, and experience of the nature
of the ceremonies performed in them suggested to me that there was
a model on which they were based. I described in the first chapter
how the towns are surrounded by walls, and the homesteads by
palings. Within the homestead, which anyone may enter if he has
business with the family, the houses are absolutely private, and no
one enters them except by invitation. Physically, therefore, their
environment is divided by a series of boundaries, which centre
upon the houses, and extend outwards through the homestead and
wards, and end with the town. Socially, these boundaries are consonant with changes in the nature of social relations, as one moves
from one division to another, in that the rules governing behaviour inside a man's house are different from those governing
relations within the homestead, which in turn differ from those
obtaining within the town.

An example of the difference between the norms of behaviour in
the homestead and the town is the rule forbidding discussion of
sexual matters within the homestead; this sort of talk must only be
indulged in at the *moras*.

The *moras* are therefore demarcated areas within which special
relationships between people, and between symbols, exist. The
homesteads and the houses are also demarcated areas within which
special relationships exist. The *moras* and the homesteads resemble
each other in their physical characteristics: just as there are gates
into the homestead there are gates into the *mora* (often standing in
isolation) which is as precisely bounded as the homestead. The

clear boundaries, the gateways, the reproduction of the *oida* in the form of the *miskata* around the *ulahita*, and the lighting of ritual fires all reproduce essential aspects of the homestead. Now the homestead is the focal point of the Konso's life, in the sense that he and his children were born in a hut upon the *oida*, it is where he eats, where his wife lives, and where his cattle and other domestic animals pass the greater part of their lives. It is highly appropriate therefore that the *mora* as 'the navel of the land' should reproduce many of the features of the homestead. Indeed, as we shall see in the description of the Logīda ceremony, the old homestead of the lineage priest acts also as a *mora*.

4. ELDERS, WARRIORS, AND SOCIAL HARMONY

In this section I shall describe two ceremonies in which the relationship between the elders and the warriors is ideally stated in ritual terms. We shall moreover be constantly reminded of those basic Konso values which I described in Chapter IV. I continue from my notes:

Some days ago the bull of the *marbara* Arfīda, which they were preparing to slaughter in Murgito, escaped and climbed up on to the platform of the *ulahita*. This offence of the bull is parallel to a bull climbing up from the *arhata* to the *oida* in a homestead. In the latter case the father of the house will die unless the bull is killed. But a bull climbing up on to the *miskata* where the *ulahita* is will cause the death of the men of the Ḥrela grade of the town. (The male potency of the bull is clearly seen as a threat to the male potency of humans in both cases.) In fact the offending bull was sold surreptitiously at Bakaule market, which caused a tremendous row; it was said that the men of this *marbara* would die. A smaller bull was given in exchange, and there was some discussion, which I did not attend, whether this animal was acceptable.

On Friday night a fire was lit in Murgito, and Ḥrela brought their spears and stood them against the smaller of the two monoliths, while the staves of the Nama Dawra were laid in front of the *ulahita*. On Saturday afternoon at about 12.15 p.m. I went down to the Mora Murgito with my diviner friend Sagara Gīya. Previously the spears had been moved to stand against the tree (in which the bones of the slaughtered animals of the hunt were placed), where the young bullock was now tethered.

As the ceremony begins someone puts the *miskata* pole in place across the top of the *mora*. The small group of Nama Dawra moves down towards the *ulahita*, and blesses as follows:

O God, O Earth; our mouths are at one; our mouths give peace; the grandfathers give peace; the mouths of the people are at one; what is evil has departed away; sickness has gone to a hidden place; may we have ntle rainge; when mouths are at one that which is evil goes far away.

Each Nama Dawra shouts these phrases in any order he pleases, so the result is a confused babble of sound.

These words are spoken in the direction first of the *ulahita*, and then of the tree and the bullock, accompanied by the aspersing of water. Ḥrela now take up their spears and fresh butter is handed round to all for anointing. Now it is the turn of the bullock to be anointed, which is done along its back by some of the Nama Dawra and others as well, sweeping their hands from head to tail. (In many such cases the sacrificial animals are given water to drink from a gourd containing water and auspicious plants, but this is not done today.) The bullock also has a garland of *halala* leaves, a long creeper which is also used to make wreaths for the heads of those who have killed a lion or leopard—Sagara Gīya is wearing such a wreath. Now the staves are brought from where they are lying before the *ulahita*, and placed under the tree where the bullock is tethered.

The supreme moment of the ceremony is now at hand, when the animal is loosed and taken to the centre of the *mora*. Many hands, but only of Ḥrela, grasp the beast by its four legs and hoist it up into the air, while it plunges about, bewildered and lowing. At this moment a *shorugata* drives his spear into its right side behind the shoulder, and it gives an agonized bellow, which is drowned in the fierce shout that echoes it from the throats of Ḥrela. Its cries grow fainter, and it is lowered to the ground. It is considered essential for the beast to cry out in this way, and I was told that if it did not the sacrifice would be in vain, and another beast would be substituted. Ḥrela begin to cut up the bullock, while the Nama Dawra of Kada and Orshāda remain sitting in the shade of the tree. Someone has tied a garland of *halala* round the base of the tree, and placed some in the branches. The fire is banked up with wood ready for the roasting of the meat, and soon the ribs and stomach, all cut into strips and hung over poles, are cooking in the flames.

Someone says to me, 'This *mora* is the navel of the land'. While the meat is roasting, many of the young men are busy cutting up and uprooting the small bushes growing around the *ulahita*. To do this is forbidden in sacred *moras*, except on occasions like today. A similar prohibition is applied to a priest's wood, which can only be cut when a priest is buried there.

Some of the earth beneath the *ulahita* has been dug away, to form a small pit, and the juniper poles loosened and one of them uprooted to make room for the pit. The intestines are brought up on to the platform, and the chyme is squeezed into the pit. This is all done rather casually, and no one takes very much notice, in spite of its ritual importance. Their thoughts seem to be fully occupied with the prospect of the imminent banquet. The sacrificial spear has been bound to the tree with *ḥalala*, and some *hansabita* placed beside it.

Cooked meats are now taken round, and one or two Kada men help in the distribution. First to be served are the Nama Dawra, of Kada and Orshāda, sitting in the shade of the tree. After them Ḫrela get their share, along with those who have just arrived, whatever their grade. I, too, am given some. After the cooked meat, the raw meat is distributed, but no one eats it in this state. Everyone cuts himself a twig to impale his meat and cook it there and then, or else pockets it to eat at home later. Besides this general distribution of cooked and raw meat, taken from all parts of the beast, and given equally to all who happen to be present, there is a more formal allocation of certain parts of the animal, as follows:

'Gulula	Hooves
'Gurula	Head (except for lower jaw, tongue and horns).
Orshāda	Tongue, prostate, scrotum, left haunch.
Kada	Hump, breast bone, right haunch.
Ḫrela	Tail (inner part).

The boys are given the lungs. The skin is divided among all those present, and priests are each given an extra long piece. The bones are also chopped up and distributed, first to the Nama Dawra, and then to all present. Some are also placed in the pit beneath the *ulahita*. The Bamalle, who used to live near Būso about 350 years ago, is traditionally given the backbone, but in fact it is no longer given to him personally, but to the head of the Ḫrele family who descend from a junior branch of the Bamalle line.

When the skin has been cut up each man present cuts a slit in his piece, and pulls it on to his right wrist.

The distribution and eating of the carcase is now complete, after about three hours. Meat is a great luxury for them, and a feast is not something to be hurried.

It is now time for the anointing of the Nama Dawra's staves. The Nama Dawra of Kada and Orshāda collect the staves into a bundle, and, crouching under the tree, form a small circle around them, every man's hand grasping them. As they anoint them copiously with butter, they bless them in the following words:[1] 'May the clouds vomit with water; now the water goes among basket-like clouds; they have become fertile; O *halibahīya*[2] cure us.' The staves are banged together on the ground five times, and on the word '*ifeete*' 'they have become fertile', they are flung out of the circle. (The circle of men probably symbolizes the womb, from which the peacemaking staves of the Nama Dawra are reborn, after their blessing and anointing, by being flung violently out of the circle.)

We are now approaching the conclusion of the ceremony. The men of Ɦrela alone take their spears and stand in two ranks facing each other, one end at the nearer of the two monoliths, and the other beneath the *ulahita* platform. Then five Nama Dawra take it in turn to walk up and down between the two ranks aspersing them with milk, using a sprig of *hansabita* as a whisk.

The first speaker, Gusiya Bukudo, a *shorugata*, blesses as follows:

People want a lion; may you kill one amidst applause, may you kill, may you kill; (to which the company replies 'kill!'); at our pool may bulls bellow three times; at our pool may bulls bellow three times; our Ɦrela want to kill; in the lion's mouth I thrust the *talboyada*;[3] may the *pagana* not become diseased; may the *pagana* not become diseased; my Ɦrela may they kill amidst applause, may they kill; I bless Ɦrela in the *mora*; may my blessing give peace; may my blessing give peace; may the bees in the land come to our fields; thus I speak.

The second speaker is the lineage priest Ɦīgo:

Listen, listen, you want beehives, you want cattle, you want millet, rows of millet; listen, listen, you want he-goats, let him come to the she-goat; listen, listen, you want gentle rain for the crops, may it come; (response: 'may it come, may it come') listen, listen, you want a lion,

---

[1] These words are a very free translation.

[2] Said by one informant to mean God and the sun together.

[3] A black cloth supposed to be thrust into the jaws of a lion in the hunt.

a decrepit lion, a lion without teeth, let him be found on the path to Sagan; listen, listen, you want beehives, and for the he-goat to come to the she-goat (response: 'let him come, let him come'). Thus I speak.

The third speaker, the lineage priest Sābo Turumalle, speaks as follows:

O Kolbe [Būso] you live in Okolla, may it be well in Okolla; listen, Kolbe, you want to kill, Kolbe, you want to kill; I will thrust the *talboyada* into the mouth of the lion; may you kill him in the midst of applause; listen, listen, Kolbe, may the fathers eat the *tada*;[1] (response: 'let them eat, let them eat, let them eat') listen, listen; O God; you want crops, let them grow in rows; (response: 'let them ripen, let them ripen, let them ripen'); listen, listen, my *sakoda*,[2] Kolbe, of Gīya, in Okolla may it be red, may it be red, may it be red; may the mothers bear sons. Thus I speak.

The fourth speaker is Ku'jo, a lineage priest:

Listen, listen, you want a blessing for Ĥrela; I as a member of Kada give a blessing to make peace for Ĥrela; may children be born on our *oidas*; may there be food on our *oidas*; listen, listen, you want cattle, the copulation of cattle, may you kill, may you kill, may you kill; may the bulls bellow, may the bulls bellow; listen listen, for Ĥrela you want lions; I will thrust the *talboyada* in the mouth of the lion; listen, listen, Kolbe, let the fathers eat the *tada*, let them eat, let them eat, let them eat; let the mothers eat the *tada*, let them eat, let them eat; let the *sakoda* be carried [here?] on the wind; listen, listen, my Kolbe wants a blessing, my blessing for them is that there be peace; may there be people on our *oidas*; may goats' fodder flourish in the land; may it flourish, may it flourish, may it flourish. Thus I speak.

The fifth and last speaker is Shan'go 'Gubale, a *shorugata*, who is about to take over the Kada drum from Sagara Gīya:

Listen, listen, Kolbe, of Gīya, may the honey-badgers slide down the trees bearing the bee-hives [and not be able to reach the honey]; listen, listen, Kolbe, of Gīya, may food come in quantities, may it come, may it come; let sickness go away to a secret place; listen, listen, let the fodder for goats flourish, let sickness go to a secret place; let the fodder for dik-diks flourish.

The ceremony ends with these blessings. The *ulahita* is tied up, and the earth replaced, and the fire in the *mora* is kept alight for the three succeeding nights; it is said that if it is allowed to go out

---

[1] The meal which sinks to the bottom of a beer gourd.
[2] A red bird.

the men of Ḫrela may suffer sickness or death. (The speakers at the blessings were all Nama Dawra. Ku'jo, Turumalle, and 'Gubale were from Kada, 'Gubale being a *shorugata*, and the other two lineage priests. Bukudo and Ḫīgo were from Orshāda.)

In order to understand the meaning of the foregoing ceremony we should interpret it as if it were a play. The bull is the symbol of virility and male ferocity, and it is vanquished and killed by the men of Ḫrela, the warrior grade. The presence of the Nama Dawra (or their representatives) symbolizes the close links between the men of Ḫrela and their seniors, who provide them with mystical protection. As befits their status they are served with meat first. The eating of a meal together symbolizes the harmony prevailing between the grades, and promotes it in the future. Just as the spears are the symbols of the warrior grade, so the staves are the symbols of the peacemaking grades of the Nama Dawra. Just as the *ulahita* is mystically revivified by the sacrifice, so the staves are given new life by being enclosed in the circle of Nama Dawra, anointed and blessed, and ceremonially reborn. At the conclusion of the ceremony the Nama Dawra and the men of Ḫrela come together in their ideal symbiosis, when the priests and *shorugatas* of each grade of the Nama Dawra asperse and bless their religious dependants of Ḫrela. The fire which burns in the *mora* near the *ulahita* for three nights is a protection for the *ulahita* against evil influences which might nullify its value as well as being associated with the domestic fire. This then is the symbolic framework of the ritual drama by which Life has been enhanced, and the forces of Death defeated.

I attended another ceremony at which an *ulahita* was erected. Since I had arrived in Būso only four days previously, in my ignorance I understood very little of what was going on at the time. Nevertheless, since the ceremony is so rare, and because the ethnographer should try to make all his important data available, I include the ceremony here, in spite of the deficiencies in the description.

I arrived in Būso on Wednesday, 9 June. The following Saturday an extremely important ceremony was held in the Mora Gomiya, adjoining the men's house at which I was residing. Some years before my arrival, there had been an *ulahita* in this *mora* which had been blown down by the wind, and it had not been re-erected. I was told that people had consulted the diviner recently, who had recommended that it should be replaced. I do not know if this had anything to do with my visit. As I have already said, *ulahitas* are normally erected only at the end of the grading cycles, so an occasion such as this is very rare indeed. The following account is exactly as I wrote it in my note-book at the time, except that I have put in a few explanatory phrases, in square brackets.

Two rows of four men, varying ages, facing each other. Leaves of *killana* [almost certainly *teemahada*] handed round by man not one of [those] sitting. He-goat is tethered and garlanded nearby. God will bring rain [so they say]. A hole is being dug near this group who have eaten their *killana* leaves; they get *yacheta*[1] seeds. A fire was lit at the beginning of the business. I have been expecting this [ceremony] for some time, and today is the first day that rain storms can be clearly seen approaching in the lowlands. In between the two rows [of men] are a couple of hides (cow). God is sending the rain for the crops, to prevent them drying up [so they say].

A number of long sticks[2] have been laid along the hides, also some green *gachetu*. Man[3] has bell on right arm. Brass head band. Eight spears[4] have now been assembled. A number of elders have black fly-whisks. The poles to be erected are young fir trees [juniper] stripped of their branches.

Everyone except a few of the eldest men who are part of the sacrificing party (but who did not seem to eat) has now split up and is standing round with the rest.

The site of this operation looks toward the Sagan river in the lowlands. It stands out like a headland from the village, but I think this has no special significance. One man[5] who (I think) gave out the food, has some *hansabita* plant in his hair, and holds a sprig of it in his (right) hand. (He later does the invoking when the rain comes.) So far there has been no objection to my asking questions and generally wandering about. The fire has been well stoked up.

Looking across to the other *mora* I can see people going about their business as usual.

The tree which they previously felled is now being cut into bits for the fire. One other chap now has some sprays of leaves. Standing with his spear. Goat getting very restive . . . [Rain now comes].

When the rain finally came the rain priest alone invoked, shaking his gown[6] and his sprig. Then, when it eased off, butter was brought, and many received it in cupped hands, on the right hand. The goat was brought up and held over the hole, previously, I think, having been

---

[1] I am not sure what these were.
[2] The staves of the Nama Dawra.
[3] The representative of the Bamalle.   [4] The spears of Ĥrela.
[5] Killano Gïya, the brother of Sagara, this year's Kada Apa Timba.
[6] A ritual act, called *hamsha*, performed when calling on rain to fall.

pushed into it [a large press of people, so I couldn't see]. He perhaps had butter spread on his head. Then, held up by his four legs, he stayed for about thirty seconds, and then had a spear pushed into his chest.[1] He looked round in a bewildered way, and gave a dreadful cry, which was echoed joyfully by the men and boys. Some more spears were thrust into him and he gave some more horrible cries. They finished him off on the ground with knives, pretty crudely, with much gurgling and shrieking.

No women of course have been present at all during the proceedings. (The number of people here has markedly increased—presumably to get some of the meat.) The only woman who passed was getting water, and she didn't stop. A pole has been put across the entrance to the ritual space, along the path. [the *miskata*]. This may have been to sit on, or also to mark off the space from women, who habitually use the path on the way to the river. [the *miskata* was put across before the sacrifice]. The old man with bell and headband seemed to take no part in the proceedings beyond that of anyone else.

They are now digging a second hole to the side (right) of the first one. The tree they are planting seems to be some sort of thorn. A few leaves left, but otherwise no roots. Plenty of small branches, but knocked about. Presumably a sign of some sort[2] relating to fruitfulness. Some of the branches have now been cut off.

The stomach [of the goat] has been cut out and held over the hole [where the fir tree will be planted] and its contents spilt into it. (It was cut open). The thorn tree has now been planted in the other hole. Some of the viscera have now been produced (I think the intestines) and they too are now being emptied into the hole. The cow hides by the way were for dismembering the goat upon. Firewood is still being brought. The hooves and lower legs have now been broken off. Now the liver, stomach, sweetbreads (?), and leg-bones are being hung on a pole and put over the fire. Whether they are only smoking them or are trying to cook them is not yet clear. Yes, definitely cooking, or burning, rather. The rain has quite finished for about an hour now. There is a small girl here, of about 2, but no-one seems to mind. A large number of children, in fact. About 50 people in all. The goat is still being cut up the while. The burnt guts have been brought back to them [the slaughterers] but I can't yet make out what has happened to them. Burnt guts have now been cut up and are being offered round to every adult present, it seems. More men coming. Must be about 70 people here now.

Children also get some of the meat. I have just been offered some,

---

[1] On the right side, by a *shorugata*.
[2] In fact it is intended to take root and support the *ulahita* with its branches.

but pleaded a bad stomach, to general laughter. Space now completely packed with people. Boy now entering covered from head to foot in creepers and cactus. The greenery is being handed in [across the pole] Now it has been thrown down into my plot [some land I rented just below the *mora*]. Some raw meat is being taken round now. Again for general distribution. Really vast numbers here now. Can't be far short of a hundred. The whole thing has been going on for about three hours. (It began with a general discussion (= furious argument) something about the distribution of meat afterwards, I think). Meat continues to be roasted. It seems plain that people are given both roasted and raw meat. Again, the pole has still not been erected. If this eating of meat had no religious significance, why did they not put it up as soon as the goat was killed? (Fortunately, the wretched carcase has been hidden from me since it was killed.) [Some time passes while eating goes on] *Ulahita* raised with fine chorus, then, as it came into position, a great shout. (This is a fir tree with its topmost branches, green. Not much bigger than 10 feet.) Old pole cut across, new one put instead. Now two lines of spear-men. Man walked between them, spraying them with milk, invoking and getting responses in chorus, as rain came down. Then final shouting and pointing with spears to heaven. According to Garide, there now follows a vigil of 3 nights, kept by 5[1] men round the fire. [This was true.] Also dancing and music. [None.] [After dark]— they have just taken a flute [a trumpet made of kudu horn, in fact] from the roof of the *mora* house, and anointed it with butter and replaced it.

5. THE PRIEST

In the preceding ceremonies I considered the role of the elders in blessing, and the ideal symbiosis between them and the warriors attained on the ritual level in the *mora*. The reader will recall that the lineage priests did not perform the sacrifices, which were carried out by the *shorugata*, but confined themselves to blessing. I shall now consider another role of the male in blessing, that of sacrificer, for the shedding of blood is closely associated with masculinity, and no woman may ever sacrifice. I define a priest as someone who, by virtue of his office, can confer benefits by supernatural means on his religious dependants. This office may be hereditary or conferred, but it will differ essentially from that of the witch-doctor or diviner,[2] in that whereas the power of the latter lies

---

[1] An ideal, not an actual number.

[2] This distinction is ideal only; among primitive peoples the functions of priest and witch-doctor are frequently combined, but it seems to me that it is a generally useful distinction, and essential in the case of the Konso.

in his knowledge of medicines and spells, or a special divinatory faculty, or perhaps possession by a spirit, a priest does not need to have any special knowledge, to be remarkable in any way for his occult attainments, or to have a personal relationship with a supernatural being. He obtains the power to bless, which is the essential function of all forms of priesthood, by qualifying for his office according to the rules laid down by the traditions of his society, and these rules need not necessarily bear any relation to the personal abilities or attainments of the incumbent. In the case of the Konso, priests are the eldest sons of fathers who were themselves priests. No woman can be a priest, nor be the means by which the office is inherited. Having succeeded to the office, the priest also succeeds to certain mystical attributes and powers. These give him a sacred status, such that a regional priest, or important lineage priest must never come into contact with death, for example; he should not attend a burial, and anyone who has been at one should not visit a priest on that day, or else should purify his feet and legs with certain plants before he steps over the threshold.

Primarily a priest has the power to bless the fields, stock, and fertility of his congregation—his lineage. Thus a priest is only credited with mystical attributes after he has succeeded to his office; quite opposite is the case of the diviner, who becomes recognized as a diviner *because* of his personal attainments in the sphere of the occult. The priest and the diviner can be further distinguished as, on the one hand, an office-holder, with public responsibilities and privileges, and on the other, a private expert, without such public duties, whose esoteric knowledge is a means of earning a living. We shall also see that the priest has virtually no involvement, at least explicitly, with spiritual beings other than God; even in this case there is no question of divine inspiration. The water-spirits of the town's wells may visit the chief priests in dreams, and it is said that the lineage ghosts also come to their priests in dreams, but these facts are only incidental to the office of the priest. A diviner, on the other hand, must have a special awareness of spiritual beings in order to operate at all. I have stressed that there is no private prayer to spiritual beings in Konso religion; in consequence the priest cannot act as mediator to God or the ghosts for any individual members of his lineage; when people are in trouble they go to the diviner, whose occult powers are used to find the cause of the sickness, or a magical remedy for an evil omen. The priest and the diviner therefore stand as the representatives of two clearly distinguishable elements in Konso religion. One element consists of public ritual, undertaken for the public good, without overt reference to spiritual beings, in which an elaborate symbolism is the operative factor in bringing spiritual benefits. In such ritual the most important functionary is the priest or *shorugata*. The other element is that which concerns the private individual, and his troubles both spiritual and physical; here the diviner is the principal functionary, and it is the action of spiritual beings or forces, such as magic, or the evil eye, which he examines as the possible cause of misfortune. The priest is concerned to bring the good things of life, and keep away the bad; the diviner on the other hand is called in when things have gone wrong, and his job is to restore health or prosperity, and to avert the mystical danger revealed in omens.

There was a noticeable difference in their attitudes to diviners and priests; priests are the official bringers of Life, and therefore preeminently respected. But diviners are definitely feared. If someone was talking to me about diviners he would lower his voice, and become ill at ease, for while a diviner is consulted for his assistance he is also the possessor of occult power, of which the Konso have a fundamental dread, whether it is in the form of divinatory skill or possession by a spirit. In Garati, moreover, the remedy for an evil dream was to make a medicine to pass the intention of the omen on to someone else, and it was said that this would often be a member of the client's own lineage, or a friend, or someone in the same ward. Naturally, I found it impossible to get any concrete evidence of cases where this had actually happened. For example, Sagara Gïya besides being a lineage priest was also a diviner, in fact the most famous dream diviner in Konso. Men even came to consult him from Burji, about fourteen hours' journey away. He held his consultations outside his homestead, in the first light of dawn, and because his remedies often entailed a hostile medicine against a kinsman or neighbour of a client, it was forbidden for anyone but him and the client to be present during the session. The distinction I originally drew between diviners and priests may seem to have been vitiated by this information, but there is good reason why a priest can also be a dream diviner, since the ghosts of the lineage return to their priest in dreams, which are supposed to be a revelation of the future, as we have seen. The skills of the diviner are many, and dream divining, in which Sagara is so eminent, is only one. Very few priests are also diviners, and when they are they are specialists in dream divining. The lineage priest Songogo in Degato was the only other one I heard of by name. In this chapter we are concerned with public ritual and with the effectiveness of symbolism, and hence with the priest; I shall consider the diviner in the next chapter, in relation to the spiritual beings in which the Konso believe.

Having shown how the priest is contrasted with the diviner in Konso religion, let us turn to examine the nature of his social status more clearly. The *ḳallu* (ritual leader) of the Macha Galla (and other branches of the Galla peoples), as described by Knutsson, is clearly similar in many ways to the *poĝalla* of the Konso, and in particular a comparison of the phonemic contents of the two words *ḳallu* and *poĝalla* throws much light on the essential meaning of the word *poĝalla*. For the phonemes 'ḳ'[1] and 'ĝ' are obviously closely related.

Knutsson writes:

. . . if we wish to link the term ḳallu with a root shedding light on its present meaning, we do not need to look beyond the Galla language. The root ḳal in Galla means slaughter, both profane and ritual (ḳallu— to slaughter, ḳalla or ḳalma—slaughter, ḳaltu—the one who slaughters). In Macha the ḳallu's ritual house is called *galma*. Phonetically g and the glottalized ḳ are close to each other in the Macha dialect. An interpretation of *galma* as the house or place of ritual slaughter seems therefore quite plausible. In this connection it is interesting to note that the terms designating the chief ritual expert among the Konso, Gauwada, and Tsamaka in south and south-western Ethiopia have the meaning of 'father or lord of the slaughter'.[2]

(Knutsson gives Haberland as the authority for this last statement.)

Similarly, in Konsiña the word *ĝalla* means 'slaughter', essentially in the form of throat-cutting, in both ritual and profane contexts. It seems almost certain that the prefix *po-* in *poĝalla* is a contraction of *apo* or *apa*, meaning 'father', the whole word meaning, as Knutsson says, 'father of the slaughter'. The use of the word *apa* in the titles of ritual offices will also be familiar to the reader in the expressions 'Apa Dawra', and 'Apa Timba'.

Great importance is attached to the fact that the lineage priests are the descendants of the first families to settle in Konso. Of

---

[1] ḳ in Knutsson's orthography is a glottalized k.
[2] Knutsson, op. cit., p. 65.

course, all the Konso are equally the descendants of these families, but because of the rules for the inheritance of surnames, only the priestly line, the senior line, retains the same name throughout the generations. There has always been a 'Gūfa, a Bamalle, a Shirto, and an Īdya. Thus the continuity of name gives a formal identity to the senior line. When I asked them how, in the beginning, the first lineage priests were able to claim their office, they said sometimes that it was because they were the first people to settle in Konso and at other times that such people would have had to be lineage priests before they came. Clearly, if the first senior male settlers could claim to be lineage priests because they had staked their claim first, there would have been no means of calling a halt to this process; all subsequent settlers from outside Konso could, on this criterion, have claimed to be lineage priests. Equally, if a man could only claim to be a lineage priest by inheritance from his father before he came to Konso, we are still no nearer understanding how the first lineage priest of any particular line obtained his office. On simple logical grounds therefore it is clear that these explanations will not do, at least taken at their face value. In reality the two accounts of the origin of the lineage priests simply express the idea that they were in existence at the beginning of Konso society, and were the ancestors of all the Konso people, but exactly how the office originated is now lost to us, in the absence of historical records.

The regional priests, the lineage priests, and the *mora* priests have distinct if sometimes overlapping responsibilities, but in so far as they are all called *poǧalla* it seems reasonable to treat the regional priests as ideal types of priesthood, as regards ritual status; thus we have a continuum from the regional priests, quintessentially sacred, through *mora* priests, who are always lineage priests as well, lineage priests, lineage priests through a junior line, and *shorugata*, to cultivators generally, who are still insiders in relation to the craftsmen, the group metaphorically at the periphery of Konso society, as opposed to the regional priests at the centre. So in order to understand the basic functions of the *poǧalla* as such, let us examine the ritual status and functions of the regional priests.

Takadi is referred to as *peeda 'Gūfa*, 'the 'Gūfa's land'. He lives in his ancestral home a bow-shot from Gaho near his sacred wood.

PLATE XII. Boys collecting *mida*

(The Kalla and the Bamalle also have large sacred woods near their homes, in which their ancestors are buried.) At the end of each nine-year cycle he sacrifices a bull in his house and erects an *ulahita*, in the presence of representatives of all the Takadi towns. He also attends the sacrifices in each town, giving permission for them to begin, and his blessing. Every year, in Pillelo, his lineage come in their best clothes to his fields outside his house, called Aramda, and till them, and then repair to his house, where he blesses them and representatives of the towns, who come after the tilling. In the month of Olindela he sacrifices a ram at a little settlement called Gahiti, which is inhabited only by his kinsmen. He cuts off the fat tail and puts it into a large horn, which he seals up to prevent the fat decaying. When the month of Oiba, the time of sowing, arrives he gives pieces of this fat to the Apa Timba of all the Takadi towns. At this time he sacrifices a ram in his house to cleanse it, and scatters the chyme on the fields as a blessing. After the young shoots have grown to a few inches high he gives his blessing to them, '*peeda indipi'gorta, ga 'gara hada iteefta*'.[1]

The Bamalle has somewhat similar functions, although in Garati the form, if not the significance, of the rituals is generally different and more complicated. At Kadabaha he receives a black substance called *irgeda* from the sky (directly from God) with which he anoints the eyes of Farīda. Every year the two sacred drums of Garati, Kadana and Dokona, are brought to his house when the great rains are beginning, by the Apa Timba of these drums, along with two black unmated she-goats, with the yellow *killiboda* fruits tied round their necks and limbs. He gives them five gourds of beer. Then he brings butter, the fat of a ram's tail preserved in a horn, and a cow's udders. With these he anoints the two drums. When the anointment is completed he places butter in the hands of all present saying '*Teedibīya teefe*', also putting some butter on the ground. He then proceeds to anoint their staves, banging them five times on the ground, saying '*opor'go*', and finally flinging them away, 'they have flourished'. He places the fat of the ram's tail in a bowl and offers it to the Apa Timba, saying as he does so '*hum!*' to which they reply '*keshi*', five times. At this time the fields outside his house, called 'Gobororo and H̃ulme, are sown. He is also the chief priest for that congeries of towns, Degato, Poro'goda, and H̃ulme, which I mentioned earlier. At their periodic hunting festival, Kařa, all the

---

[1] I am unable to translate this.

men of Ĥrela go to the Bamalle's house where he ceremonially sharpens their spears, passing them over a sharpening stone in a bundle three times, saying 'eesho', 'kill', each time.

Their religious duties are thus bound up with the grading systems, and in this respect they are obviously similar to the great *kallus* of the Borana (Kallu Oditu and Kallu Karayu), of the Arussi (Abba Muda), and the Guji. Among these Galla peoples the great *kallus* have an essential role in the regulation of the grading systems.

The regional priests all live outside the towns in isolation in the fields. It is said that all priests should do likewise, but, especially in Garati, this rule is now more broken than observed. The explanation for it that I was given stressed the danger to the townspeople from having a priest among them. When, on the death of a priest, his eldest son curses his ghost (see below, p. 254) he wears the *hallasha*, and it is said that the blast of malefic force issuing from the *hallasha* on this occasion can strike anyone in the vicinity with death. Possibly the spiritual power of the priest is regarded as temporarily out of control at this transitional time. It is also said that the ghosts which visit them in dreams are dangerous to the people living nearby. The Gīya homestead in Būso, in Idigle ward, was at the edge of the town. In the past there used to be many more people living here, and in the adjoining ward of Gomīya, but they had all died. It was said by some people that the cause of this was the Gīya family's having left their homestead in the fields outside Būso, and moved to their present site. It is also said that, as the path through the abandoned house sites led down to the well by the Elbola, the well-spirit, on its way up to visit Gīya in dreams and the lineage priest Idya not far away, might also be responsible. I think these are only partial explanations, however; we have seen that remoteness is inherently related to sanctity, and I shall develop this aspect of priesthood further in the last chapter.

The remoteness of priests is not only geographical but also extends to social relations. The great priests are not supposed to receive food or beer from the hands of anyone not of their family; and these must be made from the produce of their own fields. The present 'Gūfa is a small boy; when I visited his homestead he hid from me (I never saw him except in fleeting glimpses). His mother was clearly hostile and suspicious of me, and said that she thought I had brought something evil to harm the 'Gūfa. Eventually, when my companions and I had explained who I was

she became quite friendly. If a regional priest sleeps in another
man's house, no one else may touch that hut, without paying a fine
(so the 'Gūfa, for example, always sleeps in his own homestead). A
further consequence of the remoteness of the priest is that his wife
may never marry again after the death of her husband, or after he
has divorced her. This is supposed to be a rigid rule for the wives of
all priests, but I know of one case where the second wife of a lineage
priest, living in another town, left him and married another man.

There are a number of symbols and *materia sacra* associated with
the priest, which are very expressive of his role as the bringer of
Life. Traditionally, priests alone had phallic roof-pots on their huts,
and in Takadi this is still the case, but nowadays in Garati anyone
can have them if they are prepared to buy them, but in practice
they are only displayed by notable people, other than priests, such
as *shorugatas*. They also frequently have ostrich eggs mounted on
top of these pots, blown of course, and impaled on a stick. Since
birds and their eggs are traditionally forbidden food for the Konso
it is at first sight strange that an egg should decorate a priest's
house. But in the first place the egg is white, like the *ḥallasha*, and
clearly intended to repel evil forces (like the sprigs of juniper and
killiboda tied to all roof-pots when the huts are finished); secondly,
they are aware that birds are hatched from eggs, and in this respect
it is surely a symbol of fertility, quite consistent with the phalluses
of the roof-pot. Ostrich eggs are used to decorate Coptic churches
in Ethiopia but while this bears witness to the widespread appeal
of the egg as a fertility symbol, there is no historical connection
between the Christian use of the egg by the Copts and the use of the
egg by the Konso. Snakes also play an important part in the ritual
complex surrounding a priest. Snakes are, of course, a universal
symbol of virility and fecundity. It is said that long ago a snake
fertilized the wife of a Bamalle, when her husband had died without issue, by spitting on her, and it is also recorded that the first
men were begotten by snakes. They believe that snakes are, unless
killed by violence, immortal, since they merely slough their skins.
If a man kills a python he presents the skin to his lineage priest, as
he does with that of a lion or a leopard. In the houses of all important priests a python skin is displayed, and all priests have several
necklaces of their vertebrae to be used in their mortuary ritual.
There is a thin black snake that is apparently harmless. As I have
seen for myself, it occasionally comes into homesteads, where it

moves about with its mouth closed and finally goes away. A priest will never kill one of these, but respects it as being possessed by a family ghost. Commoner families may also respect such snakes, but it is emphasized that priests always do.

When a priest leaves his homestead and builds another, the old one is left to disintegrate, though he may remove timber and other useful building materials. There are a number of old priests' homesteads in the fields, especially in Garati, where a large number of priests have moved into the towns (the fact that one can always discover the original homestead of a priest in the fields shows that once the rule that priests should not live in towns was strictly observed, as it is to a large extent in Takadi to this day). The old homestead is never dug up and returned to cultivation. It is strictly forbidden not only to sow crops in it, but also to cut down any of the weeds or bushes that grow there, except when a religious ceremony is held there. In the same way, in the sacred *moras* there is much vegetation which may only be cut down on ceremonial occasions, and it is equally forbidden to sow crops in these *moras*. If a man disobeys these prohibitions he runs the risk of going mad. There is clearly a common pattern here, relating to the sanctity of the *moras* and the old residence of the priests. The Konso are an agricultural people, and for them the cultivation of land and the cutting down of vegetation are a necessary part of growing the crops that are to sustain them. Now it is a noticeable feature of their magic that medicines are invariably without any food value; similarly trees grown in *moras* with religious functions are never fruit-bearing species. There is, therefore, evidence in other spheres of their religious thought that lack of utilitarian value is correlated with mystical value. I suggest that in consonance with this they regard the weeding of sacred sites as a form of profanation; the field which provides material sustenance is weeded; the *mora*, or priest's house, which bestows supernatural benefits (the homestead in the fields is always the site for religious ceremonies performed by the lineage priest) is left to grow wild because this symbolizes the fertility of vegetation.[1] Priests in fact are in many ways outsiders, and associated with the wild

As the bringer of Life the priest is forbidden to kill. In Garati

[1] I give further details on the opposition between wild and cultivated plants, and the religious significance of this distinction, in my paper 'Konso Agriculture', *J.E.S.*, 1970.

many priests have disregarded this, and there only the Bamalle, the Kalla, and a few others, who have silver bracelets, or are considered to be of high status, do not kill. But in Takadi and Turo it was said that no priest should kill either in war or hunting. A priest's homestead is sanctuary, and a murderer, fleeing for his life from the vengeance of his victim's kin, could take refuge there. Correspondingly, a priest should never have anything to do with death, for death is regarded as polluting.

'Purity' in the context of Konso religion is a term which needs clarification. Their nearest word to 'pure' is *'gul'gulōda*, which in ordinary conversation generally means 'clean'. We are familiar in our own religious tradition with the extension of the concept of 'cleanness' to mean 'pure', in the spiritual sense. A virgin[1] is *inanda 'gul'gulōda*, 'a pure girl'; a sacred *mora* is *mora 'gul'gulōda*. A man who has attended a burial, or even gone to mourn at a bereaved homestead, will say *awe andi angulo*, 'today I am not clean', and will not visit the house of a priest or an Apa Timba. Similarly, the word *'jareda*, 'to wash', can be used not only in the sense of washing one's hands, but of ritual purification. At the time of Timba Tula, in Takadi, as we have seen, a man carries a turtle shell filled with the earth from a grave all through Takadi 'to cleanse the land'. When he leaves he takes it to the Sagan and throws it in. When a craftsman has performed the 'circumcision' ceremony at Gaho, the sacred stone on which he stands during this operation is cleansed with the blood of a goat. People ritually purify their homes when evil medicines are found in them, and after a battle the land is purified at the ceremony of reconciliation. When the descendants of a murderer and his victim are reconciled, there is also a ceremony of purification.

Ritual purity in the Konso religion is, therefore, closely associated with Life, and everything associated with death is the most impure of all. Thus the contrast between the priest's role as the bringer of Life and the realities of Death is greatest when he himself has to die.

When a priest dies there is no official mourning, which is greatly frowned upon. The body is eviscerated and smeared with butter and honey, two of the most auspicious substances. It remains in the house for nine days. Not only is mourning forbidden, but also it is

---

[1] Virginity is a theme in Konso ritual and cosmology which I am unable fully to explain.

obligatory for the eldest son to curse him. On the first three mornings after his father's death the eldest son comes to the gate of the
homestead in the fields, whether this was the priest's permanent
or temporary abode, with his younger brothers crouching behind
him. He is dressed in the regalia of the occasion. Down his forehead is marked a stripe of snake's excrement, a lion skin is upon
his back, and the *talboyada*, the ritual black cloth supposed to
be thrust into the lion's mouth at the climax of the hunt, is over
his head. In his hair is the *kupolīda*, the feather of a bird. On his
forehead is bound the *hallasha*, the symbol of male potency and
aggression, closely associated with the horn of the rhinoceros.
Around his neck is a necklace of snakes' vertebrae. In his right
hand is the rhinoceros horn associated with the *hallasha*. As the
first light of dawn lightens the sky, with his younger brothers
crouching behind him, the eldest son curses the ghost of his father
in this way 'God has taken your breath away; your *'gal'galta*[1] I
have broken; you have gone your way; sit in your own shade; and
God has exhausted the breath of you the father, so now bless your
children.'[2] The eldest son also sacrifices a bull and a ram. He kills
the ram by a spear thrust in the navel. He puts his hand inside the
belly and rummages with the intestines to induce death. The
burial itself is different from that of commoners. The intestines of
the dead priest are put in a separate pot, while the corpse is interred
in a basket. A special grave is dug, so that the pot of intestines is
in a small hole below the basket. The grave is not filled in, except
for a layer of timbers at the top, which are covered over with earth.
On top of this a small hut is built, consisting of a roof, supported
on a close ring of posts. This is constructed inside the homestead.
After three years the priest is exhumed and reburied in the fields,
or in his wood if he is a great priest. While there is a *shilleda* for
a grandfather, there is also a special dance for a priest, called a *mana*.[3]
On this occasion a drum is beaten.

All these singularities fall into the basic pattern of values

[1] A plant used for goat fodder; I do not know if it has any other significance.
[2] It may seem to the reader, as it seems to me, that this is scarcely a curse at
all. Nevertheless, this is how my informants described it, and their description
is supported by the use of the rhinoceros horn on this occasion, a ritual instrument chiefly associated with maleficent magic.
[3] The word *mana* is the same as that for the beehive hut, which is so closely
associated with women. I am not able to say whether this is simply an instance
of homonyms, or whether a deeper symbolic allusion is intended.

attaching to the priest. The priest is the bestower of Life, and this is totally opposed to Death. Hence the actual death of a priest is an even more frightful event than the death of a commoner. The lack of official mourning, the partial embalming, the delay in burial for nine days, and the preliminary burial in an unfilled grave inside the homestead are all clearly intended to mitigate the facts of the priest's death, to put it into slow motion as it were, and spread it over a longer period of time, and to make the process of actual physical decay as small as possible. The abuse of the priest's ghost by his eldest son is not only the result of the horror inspired by the idea of a priest's ghost, but also the expression of the rivalry which is felt to be latent between the eldest son of the priest and the father while he is alive.

In the preceding pages I have emphasized two apparently contradictory aspects of the priest's role—that of the life-bringer and man of peace on the one hand, and that of the sacrificer, shedder of blood, on the other. But this apparent contradiction can be reconciled by considering the status of the sacrificial animals—cattle, sheep, and goats.

With the very rare exception of the dik-dik sacrificed at the Kadabaha ceremony, the sacrificial animals *par excellence*, as I have already stated, are cattle, sheep, and goats, and only the males of each. These three animals occupy a special place in the Konso classificatory system. We have already seen that they live within the homestead, yet are separated from the human inhabitants, who ideally live upon the *oida*, while the animals live below on the *arhata*. A breach of this barrier by the animals is supposed to be deleterious to humans, as we have seen. Moreover, the word *pinanda* means essentially 'wild animal'; it can never be applied to cattle, sheep, or goats, which are always referred to as such; there is for them no peculiar and inclusive term.

In fact, cattle, sheep, and goats occupy a marginal status between the polar categories of the 'human' and the 'animal'. I shall first demonstrate that cattle, sheep, and goats are the paradigm species with regard to permissible animal foods, and then use this to show why it is therefore possible for the priest, who is ideally forbidden to kill any man or animal, to be essentially a *sacrificial* officer, who inherits a ritual knife for the slaughter of the ram at the Arhata Ila.

The Konso are prepared to eat many animals, and in the case of cattle, sheep, and goats they consume all parts of the carcase. But there is a large number of animals which they claim they would never eat, and for which, as food, they express disgust in many cases. The sentiment of disgust is probably universal, and there must be few people indeed, whatever their cultural background, who would not recoil from the idea of eating putrid carrion or faeces, for example. But anthropologists are familiar with an immense variety of prohibitions on food, which in many cases have no innate disgustingness, even within the native categories, to account for the prohibition. In passing, it is interesting to note that the Konso reaction to animals and animal products is different from their reaction to plants. Animals often arouse disgust when thought of as a food, but, with the possible exception of certain fungi, plants never do. Plants are dismissed as food merely because they taste nasty or are poisonous. In analysing the Konso attitude to potential foods we must therefore distinguish between plants and animals. Plants never have prohibitions attached to them, but are simply classified in terms of their taste and their effect on man. Some are never eaten by humans, and are used only as fodder for domestic animals.

There are then three aspects to their acceptance of animals as food. The first is the actual taste, pleasant or unpleasant. In most cases they would never have had any actual experience of the foods which are customarily not eaten, so we cannot say that they do not eat certain animals because they have found their flesh disagreeable. The second aspect is the appearance and characteristics of the animals, which might be such as to arouse disgust. They would never eat insects such as spiders, not because these have the reputation of tasting unpleasant, but because they are inherently repulsive. One cannot imagine any of their ancestors testing spiders or cockroaches for their possible gastronomic virtues and communicating the results to their friends. Locusts are the only exception to this, and are eaten only by children.[1] But most of the animals which they will not eat have no qualities to stimulate disgust, and we may therefore dismiss this as an explanation for their prohibition of certain animals as food.

---

[1] The fact that children eat locusts, but not other insects, shows that their elders also distinguish the locusts from other insects, since if they did not they would forbid their children to eat them, just as they forbid them to eat spiders and cockroaches. Just why an exception is made in the case of the locust I cannot say.

The following are the animals which may, and which may not, be eaten:

TABLE 45. *Permitted and prohibited animal food*

Animals permitted		Animals not permitted	
1. Cattle	Okīya	All birds (1) and eggs	Ĥambira
2. Sheep	Gaharta	Ostriches	Kuchēda
3. Goats	Teldēda	Mule	Kangeta
4. Dik-dik	Sagarita	Donkey	Ĥarēda
5. Wart-hog	Ĥarharīda	Horse (2)	Farda
6. Bush pig	Tuyoda	Lion	Garma
7. Kudu	Iligīda	Leopard	'Gīranda
8. Defasse waterbuck	Lalita	Fox	Käalta
9. Giraffe	Satauwada	Snake	various
10. Rhinoceros (4)	Orshīda	Sort of cat	Bukita
11. North-eastern buffalo	'Gura	Cat (domestic)	Adorada
12. Sort of wild goat	Taldalada	Dog	Kuta
13. Similar animal	Koprosha	Sort of dog	Kīyagīya
14. Camel	Kāla	Honey Badger	Ambita
15. Greater kudu	Urmala	Burrowing animal	Kařa
16. Gazelle	Tēla Sagana (= 'Sagan Goat')	Sort of cat	Kiroda
17. Ethiopian klipspringer	Korata	Mongoose	Ñua
18. Zebra (5)	Alulēda	Elephant (3)	Arba
19.	Kumanda	Aardvark	Ĥalaha
20.		Turtle	Kūbada
21.		Frog	Kōdada
22.		Fish	Muguja
23.		Large carnivorous water animal	Tulbēda
24.		Crocodile	Nācha
25.		Monkey	Keldīda, etc.
26.		Porcupine	Tokoyda
27.		Rat	Tabīda, etc.
28.		Hare	Kubalada
29.		Bat	Shibirata.
30.		Serval cat	Fōōda

Notes to Table 45

(1) While the Konso seem to have had chickens before the arrival of the Amhara—if one is to believe their own traditions, which are supported by the use of hen feathers in some female rituals—I was told that they were only used for their feathers. Still today many of them express disgust at the idea of eating birds' (chicken) eggs, saying they are "filth". But others have begun to imitate

the Amhara, and eat the eggs, or the meat in the form of *doro wot*, the Ethiopian form of chicken curry, but this they would seldom be able to afford. I was told that the Konso now in some cases ate the guinea fowl, *kulila*, and the francolin, *kosgorta*. These, of course, nest and lay their eggs on the ground, like chickens, and undoubtedly for this reason both these birds have become more acceptable as food. When I shot three guinea fowl and gave them to the Konso boys who were with me, they were eagerly taken away and cooked.

(2) Horses are not found in Konso, as there is no grazing for them. The Konso only know of them from school books, and from hearing Amhara talk.

(3) The elephant is now extinct in the Konso region. Donaldson Smith who passed through the area in 1895 and D'Arragon who was there in 1897 reported seeing elephants in hundreds around the Sagan.[1] Harrison,[1] however, who was in Gidole in 1901, said that the Amhara soldiers were slaughtering huge numbers for ivory.

(4) The rhinoceros is also extinct in the Konso area, and was wiped out by the Amhara at the same time, for its horn.

(5) Zebras are apparently rare around Konso.

Most of these animals are either down in the jungle along the Sagan River, or on the lowlands beyond it. Others again are rare or nocturnal. Identification in these cases was very difficult, and I relied in such cases on a picture book of Ethiopian wild life. When I could not identify an animal itself I obtained a description of its general characteristics, e.g. size, food, if it had horns, etc.

I believe it is possible to explain why some animals are not eaten on the basis of their resemblance to the paradigm animals —cattle, sheep, and goats. All three have, at least in the male, horns and hooves; they are exclusively herbivorous; they eat by day and sleep by night; and while, of course, they do not burrow holes, they live on land, not in the water or in the air. Looking down the list of animals that are eaten we can see that they all have these characteristics in common with the three paradigm animals, though not all have horns. My informants definitely stated that the horned game we were discussing 'were like cattle' because they had horns. It was this information in particular that established, for me, the association between cattle, sheep, and goats, and the other animals that the Konso eat. Similarly, I believe that the animals which are not eaten are prohibited because they differ from the paradigm animals in some or all of the characteristics I have listed above. A table of the prohibited animals will make this clearer. My informants definitely said that nocturnal and burrowing animals were bad for food. Categories I, II, V, I suggest myself.

[1] See Bibliography.

TABLE 46. *Categories of prohibited animal foods*

	I Different elements	II Carnivorous	III Nocturnal	IV Burrowing	V Human Resemblances
1. Birds	+				
2. Ostrich	+				
3. Mule¹					+
4. Donkey¹					+
5. Horse¹					+
6. Lion		+			
7. Leopard		+			
8. Fox		+			
9. Snake		+	(and general appearance)		
10. Bukita		+			
11. Cat²		+			
12. Dog		+			+
13. Kīyagīya		+			
14. Honey badger			+		
15. Kařa				+	
16. Kiřōda		+			
17. Mongoose		+	+		
18. Tubadēda	+				
19. Aardvark				+	
20. Turtle	+				
21. Frog	+				
22. Fish	+				
23. Tulbēda	+	+			
24. Crocodile	+	+			
25. Monkey					+
26. Porcupine			+		
27. Rat		+			
28. Hare				+	
29. Bat	+		+		
30. Serval cat		+			
31. Elephant? (3)					

Notes to Table 46

(1) Their dentition is allegedly 'like that of man'.

(2) No one ever suggested that cats were like people.

(3) I was told that the elephant was forbidden food; this may, of course, be a mistake on the part of my informants, especially as this prohibition has not been put to the test for more than fifty years, in all probability; in any case, it is the only animal which seems to be close enough to the paradigm animals, yet to be forbidden as food.

Cattle, sheep, and goats are thus not only the paradigm sacrificial animals, but also the paradigm animal foods. These three animals occupy a very ambiguous status in relation to man and to wild animals. We can represent them on the scale of relatedness to man as follows:

May not be eaten		*May be eaten*		*May not be eaten*
Man	Dogs, monkeys 'like people'	Cattle Sheep Goats	Wild game 'like cattle'	Wild game 'unlike cattle'

Dogs among the Konso are regarded as being in a sense like people—they are man's companions—and this is sufficient reason why they should regard eating them as unthinkable. Monkeys, often kept as pets, are also regarded as like people. Cattle, sheep, and goats are close to man in domestic terms, but on a different level of relationship; zoologically they are animals, but in terms of their relationships with men they are things, movable property. They have sexuality, true enough, and this makes them not only suitable but relevant as sacrifices, since their male potency can be utilized for supernatural purposes. Nevertheless, if we concentrate on their basic status as *things*, we can see why they should be the ideal sacrifice, and food, and why in consequence it is not a violation of the priest's ritual status as a man of peace for him also to be a priest of sacrifice. We recall that he is not supposed to go to war or to the hunt, but we need not assume that hunting and warfare are somehow cognate categories of action, conceptually opposed to the act of sacrifice. It is simply that killing bulls, rams, and he-goats is a different sort of killing from either warfare or hunting, since these animals are different sorts of animals, in that they come as close as any animal could to occupying the status of things.

The priest performs a ceremony each year at the beginning of the rains for the prosperity of his family and lineage. While I was staying in the homestead of Sagara Gīya I was fortunate enough to witness this ceremony, which took place in the form of two ceremonies, on the first day the Logīda, which concerned the immediate family, and on the second day the Arħata Îla, which was a lineage affair.

We[1] begin the Logīda at about 8 a.m. on Friday, 28 January, by washing the ceremonial paraphernalia—the *ħallasha*, the beads, and some brass armlets, and rings. Sagara's mother's brother is the chief officiant, since Sagara is only in Kada grade. The *abuya* begins by

---

[1] This description is transcribed almost directly from my notes, and I therefore use the present tense throughout.

anointing an axe with butter, and also a sharpened stick. In the days when iron was less plentiful digging-sticks were used without metal tips, and this is recalled by the use of a similar archaic digging-stick in the ceremony. Sagara also anoints the axe and stick, also the *hallasha* and beads. The beads are of two sorts, blue, called *puleda*, and red, called *furoda*. These are brought into Konso by the Borana, and the wearing of them is strictly the prerogative of the priests; the blue colour would be called '*abora*', black or dark; I refer below to the significance of these two colours black and red in relation to the priest. When the priest has also anointed the *hallasha* his mother's brother puts it on. Only when the priest has reached Orshāda grade will he wear the *hallasha* himself. Now we all—the *abuya*, Sagara, Killano his brother, Gutchulo his half-brother, Karmōde, Sagara's daughter, and another little daughter, and I—anoint ourselves, on both sides of the head in front of the ears. As we do we say 'Let us hear black things; may thorns not be in the way; may they not stab people; may cattle be born; may people be born; may the millet ripen; may God send rain.' Sagara's mother puts on the *furoda*, and the two brass armlets. A skin is lying on the ground, and on it are placed a little gourd of millet with a string around it, two spots of butter on the lip, a piece of ram's skin from a past sacrifice that lies on top of the millet, and some *ifiya* and *teemahada* stuck into the millet as well. Some food (beer and balls of millet dough) is added. When the anointing is completed, Karmōde, Sagara's daughter, gathers up the skin and its contents and puts it on her back. Now we set off in a procession to the old Gīya homestead in the fields near Būso, with the exception of Sagara, who remains at home. The *abuya* leads, followed by Karmōde, Gutchulo, the little girl, Killano, and myself. It is forbidden to talk to anyone, even to each other, until we reach the fields. The old Gīya house is a typical abandoned homestead in the fields, overgrown with weeds, and its walls broken down by trees which burst up between the stones, overhanging the dwelling and putting it into deep shade. Its distinguishing feature is a group of standing stones on the *oida*. They are nine in number: eight in a circle, with a single stone in the centre, of the usual columnar basalt. At the foot of the central stone is a *keeza*, or fireplace of three stones. This group of nine stones is a ritual house, and is to play an important part in the ceremonies which follow on Saturday. But today the *abuya* only goes inside to kindle some dry grass which is collected and put in the fireplace. They have brought a bundle of juniper bark which had been set alight in Gīya's house, and should have been still glowing (this is the usual way of carrying fire out into the fields). On this occasion the bark has gone out, and the *abuya* is grateful for the assistance of my cigarette lighter. In any case the lighting of the fire is considered achieved as soon as the grass has flared up, although it dies out as quickly as it has begun. Meanwhile the others have been clearing the *arhata* below, especially around a small black stone set in the ground. Most priests put up a small *ulahita* at this ceremony, similar to the ones erected in the sacred *moras*, except for its size, but the Gīya family chooses to regard the little black stone as its *ulahita*. As we gather around it, the *abuya* strikes the pointed stick with the axe three times, saying at each stroke *garmaë*, 'for a lion'. He then makes further blessings, which are spoken too fast for me to catch, as I do not have my tape recorder, but I hear him mention the ghosts, and ask for them not to be angry. (I was later told that he had also said 'may cattle be born, may people be born'.) He then anoints the little stone with butter, and we leave the old homestead.

As we move down to some terraces below, we are rejoined by Killano, who left us before we entered the homestead, to go down to the well. He brings back a gourd full of water, a couple of *dahanda* (gourd-plant) leaves, and some moss and slime (*kanyeta*) from the well. We come to a hollow tree, at the foot of which is another little black stone. Gutchulo and Killano go off to find some fresh juniper branches, and there is a delay in the proceedings until some are collected. When they are brought the sprigs of juniper, the *ditata*, *teemahada*, and *ifīya* are pushed into the gourd of water, so that they project from the mouth. After some preliminary clearing up we all sit on the ground (this is obligatory) and the *abuya* strikes three times on the stick, saying *garmaë* each time, and then he digs around the small black stone with it. When the ground is well dug the plants are taken out of the gourd of water and planted around the stone. The bit of ram's skin is added as well. (Just before this planting commenced we all anointed our heads with butter, on top in the centre.) The men say together 'May the millet ripen; may God send rain; may people be born; may cattle be born; may children play in the kitchens; may the fathers eat the lees; may the earth be fertile.' Then the millet is poured over the plants and the ground, and the water from the gourd is also poured over them. In the middle of the pouring dry earth is thrown over the stone and the ground beside it, then the rest of the water poured over this. The men say 'May the *killana* be successful; may the year be prosperous; may colds go away to Ala'. Finally, old leaves, stalks, and other rubbish are thrown over the stone.

Now we sit around and eat the food and drink the beer; there are no restrictions on speech during the meal, or at any time during the ceremony.

We set off back to Būso, passing the old homestead, but the *abuya* forgets to go in and put out the fire (a pure formality as it is not alight) and has to retrace his steps. As we walk through the fields we can talk, but I am told that all we can say if greeted by *Ogado!* is '*Ō!*' in reply. (This is the salutation to someone returning home after an absence.) When we come to the Gīya house we find it barred. The *abuya* calls out, and it is opened to us. We are greeted with '*Ogado*' and that ends the ceremony.

On the following morning, Saturday, the Arhata Īla begins. The Logīda was for the family; the Arhata Īla is for the lineage. *Arhata* is the lower level in the homestead, where the animals are quartered; *Īla* means 'sowing'. In order to make the account of this ceremony more intelligible, I give the relevant members of the Gīya lineage here:

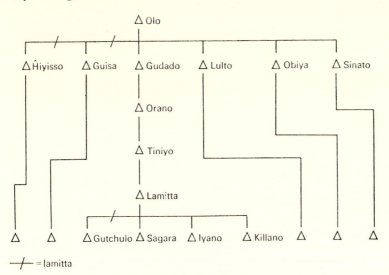

FIG. 13. The Gīya lineage

At about 9.30 we assemble at Sagara's homestead. Those present are: the *abuya*, Ḫiyisso, Koyala, Gahano, Sinabo Turshiti, Sagara, his mother, his senior wife, Ĩyano and Killano his brothers, and later Gutchulo, his half-brother. The proceedings again begin with anointing; a gourd of butter is taken round; we receive the butter in the right hand, place some in the left, and with both hands apply liberally to the head and legs. The *abuya* takes the *ḫallasha* from the gourd around which it has been hanging and ties it on his forehead. Ĩyano then brings more butter, which we apply to the temples. The blessings today at the anointing are roughly the same as yesterday. Ĩyano then offers roasted coffee beans for us to eat, and again blessings are made as we eat them. Sagara puts on his brass rings. These are obviously imported pieces of finery, and have no ritual significance. We then drink some beer, after which Sagara, the *abuya*, and another old man sit together, place their hands together round a gourd of beer on the ground, and rock it three times, spilling some each time they tilt it, saying '*Walwale*', 'May the millet ripen'. They press on it too hard, and it breaks, spilling the beer all over the ground. After a good deal more drinking we move on to Ḫiyisso's house except for the *abuya*, who remains where he was. Ḫiyisso also has a *ḫallasha*, and some white beads hung round a gourd; the *ḫallasha* is passed round among the men and anointed, as are the beads. The women drink their beer from a half-gourd cut vertically, not laterally, at this ceremony, in contrast to the men, who take theirs from a whole one.

The gourd of beer on the ground is grasped by Sagara, Ḫiyisso, and another man, and tilted three times, as before.

From Ḫiyisso's house we go on to Obĩya's, where the same procedure is followed. The *ḫallasha* is anointed, as are the beads. Butter is passed round to all present, women as well as men, and also roasted coffee beans. We then go on to Lulto's house, and though he has no *ḫallasha*, the central feature of the ceremony, the tipping of the gourd three times by the three men is performed. Next we move on to Sinabo's house, and then to the homestead of Ganiyada neither of whom have *ḫallashas*, but where the ceremony of tipping the gourd and the anointment takes place as in the other homesteads.

When these visits were completed we returned to Gĩya's home for lunch. (We did not visit Guisa's homestead, partly because he is now too much concerned with trade, which is regarded as separating him from his lineage, but also, I think, because he is a *nama saytana*.)

While I had some lunch Sagara changed his five iron rings, with Killano's help. He told me that there was no necessity for him to do it on this day, but the rings were worn and he might as well replace them now as at any other time. When I had finished my lunch the lineage members we had visited in the morning, as well as the Gīya family and the *abuya*, with a horde of women and children, set off for the old Gīya homestead in the fields, where the ceremony had taken place yesterday.

When we arrive a proper fire is lit inside the ritual house of standing stones, instead of the purely formal affair of yesterday. Sagara blesses 'May the millet ripen; may God send rain; may the *killana* be successful; may people be born.' He casts some millet seeds around, as well as *ifīya* and *teemahada*. Then he and the *abuya* anoint the same axe and digging-stick that were used in the ritual the day before. Coffee beans mixed with butter are handed round.

Another fire is started a few paces away from the ritual house. The *abuya* and Sagara take their places within the house, and at the entrance is a wooden bowl, containing a rhinoceros horn, the lineage knife used by the priest on such occasions, *ifīya*, *hansabita*, *teemahada*, salt, and coffee beans. Only the *abuya* and the priest sit inside, says Sagara, because this is the priest's house. A ram in the meanwhile has been tethered on the *arhata* below. I think, but am not sure, that it was made to drink from a half-gourd of water and *ifīya*, since it is a sacrificial animal. There is no garland upon it.[1] Now it is brought up on to the *oida* and held on its back in the entrance of the house, with its head facing outwards, and Īyano holds its jaws tight shut so that it shall make no noise as it is killed. Sagara, still inside the house, reaches over the animal's body and makes a cut on its throat with the lineage knife, laying sprigs of *ifīya* and *hansabita* along the knife as he does so. As soon as he has marked the skin, for the knife is very blunt, he draws his own personal knife and flays off a section of the skin of the throat, and then plunges the knife deep into the throat, so that the point grates on the bone of the vertebrae. The blood flows slowly out into the long wooden bowl underneath the head, and Īyano has to hold on to the ram's jaws desperately as it writhes. As Sagara drives the knife into its

---

[1] This perhaps suggests that garlands of *halala* are associated with war and hunting.

throat everyone spits[1] and says 'May people be born; may they suck the breast and prosper.'

While the carcass is being dismembered, Sagara supervises the cutting of a branch which is to act as the roof for the ritual house. A few bunches of dried grass are also collected and tied on to the branch to signify thatching. A pot is now boiling on the fire outside the house, ready to cook the meat of the ram. Sagara and the *abuya* are sitting inside the house, drinking beer; the bowl of water containing the *ifīya*, *ḥansabita*, and other substances is now tipped outside the house. While all these preparations are going on the boys have been getting bored, and are climbing a tree in the homestead, collecting fruit. When the intestines and stomach are removed Sagara goes over to haruspicate with them. They are then taken over to the little black stone on the *arḥata* and slit, so that the chyme pours all over the stone, making a heap which buries it completely. All the bones, the head, and the stomach skin are wrapped in the hide, and placed at the door of the house. The gravy from the pot boiling over the fire is poured into a long bowl, and Killano takes a gourd and, filling it from this bowl, carries it down to the other little stone which was the scene of the vegetable offerings of the day before, and pours it over this stone. The boiled intestines and other parts are then poured out of the pot into the bowl, and cut up. Millet balls are handed round, and people say 'Together let us suck'. The meat is divided into piles on the skin, and then it too is handed round. A bowl of special meat, including the neck, is taken into the house by Karmōde, Sagara's daughter. As we begin to eat (I am given meat, as always at sacrifices), everyone says 'Let it become big'. This is the end of the ceremony at the old homestead, although the actual eating goes on for some time. Eventually we all rise and make our way back through the fields: there is no prohibition on our talking as we do so. When we arrive at Sagara's house we roast some meat of the ram, which is eaten there and then, and the *abuya* finally takes off his *ḥallasha*.

Sagara then has a black ram brought up onto the *oida*; a bowl of water containing *ifīya*, *ḥansabita*, and *shelaĝda* is ready, also containing the lineage knife. His mother puts butter down the ram's back, and Sagara and the *abuya* also anoint it, saying '*Tambōsh!*'. Then his mother anoints if again with water, while we all anoint ourselves with butter. The ram is made to drink from the bowl, with

---

[1] Spitting is a sign of blessing.

the plants in it, and when he has done this he is placed tail first in the doorway of a sleeping hut, lying on his back. He is taken right inside, so that none of us sitting outside can see. This is clearly intentional, as they ask to borrow my hurricane lamp to see by, and when I get up to have a closer look inside, they ask me to sit down.

The significance of most of the ceremonial acts in the Logīda and Arḫata Īla seems fairly clear. Since I have now described the basic sacrifice performed by the lineage priest, we are now in a position to make an analysis of the themes in Konso ritual generally.

6. SOME THEMES IN KONSO RITUAL

(a). *Sacrifice.* The word for a sacrifice is *killōda*, but it does not appear to function as a verb, since to say 'he sacrifices' they would use '*killōda igōni*', 'he makes a *killōda*'. The animals sacrificed are bulls, rams, and he-goats, and, at the Kadabaha, the dik-dik. No female animals are ever sacrificed. The Konso themselves have no theory of sacrifice which explains the process by which the ritual killing of animals benefits the participants in the sacrifice. We have then to collect together all the available data relevant to sacrifice, and see what themes appear which relate to their culture as a whole.

For any ceremony related to the *ulahitas* of Ḫrela a bullock or a goat is obligatory as a sacrifice; the priest sacrifices a ram in ceremonies which concern him as the head of his lineage. The ram is specifically associated with the priest. The only other sacrificed animal is the dik-dik, which clearly represents the animals of the chase. I shall consider the dik-dik later. Ceremonies which celebrate successful huntings, such as the Kaṛa, or the Hopa, require the sacrifice of a bull or goat.

The great regional priests also perform special sacrificial rites of their own. At the Pariyada[1] ceremony, the Bamalle stabs a black he-goat in the navel with a '*jika*, the ancient barbed spear of Konso, and puts its blood on the foreheads of Farīda boys from Degato. At an Argamīda reconciliation ceremony a dik-dik is brought alive to the Rufe wood and the Bamalle stabs it in the navel. On the same occasion the Bamalle stabs a red bull in the ribs, and it is supposed to cry out. When Venus rises in the early hours before dawn the Bamalle's lineage brings a goat up to his homestead high on the Ḫonso hill, before the planet is due to appear. The goat is held up,

[1] The counterpart in Degato of the 'Ganōda in Būso.

and he stabs it three times in the ribs, when it screams. He then takes his sacred spear, the '*jika*, and goes out with his lineage to a promontory overlooking all the land. When the morning star rises over the mountains in the east, he stabs at it three times, saying at each thrust, 'Thus I strike; I have defeated you'. We should remember that the Evening/Morning star, Moha, is referred to as a priest, because of its association with rain. As the utterances at the time of striking with the spear show, it is thought of as threatening the influence of a great priest like the Bamalle.

At the Kařa hunting ceremony, celebrated in Degato, there is a concluding sacrifice in the Kitole *mora*, where the Bamalle kills a red bull. It is held up, and the Bamalle stabs it in the navel, when it screams. The Kalla and the 'Gūfa seem to have fewer sacrificial duties, but this is possibly due to my relatively smaller amount of information on them in comparison with the Bamalle. Moreover, they both kill a ram each year, like all the other lineage priests, at the beginning of the rains. At the death of a priest, his eldest son kills a ram by stabbing it in the navel, and rummaging in its intestines.

The killing of a bull after the death of an adult does not seem to be a ritual killing of the same type as the preceding ones, since it is explicitly said to be to placate the ghost of the departed, who will return to the surviving relatives in a dream if a beast is not killed within a few months. But on such occasions there is apparently very little accompanying ritual.

Beasts which are killed on ritual occasions in the *mora* are invariably garlanded and are usually given water to drink in which auspicious plants are placed. Only priests can sacrifice on behalf of the lineage, and their knives for this purpose are inherited from their fathers. But the sacrifices for Ĥrela appear to be performed by *shorugata*. No Farīda can sacrifice. In every sacrifice the resulting meat is always eaten by the people concerned, as I described in the Murgito ceremony. There are no burnt offerings, nor any other sacrifices where the animal's flesh is left to be consumed by spiritual beings.

But sacrifice is not confined to animals. It is clear to me that the *ulahita* is a vegetable sacrifice. It is the most prominent evergreen tree in Konso, favoured for building houses, as it is very strong and supple, and resistant to boring insects. For these reasons it is clear that the Konso think of it as endowed with powerful vitality. When

I asked some of them why they only put up juniper trees from which the roots have been cut, so that the tree died, they said that if the juniper trees of the *ulahita* died Ḟrela would live, but if the trees lived Ḟrela would die. The juniper is simply a generally auspicious plant which by virtue of its properties is highly suitable for sacrifice. The priest erects one for his lineage. In a public *mora*, *ulahitas* are devoted to the well-being of Ḟrela, and no woman of child-bearing years is supposed to touch one, or sit beside it. This is because of the weakening effect of females, in their sexual and emotional aspects, on men. But the priest's *ulahita*, which is devoted to the well-being of the lineage and thus is not concerned so specifically with male virtues, can be touched by women, and at the ceremony of its erection every year women have to be present. There are a few other occasions when vegetable sacrifices are made, and which differ from those involving the *ulahita* in that they seem to be placatory. At the cleaning of the well near Būso which I attended, certain plants were placed at the top which I was told acted like a goat, in that they were intended to placate the spirit of the well, so that it would not be angered by having its home disturbed. People may put out millet balls for the ghosts of their ancestors in their homesteads, on the advice of the diviner, but this is very rare in my experience. I was also told that the practice of spitting out a small quantity of beer when beginning to drink was an offering to the ghosts. Apart from these minor rites, however, the *ulahita* is the true counterpart of the animal sacrifice.

In looking at sacrifice among the Konso as a whole, we can see that it is only male animals which are killed, and the most vital of the trees. It might be objected that the dik-dik is not a very impressive animal; it is clearly a symbol of all wild animals, and associated with success in hunting; but though the Konso glory in their hunting achievements, it would be asking too much to expect them to catch a lion or leopard, and bring it back alive to Damalle *mora*, hold it up in the air, and stab it!

I was struck by the emphasis which was placed upon the necessity for the bull or goat to scream when killed at a ceremony for Ḟrela, and the necessity of substituting another if the first did not scream. The scream of the bull or goat is one of submission, and the shout of Ḟrela is one of triumph. On this occasion sacrifice is an act of war. The fact that the sacrificial animal for Ḟrela grade is the bull, admired for its virility and strength, which screams as it dies, to the answering shout of the young men, suggests to anyone watching that a victory is intended. For the bull is seen in two aspects. One is as a perfect victim. Not only is he a male animal, and the epitome of the male virtues, but he is made more auspicious by symbolic acts at the time of the ceremony—the anointing and garlanding of the animal, and perhaps the offering of water and auspicious plants for it to drink. Moreover, the bull will always be red or black; white is an inauspicious colour, the colour of death. No white animal, or partially white animal, will be sacrificed. Secondly, the bullock which was killed was also seen as a rival. In this aspect its male potency is contrasted to that of man, and it was because it had climbed up on to the *ulahita* platform that it menaced the masculinity of Ĥrela with its own. They explicitly compared the action of the bull to when a bull climbs up on to the *oida* of a homestead. A bull which does this threatens the master of the house, and has to be killed. Similarly a ram which enters the sleeping-house of the man has to be killed. In its second aspect, as a rival of man, the bull also has to be killed.

But this consideration can hardly apply to the killing of the juniper trees. As they have no sexuality, they could not be a rival of man in this respect. It seems to me that they are killed because they are in the plant world the counterpart of the bull, at least in their strength and vitality, and thus make worthy victims.

Those with whom I discussed sacrifice were very emphatic that bulls and goats sacrificed in the *mora*, for the benefit of Ĥrela in fact, should scream, whereas the ram killed at the Arĥata Īla must be kept quiet. At the same time we saw that the bullock killed in Mora Murgito was held up in the air, while the ram which Sagara Gīya sacrificed was held on the ground. These facts suggest that the sacrifice of a bull in the *mora* has a significantly different interpretation from that of the ram. The death of the bull, as I have suggested, is seen as a symbolic victory for Ĥrela. But why do they lift it up in the air, and why do they hold the ram on the ground? I suggested to Sagara Gīya that the bull might be intended as a present to God, while the ram was a present to Earth. This he immediately agreed with. A more precise explanation of the elevation of the bull is that symbolically it suggests a rain cloud, but this, of course, would still establish its relationship with Waĝa, even though at a higher level of generality. In the circumstances of the Arĥata Īla it seems reasonable that the sacrifice of the ram on the other hand should not be seen as a victory but simply as the release of its vitality, since the ceremony is directed to the well-being of flocks and fields, not to that of the warrior grade. For these purposes it is appropriately held on the Earth, not in the air. What interpretation should be given to its silence enforced by holding its jaws shut? We have seen that silence and peace are believed to be closely associated with the fertility of the fields, and I have also suggested that the *mora* sacrifices are symbolic acts of war. But war would be quite inappropriate in a ceremony for the fields, and hence the ram's jaws are held shut.

We have seen that the stomach contents or chyme of the slaughtered animal are poured into the hole of the *ulahita*. At the Arhata Īla the chyme of the ram was similarly poured over the black stone which acted as the *ulahita* of the lineage. Clearly it is not intended to make the *ulahita* grow. The roots are cut off, and religiously it is essential that the *ulahita* should die. Moreover, as we have seen in the case of the Arhata Īla sacrifice, the Gīya family uses a black stone as an *ulahita*, which could never grow at all. What they are doing in fact is taking the food which was to have nourished the beast, and made it nourish the *ulahita*. But the nourishment is purely symbolic.

(*b*) *Numbers*. The frequency with which numbers appear in ritual contexts is on the face of it surprising, for numbers are of all human concepts the most general, and the most lacking in any intrinsic religious associations. Before considering their symbolic meaning, it is necessary to say something about the Konso numerical system in general.

Like that of many other peoples, it is based on ten, as follows:

1	taka, toka
2	laki
3	sessa
4	afur
5	kien, chien, hien
6	le
7	tapa
8	sette
9	sagal
10	kudan
11	kudanga taka
12	kudanga laki

20	kunda laki
21	kunda laki taka
30	kunda sessa
31	kunda sessa taka
100	dipa
110	dipa taka (ga) kudan
321	dipa sessa, kun'da laki taka
1,000	kuma

From 11 to 19, 10 is used in combination with the numbers from 1–9, *kudanga* simply being a fusion of *kudan* and *ga*. (The ordinal form also transposes the n and d, *kundata*.) At twenty, *kunda laki*, the literal meaning is 'ten times two', and so on until 100 is reached. At 100 a new term is introduced to avoid the complexity of saying 'ten times ten', and the same is true at the 1,000 level. There are also ordinal and distributive forms, the ordinal adding '-ata' as a suffix, and the distributive '-a'. It is an interesting linguistic point that while most Konsiña nouns, adjectives, and infinitives end in a consonant +a, the numbers from 1 to 10 are a marked exception, 7 of them having different sorts of ending.

We can see from the description of their numerical system that they are quite capable of handling complex combinations of words to express numbers. In their calculations they can do addition by the interposition of *ga*, 'and', and multiplication, though quite rare in my experience, is possible by using distributives, up to ten, that is, or by treating the second number as an adjective, as in the case of *dipa sessa*. I have never heard subtraction practised, though I suppose it could be done by saying something like '*kudan deza afur gideda le*', 'ten less four means six'. Division is, I think, impossible for them, except by such clumsy locutions as 'twelve shared into four'. I have never heard this said. When they have any complicated calculations to perform, such as dividing money between several people, they invariably reckon by using small stones, or pellets of sheeps' or goats' dung, and distributing a given number into heaps, each of which represents a person's share.

But while they can be described as fairly sophisticated mathematically, this does not begin to explain why numbers should have mystical significance for them. Before giving my explanation for the ritual significance of their numbers, I shall set out the associations which each number has, and the contexts in which each is

XIII. Town gate at Tafa

used in ritual. It is important to note that only Garati and Takadi have a system of ritual numerology, which is essentially the same in both cases. There is no evidence that Turo has ever possessed this system. When I inquired there I was told that odd numbers were bad, and even ones were good; but this is an Amharic belief, which has clearly filled a vacuum which does not exist in Takadi or Garati, because they already had a different system of numerical symbolism before the Amhara came to Konso—one which does not distinguish between even and odd numbers as such.

1.

Frequently 1 stick, inscribed with 2 rings, is placed on women's graves, both in Garati and Takadi.

There was no clear idea in either region that it was either auspicious or inauspicious.

2.

In some areas, especially in Takadi, women's graves have 2 sticks, each with 2 carved rings, and 2 stones. Some people in Garati thought it was a bad number, but this was not a general belief.

3.

(i) In Garati and Takadi 3 sticks, each with 3 rings, are placed on men's graves.

(ii) A vigil of 3 nights is kept at a new *ulahita* (Garati).

(iii) A roof-pot is raised 3 times to the word *keesho*, 'I pour', when a house is completed (Garati).

(iv) 3 men take the gourd and rock it 3 times at the Arhata Ila (Garati).

(v) The *abuya* strikes the stick with the axe 3 times at the Logīda (Garati).

(vi) The priests' wives jump up and down 3 times at the *sōla* dance (Garati).

(vii) When the eldest son dies, the father and *abuya* walk across the grave 3 times, then stamp slowly with the right foot 3 times (Takadi).

(viii) There are 3 days of mourning for boys and girls (Takadi).

(ix) 3 stripes of *kanyeta* are drawn across each of a woman's breasts when the *sōgeda* is completed, and she has started to leave her homestead (Takadi). In Garati soot is used.

(x) At the *sōgeda*, 3 people, the mother, the virgin, and the grandmother, go to the gate of the homestead, and collect 3 things—*mida*, wood, and fodder.

(xi) The bride brings 3 girl friends with her to the wedding (Garati and Takadi).

(xii) 3 men watch the body of a dead priest for 3 months.

(xiii) The Bamalle stabs at Moha 3 times. At the same ceremony he stabs a goat 3 times (Garati).

(xiv) At Kařa, the bundle of spears is passed over the sharpening stone 3 times (Garati).

(xv) After the death of a priest, on 3 mornings his eldest son curses him (Garati and Takadi).

(xvi) The afterbirth is buried to 3 blows of the axe on the stick (Garati).

(xvii) The spears of the dancers are raised 3 times in the Hopa dance (Garati).

(xviii) A priest is exhumed after 3 years (Garati and Takadi).

(xix) The *sōgeda* takes place in the 3rd month (Garati and Takadi).

It was always said that 3 was a very good number in Garati and Takadi. The fact that 3 sticks are placed on a man's grave does not mean that it is a bad number; here 3 is indicating the sex of the dead person.

4.

There are no occasions that I know of where 4 occurs with any significance. It was sometimes said to be rather bad, and some informants in Takadi said that it could be bad for women.

5.

(i) Lineage priests in Garati, and Nama Dawra in Takadi, have 5 iron rings on their wrists.

(ii) The Bamalle gives 5 gourds of beer to the Apa Timba at the anointing of the drums.

(iii) The Bamalle bangs the staves of the Apa Timba on the ground 5 times.

(iv) He offers them food 5 times.

(v) 5 *shorugatas* and priests give blessings at the reconsecration of the *ulahita*.

(vi) The staves of the Nama Dawra are banged on the ground 5 times.

This number is always asserted to be very good, both in Garati and Takadi.

6.

(i) Parents who have 5 boys and 1 girl, or 5 girls and 1 boy, are likely to die. 6 boys or 6 girls are harmless combinations, as is any other combination making 6 (Garati and Takadi).
(ii) A woman is mourned for 6 days in Garati.
(iii) A woman has 6 little stones put in a gourd on her grave (Takadi).
(iv) A woman does not eat from a bowl in which there are 6 balls of millet (Garati and Takadi).

This number is said to be very bad for women both in Garati and Takadi.

7.

(i) I was told that 7 sheaves of grain were the tribute to the Nama Dawra in Degato. This was the only mention of it I encountered, except for some magical prescriptions of a diviner; there is good reason to believe that she was influenced by Amhara beliefs.

It was generally said to be good, but it has no place in ritual. I do not think it is traditionally a significant number in Konso. At present its main association is with the 7 days of the week.

8.

This number has even vaguer associations. I could not discover any ritual occasion in which it figured. The general opinion of it in Garati and Takadi was that it was quite good.

9.

(i) A priest remains for 9 days in his house before burial (Garati and Takadi).
(ii) No religious ceremony is held on the 9th day of a month (Garati and Takadi).
(iii) A man is mourned for 9 days (Garati and Takadi).
(iv) In Takadi, the Gūfa is mourned for 9 months.
(v) A man has 9 little stones put in a pot on his grave (Takadi).
(vi) A man does not eat from a bowl with 9 balls of meal (Garati and Takadi).

(vii) The Takadi cycle is, and the Garati cycle was, based on 9
years.

The universal view in Garati and Takadi was that 9 was a very
bad number, and especially associated with the death of men, as 6 is
with the death of women. Sagara Gïya was the only man I knew
who disagreed and said that 9 must be good, because it was the
basis of the cycles in Garati and Takadi, but he had rather eccentric views on a number of points of ritual, and it is certainly true
that on this question his opinion was purely his own.

No other number had any mystical association that I could discover, except that the 10th year after the end of each 18-year cycle
was supposed by some people to produce a bad harvest.

The following numbers therefore have important ritual associations: 3, 5, 6, 9. 1 and 2 are important, especially for the argument
which follows, but apart from their association with women's
graves they are neither auspicious nor inauspicious. 3 is very good,
as is 5; 6 and 9 are the numbers of death, while 9 has the apparently
contradictory characteristic of being the basis of the grading cycles.

I think it is fair to ignore 4, 7, and 8, since they have no place
in ritual; if these numbers were really significant in Konso numerology it is certain that they would have in place. Their rather
commonplace ratings confirm the supposition that they can be
treated as irrelevant.

Why should numbers, the most abstract of human concepts have
such emotional associations? Lucky and unlucky numbers are of
course found in a large selection of societies, though no individual
number has any universal significance. As a preliminary to our
investigation of Konso numerology, we can safely state that the
numbers in question can have no possible innate symbolic characteristics of their own (unlike columnar basalt, for example, which
seen in the form of isolated pillars would suggest the erect penis),
and that they must have an association with fundamental Konso
values. I shall argue that the values which give these numbers
their associations and their ratings as auspicious and inauspicious,
centre on their beliefs about sex and fertility, masculinity, and
femininity, which as we have seen in the chapter on values are basic
in their culture.

The numbers 3 and 2 are associated with men and women respectively. We can deduce this because 3 sticks with 3 rings on each

are placed on men's graves, and either 2 sticks with 2 rings each, or 1 stick with 2 rings, on women's graves. Originally, all women's graves would have had 2 sticks, as can be shown from the correlation of the 3 rings on each of the 3 sticks of men's graves, and the 2 rings on each of the 2 sticks of women's graves, and the retention of 2 rings even on the 1 stick that is often now placed on a woman's grave. It is likely that in many cases, once the original significance of the 3 and 2 had become blurred, 2 was felt to be insufficiently distinct from 3, and consequently 1 stick alone was utilized. Certainly now they do not know why 3 sticks are placed on a man's grave, and 2 on a woman's, apart from the obvious fact that this indicates the sex of the dead person. I think it is clear however, that when the custom was initiated, 3 stood for the male genitalia, the penis and two testicles, that is, and 2 for the most obvious features of the female genitalia—the *labia majora*. From what we have already discovered about their different attitudes to male and female sexuality, it is not surprising that they should rate 3 as a very good number and 2 as indifferent to poor.

Having become associated with masculinity 3 has clearly become generalized in its significance into being simply an auspicious number in ritual situations which have nothing specially to do with masculinity or procreation.

As we know, 5 is also an auspicious number. Again relying on the touchstone of relevance to procreation, I interpret its basic significance as derived from the addition of 3 and 2, the male and female symbols, that is, which thus linked denote copulation. In my interpretation I eschew any purely mathematical combination of numbers to explain why a number has a mystical significance, but in this case the addition is so closely related to the biological function of the sexes that it seems the obvious interpretation of 5, against the background of the Konso value of fertility, and their mathematical awareness. Like 3, 5 has also become generalized as an auspicious number, though it is interesting to note that in Garati 5 iron rings are the insignia of the lineage priest, on whose blessing the fertility of his lineage depends.

I shall pass over 6 at the moment, as it is the most difficult number to understand, and consider 9. I said earlier that purely mathematical considerations cannot be decisive or even relevant in understanding the significance of Konso ritual numbers. We might be tempted to explain 9 as the product of 3×3, a perfect square, but this sort of interpretation would be quite unrealistic. Not only is 9 the symbol of death, it is also the base number of the Takadi cycle, and was the base number of the Garati cycle. We have to produce an explanation, therefore, which relates the number 9 to death (especially of men), to the number of years in the two grading cycles, and to fertility.

The Konso believe that babies are born in the 9th month of gestation. In fact, of course, they are born in the 10th, but they begin to count from the time when the menses first do not appear, thus excluding the first two weeks or so from their reckoning. Furthermore, there is a high infant mortality rate among the Konso, which extends to the mothers as well. The mission clinic tells me that this is due to the lack of development in the pelvis, caused by the calcium deficiency in their diet because there is so little milk. Apparently in other parts of Ethiopia, especially among the Borana, who live on milk, there is nothing like the same difficulty in childbirth for their women. If 9 is significant because it is the number of the month in which children are born, then we can explain why it is the basis of the Takadi and Garati grading cycles—it is symbolically appropriate that the period of the grades should be that of human gestation, expressed in years, that is, not months. Similarly it is a bad month, because instead of bringing life it so often brings danger and death, not only of the eagerly awaited child, but sometimes of its mother as well.

How, on this basis, can we explain the fact that the morbid numbers are two, and not one—with 6 as well as 9—and also the fact that 9 is associated with men, while 6 is associated with women? We must not forget that 9 and 6 are closely associated with days of mourning, 9 days or months for a man, and 6 for a woman. Now it is consistent with the different statuses of the sexes for them to allocate a longer period of mourning to a man than to a woman. The problem is, why did they choose 6 as the morbid number for a woman? and why is it supposed to be fatal for the parents to have either 5 boys and 1 girl or vice versa? Since the hypothesis of the mystical numbers has served so well in explaining 2, 3, 5, and 9, one would be irrational to discard it at this stage and look for some other interpretation. We must explain it on the same basis as all the other numbers.

It is predictable that they should wish to differentiate the days of mourning for men and women, and the difference in morbid numbers for women and men is consistent with the symbolic division between the sexes that the Konso make generally. But while 9 has clear associations with birth, 6 has not. True, it is believed in Turo that while boys are born in the tenth month, girls are born in the ninth, but no one could believe that girls are born after only six months. We have then to explain why 6 is associated with the death of women, as opposed to men, why it is dangerous to have 5 children of one sex and 1 of another; and the explanation has to be fundamentally related to fertility and the relations between the sexes. We saw in the chapter on values that homosexuality is a problem of which they are keenly aware. If we accept, as seems obvious, that 5 is the sum of 3 and 2, and symbolizes normal procreation, then 6 is the sum of 3 and 3, the sexual union of two males, sterile, unnatural, and (most important in relation to the present argument) fundamentally hostile to women. In these respects 5 is the opposite of 6, and is separated from it by only one digit, so while 5 is a very auspicious number it becomes converted to a very inauspicious number by the addition of 1. Hence the significance of having 5 children of one sex, and 1 of the other. While the reader may feel that this is rather an elaborate explanation, I think it is the only one which does justice to all the facts.

(c) *Colours*. There are three principal colour words, *äada*, white, *abora*, black, and *adima*, red. *Äada* also means light in shade, and *abora* dark. Thus a *kiliboda* fruit in its green state will be called *abora*, dark, and when it turns a bright yellow it is referred to as *äada*, light. Sometimes yellow is referred to as *pudiyada*, and *ilauwa* is used for blue or green. But these words are very seldom used in conversation. Black, white, and red are sufficient for them, since in the simple ordering of their lives colour is never important in differentiating objects. They do not have to say 'Pass me the blue book, not the green one', and they are not moved to exclaim 'what lovely mauve flowers those are'. In our world of advanced technology colours have a vast role as ornaments, indication marks, and signals—uses which have no relevance for them. They display no awareness of beauty, and while they have names for almost all plants, show no interest in their colours—as qualities to be admired for themselves—but merely note them as helping to distinguish one plant from another. I once picked some striking plants, with brilliant red flowers, which grow as weeds in the fields, and put them in a glass with water. 'What are you doing with that useless rubbish?' they asked, 'I like to look at them', I replied, which produced the roars of laughter I expected. Of course they are aware, sensorily speaking, of the vivid green of the crops, or the blue of the sky, but they do not have any occasion to refer to the colour of these things specifically. If they want to talk about millet they say *unda*, if about the sky they say *monda*, and leave it at that. The platitudes with which we are familiar in logic books like 'the sky is blue' and 'grass is green' would never occur to them.

Red, white, and black then are their only important words, bearing in mind the extended meaning of *äada* as light in shade, and *abora* as dark. Black is for them a very auspicious colour; red has a somewhat ambivalent rating, but is regarded as predominantly associated with meat; and white is a symbol of death.

White, in Konso thought, is explicitly said to be bad because it is the colour of cotton, which ripens in the dry months when the earth is parched, and the water in the streams and wells begins to fail. It is also the colour of bone, of death, in fact. White occurs in ritual and magic in contexts which relate to cursing and death. The *'goita*, or conus-shell which composes the base of the *hallasha* is white, as is the metal phallus. As we have seen, the *hallasha* is used to curse the ghost of the dead priest and, on other occasions, thieves who have escaped undetected. At a *shilleda*, the dancers often daub themselves all over with a white clay. Drums, which are beaten among other occasions at a *mana*, or mortuary ceremony for a dead priest, are also white. Nor can it be a coincidence that their shields are also coloured white with this substance, to afford some magical protection in battle for their bearers, against the evil eye of opponents. In the fields one often sees amid the ripening crops a stump of tree in the forked branches of which the owner of the land has put a piece of bone, or a white rock. A white cotton thread is often strung round a homestead, or over a gate, to protect the inmates against the evil eye. One often sees the top bones of cattle skulls, with the horns still attached, put over the gateways into homesteads, not only to indicate that they are able to afford meat, but also to ward off evil influences. No white beast is ever sacrificed.

White, therefore, is in itself a symbol of death. But, as we have seen, it can be used both to curse, and to ward off the maleficence of the evil eye. In the same way fire can be used to burn the hair of an enemy, with the intention of killing him by magic, and to burn an evil medicine-bundle placed in one's homestead. Therefore, we must distinguish between the essential significance of a colour (or any magical motif, for that matter), and the ends to which it may be used. Once we recognize this distinction, we can understand that both in offensive and protective magical situations the essential meaning of white is the same; it is simply the purposes for which it is being used which differ.

Red is associated with meat and blood, and so generally is considered a good colour, as the blood and meat in question will be those of an animal being cut up for food. But on some occasions it may be the blood of man; there is a type of rainbow which seems not to rise into the air, but to stain a piece of ground red. It is said that where this patch of red light appears to fall, a man or a game animal will be killed. But since its primary association is with meat it is basically an auspicious colour. In ritual it plays a very insignificant role, and I cannot think of an occasion on which it is preferred to black.

Black, as I have already remarked, is a very auspicious colour. I described in Chapter II how rain over Konso had a very different aspect from the rain of England, how the black thunderclouds move over the mountains, carrying torrential downpours beneath them. There can be little doubt that the auspicious quality of black for the Konso derives from its symbolic association with rainclouds. They never told me explicitly that they believed black was good, though they were consciously aware why white was bad. The fact that white and red are associated with things and phenomena which are very important in their way of life is presumptive evidence that black, too, must be associated with something equally significant in this respect, and the colour of rainclouds is the obvious explanation. One reason why there is no explicit relationship between black, or dark, and rainclouds in their minds, is I think because, whereas white symbols are all strongly related to death in their ritual, black symbolism is less specific in its connotation, and more generally beneficent. For example, at the Logida, we anointed ourselves with soot on the temples just in front of both ears, saying 'dakīdabora'. A woman in Garati who has just emerged from seclusion after the birth of her child, has three stripes of soot on each breast. The Nama Dawra at the Sōla have black spots on their foreheads; a man who has killed a lion may put a smear of soot around his left eye. The lineage priest's five iron rings are made of iron, which is called a black metal. The Bamalle prays to God at the Kadabaha, and receives a black substance, *irgēda*, with which he anoints the Farīda boys who are to be promoted to Ĥrela. A black cloth, *talboyada*, is apparently thrust into the lion's jaws at the kill. At the old Gīya house where the Logīda and Arĥata Īla were held, there is a black stone, which acts as the *ulahita*, and upon which the chyme of the ram is poured out. When a well-spirit, *ella*, is propitiated, a black sheep is taken to the well, and made to urinate into it. Urine, as we have seen, can be the symbol of rain, as when rain is said to be the urine of the *poĝalla* Moha, the evening star, and in this well ceremony the black sheep is the rain cloud and its urine is the rain. But, in most cases the black objects and substances have no special association with rain in the rituals. They are merely 'good' in the general sense.

Black, therefore, is specifically, if implicitly, associated with rain, and its significance in symbolic contexts is one of general auspiciousness. Red has two important associations—with the blood of animals, and hence their meat, and with the blood of men, and hence with warfare. Its meaning, therefore, depends on whether it is associated with food or with human bloodshed. White is specifically, and explicitly, associated with death. But while, unlike red, it is not ambivalent, it can be used with different magical intentions—to protect oneself or to attack an enemy. Thus the ambivalence of white derives not from its significance, which is clear and unambiguous, but from the social situation in which it is used. In many cases also, colours are used to express auspicious or inauspicious states, without the intention of changing them.

7. THE EFFICACY OF SYMBOLISM

I should like to digress here from my main theme and try to throw some light on the problem of why they should believe in the practical efficacy of symbolic action, which I believe is related to their lack of our conception of the subjective and the objective.

Lienhardt, writing of the absence of a concept of 'mind' among the Dinka, says

The Dinka have no conception which at all closely corresponds to our popular modern conception of the 'mind', as mediating and, as it were, storing up experiences of the self. There is for them no interior entity to appear, on reflection, to stand between the experiencing self at any given moment, and what is or has been an exterior influence upon the self. So it seems that what we should call in some cases the 'memories' of experiences, and regard therefore as in some way intrinsic and interior to the remembering person, and modified in their effect upon him by that interiority, appear to the Dinka as exteriorly acting upon him, as it were the sources from which they derived. Hence it would be impossible to suggest to Dinka that a powerful dream was 'only' a dream, and might for that reason be dismissed as relatively unimportant in the light of day, or that a state of possession was grounded 'merely' in the psychology of the person possessed. They do not make the kind of distinction between the psyche and the world which would make such interpretations significant for them.[1]

He continues on p. 151:

It is perhaps significant that in ordinary English usage we have no word to indicate an opposite of 'actions' in relation to the self. If the word 'passions', passiones, were still normally current as the opposite of 'actions' it would be possible to say that the Dinka Powers were the images of human passiones seen as the active sources of those passiones.

The Konso have no words for 'experience', 'the self', 'mind', 'objective', or 'subjective', or any of the other terms necessary for a metaphysical discussion. However, it is possible to deduce something of their concept of the mind and mental processes, in relation to the objective world, from the way in which they refer to stupidity and intelligence. A stupid person can be said to have an empty head, *matādi pāda bata*, 'his head is space only', or *matādi igokōgi*, 'his head is hard', or *matādi ḍaga bata*, 'his head is only rock'. In contrast to this, a clever person has a soft head, *matādi inukulli*, or *isha mindolīda*, 'he is a forehead person'. The intelligent person is thought of as receptive to impressions, as earth or clay can be receptive of footprints or other markings. The stupid person is not receptive, and in this respect resembles rock. Moreover, the head is thought of as the seat of thought—the expression *mindolīda*, 'forehead person' brings this out very clearly. They would certainly agree that the brain, *nurheda*, is what is used in thinking. Without therefore involving themselves in any precise definitions of mental functioning, they think of the person as receiving impressions from the world around him, and thinking about them by processes that go on inside his head. They would say, referring to the workings of a man's conscience, for example, that he is ashamed, that he

[1] Lienhardt, op. cit., p. 149.

knows he has done wrong, or that he is afraid, and that as a result he may try to rectify his fault, as by returning something he has stolen.

But while they distinguish man as a perceiving entity from the exterior world, they seem to have no conception of the mind as capable of generating its own images, as in dreams or hallucinations. There is certainly no awareness of the subconscious. Consistently with this, it seems that they would regard the emotive and conceptual impact of a symbol as inhering in the symbol, and not, as we would, as a reaction produced in our own minds.

What the Konso would describe as the ghost of a dead man in certain circumstances, we would certainly interpret as an after-image or hallucination. For example, I was once told that when people shot their enemies with rifles, especially down on the Gomīda plain, the killer never saw the ghost of his victim.

When you shoot him he just falls down, and that is the end of him. But when you find an enemy, and smash his head in with a rock, or spear him to pieces, he is screaming for mercy, and in the agonies of death. Then you run home as fast as you can, not stopping for anything. And when people ask you why you are running, you just say 'I have killed a man', and go on running until you get home, when you go and hide inside your hut. But you can't escape the ghost of a man you have killed in this way. It will be there with you in the hut.

We should say that the 'ghost' is simply a strong visual impression, or even an hallucination brought about by the vivid and bloody sight of an enemy killed in close personal combat; the fact that no 'ghost' is experienced when one shoots an enemy, a far more impersonal and less impressive death (for the killer) would for us be strong evidence that there was no genuine supernatural entity which appeared in such cases. But for them the vividness of the hallucination, and its immateriality mean that it has some other origin than in the mind of the beholder. The same is true of dreams, which are often vivid and even terrifying. While the dreamer seems to have travelled abroad during these experiences he knows quite well that his body has remained in the same place, yet because of their vividness and unpredictability he cannot treat dreams as purely subjective mental activities. It would be hard to demonstrate any belief in 'vital force', or any other immanent supernatural power to explain their belief in the efficacy of their symbolism. For it would be difficult enough to explain how such a force could be present in physical objects like *hallashas* or soot, and be absent on mundane occasions, and even harder to show how a number or a colour could ever be the vehicle of such a force. Moreover, there is no reason to suppose that the Konso believe in such a force, as it is never referred to. So it has no use as a hypothesis. But they do not regard their symbolism, as the outsider would do, purely as symbolism; for them it is also efficacious in changing the real world. Just as dreams and hallucinations are mental experiences which, by their clarity and force, are believed to possess objective reality, so their symbols, in ritual contexts, also possess a clarity and force in the expression of Life and Death which for them is objectively real. They clearly consider their experience of the signification of symbols to be a real force. What they suppose to be the power of symbolism is in fact a projection of the impact these symbols make upon their minds, into the real world. These considerations would also apply both to ritual medicines and magic.

There is thus no 'inner mystical nature' of the objects used which is thought to be released in magic or during rituals. In ordinary circumstances the bullock is just a bullock, the *ḥalala* which garlands it is just a plant, and the milk aspersed over Ḥrela will be simply milk. In the same way, those in England who believe that it brings bad luck to open an umbrella in the house would not suppose that there was some mysterious force in umbrellas which was released only by opening them inside houses; this would completely misunderstand the nature of such beliefs. The components of Konso rituals—the plants, the sacrificial animals, and the colours and numbers, for example—only have these auspicious properties within the context of the ritual, because they are all assembled in one place, for one purpose, in accordance with anciently prescribed rules, which all serve to separate them from their mundane aspects. On these occasions, within the precincts of the *mora*, their symbolic, not their physical, properties are the important ones, and take on a life and potency of their own.

Though it might be suggested that the evil eye is an example of a belief in supernatural force, and therefore constitutes an exception to the theory of the nature of mystical action I have been advancing, it can easily be shown to be just another example in which the workings of the mind have not been explained by the Konso in subjective terms. They are naturally aware of the strength of emotions, both for good and evil. Human nature being what it is, destructive and hate-filled thoughts are more vivid than beneficent intention, but nevertheless both the power of the evil eye and the power to bless are surely different aspects of the same phenomenon. They attribute to emotions, whether friendly or hostile, an objective reality which we should deny; blessing and cursing are therefore supposed to be effective in the real world, either to bring health and prosperity, or to destroy them, and this applies to the special case of the evil eye.

Thus symbols are effective for the Konso because, like dreams and hallucinations, they regard the emotive and conceptual power of symbols as inhering in the symbols, as being 'out there', and not as subjective reactions of their own minds.

PART II. EARTH

As I have said previously, God and the earth are regarded as independent entities. The following myth puts their relationship very concisely:

Long ago God and the earth were challenging each other. God said, 'I am the greater', and earth said, 'I make the plants sprout, and the crops ripen, and give food to the goats and the cattle. Everything flourishes through me. I am the greater.' Then God said, 'I will send rain for seven days, and I will stop raining for one day, and all the plants and all things that you support will dry up.' Earth said, 'I don't need even one day of your rain.' So God rained for seven days, and He withdrew His rain for one day, and everything dried up on earth. And earth said, 'I am beaten.'

When I asked who created the earth, the invariable reply was that it had been in existence when the first man saw it, so how could anyone tell who had made it. While the earth is thus regarded as not created by God, it cannot cause the plants and animals to flourish without His rain.

Of course, rain is as much a physical necessity as earth, but perhaps the point is that while the earth needs rain if it is to be fruitful, God cannot sustain Life without the earth. They are thus independent but complementary. Rain, moreover, in so far as it is an instrument of God's judgement, has a moral aspect which the earth lacks entirely.

The sun, on the other hand, is regarded as being hostile to growth; it is not thought of as ripening the crops, but as destroying them.

One day the Sun and the Rain were arguing. The Sun said, 'I am stronger than you'. The Rain said, 'No, I am stronger than you'. So the Sun said, 'We will have a contest'. The Rain then rained for seven days, and all the ground was soaking, water everywhere, the paths nothing but mud, and big pools in all the fields. Then the Sun shone down fiercely with all his might on the next day, and by evening time all was dry again, as if the rain had never been. So the Sun showed that he was the stronger of the two.

In view of this disassociation of God and the earth, and what I shall argue is the close association of the earth with women, I shall at this point set out the evidence for the antithesis between God and women.

1. GOD AND WOMEN

Sagara Gīya once said to me that God disliked women, and gave this as a reason for their exclusion from the *moras* at sacrifices. I was also told (as I mention above) by a number of informants that women were excluded from these occasions because they married into other towns, and might betray the secrets of these ceremonies to their husbands' towns. Now at the level of my immediate observations both these statements are certainly false. Women are excluded from sacrifices in the *moras* because these sacrifices are for the benefit of the warrior grade, Ĥrela, and women are thought, as I have said before, to have a weakening effect, both emotionally and physically, on men. Sexually mature women are forbidden to sit near the *ulahitas*, even when there is no sacrifice taking place. Moreover there are no secrets in the ceremonies, and in any case most women marry within their own or friendly towns, as I have shown. When I repeated Sagara Gīya's statement that God disliked women as a reason for their exclusion from the sacrifices in the *moras* to Apo Okato, my best informant in Degato, he laughed and said that some people liked to deceive me, and that it was nonsense. The *moras* were for men, he said, and women simply had no place in them. As an observation upon daily life this is quite true. But at a higher level of generality Sagara Gīya's belief that God dislikes women is more defensible, and is related to the statements that they are excluded from the *moras* because they will marry in other towns.

To show that God disliked women Sagara Gīya gave me the following text.

Long ago a Kalla had two wives. One wife was in one hut[1] and one was in another, while the Kalla slept in a third hut. In the night God and the Kalla used to talk together. The junior wife said [to herself], 'Kalla and the other wife are talking together [with the implication of sexual relations], I will go and watch.' In this hut [where the Kalla was] there was a big trough for beer making; and the junior wife hid inside this trough. The Kalla did not know this, and God came in the night, and said, 'Kalla, what is stinking inside this hut here?' The Kalla said, 'I don't know.' God said, 'Wée! it stinks, I am going away.' The next day the Kalla looked inside the trough, and the junior wife was dead inside it. After this time God did not come to stay at the Kalla's house. Long ago He came in the form of rain and mist, and when someone was dead He came down as a mist, and bore the dead body away, but after this incident He never came again.

The result was that people had to bury their dead in graves.

This text shows clearly how a woman by her jealousy and curiosity caused God to withdraw from contact with mankind.

Thus the statements that God dislikes women, and that they are excluded from the ceremonies in the *moras* because they marry men of other towns, to whom they might betray the secrets of the ceremonies, while false at the level of immediate observation, are, at the highest level of generality, both true. They offend God, the ultimate source of order, perhaps because of their feminine characteristics of quarrelsomeness, jealousy, and inquisitiveness, but, more significantly, because they are also 'outsiders' in relation to the established social order since they are not permanent members of the town of their birth (at least, this is how they are imagined), or of their lineage, but fluid elements in society, because they marry into other towns and lineages, whose stable elements are essentially male. Moreover, as the beer trough motif brings out, they, like the earth, represent the physical basis of society, as opposed to the moral.

So if we regard the sacrifices in the *moras* as sustaining the whole order of things as the Konso conceive this to be, there is also some truth, again at the highest level of generality, in saying that they are excluded because they marry men of other towns.

2. EARTH, WOMEN, AND FOOD

Earth is regarded as the source of food, and this basic function is emphasized by its symbolic opposition to graves. It is said that

[1] Or 'homestead'; *tiga* can mean 'hut' or 'homestead'.

XIV. Sagara Giya

before God went to live far from men the dead were not buried in the earth; God came down in the form of a mist and carried away the corpses; but since His estrangement from humanity it has become necessary to bury people in the earth. This contradiction between the life-giving properties of the earth and its necessary functions as a receptacle of the dead was the explicit reason given me in Turo for their custom of burying everybody in groves of trees, and not in the fields; while in Idigle the *dina* around the town is used to bury everyone, cultivators as well as craftsmen. There is a legend according to which, 'The earth and man were once talking together. The earth said, "Now, while you are alive, you eat me, but when you are dead I shall eat you, in the grave".'

It seems clear that there is an association of earth with women through their function of providing food for their babies and their families. Women's chief occupation is, of course, the preparation of food and beer, although when necessary they work in the fields with men. The fetching of water from the wells is also their prime responsibility. But the grindstone is particularly closely associated with them, to such an extent that no man may ever use it, on pain of being laughed at as a *sagōda*, an effeminate man. Perhaps the grindstone has phallic associations, especially as the woman kneels almost astride it. Two other instruments, however, the pestle and mortar and the winnowing tray, while equally closely associated with women, in the sense that it is women who normally use them, are used by men occasionally without stigma, though the winnowing tray requires a great deal of practice. Men are not forbidden to make food, and when their wives are ill they will do so, but they never make beer, which they are forbidden to prepare.

Pots, in particular, are very closely associated with women. Pottery is specifically a female craft, and in some areas pots are placed on their graves. It seems likely that the pot is seen as symbolizing fertility (a womb-like vessel), earth (the material from which it is made), women (who make and use it), and nourishment (what it contains). There is a legend that the secret of using malted grain was brought to Konso from the neighbouring Burji people by a woman potter. (Still today almost all the potters are women from Burji who have married Konso craftsmen.) Now the Burji and the Konso are highly skilled agriculturalists. It seems unlikely that the discovery of malted grain was really introduced in this way—accidental discovery, through the leakage of rainwater into a granary of millet, would seem a more plausible explanation. The real point of the story is, therefore, probably symbolic, providing another association between women, beer, and pots. (I shall discuss the significance of beer in a moment.)

Every Konso hut has a broken pot on its roof, as shown in the diagram:

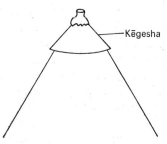

The pot is placed there by a *shorugata*, and is hung with *kiliboda* fruit and juniper branches. Beer is also poured over it; pouring beer, as we have seen, is the main form of libation. It is said that the pot is to keep out the rain, but since it is open at the top this seems rather unlikely. This unadorned roof-pot is paralleled by the phallic roof-pot of the men's club-houses, and the priests'. The peculiar upper part of the thatch called *kēgesha*, shown in the diagram, seems to have no structural significance. Perhaps, in view of its appearance and its resemblance to the *hallasha*, it would not be too fanciful to suggest that it is a phallic symbol, and that in conjunction with the pot it is a symbol of fertility.

The pot motif establishes a relationship between sexual fertility and nourishment. There is also a clear relationship between nourishment and blessing. Beer, honey, butter, and milk are all auspicious, and used for blessing. More particularly for our purpose in examining the relationship between the female, nourishment, and blessing, we find that breasts, udders, navels, and the womb are also important links between women and blessing. The speeches at the Hora Dehamda refer several times to the seven breasts of the town—the seven most important lineage priests; the udders of a cow are used in the anointing of the Garati drums by the Bamalle; the Kidoma, the chief sacred stone of Garati, is referred to as 'the navel of Garati'; and *moras* in general are referred to as the navels of the land. It also seems likely that wombs are

symbolized in the circle of women at the Sōla dances (to be described below, pp. 300 ff.), in the circle of Nama Dawra at the anointing of their staves in the *ulahita* ceremony (above, pp. 236 ff.), and in
the *miskata* circles of stones in the more important *moras*, and on the
oida of the old Gīya homestead. Thus breasts, wombs, and navels,
the tokens of man's physical dependence on the female, are symbols
of blessing as well as of birth. But it is to be noticed that women
themselves never bless; at least, this is the ideal picture presented
by my informants. Women are physically necessary to society, but
men must provide that social cohesion and order of which blessing
is an expression.

The role of the *abuya* in blessing is significant here. As I suggested earlier, the *abuya* is regarded as the male closest to the mother,
rather than her father, since brothers are seen as closer to sisters
than fathers to daughters. The Konso frequently stressed to me
that the *abuya*'s chief function was to bless his sister's children.
They recognize a man's ties with his mother's immediate kin, and
therefore the appropriateness of receiving a blessing from them, as
well as from his own lineage. His mother, however, is a woman, and
cannot bless herself; her brother therefore acts as a male substitute
for this purpose.

As we have seen, women also have a very close association with
beer, while men never prepare it. Beer is also the prime substance
used in libations. It is possible that since beer is red (except for
a small amount made from white millet) and women have an association with blood, as we saw in the myth about God's estrangement
from humanity, the link between beer, women, and fertility
is provided by the concept of menstrual blood. Unfortunately
I was unable to obtain any data on menstruation, apart from my
own observation that women are never secluded during their
periods, so this interpretation of beer must remain problematic.

The ritual use of food among the Konso exemplifies the principle
that there is a radical distinction between the making of food and
its bestowal as a symbol of blessing, between the physical basis of
society and the social order itself. Thus the Bamalle gives food
to the Apa Timba, and the fat of a ram's tail; the Apa Timba
of the Garat drums send food to the Apa Timba of the Kada
drums in the eight central towns of Garati; the 'Gūfa gives the
fat of a ram's tail to the representatives of the Takadi towns; the
husband gives his wife butter and honey for the first three months

after their marriage; food is given to the boys of the ward at the
sōgeda ceremony (see below, pp. 296 ff.); the bachelors take food in
the Kolalta ceremony at Degato; at the Pariyada ceremony at Degato
the elders give food to an orphan; beer is used to bless at the Logīda
ceremony, and is poured on a new roof-pot; and the lineage priest
gives food to his ward and lineage at his accession. The preparation
of food, however, is a sign of ritual inferiority. In the normal way
wives prepare food for their husbands, but at the Sōla, in which the
mothers in Kada bless their sons in Farīda, these roles are reversed,
and the men prepare food for their wives, and bring it to them at
the places where they are sleeping. In Takadi, when a grandmother
dies her unmarried grandsons prepare the food for the mourners.
At a sacrifice for the reconsecration of an *ulahita*, the young men
of Ḣrela butcher the bull and prepare and offer the meat to their
seniors of Kada and Orshāda, the Nama Dawra, who take no part
in the preparation of the food.

Refusing to eat with, or to accept food from, a class of persons is
a clear indication of social and ritual distance. Thus the Kalla, the
Bamalle, and the 'Gūfa will not accept food, except butter, milk,
and honey, from anyone else, and may only consume food and beer
made from grain grown in their own fields. In the same way the
cultivators used not to eat or drink with craftsmen. Commensality
is an indication of social and ritual equality. Men and women on
ceremonial occasions such as the Logīda eat separately, and this
used to be the case domestically as well, when the husband ate first
and alone.

Women also have an important symbolic association with the earth
in terms of fertility. In a wood just outside the town of Olanda there
is a sacred stone called the 'Daga Shé. It is unique among the Konso
sacred stones in normally being totally buried in the ground, being
dug up only for ritual occasions. These are primarily of two sorts.
When women are barren they go to the 'Daga Shé and make ritual
offerings of meat, under the supervision of some Nama Dawra so
that they may conceive; and the descendants of a murderer and
his victim make peace on it. The 'Daga Shé therefore establishes a
link of the clearest sort between the earth and female fertility.

The association between the fertility of women and the earth is
also established through the symbolism of the gourd, which is seen
as a womb.

There was in the beginning a great gourd in the well called Kō'jira.

God planted it. It grew bigger and bigger until eventually it burst. Inside were a pair of tongs, a hammer, a priest with a silver bracelet, a man digging the soil, a man scraping skins, and a man making cloth. The priest's name was Lohoba. He settled near the well, and his descendants went to the various areas round about.

(This story was told me by a blacksmith.) While it is said in this story that God planted the gourd, this is formally speaking an extraneous element. The gourd motif also occurs in the tradition that the first ancestor of the Shirto family was born from a dark or black gourd.

3. WOMEN AND WATER; BLOOD AND EARTH

Water manifests itself in two forms to the Konso, as rain and as well-water. As rain it is clearly and explicitly associated with God, and peace. As well-water I shall argue that it is associated with women. Blood, too, has a dual aspect. The blood shed in warfare, the blood of humans, is inauspicious, but the blood of animals, the blood of sacrifice and food, is auspicious.

We can see the difference between the two sorts of blood in the details of the circumcision of the old men at the end of the nine-year cycle in Gaho. They stand on the sacred stone 'Shila', and the blood of their penises falls upon it. This blood, human blood, is inauspicious, and purified by animal blood, that of a sacrificed goat. Again, at the ceremony of reconciliation after a battle, the earth is cleansed from the blood spilt upon it by the blood of a sacrificed bull. Thus human blood defiles the earth, while animal blood purifies it. But the type of blood seems irrelevant in the case of water. No blood must ever be allowed to fall into a stream or well, nor should the carcase of a beast or man be carried across one. It is also said that red cattle should not be driven over a stream; in all these cases the water is liable to dry up. In the same way quarrelling can also make wells and streams run dry. Well- and stream-water therefore, like rain, have an association with peace. But, as the following myth illustrates, there is also a close association between well-water and women. We recall that women are forbidden not only to slaughter animals, but also to engage in iron-working, which is associated with warfare. Thus women are symbolically opposed to blood in both human and animal forms (if we except the problematic association with menstrual blood). Well-water is perhaps the female counterpart of rain, the water of God.

Long ago the well Ħambara [Ħambara now is near Gaho about
three hours' walk away] was here beside the Elbola; they dug the well
for this water; every day it was taking hold of people and they were
falling in. Therefore the town brought some of the earth from which
pots are made, and threw it into the water. This water came out of the
well and became a sheep, and went up there to Gaho, to the Omida
house. The family said 'Whose sheep is this?' And they went to the
diviner, who said 'Cut the throat of this sheep, and do not let its flesh
touch the earth, and do not let its grease fall to the ground.' This is
what the diviner told the family. So the family killed the sheep and ate
it. On another day there was a dance, and one of the daughters came
and took some of the grease[1] and smeared herself with it. And at this
time a little of the grease fell onto the ground. And the grease grew
bigger and bigger and spread out. She covered it with a hide and with a
bowl. This grease turned into water, and spread wider and wider. The
girl screamed and called the people. Their homestead was big, and
there was a bull inside, and an old woman. This bull was floundering
in the water, and the knife for cutting the tether would not cut. The
grandmother climbed up on the bull and said 'Our bull is dying; I will
die with it.' And the bull and the old woman were submerged in the
water. Then the water was called Ħambara; thus the sheep made the
well and the family had to leave.

Thus the water turns into a female sheep, which is rendered
into grease, and which the action of a girl turns back into water
again. The fact that the diviner warned against allowing the grease
to touch the earth, and the consequences when this advice was not
adhered to, suggest that there is felt to be an association between
the earth and water, in so far as both are essential for life. In this
connection it is perhaps relevant to observe that there is a clear
association between vegetable life and wells. On the occasion of
cleaning the well at Buso, vegetable sacrifices were made. The walls
of the well were thickly overgrown with weeds and vegetation, and
there were large accumulations of weed and slime in the water.
Before they began clearing the vegetation they placed a branch of
juniper, a green gourd with *kiliboda* fruits hung around the neck,
and a branch of *ilalasha* leaves with *kiliboda* fruits around the base,
all upon the top of the wall. They said that these were the same as
a goat sacrificed in the *mora*, and were intended to placate the spirit
for disturbing it.

---

[1] The grease referred to is that which is made from the fat tails of the sheep
by cutting them into strips and boiling over a fire. Women use it and butter as
a cosmetic for the hair; it is believed to make it grow.

The words for well and for water-spirit are the same, *ella*, but
in the myth reproduced above, there is no unequivocal mention of
the spirit throughout the story, since the word for water is *bisha*,
and this is the word used in the text, not *ella*. It is the water which
is described as pulling people into the well, not the spirit, and there
is no mention of the spirit turning into and possessing the sheep,
but rather of the water doing so. And when the girl allowed the
grease to fall on the ground it turned into water. Yet they have a
number of quite explicit beliefs about well-spirits. They are not
considered evil, but may bring about people's deaths by causing
them to fall into wells. (Such spirits also inhabit artificial cattle
pools. The Sagan River is also supposed to have many *ella*, but they
do not believe that these spirits inhabit ordinary streams, even
when these run all year round.)

They were very insistent that I should not photograph the well
in Būso, as the spirit would go to the important lineage priest Īdya
and complain. This was the only occasion when I was forbidden to
photograph anything, but in other towns I was told that it was bad
for wells to be photographed. They also believe that wells can be
jealous of each other. At Degato there were three water holes, and
it was said that when drawing water from one a person should
never talk about the other two. Similarly in Gaho, the three wells
Ĥambara, Kodola, and Ĥarasho were all friends of each other, but
all enemies of the nearby well of Bahale, belonging to the town of
Tēbana.

Wells, in fact, unlike the earth, are not under the control of man—
they appear and disappear as they please. So while, like the earth,
they are exploited to sustain life, they have an important association with the uncontrollable forces of the wild, and hence it is appropriate for spirits to dwell in them. The cosmological significance
of the wild will be explained in more detail in the last chapter.

4. AUSPICIOUS ASPECTS OF WOMEN

As we have seen, women are of ambivalent status, in some respects being outside society, and in others being the basis of its
survival. This second aspect is, of course, most evident in their role
as the bearers of children, and newly delivered mothers are most
auspicious, as we shall see in the following description of a *sōgeda*
ceremony. But it seems that in Garati they recognize the social

as well as the physical aspect of maternity, so that mothers as a category may properly bless sons as a category, in a ceremony known as the Sōla, though the manner in which they bless is quite different from that in which the elders do so, most noticeably in lacking almost any verbal content. The auspiciousness of female fertility is demonstrated in complex ritual form in the ceremony of the *sōgeda*, when the mother and child emerge from seclusion in the third month after the birth. As we shall see, the newly delivered mother is seen as a source of beneficent influence on domestic animals and the boys of the ward.

When a woman has given birth, she remains secluded in her homestead with the baby until sometime in the third month. There are a number of reasons for this. It is believed that evil spirits will try to kill the child if it is a boy, and when it is only a few weeks old it is supposed to be particularly vulnerable. A boy may be given a girl's name, to trick the spirits into thinking the child is a girl; they are supposed to have less interest in killing little girls. While this belief is consistent with the higher status of men in Konso, it may also derive from the higher death rate of boy babies. They also say that if an *edanda* boy is born in a *ȟauda* hut he will thereby deceive the evil spirits into thinking he is a craftsman, and so not worth their attentions. I knew a man whose father was called 'Sagoda' for the same reason. So the fear of evil influences upon the newborn baby is one reason for its initial seclusion with the mother.

But the baby is also regarded as still mystically tied to the mother until the coming-out ceremony. The symbol of this bond is the remains of the umbilical cord, which are said to be still attached to the navel. In fact, by the third month the remnant of the umbilical cord will have fallen off, so the references to it are really symbolic and the emphasis on the 'third' month is yet another example of the auspiciousness of 3. It is said that when the remnant of the umbilical cord is ready to be detached the *sōgeda* takes place, and the child is given its name, and becomes a member of society. Before the *sōgeda*, if the child dies it is buried without formality, but a child which dies after the *sōgeda* is mourned as is any young unmarried person. I was fortunate enough to attend a *sōgeda* ceremony in Gaho, which I now describe.

During the day, women friends of the couple, particularly from the ward and the town, and special friends from elsewhere, bring gourds of millet, with sprigs of the coffee bush stuck in the top. The woman's mother and her brothers come, but it is not the custom for her father to do so. If the husband is living in a separate house from his parents, they both come, but in this case, as he is the eldest son, they are there anyway. His friends also come, to drink beer, but bring no gifts. As the day draws to a close most of the visitors begin to move off back to their own homes, and there is a lull in the proceedings until it is quite dark except for a thin crescent moon just above the horizon. During this time an old woman (always a grandmother) of the ward has cut off the dried umbilical cord and put it in a little gourd up in the rafters of the mother's sleeping hut. As the most important part of the ceremony is about to begin, there are in this hut, besides the mother and her child, her mother, her husband's mother and sister, and the old woman of the ward, referred to as the *hīyatōda*, 'the birth person'.

The *hīyatōda* first stands the wife in a bowl of mud brought from one of the wells (this special mud and slime from wells is called *kanyeta*, a most auspicious substance), and smears her lower legs with it up to the knees. Then the *hīyatōda* takes a staff to the top of which are tied *ifīya* and *hansabita*, also with *kanyeta* on it, and strikes the centre post of the hut with it three times, saying at each stroke 'May her belly be full and not be hungry'; the same is done to the left door post. She then strikes it three times between the wife's breasts. Now the *hīyatōda* smears more *kanyeta* on the mother's body and arms, omitting the head and face. She then brings the *kora*[1] and butters it, saying '*Ambado*'; the *kora* is hung over the mother's shoulders.

A young sheep which has never been served is now brought to the doorway of the hut; here its head and buttocks are struck three times alternately with the same staff, the *hīyatōda* saying "*gās!*" each time. In fact the animal is struggling so violently under this treatment that we are obliged to let it go, but theoretically we should have completed the three strokes on head and tail. The mother then takes some soot and marks a stripe down her forehead and nose, while the other women put the stripe along their foreheads, except the husband's sister, who marks herself like her sister-in-law. Then the mother puts the *kora* over her skirt. This skirt is not the usual rather short affair, but reaches to well below the knees, and is formed of a large skin which is wrapped around the

---

[1] The piece of skirt which covers the buttocks beneath the main skirt.

woman, and not cut away anywhere. Tied with a leather belt it
is very similar to a rather old-fashioned European skirt. Such
skirts are worn when women have ended their seclusion, in Būso
at the Sōla ceremony for women, and often by grandmothers.The
mother also puts on a black goat-skin as a cloak; this also is ritual
dress for women; the women at the Sōla in Būso wore exactly
similar dress.

Now that she has been properly anointed and dressed, and has
received the blessing of the *ĥiyatōda* with the staff of auspicious
plants, it is time for the mother to emerge. The *ĥiyatōda* comes
first, secondly the husband's sister, then an unmarried girl, and
finally the wife herself. They go to the entrance of the homestead and collect *mida*, fodder for the sheep, and some kindling
wood. The fodder is given to the sheep by the wife; the kindling
wood is set on one side. After this they go back to the house and
warm up some food; after they have eaten of this, they place the rest
in a long bowl, and thrust it towards the door three times, saying
'*Tuno*'. At the third thrust the bowl is thrown outside, and the little
boys of the ward and some of the relatives, who have been chat-
tering eagerly in expectation, all make a dive for it and grab what
they can. Several of them have their faces pushed in it for fun by
some of the older people present. At this time the husband comes
to sit in the hut, as the naming is about to take place. The name
has been decided on in discussion beforehand; now the *ĥiyatōda*
pronounces it first, then the husband. After this a gourd of beer is
passed round among us for our blessings, and we each say 'May
a bull be born on the *oida*'. The ceremony is now at an end.
Throuhout this ceremony, a gourd bowl of *mida* is at the door of
the hut, and a little *ĝama*, all wet, and a gourd of *kanyeta*, standing
on a leaf of *ensete*.

I have already explained the seclusion itself as a means of protecting the child against malevolent spirits and the evil wishes of
jealous humans. It is also a recognition of the fact that the newborn
baby is still tied so completely to its mother that it cannot at once
be accepted as a separate person in its own right. The severance of
the umbilical cord on this occasion marks the ritual separation of
child from mother, and the giving of the name signifies his appearance as a person in his own right, at whose death mourning rites
would be due.

At the *sōgeda* why do women and not men bring gifts? We might expect that the husband's friends would bring him something. The fear of jealousy, by people and spirits, hangs over this ceremony, because of the birth of a son to the mother. It would be appropriate therefore for women to bring gifts to show the benevolence of their feelings to the mother, but since men do not have babies they are less likely to be suspected of harbouring jealous thoughts of the new mother.

The role of the young sheep is interesting. The place of cattle, sheep, and goats is on the *arhata*, the lower level of the homestead, while the family lives mostly on the *oida*, the upper level. If a bull climbs on to the *oida*, as I have mentioned before, it must be slaughtered, or the father of the house will die, and the same will happen if a ram enters his sleeping house. The female counterparts of these animals can similarly threaten the wife. On this occasion an unmated sheep is deliberately brought into the doorway of the hut. I do not think that it is regarded as ritually dangerous. The staff with *ifiya* and *hansabita* is used to bless the mother, and has only auspicious qualities. It could hardly therefore in the same context be used with ritually offensive intentions to the sheep. It is surely intended to confer the same fertility on the animal as on the woman. Unfortunately the expression '*gās!* is beyond my powers of translation. The object of the whole ceremony with the staff is probably one of general blessing, on the house, the women, and the domestic animals.

The unmarried girl, officially, and perhaps in reality, a virgin, is present, I think, because of her sacred quality. They have a definite concept of virginity as something good in itself, and a virgin is called *inanda 'gul'gulōda*, 'a pure girl'. Old women have an important role on occasions to do with birth because of their experience in such matters, which would obviously be more relevant at the birth itself, but also, one may suppose, because they have proved themselves fertile, and their children have done likewise, to make them grandmothers. But, being beyond childbearing, they are no longer liable to feel the envy of a mother which a younger woman would feel.

The procession to collect *mida*, fodder, and kindling wood symbolizes, of course, the recommencement of the mother's normal life. As she does this she is accompanied by her two guardians, the virgin and the old woman.

The giving of food to the young boys echoes a similar custom in

Degato, where boys or unmarried men are given food, or allowed to steal it, on certain ceremonial days. A woman who has given birth is considered peculiarly auspicious, and people will come to her house to receive butter from her hands with which to anoint themselves. So the giving of the food from her house to the boys can perhaps be considered as a blessing on the young men of the ward.

In Garati the benedictory role of Kada is not confined to men. In a number of towns a ceremony called the Sōla is performed, in which the women of Kada bless their children in Farīda. This ceremony is unique in Konso, as the only one at which women not only attend (they are essential participants in the Arĥata Īla and the Logīda, for example) but are also the primary actors, and from which men are virtually excluded, except for the Nama Dawra. It does not take place in Takadi or Turo, and within Garati itself is perhaps not found in every town. My servant, Garide, concluded his exposition of the Sōla by saying 'This is the ceremony for all the region of Garati', and since he came from Patangaldo he was presumably speaking the truth for this town and Olanda. It used to take place in Degato, and therefore in Poro'goda and Ĥulme, but has now lapsed, according to one informant, because people were no longer prepared to contribute the necessary food and beer. It is still held in Idigle and Keľdime, but I have no reliable information for the other towns.

The Sōla in Būso is performed every year, but at no set time. Indeed, when I was there it was held at the beginning of Keesha, an inauspicious month. It was stressed that the only deciding factor was the amount of work on hand in the fields, and that in consequence the only period when it was never held was during the great rains, Kadana.

Garide said this of the women who took part:

The women with children, the mothers of Farīda, they perform the Sōla. The mothers cease to perform the Sōla dance after their sons have attained Ĥrela, then there is no dancing. Different people with children in Farīda now perform the ceremony, and their predecessors are in Orshāda. Orshāda is in front of Kada, Orshāda is big; in front of Orshāda 'Gurula is big; in front of 'Gurula Ukuda is big. Thus they show respect to people, and call them 'big people'.

The ceremonial procedure is as follows. In the month before it is to occur the Kada women (in consultation with the Kada

Apa Timba, I was told) decide when the ceremony should take place. They then go in procession through the town to call at the homes of the Orshāda women to inform them of the arrangements. These women in the procession are called *Hīga*. On the evening before, the *saleda*, the town crier, makes the final announcement. On the first day there is no dance, and in the evening the women of both grades go in ceremonial dress to the lineage priests' houses. Those of Sessīdi dual division go to the home of the lineage priest Turumalle, those of Pishmalli to Īdya, and of Ifada to Kū'jo. The women wear hen feathers in their hair; Kada women have great waving sprays of feathers projecting all round their heads, while Orshāda women have them only above their ears. They all wear black goat-skin cloaks, ornamented with cowrie shells, and their skirts are not of the usual pattern, but are all of one piece, of skin, reaching below the knees, and fastened by a belt. This type of skirt is used both in Garati and Takadi by women who have just emerged from seclusion after giving birth to a child.

The boxes for the feathers, in which they are normally stored together with a white powder to preserve their colour, are made of bamboo tube, closed at each end with a piece of leather, and called *ḥadila*. They are of some ritual importance, and only the Orshāda women carry them, clan by clan, or lineage by lineage—the use of the word *kaffa* makes it hard to decide which. The bamboo tubes have small gourds of coffee beans attached, and neither tubes nor the gourds may be touched by anyone but their guardians.

On this first evening the women's husbands collect food from the ward[1] and take it to the lineage priests' homesteads, where it is shared out among the women, while the men return home. The women sleep at the priests' homesteads, wearing their feathers and sitting bolt upright, I was told, for fear of the mystical consequences —sickness or death—which should befall them if their feathers were knocked off.

In the morning dances are held, first at the priests' houses (their ancient homestead sites in the fields in the case of Turumalle and Kū'jo, who have moved to live inside Būso), and then at the Mora Tara'jo, a sacred *mora*. The women walk in silent procession to and from the *moras* used in the Sōla. I have dealt with the symbolic

[1] Exactly by whom food is given in the ward is not clear from the accounts. There is either a general collection from the households of each ward, or the husbands simply knead the cooked balls of millet in their own houses.

meaning of silence above, pp. 230 f. The Orshāda women precede
the Nama Dawra of Orshāda and the women of Kada precede the
Nama Dawra of Kada. It was stressed that this procession was in
order of birth, and there should be no 'jumping the queue'. It
will be noted that the women on this occasion take precedence over
the men. When they have all arrived in the *mora*, the Nama Dawra
and the women of Orshāda sit on the stone benches around the
mora, while the women of Kada perform the dances. The most
striking feature of these dances is that the wives of the lineage priests
and the *shorugatas* (their grades are not clear in my informants'
accounts) stand inside a circle of women, one by one, and jump up
and down three times. The women all sing a number of simple
songs of blessing for the young men, clapping and bowing to the
centre as they do so. The Konso are a dramatic people, and these
rings of black-cloaked women with their white feather head-dresses
tossing to and fro, in the *moras* or out in the fields, was one of the
most compelling sights I witnessed among them. Some of the songs
which accompany the dances are as follows:

> There is clapping among my Kada, and my Kada is borne shoulder-
> high[1] do not refuse (whom?) a lion.
>
> Kandillo (a man) our boy, bless him with a lion, he kills a lion.
>
> May a lion come to the Kadiya pool.
>
> Gahano our boy, Kalabo our boy, bless them with a lion, give
> them a lion.

The object of this dance is to bless the young men of Farīda and
with this in mind we may perhaps explain the circle of women as
a ritual womb, and the jumping up and down of the priests' wives as
symbolizing the hoped-for growth of the sons of the Kada women.
(It is worth remembering that officially Farīda should not be hunting lions, or at least taking the honour of killing them. While a strict
interpretation of the original text of these songs means 'give them
a lion', it is perhaps not impossible that the real meaning is 'may
they have the courage of lions'.)

When the dances in the *mora* on the first day are finished, roasted
coffee beans are handed round and eaten by the women concerned
in the Sōla, and by the Nama Dawra, but by no one else. While other

---

[1] See below, p. 303, for an explanation of this.

men are allowed to watch the Sōla, they do not participate. Then the women return in silent procession to the priests' homes, in the same order as they came, to spend the night (the second) in the same way as the first, and their husbands bring them food as they did the night before.

On the morning of the third day their husbands bring broken gourds, of the type generally used to collect rubbish, to the priests' homes, and the women cast stones into these gourds. The men thereupon take the gourds to the gates of the town and throw the stones away. Dances will then take place on this day. In the evening the women will sleep at the homes of some of the Nama Dawra. On the morning of the fourth day the ritual of the stones is repeated, and the women then go to homesteads in the fields (not of the priests apparently) where they dance. Where they sleep on this night I do not know. On the fifth and last day there is no stone ritual, and dances of the same type are held in Idigle and Tara'jo *moras*. At the end of the dancing on this day the Nama Dawra are carried round on the shoulders of the young men of Ĥrela, and this dance is called a *heemasha*. When it is finished, roasted coffee beans are handed round to everyone present, even including outsiders such as myself.

It is worth noting that if important work in the fields becomes necessary during the period of the Sōla the ceremony can be interrupted for a day or more.

Every year the Apa Kadana (the holder of the Kadana drum in Garati for that year) gives to each town a piece of cooked millet dough wrapped in straw (to keep out the rats). It goes to the house of the Kada drum-holder, not that of the Ĥrela drum-holder. This food is apparently eaten at the Sōla, and Ĥrela, therefore, have no part in this. It is not sent to all the Garati towns, however, but only to the central eight.

In the Sōla, therefore, women enjoy the opportunity to dispense their beneficent powers to Farīda, and to the town as a whole—as is symbolized in the general distribution of coffee beans at the last ceremony, and by their visit to the fields. The stones which they cause to be cast out of the town gates are clear symbols of evil. At the last ceremony, moreover, the traditional order is reasserted by the performance of the *heemasha*, when the Nama Dawra of Kada are carried round on the shoulders of their juniors in Ĥrela, and the men once again occupy the centre of the stage.

Social institutions	Values	Ritual content
Priests	Peace	Staves of *Nama Dawra*
		Silence at rituals
Nama Dawra		Commensality
		Content of blessings
Kada and Orshāda grades		Prohibition of quarrels in front of priest
Drums		Priest forbidden to kill
Ĥrela grade	Virility	Ulahita
		Phallic roof-pot and *kĕgesha*
Harriyādas		*'Daga 'deeruma*
		Ĥallasha
Men's houses		Rhinoceros horn
		Number '3'
Wagas		Sacrifice of bull and goat by Ĥrela
		Spears
		Content of blessings
The grading systems	Seniority	Power of elders to bless
		Ritual role of *abuya*
Generational status		Grading ceremonies
Status of eS		
Priests	Life and Fertility	Number '5'
		Black, Red
Nama Dawra		Water, milk, honey, butter, soot
Drums		Various plants
		Sacrifice of ram by lineage priest
Grading systems		Arĥata Îla
		Sōla
		Sacred *moras*
		Wild vegetation
		Ostrich eggs
		Grass lawn of priest

6. CONCLUSIONS

The major themes of this chapter—notably the relation between
God, social order, and men; and women, physical fertility, and the
earth—have already been set out, and need no further recapitulation
here.

But we are now in a position to see how their values are expressed
in their rituals, on the one hand, and in their social institutions

on the other. It will be observed that some institutions are related to two values; the priests, for example, to peace and Life. This cannot be explained in terms of values, but rather by the relationship between priests and peace in their total cosmology, which will be reviewed in the last chapter.

VIII

DIVINERS AND MAGIC

A *killana*, religious ceremony, or *killōda*, sacrifice, is essentially social; that is, it is performed by elders, priests, or *shorugatas* in public, with the object of conferring benefits on some group of persons by supernatural means. But these rituals necessarily take no account of the afflictions of the individual, the failure of his crops through disease or pests, evil dreams, the discovery of a bad medicine in his homestead, or sickness. In such case the private person has no recourse to prayer among the Konso, nor even to a standard repertoire of magical substances. He normally consults a diviner, a *suaita*, whose status is essentially achieved and individualistic. As I pointed out in the last chapter, unlike the priest, in Konso the diviner achieves recognition by virtue of his character and personal achievements in the realm of the occult. Thus while a priest may only be a male who inherits his office by primogeniture, a diviner may often be female, and the children of such a person are not believed necessarily to inherit their parent's powers.

The roles of the priest and the diviner, however, are not mutually exclusive. As I have mentioned before (p. 246), Sagara Gīya is a priest and a famous dream diviner; the explanation my informants gave me for this was that as a priest he has special access to the ghosts of the lineage, who visit him in dreams. (This seems to be something of a rationalization, in view of the facts that so few priests are dream diviners, and that there is no clear theory of dreams meaning they are closely associated with ghosts.) Whatever the explanation, it is not incompatible with his office for a priest to be a dream diviner.

Diviners may also be consulted by towns, on when to perform an important ceremony, for example. When I first arrived in Būso I lived in a deserted men's clubhouse at the Mora Gomīya. Some years before there had been an *ulahita* there, which had been blown down by the wind and never re-erected. Before I arrived it had been decided to put it up again, and it was the diviner who had been consulted on this. It would not be true therefore to say that the diviner is of necessity only concerned with individuals; when the well-being of the town is threatened by evil magic, or there is some doubt as to when to hold a ceremony, a notable diviner will be consulted. But in practice a clear distinction can be drawn between the work of the diviner, which is the operation of supernatural beings and forces, and that of the priest, which is associated with the traditional ceremonies, and not related directly to supernatural beings and magic.

The diviner thus has two related functions. First, a consultation with him is a substitute for the private prayers to God which are found in other religions; secondly, in the course of this consultation he has to unravel the tangled web of causation that results from the activities of the various supernatural entities—God, ghosts, evil spirits, water-spirits, witches, and sorcerers.

The diviners I knew were people of strong personality, and seemed to have, for what the observation is worth, expressions of peculiar penetration, especially in their eyes. They are clearly of unusual intelligence, and abnormal sensitivity. Their knowledge may be used in divination, of which traditionally there are several forms: by stars, haruspication, dreams, the drift of smoke, the fall of coffee beans, and, more recently, spirit possession. He is called in to detect the work of the evil eye, and the whereabouts of bad medicines hidden in a homestead by an enemy. He will advise on the correct medicines to avoid the evil consequences of omens, and evil magic, and his remedies may be used by towns as well as individuals.

The sort of problems that are brought to the diviner are a cross-section of the pains and difficulties of everyday life. This is a list I made in the course of attending a diviner's consultations in Gaho. (The diviner in question was called 'Gondina, and I shall describe her case later.)

1. A man has a daughter who is ill—'all her skin hurts', a common symptom of influenza and other feverish conditions.
2. A man dreamt of the ghost of his father.
3. A woman has a child delayed in birth.
4. A woman's husband is going to Sidama. She wants to ensure that all will be well with him.
5. A woman dreamt of falling over a cliff, and climbing up again.

6. A man will shortly marry, and wants sons.
7. A woman's daughter has recently married and wants a son.
8. A man has a headache, and toothache.
9. An Ogdomīda girl is to marry a Kerdita boy. These clans are closely associated in Takadi, and so ritual precautions must be taken.
10. A man had seen a red snake on the path, without killing it.
11. A man's brother's son refuses to suckle.
12. A woman dreamt that she fell into the River Sagan and was carried away.
13. A man has a daughter whose delivery is overdue.
14. Another diviner has a rebellious and disrespectful son.[1]
15. A woman's husband has left her, and calls her a whore.
16. A girl has a headache, and painful legs.
17. A girl, who used to be mad, has brought a goat as a present to 'Gonḍina for curing her. (The present is actually intended for the *īyanna*.)
18. A man's fields are infested with ants.
19. A man's son has stomach-ache.
20. A man dreamt that he was sitting by a well with three women who are in fact dead.

In assessing the work of the diviner, I shall first consider the Konso theories of disease.

I. DISEASE AND THE SUPERNATURAL

The Konso have very few purely physical medications, but this is not because they believe that all disease is produced by supernatural causes, but simply because they know of very few medicines. Their most common means of removing pain, in any part of the body, except the head, is to burn the affected region with the hot tip of a fire drill or a glowing ember. They are also familiar with the Amharic *kosso*, which is a violent purgative for tapeworm. They accept the fact that *ferenji* medicine can cure them, but without understanding why. Nevertheless, they are not wholly concerned with the medicines, but partly with who administers them. I used to treat them for conjunctivitis, dysentery, headaches and malaria, and the usual cuts

---

[1] Diviners cannot solve their own problems; they must go to a colleague for help.

PLATE XV. Sacrifice

and burns, in which I am glad to say I was invariably successful. This was because the injuries and diseases in question were themselves simple to treat, and the people had mostly never previously been given modern antibiotics, and reacted very favourably to them. But many of them refused to go to the mission clinic, and insisted that I should treat them. This was partly because I never accepted any payment, while the clinic of course was bound to charge for its medicines to support itself, but also because I had a better record of success than the clinic. Logically, it is obvious that this was (*a*) because the clinic had many more patients than I did, and (*b*) because many of its patients were far more dangerously ill than any I saw, and some of them bound to die in any case. But Sagara Gīya, for example, would never go to the clinic, and relied on me for treatment—reasonably enough, from his point of view, as, understanding nothing of the principles on which European drugs worked, he had to judge solely by results. He had never known me to fail, whereas many people who had been taken to the clinic never came back alive. There were many other people who feared the clinic for this reason, saying that it was a bad place because people died there.

They can provide explanations of some diseases in terms of what we should call 'natural causes'. For example, they believe that malaria is caused by the bite of mosquitoes, and this is not the result of mission teaching. They reason that since there are no mosquitoes in the Konso Highlands, but only down in the lowlands, and since people begin to show the signs of malaria only after visiting the lowlands, the mosquito must be responsible. They vaccinate themselves against smallpox by cutting the wrist and rubbing the fluid from the ulcers of a smallpox victim into the incision, and binding it up with a leaf. 'The person will get smallpox from this, but he will never die, and he will never have smallpox again. People who catch smallpox without having this treatment often do die.' I asked the mission if they had taught them this technique, but they assured me that they would never recommend anything so potentially dangerous. In their prayers and blessings, they ask that colds and bronchial conditions go to Ala, the high mountain near Gidole overlooking Konso. This is, I think, because this mountain, cold and wet, is associated with running noses and colds, among its inhabitants, and is therefore seen as the home of these conditions.

But in many cases they can give no explanation either in terms of natural causes or of supernatural action for disease. For example, when I asked Sagara Gĩya, who was in the throes of dysentery, where the disease had come from, or who had sent it, he replied that it just came, and there was no agency responsible for it.

There is, however, a class of diseases which is attributed to the action of evil spirits, ghosts, magic, or witchcraft.

Dōdita, characterized by a sudden attack of stabbing pains in the side, and a bloody flux from the nose and mouth, is said to occur chiefly on the plains between Konso and Gidole; these plains are the haunt of evil spirits, and the angry ghosts of strangers who have died in Konso far from their own people, and who are the enemies of living men as a consequence. This illness is probably pneumonia. *Kawarĩda* is a feverish complaint, with a spasmodic stiffening of the back and neck muscles, and, I am reliably informed, is probably a type of Rift Valley encephalitis. It is supposed to be caused by the shadow of a large buzzard, called Kawarĩda, passing over a man. The bird itself, however, is also the vehicle of an evil spirit. Severe headaches are said to be the work of evil spirits. *Pabelda* is the condition when a person talks in a different voice, as a result of spirit possession. Insanity is supposed to be the work of evil spirits, in many cases, as opposed to idiocy, which is God's doing. A man cutting down a tree under which an evil spirit likes to sit may be sent mad, and anyone killing a turtle or a snake found near water may become insane, since these creatures are frequently the vehicles of water spirits.

The ghosts can also cause sickness, though of less specific kinds. God is thought of as responsible for the death of sinners, and he may be appealed to in a dispute, so that the liar will be struck by his vengeance; but, punishment apart, He is not thought of as producing any particular sickness. Evil spirits, as we have seen, cause diseases which are associated with the malfunction of the mind.

The other supernatural influences which can cause sickness are magic and witchcraft. I adopt here Evans-Pritchard's distinction between magic as operating through the agency of certain physical substances, or 'medicines', and witchcraft as operating purely by psychic emanations from the person possessing the power to bewitch. The evil eye is the only manifestation of witchcraft, so defined, among the Konso. It can cause food to stick in the throat, beer to be spoilt while it is being brewed (a burning brand may be passed over the dough and the cooking pot to counteract it), crops to dry up (where other people's are flourishing), and children and calves not to suckle. It is said that the motive for the use of the evil eye is envy, of health ability or possessions. When I was having some *waga* statues made for me, the man who was carving them hid them under some straw in a sheep pen while they were in his homestead, and made me promise to keep them well hidden in my hut until I left. He said that if they were to be exposed to public view, someone with the evil eye would cause him to break an arm or leg, because of the envy they would feel at his skill.

One will often see pieces of bone or white rock in the forks of trees out in the fields, put there to protect the crops. On one occasion near Gaho I saw a little figure of a man, rather like the *waga* statues, designed to protect the crops from the evil eye. A person with the evil eye can be detected by a habit of praising fields, or livestock, or children. The daughter of an informant of mine was said to have the evil eye. For example, one day she said of a kite flying overhead, 'That's a nice bird', whereupon it straightway fell dead to the ground. In the normal way, of course, it would never occur to anyone to make such a remark, or, for that matter, to compliment someone else's children or livestock.

A *koima*, someone with the evil eye, will only be talked about in whispers, partly because it is a very serious offence to accuse someone of being one, but also, one may surmise, because people fear that if the *koima* hears them, they will be next to suffer from his or her attentions. Because witchcraft and magic are so serious, and therefore talked of only in whispers, it is hard to make any estimate of how frequently they are considered to be the cause of misfortune. One cannot reliably judge from the precautionary measures taken against harmful supernatural influences as a whole. Some diseases therefore the Konso regard as of purely physical origin, others they have no opinion about, and yet a third category they believe to be caused by supernatural means.

2. THE DIVINER AND MAGIC

The diviner is necessarily an expert in the use of magical substances, since he must understand their significance when they are used against a client, and their potential as counter-magic for the benefit of his client. Many magical substances can be used both as hostile and as protective medicines, a duality of role which we also observed in the case of the colour white. For example, it is said that one can kill an enemy by burning his hair, but fire can also be used to burn evil medicines left in one's homestead or on the path, and so destroy their influence. The cursing powers of white substances, such as white rock or bone can also be used to counteract the evil eye, as we have seen. The following are the medicines most commonly used in magic.

TABLE 47. *Magical substances*

1. *Shalōda*	cotton thread	Protects against evil influence; is also a general bad medicine
2. *Lafta*	bone	Protects against evil influence; is also a general bad medicine
3. *Paldita*	white rock	Protects against evil influence. Is specially used to protect crops from the evil eye
4. *Herōda*	married woman's anklet	Used as a symbol of a woman in offensive magic
5. *Kōka*	red-headed lizard	Used as a symbol of a man in offensive magic
6. *Alga*	a smaller lizard with light stripes along its flanks	Used as a symbol of a woman in offensive magic
7. *'Gitanda*	an old hide, used for burials	A symbol of death in offensive magic
8. *Argīda*	a large broad-leaved cactus	A symbol of a man in offensive magic
9. *Elelita*	cowrie shell	A symbol of a child in offensive magic
10. *Maraita*	small plant	A weakening medicine in offensive magic
11. *Kilibōda*	plant with bright yellow fruit	The most generally used protective medicine
12. *Razotta*	small plant	A weakening medicine in offensive magic
13. *Tamada*	earth-bee honey	Produces confusion of speech
14. *Ḥarabata*	spider's web	Produces confusion of the eyes
15. *Nirfa*	human hair	If burnt by an enemy the owner will die

16. *'Dila*	charcoal	If placed in a medicine bundle, is a symbol of death, but can also protect against evil influences, as in beer-making against the evil eye
17. *Dūsheda*	froth produced by the praying mantis	Transfers disease by being passed over a sufferer's body.
18. *Algita*	sharp-pointed cactus like sisal	Symbol of Ĥrela grade in offensive magic. Can be used also in protective magic
19. *Furma*	large brown beetle, with a curved horn at the front of its head	The symbol of a priest in offensive medicine
20. *Ditata*	stout plant with tough wood	Symbol of Ĥrela grade

These medicines would all be referred to as *kodagoda*, and are only used in magic. They would be regarded as quite inappropriate for ritual purposes. It will be noticed that they either convey some form of sickness or death, or stand for some category of person. It was never suggested that invocations or spells were necessary to ensure their effectiveness. Medicines of this sort are invariably put together in groups. For example, the medicine-bundle placed in the path near Būso at the time of the Ĥora Dehamda was composed as follows:

Argīda
Paldita
Tibita (a plant used for goat fodder; significance obscure, but suggestions that it causes social disharmony)
3 pieces of *Algita*, skewered by a piece of *Ditata*
Farada (a locust, signifying children)
Furma
Dūsheda

There are thus a number of maleficent medicines—*paldita*, *tibita*, *dūsheda*, and the piercing of the 3 pieces of *algita*, by a stick of *ditata* (the 3 here signifying the masculinity of the *algita*); there are also a number of medicines symbolizing social categories; *argīda*, *algita*, *farada*, and *furma*, standing for men, Ĥrela grade, children, and priests respectively.

An example of protective medicine is a spike of *algita* (the sisal-like cactus) painted with red and black stripes, impaling a *kilibōda* fruit. This was outside a man's homestead, by his store of thatching grass. It can be seen that this combines the aggressive symbolism of the male symbol of the *algita*, and the light-coloured *kilibōda* fruit, with the auspicious colours of black and red. Magic therefore uses not only aggressive symbols in protective medicine, but also uses auspicious symbols as well.

In religious rituals, however, there is a different set of medicines, of which the following are chiefly used:

TABLE 48. *Ritual substances*

naba	soot	Used for anointing
dada	butter	,, ,, ,,
kanyeta	well-slime	,, ,, ,,
animal blood		Used for purification
Sagan or well-water		Used for aspersion
pipe-water		,, ,, ,,
milk		,, ,, ,,
beer		Used for libations
juniper		Vegetable sacrifice
ifīya		Strong-smelling auspicious plant. Used in many capacities as a beneficent symbol
hansabita		Strong-smelling auspicious plant. Used in many capacities as a beneficent symbol
halāla		A creeper, used as a symbol of general bravery, and of lion killers

Coffee beans, roasted, are often passed round as a ritual food, and salt is also eaten on similar occasions.

It will be noticed that millet and other solid foodstuffs have no part in ritual. On the other hand, certain liquids—animal blood; milk, and its derivative butter; water, and its derivative beer—are very important in ritual. It seems likely that these three liquids are regarded as the source of life, upon which not only human but also vegetable life depends.

While ritual substances are not on the whole the same as those used in magic, their mode of operation is precisely similar. In both spheres of action they form a simple symbolic language to express ideal situations which it is hoped will come to pass. In the case of magical substances, as with those used in ritual, it is realized that in essence they are ordinary material objects. Only when they are combined together for certain purposes, in certain ways, on particular occasions, and with certain intentions, do their symbolic properties have the power to change the real world.

3. DIVINERS AND SPIRITS

Many of the modes of divination among the Konso, such as haruspication, observing the drift of smoke or the fall of coffee beans, or star-gazing, are more matters of simple technique than the product of direct inspiration, but even these forms of divination are regarded as ultimately efficacious because of the occult powers of the diviner; I do not think they regard such techniques as communicable in the same way as weaving or ironworking. This is the source of the diviner's ambivalent position in Konso society. For supernatural power is, in their world-view, something potentially outside social control—in the last chapter I emphasized the long hair which is usually worn by diviners, and its asocial symbolism.

In fact, Konso tradition is opposed to the use of spiritual beings for assistance in life; they have always relied on the relatively technical processes of divination and magic for the solution to personal problems, and on religious ceremonies for promoting the general well-being of the group.

The diviner, therefore, is socially useful, but his power is inherently dangerous, and an unscrupulous person who is by trade skilled in magic and the occult may be tempted to use them for his own ends. The *nama saytana* is an example of someone who has taken to an extreme degree the propensity of diviners to have associations with supernatural beings and the forces of the wild.

The question of evil spirits has been complicated in Konso by the use of the word *saytana*. In Amharic this not only means Satan, the Evil One, but a demon, and this is the sense in which the Konso use it. They have no idea of a Bad God. A *nama saytana* is someone who is possessed by an evil spirit. Apart from the woman diviner, 'Gon̄dina, whose case I describe below, I only once saw a woman in a possessed state, while I watched through the palings of her homestead. She was running about and crying out unintelligibly. I was told that some people when possessed would climb up trees at night and eat fire. In such cases of possession the man concerned will enter into a cult relationship with his spirit, and make periodic sacrifices to it. All such manifestations of supernatural power are greatly feared, and *nama saytana* are not persecuted in consequence. (White men are supposed to drive evil spirits away by their very presence. When the Italians were in Konso it is said that the amount of spirit possession was quite small, but after they left it increased enormously, until the arrival of the missionaries, when it diminished again. A priest of Ma'jella asked me to go up to his home, where I gathered his wife had died as the victim of an evil spirit a few months previously. My presence was wanted to drive it away for good.)

Diviners are not regarded as *nama saytana*, but they have close similarities. This is especially so in the case of diviners who claim to be possessed by an *īyanna*, a good spirit, which is a Galla cult of recent origin.

It seems almost impossible that the *īyanna* cult of spirit possession existed among diviners until the Amhara pacified the region. The simple reason for this is that possession by an *īyanna* is an explicitly Galla phenomenon. The seances are always conducted in Galliña, and the spirits concerned are said to come from outside Konso—'Gondina's spirit came from Addis Ababa, she told me. The word *īyanna* is a Galla word, and my informants were agreed that this *īyanna* possession is a modern phenomenon. For if possession among diviners were indigenous in Konso, it would obviously, among other things, be conducted by means of the Konso language, and have some other name than *īyanna*.

Because hitherto only evil spirits have figured in Konso spirit possession the present *īyanna* cult is still regarded with great suspicion by the majority of the people, only mitigated by the fact that such diviners are believed to bestow real benefits. Even the diviners themselves are liable to say that each other's spirits are evil, while their own are, of course, good spirits, or *īyanna*.

While I lived for three months in the home of one of the most famous diviners in Konso, Sagara Gīya, the secrecy of his consultations, to which I have already alluded, prevented me from observing him in the course of any of them. I tried to overcome this by asking him to give me the interpretation of some of my own dreams, with the appropriate medicines if they were inauspicious, but he replied that *ferenji* dreams were not the same as Konso dreams, and he didn't know how to deal with them.

The only diviner whose seances I was able to attend was the woman called 'Gondina who lived in Gaho. She was possessed by an *īyanna*; and I had no difficulty in attending the seances at her house:

in fact, she invited me to come. While, as I have said, the *īyanna* cult which she practised is an innovation, the kind of problems brought to her, and the Konso magical remedies she gave are typical of the *modus operandi* of the traditional Konso diviner.

I realized 'Gonḋina was a remarkable woman as soon as I saw her, not only by her shoulder-length ringlets (the mark of someone with an *īyanna*), but also by her commanding face and manner. Konso women are by no means shy and self-effacing, but 'Gonḋina was almost masculine in these respects, not least in her deep and powerful voice. She was also clearly of unusual intelligence. She had been born in Kusume, an area to the north of Garati, bordering on Turo, and then married a man in Būso. He left her after some time, and Sagara Gīya told me he had wanted to marry her (which would have produced a formidable combination!), but his other wives objected so strongly that he was obliged to give up the idea. She then married a man in Poro'goda, a marriage which also broke up, and later a man in Īyedi, who also left her. Finally she went to Gaho, where her new husband also decided that he could stand no more. In all her marriages, I gathered, her possession by the *īyanna*, which began when she was quite young, was the chief reason for her husbands' leaving her.

When I met her she was living with a small son and daughter, her eldest son being at school in Addis Ababa. She also had a middle-aged 'spinster', called Garide (the only one I met in Konso), who did most of the work around the homestead, and a girl, Gahadeeya Onyo, of about twenty, perfectly cheerful and normal, who also helped with the household work, and played the drum and bells during the seances.

Her homestead consisted of a large hut, and a smaller one, and a rough animal shelter, for daytime use. She had no cattle, but at night her chickens and goats were taken into the large hut, where the cooking was also done. In these two respects her mode of life was untypical of the Konso, and resembled that of the Amhara.

Her larger hut, where the seances were held, was divided into a large outer section, and a smaller inner room, where she sat when possessed by the spirit, and slept. The centre pole was covered in bundles of juniper and other auspicious plants, and over the door were many bones from feasts and sacrifices. A low platform ran round a large portion of the outer wall on the inside, where those who had come to consult the spirit could sit. Normally she invoked

the spirit on Saturday evenings, and it came again on Sundays,
when she held her real seance.

I continue from my notes:

I visited 'Gonḋina at about 8.15 p.m. tonight (Saturday). The
sagōda[1] (a young man from Fāsha) and 'Gonḋina's two children were
there, and later two other women came in. 'Gonḋina had a drum, made
of a tin, with a hide stretched over one end. There was a fire burning.
She was quite normal and cheerful. I gave her a present of incense,
which was gratefully accepted. We sat there singing and beating the
drum for some time, and coffee was served.' Gonḋina also danced with
a spear and an iron-tipped walking stick. She asked me if I had my
little bell (which I had bought that day at the market). I went and got it.
After showing it her, she gave me her big bell to play. After a while,
and much dancing, she appeared to be dizzy, and said that the spirit
was coming. Garide aspersed water over the house, over the people,
and on the partition. She ['Gonḋina] danced some more, and then
began to toss her head about, lashing her ringlets, burbling and
warbling, with convulsive movements of her body. Her voice immediately became the hoarse croak that signified the presence of the
spirit. Some of the women went and kissed her feet. She said *'asham!'*
(a Galla greeting, used very generally in Konso) many times, to which
we all replied. She was offered incense by Garide, and snuffed up the
fumes avidly from the bowl. She expressed displeasure, in Galliña,
that some children had been throwing stones at her black chickens.
After a lot more dancing, during which Garide went out and placed
incense in three hearths in the garden outside, she eventually spun
round, and lay exhausted by her little partition. The *īyanna* had then
gone, and she spoke again in her usual voice, and continued to behave
quite normally for the rest of the evening. The possession had lasted
for perhaps an hour. When it was over we had more coffee, and talked
of everyday things, such as the fighting with the Borana (of which
there was a large amount at that time). We dispersed at about 10.45 p.m.

But the details of the ceremony varied from week to week. A fort-
night later I recorded the following details:

Went to 'Gonḋina's tonight; got there about 8.15. Two men were
there, Garide, Gahadeeya, Gahadeeya's mother, an old woman, another
woman, and 'Gonḋina's two children, besides my companion and
myself.

---

[1] 'Gonḋina herself is sexually 'indeterminate', one of her assistants is a
spinster, and *sagōdas* are prominent among her visitors. This seems good
evidence for an association between the absence of clear sex role and interest in
spirit possession.

We had some singing and dancing, and then after about only a quarter
of an hour 'Gondina became possessed. The dancing went on for some
time; she was on her knees. Then she arose and signalled for silence.
The spirit said that it was angry at having been called down at a time
of death, which was God's doing (as she was speaking in Galliña I had
to get a rough summary afterwards from my companion, who was not
the best of informants). There had recently been a death in Gaho, and
it was said that the *iyanna* would be angry if called upon at such a time.
(It is a general belief in Konso that a diviner should have nothing to do
with death, like a priest.) She continued dancing, and suddenly flung
a spear with great force into the door-post. Then, as she continued to
dance, she placed her right foot on the glowing coals of the fire on the
floor. She kept it there for about eight seconds. As the dance continued,
she returned to the hearth, and placed the same foot on the coals again,
for a similar length of time, without showing any signs of knowing
what she was doing. When Gahadeeya tried to go out she beat her back
with the butt of another spear, and cursed her in Galliña. During this
time no obeisances were made, nor was she offered incense or coffee.
There were only a few greetings of '*asham!*' Finally, when she was over
at the door, she collapsed more or less helpless and had to be assisted
to a seat—the spirit had gone. She asked how the spear had come to be
stuck in the door-post.

She displayed no signs of injury on the sole of her right foot, nor
any pain, and was quite unaware of what she had done. I found her
performance this evening frightening and sinister.

We now began to talk normally; apparently the spear had been
thrown into the door-post to stop anyone leaving. She asked me why
the spirit had come, as she was not supposed to call on it at a time of
death. I said I didn't know. When coffee was ready she prayed in
Galliña, and flung a handful of parched grain across the room. After
coffee the usual incense was taken outside to the three '*arsa*' or fireplaces
in the garden, and some was burnt inside as well.

While we were drinking coffee she became aware of an evil spirit
and told it to go away. Apparently it had come for a drink at the well,
and, hearing the music and dancing, wanted to come in. She forbade it
to do so. It asked for tobacco, so she went out and gave it some, holding
a conversation with it in Galliña. I asked her what a *saytana* looked
like. 'They are like a man, except that they have legs and feet of straw,
big chests, and very big eyes.' We finished at about 10.30 p.m. Her
possession tonight lasted only about half an hour.

This was the most dramatic instance of possession I ever witnessed in 'Gondina's house. On some evenings when I went,

however, the *īyanna* never came at all, either because there was
too much joking, or because 'Gondina was not feeling well enough.

Every Sunday she would begin beating her drum, often before
six in the morning, and would become possessed almost immediately. But on these occasions I think the possession was simulated.
For instead of its lasting only half an hour to an hour, she would
speak in the deep hoarse tones which signified possession for as
much as ten hours at a time. Her possession on Saturday evenings
was marked by an apparent ignorance of what was going on around
her, and it seemed that the trance needed to be sustained by violent
physical activity; but on Sundays she had to answer questions
about difficult personal problems, and as well as doing this to her
clients' apparent satisfaction, she showed an acute awareness of
what was going on in the main part of the hut (on Sundays she sat
behind her partition). She was also unable to sustain her trance on
these occasions by dancing. While the spirit was supposed only to
know Gallina, she spoke to me in Konsina, as she knew that I had
no Gallina. For all these reasons I think that her trance on Sundays
was simulated, whereas her behaviour on Saturday night was an
example of an abnormal mental state.

On Sunday mornings all those who had problems they wished to
put to the *īyanna* came to 'Gondina's house at any time after
dawn, and sat with the other clients until their turn came to ask
their questions. 'Gondina spoke in Gallina, and had an old woman
who was always there to act as her interpreter. I give an account
from my notes of a typical seance on a Sunday morning:

I went along with Sheereda [my informant who spoke Gallina] at
about 7 a.m. There were six or seven other people there besides ourselves; the old woman who was translating, Garide (who poured coffee),
the girl, Gahadeeya (who rings the bells), and the two *sagōda* from
Fāsha, both wearing their skirts. There were various other women who
came in from time to time. Besides them there were two men from Tebana,
one from Kamole, and one from Gaho, one other man, and ourselves.

The diviner is hidden behind a screen and has her drum and her
bell. It seems permitted for people to go in and see her and pay their
respects. She sings, and the congregation accompanies her with a simple
refrain and clapping, and with the bells. The diviner brings the song to
an end with the rapid ringing of her bell, and then answers questions.
Her voice is extremely deep while she does so, and she speaks in Gallina,
with a few lapses. Someone then interprets. But I could detect no signs
of possession. She was quite capable of waiting until the translation was

completed, even if something delayed it, and of making remarks, more in her normal voice, and in Konsiña, especially to me this morning, asking me to drink coffee, and if I would like to marry this girl or that, and being generally frivolous. When coffee was served she drank hers along with the rest of us, though it was passed to her through the screen, and there was a long silence while she drank it. She was asked questions by each client in turn, but took some time in answering, as every few minutes she would break into song.

The first client I heard was the young man from Tēbana. He said he was ill, and she asked him if he had looked into a grave, and he said, no. But he had seen a red snake in the path, though without killing it. She said that this snake had an evil spirit, and this caused the client's sickness. He was to take a red cockerel, a white he-goat, and kill both at Orballe (a piece of land near-by) by cutting their throats. He was to take the goat back to his house, and leave the cockerel on the path. Then he should take three stones and pass them over his head, and throw them away. He should also take *kukubtoda*,[1] rub it between his hands and hold it against his belly. She gave him some salt, which he was to bite up and spit inside his shirt.

The man from Kamole had a daughter who was ill with a feverish condition, perhaps influenza—'all her skin hurts'. 'Are there two other daughters?' 'Yes, one alive, and one dead.' 'It is the ghost of the dead sister that is causing the sickness. Does the path to your house have a banana tree or a coffee bush?' 'Yes, a banana tree.' 'The ghost hid behind this banana tree and as the girl went out to watch the goats it struck her with sickness.'

To cure this the father was to get a piece of *rēgambīda* wood, two small stones, some *shelagda*, and *otīda*, and throw them in the path. He should also take a locust, kill it by biting it, and hold it to the sick girl's chest, and burn some mantis froth (*dūsheda*). Then the girl would get well.

It would be tedious, and uninformative, to recite any more cases. It was clear to me after studying the details of more than twenty that there were certain common medicines which I have already described in the previous section on Konso magic. (Even though the *īyanna* was a Galla, he recommended Konso medicines!) But there was no evidence that the medicines were adjusted to the specific complaints.

While, as I have said, the *īyanna* diviner represents an innovation in Konso religion, and one which is frequently deplored, we may say that it exemplifies the traditional aptitudes of the diviner but to an exaggerated degree.

[1] A plant.

IX

THREE CATEGORIES OF OUTSIDER: GOD, EARTH, AND THE WILD

THE problem of understanding its own origin faces every human society, for there is an inherent impossibility in explaining a whole in terms of the actions of any of its parts. We frequently find therefore that some external agency, such as a god, culture hero, or conqueror, is postulated as the creator of the total social order. But such beings are of necessity outsiders. Among the Konso, as we have seen, God is regarded as the ultimate source of order, both conceptual and moral. In the beginning He laid down the laws which should govern men's conduct, but then He went far away, and delegated the responsibility for maintaining the moral order to the elders, though He retained the power of punishing sinners by sickness and death. He is essentially a remote Being, and there is no idea of praying to Him, either corporately or individually. 'Prayer' in Konsiña is the same word as 'request', and for particular groups or persons to establish the relationship of petitioners with God would mean that He was no longer an outsider, the impartial maintainer of the total social order. It is therefore highly significant that God is very closely associated with the sky, for it is only those who look down from high places who can see the totality of things laid out below them. The Konso are not the only people to perceive the appropriateness of beings who create order dwelling in high places. The sky-God is one of the most familiar elements in African cosmologies, and, indeed, is found outside Africa. We recall, for example, that the two major instances of law-giving in the Scriptures—Moses receiving the Ten Commandments, and Christ's Sermon on the Mount—both occur on mountains.

But the Konso do not believe that God ordained the grading systems or the towns. While He laid down the principles of right conduct, not only are they aware that they have altered the rules of their grading systems at various times in the past, but the legend of their origins clearly states that the people decided to borrow them from the Burji. There is thus no doubt in their minds that the systems are of human origin. (Nevertheless, while the rules are of human origin, the systems are clearly regarded as expressing fundamental truths about the nature of human society—the dependence of age-groups on generational/sibling seniority—and hence as being a true basis of social order, of peace, in the widest sense of the term.)

Again, the Konso clearly believe that their ancestors formed the towns for self-protection. Whether they are correct in this belief or not is irrelevant for our purposes; the point is that according to their own traditions the towns were formed by men, not God.

But they clearly feel that their grading systems and towns require the mediation of priests and Nama Dawra; we have seen that the regional priests give permission for the new cycles to begin, and act as peacemakers between the towns. Now the best mediators are outsiders and there is considerable evidence to show that the regional and lineage priests are regarded as outsiders. We have seen that the regional priests, and ideally the lineage priests, live outside the towns in the fields. It is said that the ancestors of the town of Lehīda, whose men act as peacemakers in Garati, originally migrated from Takadi. The ward of Ifada in Būso, who have a peace-making role within the town, are regarded as only partially integrated into the town, and there is even some doubt as to whether they are members of either dual division. At the Sōla ceremony the women of Ifada dance by themselves. There is thus a clear association between being outside society and having the role of mediator. The regional priests not only mediate in the quarrels of the towns, but also by giving permission for each new cycle of the grading system to begin they are also clearly regarded as providing a link, a mediation, between the discontinuity of the successive cycles. The lineage priests, besides exemplifying the role of eS in an extreme degree, which, as we have seen, is a mediator's role, mediate also between the members of the lineage. But the elders, unlike the priests, do not mediate between any of the component elements of society. They are the sources of wisdom and moral authority, and in this respect analogous to God, and therefore corporately they can bless, but individually they can not, and no taboos attach to them personally, as they do to the priests. Everyone can become an elder in the course of a normal life span.

Yet outsiders such as the priests are of a different nature from outsiders such as God, for there is an inherent difference between creating order and mediating between the component parts of that order. The creator of order stands above society, but mediators are outside 'on the ground'; the Konso in fact consider them to be related to the forces of the wild, which are inherently outside social control. The old homesteads of priests must never be cultivated, and the large woods which adjoin the homesteads of the regional priests must never be cut, except when a priest is being buried there (though priests may give trees to lineage members, or to towns for ritual or profane purposes). The vegetation which springs up in sacred *moras* must never be cut, except during a ritual, and we find that the most sacred *moras* are out in the fields—the Mora Murgito in Būso, for example, is on the edge of the town, and the Mora Hirle, which is now contained within Idigle—see Map IV— has been swamped by the expansion of the town, and was once in the fields. The *moras* of Damalle and Mirig, in Garati, Oibatale in Takadi, and Teera in Turo, are all out in the fields, and, moreover, are all covered with dense vegetation. I drew attention earlier to the manifest contrast between the wild vegetation of the *moras* and the cultivated fields, and said that sacredness was clearly associated with the wild, as opposed to the utilitarian and the domesticated.

Now in discussing the clans we saw that they were divided into Odīya, of God, Teedibīya, of Earth, and Kāālo. I was told in Idigle that Kāālo meant 'wild animals'; in Būso they did not use the word 'Kāālo', but 'Sagan'. We have already seen the importance of the principles of God and Earth in their cosmology, and so we may conclude that Kāālo or Sagan is a principle of equal significance. The Sagan is associated in their minds with the jungle, wild beasts, enemies such as the Borana, and evil spirits. These are all forces which are outside social control, and thus it is fitting that priests should be identified with them. But Kāālo, the Wild, is inherently ambivalent. The nature of this ambivalence can best be appreciated by considering the Konso attitude to another kind of outsider, who has important resemblances to the priests—the white man. When I first arrived in Konso, and was making arrangements to live in Būso, the mission, who were conducting the negotiations on my behalf in Amharic, told me that the people were opposed to my living there because, as one teacher translated their objection, 'I would harm their religion'. After I had been living in Būso for a few weeks one of the men said to me, 'You are a priest; you can

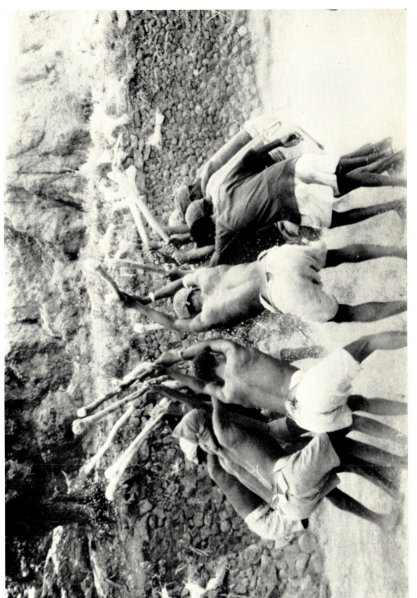

XVI. Threshing wheat

bring the rain'. When I had left Būso, and was living in Degato, I met some old acquaintances from Būso, who said that they were sorry I had gone, as there had been no quarrelling or sickness while I had lived among them (something of an exaggeration, I may say!). Now the outsider, of the type represented by the white man, the total stranger, who comes to an alien society without previous ties with any particular persons or groups within it, while he may be seen as the embodiment of anomie, the destroyer of the existing order, is also potentially the friend of all men, the ideal mediator and peacemaker. He has that divine attribute, impartiality. We are familiar in the ethnographic literature with numerous instances in which foreigners have been made priests, rain-makers, or kings by their adopted people, and this may also explain why the original Kalla, if he was really an Amhara, was given exceptional ritual status. It also throws light on the otherwise rather cryptic explanation given me by the Kalla of the high degree of mobility of his ancestors—'They moved about to make themselves big.' The familiar theme in European legends of the stranger who proves to be a prince, or the devil, in disguise, is clearly related to this ambivalent quality of outsiders.

Priests thus derive their efficacy from their status as outsiders, which, in the case of the regional priests, is maintained at the level of social interaction by strict taboos against their accepting food or drink from other men, against their sleeping in another man's homestead, and against marrying a first wife from any of the towns of their own region. But their status as outsiders and mediators is also inherently linked with the Wild, with those forces which are outside social control, and therefore ambivalent. The Wild can provide society with its mediators, but also with enemies, in the form of hostile tribesmen in ambush, fierce wild animals, and evil spirits. We have seen that while priests are regarded as wholly on the side of social order, their presence among men is regarded as dangerous, especially when a priest dies and the spiritual powers which were controlled by the bonds of social responsibility are released by death. The spiritual powers of priests are thus inherently dangerous. This is much more marked in the case of diviners. As we have seen, the diviner is associated with evil spirits, he can talk with ghosts and interpret dreams. I suggested earlier, following Lienhardt, that the Konso lack our model of the subjective and the objective, and while to us dreams, hysterical or dissociative states, and hallucinations are manifestations of the individual subconscious, to them, and apparently to most primitive peoples, these phenomena are what we should call objectively real. Now, whether one takes the European or the Konso approach to such phenomena, they are basically unpredictable; one cannot tell when one will see a ghost, or dream an inauspicious dream, or be seized with madness, and consequently, being beyond any kind of social control, they are a mode of reality which is essentially part of the Käälo complex. A *nama saytana*, while he may be able to induce in himself a state of 'spirit possession', like the diviner, is, while in such a state, not regarded as amenable to social control. Magic and witchcraft, as the means by which individual malice is expressed, by anonymous and secret means, are also clearly seen as analogous to the forces of the wild. Fire and white substances, the primary magical weapons, are inherently destructive—whether one regards a particular use of these medicines as good or bad depends on whether one is the user or the victim. As we saw, magical substances differ from those used in ritual, the latter being inherently auspicious. Diviners therefore are definable in terms of the Käälo complex; their powers are those of the socially uncontrollable forces of the wild (in this case, of what we should describe as the individual psyche), who are tolerated because they are useful, but who are inherently dangerous.

It is possible for priests to act as diviners, as we saw, but there is another point of association between them. The present 'Gūfa is a small boy whose father died a few years ago. His hair hangs down to his shoulders, and will be cut only when he reaches Ĥrelita grade. At present he can bless, but only under his mother's supervision. Now it is a mark of someone who is possessed by an *īyanna* to leave his hair uncut in an exactly similar manner. I have argued elsewhere, in my paper 'Social Hair',[1] that long hair is a symbol of being outside society and of association with sanctity and/or animality, and that cutting the hair = re-entering society, or the imposition of social control. The long hair of the 'Gūfa and the diviner possessed by an *īyanna* are examples of this phenomenon, and also of the resemblance which is felt to exist between the priest who is not a member of the adult grade and is incapable of assuming full adult responsibility, and a type of diviner.

There is a third class of outsider, whose characteristics I have already discussed at length—women. As we saw in the chapter on

[1] *Man*, 4 (1969).

God and Earth, women are regarded as passive instruments, necessary for the physical survival of society by their fertility and their role as the providers of food, and in this respect are closely analogous to the earth and domestic animals. But while they provide the physical necessities for survival, and as such are beneficial, the earth, women, and domestic animals are essentially passive in relation to the social order, organized in ways over which they have no control, and about which they are not consulted. We recall that there are three categories of animals, those like man which may not be eaten; wild animals, which also may not be eaten, but are hunted, and in this respect are analogous to enemies, and domestic animals, which are treated as things, and may be eaten. In ritual, the symbols of fertility, while mainly feminine in association, are manipulated by men. Even in the Sōla ceremony which recognizes the social significance of the maternal role, women do not verbally bless. Ideally women are silent; men speak, and bless, for speech is the means by which the social order is made articulate and maintained. Women, it may be remembered, like craftsmen, and white men, are forbidden to touch the sacred drums, the symbols of the social order.

The Konso have thus identified three categories of outsiders. These are God, the creator of order; the Wild, outside the control of society, from which come mediators and destroyers; and the Earth, the passive provider of physical fertility and food, beneficial, but needing to be socialized and manipulated by men. It is clear that these categories are not mutually exclusive; they are more like dimensions or axes, and some persons or categories occupy a position between two, rather than being unambiguously located in one. Thus the regional priests and lineage priests approach the 'God axis'; it is said that 'God encircles a priest'. Women, while resembling the earth in many respects, are also seen as fluid and uncontrolled elements in society, and in this respect approach the 'Käälo axis'; and other examples could be provided, such as the craftsmen, and Farīda.

These three cosmological categories of outsider provide the dimensions in relation to which the crucial categories of elders, priests and diviners, and women are located in their society, and manifest the three ways in which they conceive their society to be related to the world around it. The Konso clearly believe that the principles of God, Earth, and the Wild express fundamental truths about reality. Moreover, we can see that in view of their basic nature these principles are relevant for all societies, though the extent to which they can be used cross-culturally, and shown to operate in other societies is, of course, a subject for empirical investigation.

It might be argued however, by traditional functionalists, that God is a projection of the social order; the earth, mystically conceived, of the female role in society; evil spirits of anomie, and ghosts of the lineage. But the Konso do not make the clear distinction that social anthropologists do between society and the supernatural, or society and nature. For analytical purposes it is sometimes necessary for us to treat the data as though these were discrete ontological realms, but it must have become clear in the course of this monograph that for the Konso these three realms so deeply interpenetrate one another that it is meaningless, in the last resort, to talk of their religion on the one hand, and their society on the other. Readers who disagree may care to ask themselves whether the generation-grading systems, the Nama Dawra, the lineage priests, and the elders are social or religious institutions. As Lienhardt has shown us, in *Divinity and Experience*, for the Dinka the source of the form and characteristics of supernatural beings is the totality of man's experience, and not just his social life, and the same is true of the Konso. The principles of God, Earth, and the Wild are cosmological, not merely social; that is, they are based on the Konso's experience of the sky, the earth, and the bush, as well as on their experience of social life. Therefore we are here dealing with their experience not of society alone, but of their total environment, physical as well as social, and on the evidence we have it would be inadmissible to say that it is only their experience of living in society which is projected into their cosmology. As Evans-Pritchard says, 'It was Durkheim and not the savage who made society into a god.'[1]

Moreover, while there is no doubt that their cosmology is related to their total experience, it is as absurd to claim that it merely reflects it as to claim that Keats's 'Ode to a Nightingale' merely reflects his experience of nightingales. Reflections, by definition, are passive, dependent variables, but poetry is a creative act of the imagination, and it is clear that the cosmologies of primitive peoples are creative too, and no mere passive reflections of their society or even their total environments.

[1] E. E. Evans-Pritchard, *Nuer Religion*, p. 313.

POSTSCRIPT

I T has been a constant theme of this monograph that societies are systems of ideas as well as systems of action, and that therefore they are more appropriately treated as rule systems than as organisms. In analysing a rule system we are concerned with establishing those rules which are of greatest generality, and I have tried to show that values have this status. It might be objected, however, that values are too vague for the purposes of clear and rigorous analysis. Yet anyone who reflects on the course of European or American history, for example, is bound to give them a central place in his analysis. The Constitution of the United States, or the French Revolution, is quite inexplicable without an understanding of the contemporary ideas of liberty, equality, justice, and democracy. Values are, of course, in a sense vague, in so far as it is possible for different ideologies or societies to differ about what constitutes liberty or equality, for example, but it would be absurd to claim that people and their institutions can only operate on the basis of clearly defined ideas. Moreover, it is the very vagueness of values which is the basis of their generality, and which allows a society to change, over time, while allowing the members to feel that it is essentially the same. A society requires a body of very general principles to give it coherency while retaining flexibility. On the other hand, as we have seen, values are not analogous to axioms in a deductive system. In the first place there may be conflicts between them, as between peace and virility, or individualism and co-operation; and secondly there is no necessary relation between the existence of certain values and any specific institution.

We have also seen that certain other principles—God, Earth, and the Wild—are fundamental to Konso society in so far as they express the relationship of elders, priests and diviners, and women to the Konso social order. To this extent therefore values are not the only basic principles of their society, and it is probable that all societies also have certain organizational principles which relate crucial categories to the social order.

Thus Konso society 'makes sense', and is not a mere jumble of customs and institutions; but it is not an organism, or, for that matter, a structure. 'Structure' is a concept which has generated more dense metaphysical smoke than any other in our discipline. I have preferred therefore to limit its use to a narrow range of institutions such as the grading systems, in which the component parts are highly integrated by a body of rules, such that they are interdependent, as are business corporations in our society. To suggest that total societies are, in this sense, 'structures' is clearly absurd.

Not only have I largely dispensed with the notion of 'structure' as an analytical concept, but also with that of 'function'. The functionalist point of view rests upon the belief that societies are integrated systems, in the same sense as organisms are. This being so, there must be an inevitable tendency for institutions and customs to be evolved which do not contradict one another but which, on the contrary, tend to consolidate one another in a state of harmony. But many analyses which purport to show that such-and-such institutions *support* the existing social organization are really only saying that these institutions are *consistent* with the existing social organization—quite circular, in fact. I have attempted to show, however, that we must distinguish the overt rules by which a society is governed—values and belief systems—and which give it coherency at the conceptual level, from the consequences of their working-out through institutional logic. The best illustration of this difficult point is the question of the cross-cutting membership of wards, lineages, and working-parties which, while they may have the *effect* of increasing solidarity, cannot be explained by this, but rather by the individualistic values of the Konso. For explanations in terms of the solidarity produced could only be well founded if it could be shown that societies have an inevitable tendency to produce harmonious organizational forms. But as I pointed out in the Introduction, social harmony is, in the first place, not a universal norm, but culturally relative, and what is considered an acceptable level of violence or conflict in one society would be regarded as complete anarchy in another. Secondly, as we have seen in the case of Konso society, it is perfectly possible to have endemic conflict and disharmony, which the people regard as deplorable but unavoidable, as in the case of inter-town warfare, or the hostility between the dual divisions. They have developed institutional forms which inevitably produce conflict, and for which there is no remedy within the system. The system of town relationships is an organizational blind-alley from which there is no escape, into which they have been forced by the logic of choice-situations and stochastic processes.

Another example of the distinction between the processes by which institutions evolve, and the value and belief systems, is the status of the men's houses. It is highly likely that these originated as guard-rooms on the town walls, since in very many cases one finds that they are located on old walls, even where these are well inside the towns as they now exist. It would obviously have been militarily advantageous for bodies of armed men to have slept on the walls at night. But, assuming that this was their origin, causally speaking, resulting from the technical institutional demands of the military situation, their *significance* in terms of the Konso world-view has quite transcended their military purpose, and they are now seen, consistently with the Konso obsession with virility, primarily as a means of preserving their strength and manhood. The status of the craftsmen is yet another example of this extremely important distinction between the conceptual rules of the society, and the nexus of social relations and institutional logic. Their relations with the cultivators are grounded in the different modes of production by which craftsmen and cultivators support themselves, but the *status* of craftsmen derives from the value system.

Functionalist explanations are especially useless in accounting for ritual behaviour. We have seen that there is no evidence that ritual reinforces social solidarity, except in the ceremony of the Hora Dehamda, which is explicitly devoted to this end, and is composed mainly of hortatory speeches. On the contrary, people only attend rituals when a certain level of solidarity already exists between them. Solidarity is the product of day-to-day relations, not of occasional ceremonies.

The functionalist faith in inherent tendencies in every society towards harmony and social solidarity not only often assumes that 'whatever is, is necessary', but sometimes goes to ridiculous lengths to prove that conflict ultimately produces its opposite, rather as though one were to argue that dry-rot was structurally beneficial to a house because it induced the owner to repair it. This is not to say that there is not a 'strain to consistency' in societies, but I suggest that such consistency is due to the fact that human beings are rule-following creatures, and not merely sophisticated billiard balls interacting. What we must try to distinguish is the nature of the rule systems—values and cosmologies—on the one hand, and the logic of institutions on the other. To return to the analogy of the 'game', we must distinguish between the rules of the game of billiards written in the rule book, and the physical laws which govern the interaction of the balls on the table.

To sum up, therefore, I would say that the consistency and coherency of all societies with which ethnographers are familiar are not the result of some mechanistic process of integration, but derive from the human need for some general body of rules by which to order their lives. But institutional logic has its own processes which are in many cases not foreseeable by the people, and its working-out may produce deep contradictions within their society.

GLOSSARY OF KONSO WORDS USED IN THE TEXT

Apa Timba, Apa Para   'Father of the drum', 'father of the year', the holder of a sacred drum.

arĥata   The lower level of the homestead, on which the animals are housed. See *oida*.

balabbat   Town headman, appointed by the Ethiopian government.

ꝺaga ꝺeeruma   'Stone(s) of manhood', pillars of columnar basalt, phallic symbols, erected to commemorate successful battles.

dina   The wood surrounding a town.

ēdanda   Cultivators, a hereditary class.

ella   Water spirit.

Farīda   Most junior grade, containing young men and boys, forbidden to marry and in other ways excluded from adult status.

ĥallasha   Phallic forehead ornament.

harriyāda   Named non-recurring sets, synchronized with the grading system.

hauda   Craftsmen, a hereditary class.

hīyoda   Council of elders, an elder, a leader.

Ĥrela   The warrior grade.

īyanna   Beneficent spirit, possessing certain diviners. The cult is of Galla origin.

'jika   Ancient type of barbed spear now banned for martial purposes, and retained only for ritual.

Kada   Grade above Ĥrela, with responsibilities for blessing.

kaffa   Clan or lineage.

killana   Religious ceremony.

marbara   Working party of friends who band together and cultivate fields for payment. See *parga*.

mida   The foliage of the *shelaĝda* tree (q.v.) chiefly cultivated in towns, and used for food.

miskata   Small enclosure within a sacred place, from which women are excluded. Also, a pole placed across the entrance to a sacred place during sacrifice.

mora	Demarcated public place, both profane and sacred.
Nama Dawra	Official peace-maker.
oida	Upper level of the homestead, on which the humans live. (See *arĥata*.)
oritta	Evil spirit.
parga	Smaller version of the *marbara* (q.v.).
poĝalla	Lineage head and priest.
saga	Blessing.
sagōda	Effeminate man.
Saleda	Town-crier.
seega	Male dance in which two parties pretend to attack each other, run through each other, and re-form on opposite sides of the *mora*.
shorugata	Head of an eminent family, with quasi-priestly responsibilities.
shelaĝda	Tree from which *mida* (q.v.) is hooked down for food. See Plant Glossary.
suaita	Diviner.
ulahita	Dead juniper trees mystically associated with Ĥrela grade.
waga	Carved wooden mortuary statues.
yaĝa	Fermented millet beer.

GLOSSARY OF IMPORTANT PLANT NAMES

I. RITUAL

ḥansabita	*Labiatae: Ocimum suave.*
ifīya	*Labiatae: Becium?*
kiliboda	*Solanaceae: Solanum incaneum.*
piribirta	*Cupressaceae: Juniperus procera.* Hochst. ex. Endl. (Juniper).
teemahada	*Celastraceae: Catha edulis* (khat).

II. FOOD

ashargirteda	*Papilionaceae: Cajanus cajan* (L.) Millsp. (chick-pea).
hidana	*Dioscoreaceae: Dioscorea* (yam).
kapa	Wheat.
longa	*Araceae- Colocasia esculentum* Schott. (taro).
okāla	*Papilionaceae: Vigna.*
pagana	(*a*) *Araceae: Arisaema* Mart (Indian Turnip). (*b*) *Taccaceae Tacca involucrata* Shum.
pare'ja	*Gramineae: Eleusine coracana* (finger-millet).
poĝoloda	Maize.
porda	Barley.
shelaĝda	*Moringaceae: Moringa stenopetala* (Bak.F.) Cufod. or, less probably, *Moringa oleifera.*
sufeda	*Compositae: Helianthus annuus?* (sunflower).
unda	Millet.

INDEX

abortions, 141, 142, 188, 189, 196
adultery, 116
age-grading systems, 217, 218. *See also* generation-grading systems
agriculture, 22, 25, 120; cycle of activities, 171; in relation to grading systems, 219–20; plough, 41
alliances, inter-town, 56
Amhara, conquest and administration, 5, 7, 9, 28, 62, 64, 71, 134; results of, 7–8, 22, 81, 140, 152, 172, 187, 224
anarchy, 129
ancestors, 87, 134, 158, 161, 323
Apa Para (Father of the Year), 72, 73, 76, 77, 84
Apa Timba (Drum Father), 72, 76, 122, 229, 247, 249, 253, 291, 301
Azaïs, F., 28

*balabbat*s, 114; heredity of office, 71; as tax collectors, 66
battles, causes of, 53–5; ceremonies associated with, 56; conventions, 55; lists of, 54
Baxter, P. T. W., 16 n., 132, 144
Beattie, J. H. M., 18
bee-keeping, 27
begging, 138
blood, dual aspect of, 293
Bohannan, P., 14
Borana (division of Galla tribe), 1, 3, 8, 21, 25, 38, 39, 131, 135, 144, 147; pacifism of, 16
burial, 65, 156 ff., 289; of child before *sōgeda*, 296; obligations of ward members, 65, 98
Burji tribe, 1; women potters, 3

Campbell, J. K., 18
childbearing, 278; prohibitions on, 193, 199; ritual after, 296 ff.
circumcision, 142, 193, 196, 199, 293
clans, 87–93; alliances, 88; historical aspects, 92; incest in, 88; inter-marriage prohibitions, 89, 92; ritual division, 89, 90, 324; sizes, 88; totems, 90–2
colour, 279; awareness of colour, 280; significance of black, 261, 281, 282,

314; significance of red, 261, 281, 282, 314; significance of white, 280, 282, 326
conversion to Christianity, 6–7
Coptic Church, 5
Coulton, C. G., 231
Councils, 128, 133, 188
Craftsmen: burial, 144; contempt for, 38–9, 49, 131, 140, 296; exclusion from grading systems, 141; exclusion from sacred enclosure, 232; marriage, 140, 141; mobility, 145–6; physical characteristics, 140; reason for prejudice against, 135. 144; status of, 139–47, 327

dancing, 32–3
Darragon, 42, 258
days of the week, *see* time-reckoning
death, attitude to, 130, 135, 160, 161; life after, 161; death of a priest, 49, 158. *See also* burial
divination, 176, 177, 228, 241, 245, 246, 306–8, 311–12, 315 ff.; star-divination, 178, 307, 315
divorce, 88, 116; of priests, 251
dreams, interpretations, 161–3, 284–5, 316, 325
drums, sacred, 42, 47, 48, 60, 63, 125, 190, 249; association with authority, 51; as symbol of social order, 164, 327; cycle of, 57, 73, 74, 199, 200; in relation to generation grades, 198; occasions of use, 49, 193. *See also* Garati, Takadi, and Turo
Dyson-Hudson, N., 66 n., 93

Earth: as source of food, 288; for burial, 289
education, 6
Elders, Council of, 40. *See also* Councils
emigration, 9
Evans-Pritchard, E. E., 15, 310, 328
evil eye, 307, 310, 311; spirits, 315–16, 324

family, 103; cognatic ties, 108–9; polygyny, 104–5; relationships in, 103–4; status of eldest son, 109 ff.